Praise for S

"By simultaneously weaving the voices of actual Somali immigrants with those of social scientists, this anthology will significantly contribute to our understanding of the complexities of the global Somali diaspora—particularly at a moment when almost in every corner of the globe, from Johannesburg, South Africa to Lewiston, Maine, Somali immigrant communities are facing increased cultural and religious scrutiny."

—ABDI KUSOW, associate professor of sociology, Iowa State University

"This book is a timely documentation of the journey of Somalis into Maine, capturing the voices of the people and their stories in the diaspora. This analytical narrative of Somali secondary immigration demonstrates the lives of immigrants as they settle in their new adopted homes. For generations to come, these stories will inform the perceptions of those who have moved to 'new lands' and will educate others who are yet to experience this life-changing moment."

—ABDI ROBLE, founder and photographer of the Somali Documentary Project; visiting scholar at the Center for African Studies at Ohio State University

"In this eclectic, wide-ranging mix of academic essays, personal reflections, autobiographical narratives, and interview excerpts, the Somali Narrative Project has produced a wonderfully intimate portrait of Somalis' lives in Lewiston, Maine. The collaborative work between young students, older scholars, and community members offers a compelling model of how to blend humanistic and empirical research on immigrant experiences."

—CATHERINE BESTEMAN, professor and chair of the Department of Anthropology, Colby College

"This book on the Somali story in Lewiston, Maine, is a valuable resource for all who live in our increasingly diverse state and in other states experiencing immigration growth. We learn that Somalis are looking for the same things all Maine people seek: quality of life."

—LARRY GILBERT, mayor of Lewiston, Maine

"The Somali Narrative Project is a model of creative, active learning that engages students in the important roles of storyteller, historian, and emissary. The anthology that emerged from this faculty-student collaboration is a rare combination of young immigrant voices and accessible scholarly studies that creates a counter-narrative to the contemporary story of the Somali diaspora in Maine."

—DANIEL F. DETZNER, professor of postsecondary teaching and learning, University of Minnesota; author of *Elder Voices: Southeast Asian Families in the United States.*

"The history of African immigration to the United States is vexed by the concurrent history of slavery. And yet, today more than ever, Africans seek refuge on American soil in some of the unlikeliest of places. *Somalis in Maine* weaves together this complicated history through the words of Somali immigrants themselves, as well as through scholars who want to understand why Maine, considered the 'whitest state in America,' has become home to this particular group of Africans in the diaspora. At once moving, compelling, and complex, *Somalis in Maine* represents a watershed moment in African diaspora studies."

—E. PATRICK JOHNSON, professor and department chair, Department of African American Studies, Northwestern University

"At the core, these narratives are a window into building an open dialogue rather than shutting people into neatly defined stereotypes. *Somalis in Maine* shows us a community in the midst of change. Like all oral narratives, these stories subvert the mainstream commonly held beliefs and sound bites that focus on conflict and misunderstanding, and show us a displaced community of Somalis in the process of building and rebuilding their lives."

—JUDITH SLOAN, radio producer, actress, and coauthor with Warren Lehrer of *Crossing the BLVD: strangers, neighbors, aliens in a new America.*

"This is a precious and beautiful book that honors the power of 'small stories' in 'small spaces' that traverse time and place to touch us all with the urgency of their importance, the soul of their humanity, and the grand eloquence of their meanings. The stories of Somalia and the Somali Diaspora deserve our attention because, as this compelling book demonstrates, they contain and perform those universal, yet unique and poignant moments of culture, identity, and belonging in the making. This is a book of life and breath encounters—of the foreign, the familiar, and the in-between—told through the voices of Somalis and those who know how to listen with the heart and learn with purpose."

—D. SOYINI MADISON, PhD, professor of performance studies and anthropology, Northwestern University

"*Somalis in Maine: Crossing Cultural Currents* is a fascinating book about the experiences of Somali refugees who ended up in Maine. It provides a wide range of perspectives and voices, ranging from young Somali Americans who talk about various aspects of their lives in past and present to academic scholars who describe and analyze their conversations with Somalis living in Maine. As such, it is a rich compilation that does full justice to the complexities of having to flee your own country, living as a refugee in the region, and 'becoming' a Somali American upon resettlement. The book offers a rare insight into people's motivations, dreams, fears and the challenges they face in building life from scratch. As such, it is a highly recommendable read."

—CINDY HORST, senior researcher, Peace Research Institute Oslo

"When a project draws different members of a diverse community into a broad but focused engagement, it can both reflect and shape that community. This book represents such a project. The Somali American experience in Maine is here presented by youth and grown-ups, students and professors, and administrators and artists whose (his-)stories derive from both sides of the hyphen. They come together in this book to tell us about what they have learned from and about each other. Apart from delighting and informing a general readership, it will also serve as a great teaching text."

—LIDWIEN KAPTEIJNS, Kendall/Hodder Professor of History, Wellesley College

"*Somalis in Maine: Crossing Cultural Currents* enhances our understanding of recent immigration in the United States by exploring the experiences of East African Muslim refugees in Maine. Through a combination of scholarly essays and first-hand accounts by Somali community members, this work sheds light on pre-migration experiences in Somalia, regional migrations in Africa, migration to and re-migration in the United States, and settlement and community formation in Lewiston, Maine. *Somalis in Maine* illustrates well the challenges that Somali immigrants have faced in all of these aspects of the migration experience. This work also considers the tensions Somalis have faced within their own community as they have sought to adapt to life in U.S. society. Like the French-Canadian immigrants who preceded them to Lewiston, Somalis appear to be actively negotiating the terms of their entry into U.S. society, thus challenging contemporary notions of the process of assimilation."

—MARK PAUL RICHARD, State University of New York at Plattsburgh; author of *Loyal but French: The Negotiation of Identity by French-Canadian Descendants in the United States*

"This extremely well-written book makes a noteworthy contribution to the study of ethnic Americans. Significantly enhancing the authors' thorough documentation of the complex dynamics of newcomer and community interaction is their extensive utilization of the rich tradition of Somali storytelling to elicit multiple voices and diverse perspectives. This collaborative involvement between trained objective observers and those caught between two worlds does more than deepen our understanding of this mostly unknown group. The authors' research approach and the resulting recorded dialogues also should serve as a model for future ethnographers wanting to present an accurate, even-handed, and mutually beneficial study of a people."

—VINCENT N. PARRILLO, professor and graduate director, William Patterson University; author of *Strangers to these Shores*

Somalis in Maine
CROSSING CULTURAL CURRENTS

Edited by
Kimberly A. Huisman
Mazie Hough
Kristin M. Langellier
Carol Nordstrom Toner

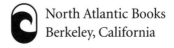

North Atlantic Books
Berkeley, California

Published by
North Atlantic Books   Cover photo by Samantha Appleton
P.O. Box 12327   Cover and book design by Suzanne Albertson
Berkeley, California 94712

Copyright acknowledgments are printed on page 359.

Printed in the United States of America

This is issue number 69 in the Io series.

Somalis in Maine: Crossing Cultural Currents is sponsored by the Society for the Study of Native Arts and Sciences, a nonprofit educational corporation whose goals are to develop an educational and cross-cultural perspective linking various scientific, social, and artistic fields; to nurture a holistic view of arts, sciences, humanities, and healing; and to publish and distribute literature on the relationship of mind, body, and nature.

North Atlantic Books' publications are available through most bookstores. For further information, visit our website at www.northatlanticbooks.com or call 800-733-3000.

Library of Congress Cataloging-in-Publication Data

Somalis in Maine : crossing cultural currents / edited by Kimberly A. Huisman ... [et al.].
        p. cm.
    Includes bibliographical references and index.
    Summary: "Containing personal stories, ethnography, and reflective essays, Somalis in Maine explores the unique cross-cultural interactions and collaborations between Somali refugees and Americans in the town of Lewiston, Maine"—Provided by publisher.
    ISBN 978-1-55643-926-1
    1. Somali Americans—Maine. 2. Lewiston (Me.)—Ethnic relations. 3. Maine—Ethnic relations. I. Huisman, Kimberly A., 1967–
    F29.L63S66 2011
    305.89'3540730741—dc22   2010048314

            1 2 3 4 5 6 7 8 9 SHERIDAN 16 15 14 13 12 11

Acknowledgments

This book is the result of a collaboration we call the Somali Narrative Project. Begun in 2004 in response to the arrival of Somali refugees in Lewiston, Maine, the collaborative involves University of Maine faculty members and Somali students as well as members of Maine's Somali community. We would like first of all to thank the Somali people who shared their stories with us. We dedicate this volume on crossing cultural currents to them and their families. We acknowledge especially those Somalis who helped introduce us to Lewiston's Somali community—Qamar Bashir, Fatuma Hussein, and Ismail Ahmed. Lewiston's Deputy City Administrator, Phil Nadeau, graciously offered us his insights to the city's response to the Somali settlement. We are also deeply grateful to all of the Somali students who worked with us in reading, interviewing, performing, and telling stories, particularly our initial three students, Nasra Mohamed, Safia Nur, and Ismail Warsame. We would like to thank those who provided us with grants and other financial support, including the Maine Humanities Council, and the following units from The University of Maine: the Women in the Curriculum and Women's Studies Program, the Center for Excellence in Teaching and Assessment, the Office of Equal Opportunity, and the Sociology Department. Our friends and colleagues helped in a variety of ways: Steve Barkan, Laurie Cartier, Angela Hart, Cate Colombo, Ann Schonberger, Bob White, Jason Crain, Kevin Johnson, Eric Peterson, Deborah Pearlman, and Chrissy Fowler. Many work-study students helped with interviews, transcriptions, technology, transportation, and research—we thank them all. We are also indebted to Katherine O'Flaherty for her careful proofreading, and to our editors: Erin Wiegand for shepherding us through the publication process and Lindy Hough for first recognizing the value in our project, and copyeditor Denise Silva and editorial director Jon Goodspeed for their advice and careful attention to detail. And finally, our sincere thanks to the contributors to this volume. Without these people and these programs—and without each other's synergistic strengths—we could not have produced this book. To all, *mahadsanidiin*.

Contents

Preface

This story of Somalis in Maine begins in the middle, where all stories must begin. For wherever we start our telling, the story is already underway and unfolding in time, its ending still unfinished and unforeseeable. Whether or not one has personal experience with Somalis, ideas and images about them are already forming as a narrative. What one knows about Somalia may be seen primarily through media stories with images of starving women and children, the violence of the civil war, the lawlessness of piracy off the Somali coast, and alleged links to al-Qaeda. And what one has learned about Somali immigrants to North America is often through media reports about social problems involving race, religion, and economic tensions in cities, schools, and work settings. Despite their relatively small numbers as refugees and immigrants, Somalis have attracted attention nearly everywhere the global diaspora has taken them. Lewiston, Maine, for example, was a site of national and international media attention in 2002 around an episode, documented in a film titled *The Letter: An American Town and the "Somali Invasion"* by Ziad H. Hamzeh, that emerged around the rapid migration of Somalis to that small city. Somalis are now a part of Maine's story as they settle into the state and contribute new chapters to its immigrant history. This book is an invitation both to listen to some of that history and to refocus the montage of negative images by entering into cultural currents that carry new voices and views of Somalis in Maine.

Stories travel and Somalis travel. As one young narrator, Khalid Mohamed, says in his story, "we are natural-born nomads." The migration to Maine was fueled when Somalis fled the collapse of their homeland in the Horn of Africa, where civil war has raged for two decades and continues today. Somalis move within an unprecedented global flow of refugees, one that reflects a predominance of Africans, Muslims, and women and children. Somalis are among those refugees who have witnessed many horrors and suffered great losses. As they have made the long and dangerous journeys to escape war, famine, and the ecological breakdown of their homeland, they have experienced the trauma of deaths, dislocations, and separations from family. Years spent in overcrowded and under-resourced refugee camps, such as Dadaab and Kakuma in Kenya—where some have passed their entire childhoods and all await resettlement or return to Somalia—

add to the trauma. Families fortunate enough to be resettled across the globe then face daunting challenges of meeting needs for safety, housing, health care, education, and employment in their new homes. Movement over borders challenges both refugees and host countries to make cultural crossings: Somalis to learn about their new homes and how to make their way in them; and host countries to learn about their new neighbors and ultimately more about themselves, too.

The Somali diaspora crosses continents and nations, for example, the United Kingdom, Russia, Australia, Canada, Italy, and Sweden. Many Somalis resettled in the United States were first located in large cities, such as Atlanta, Boston, and Anaheim, California. And although not all Somalis are pastoral nomads—many come from urban settings such as Mogadishu—most do travel until they find themselves together, so that large communities of refugee and secondary immigrants are now established in, for example, Minneapolis, Minnesota; Columbus, Ohio; and Lewiston, Maine. Most Somalis in Maine are secondary migrants who passed through primary sites of resettlement to begin arriving in 2001 when stories of its attractions were circulated through the extensive oral and internet networks of the diaspora. In 2003, ethnic Bantu, a minority and marginalized group of subsistence farmers from southern Somalia who were particularly vulnerable to the violence of the civil war, joined the growing population in the twin cities of Lewiston-Auburn in south-central Maine. Some Somalis stay on to become new Mainers, while others move on to new places to call home.

The history of the Somali diaspora has yet to be written in its more holistic dimensions and many local variations. This book does not attempt to compose this still-emerging diasporic history, but it does extend a kaleidoscope of voices and views on Somalis in Maine. In addition, we offer resources to situate and contextualize these Maine stories in a larger cultural narrative. This preface is followed by two maps. The first locates Somalia's international boundaries and the more extensive and fluid ethnic boundaries of its peoples living in Kenya, Ethiopia, and Djibouti (see figure 1). The second locates Somalia in the context of Africa and Islam (see figure 2). A chronology of Somalia's history and diaspora follows, highlighting some of the key events in its trajectory. Moments in the chronology and points on the maps flicker through the stories, essays, and interviews in the book, intimating the layers of history and threads of culture that quilt the pattern of Somalia and the diaspora. For readers who wish to pursue wider and deeper information, the endnotes and bibliography cite numerous research references.

Where and when do we enter the cultural currents of the Somali story as editors of this volume? The Somali Narrative Project (SNP) was founded in 2004 to address the rapid change and cultural tensions that emerged in response to the migration that brought Somalis to Maine. The Somali Narrative Project is a collaboration between the editors, who are University of Maine faculty, and Somali students and Somalis in Lewiston-Auburn. Faculty members bring the perspectives of several disciplines—sociology, history, communication, performance studies, women's studies, and Maine studies—to the project. Student members are a changing cast of young Somalis studying many curricula as they pass through the University of Maine. From the outset, the central concern was that our work be community-based, mutually beneficial to participants, and student-oriented. We heard repeatedly from Somali elders, parents, youth, and our own Somali students that "people don't understand our history and culture and religion." To address this gap, the project developed three interrelated goals: (1) to document Somali immigration to Maine through narrative interviews that create, in one Somali's words, "a library of real stories"; (2) to improve intercultural communication by promoting dialogue with and understanding about Somalis; and (3) to engage in community advocacy projects that respond to needs identified by members of the Somali community. The project has evolved over time to embrace the conversations, storytelling, and writing contained in this book. We hope this volume moves toward these goals by creating opportunities for greater understanding, deeper dialogue, and positive change that enhances the intertwined futures of Somalis and Americans. The cultural flow that mingles local and global currents is changing not only Somalis and the story of Maine but also the United States as Somalia is inserted in the North American narrative.

Somalis in Maine speaks in multiple voices and diverse perspectives of Somalis and non-Somalis as we all navigate the confluence of cultures that intermixes people and histories. We have organized the book into five sections that feature dimensions of crossing cultural currents. Each section is headed by a quotation from a Maine Somali that describes an aspect of Somali diasporic experience. Each chapter in each section alternates with first-person stories by Somali students with whom we have worked. Somalis are born storytellers who come from a rich and abundant culture of oral traditions. These stories emerged in workshops with young Somalis that were facilitated by the Somali Narrative Project in 2009 and 2010. We have dubbed this group of storytellers the "1.5 generation" because they have been in the United States and Maine longer than our first group of students who helped found the project. Hence the memories of Somalia these narrators carry are already quite distant to them, recalled or repressed as shards of experience that cross geographies and cultures.

Throughout the book we offer photographs to visually complement the verbal stories and analyses. We do so with the caveat that documenting Somalis with photographic images is itself a complex demand and a delicate cultural negotiation. Photographing Somalis relies first of all on the dynamics of interpersonal trust and mutual relationships built as we interacted over several years. But photographs may also invoke historical and religious concerns. As a people traumatized by their recent history, as refugees subjected to the commands and surveillance of bureaucracies, and as the objects of media attention that almost always casts them as victims or in negative light, Somalis are justifiably wary of the camera. Moreover, as devout Muslims, many share an Islamic caution about creating images. Hence, photographing Somalis absorbs several cultural tensions; and we are sincerely appreciative of the photographs used by permission here.

Part I, "'The Water in Maine Is Sweet," explores contexts and dynamics of cultural contact. Chapter 1, by historian Mazie Hough, asks the diasporic question "why now?" to explore some of the intersecting currents of internal and global history that contribute to bringing Somalis to Maine in the early twenty-first century. This brief historical introduction sets the stage for examining some of the specific complexities of cultural contact between Somalis and their host communities. "The water in Maine is sweet," the quotation of a Somali poet who lived in Lewiston, echoes the poetic language characteristic of Somali oral tradition as well as the first and most persistent question asked about this immigrant group—"why Maine?"—given the enormous climate differences from Somalia, the state's perennially weak economy, and its homogenous population as the "whitest" state in the United States. Sociologist Kimberly A. Huisman's essay examines the culturally specific pattern of secondary migration by looking at the decisions Somalis present for coming to and for leaving Maine as well as their remarkable social networks. Then Phil Nadeau, a city administrator in Lewiston and public policy researcher, takes up the city's response to the Somali migration, detailing the initial and ongoing efforts to meet their needs. His analysis of policy issues around secondary migration and literacy outlines continuing challenges that face the city and Somalis, particularly with regard to employment.

Three Somali writers author the chapters in Part II. Its title, "We Are Not Under the Tree," is a quotation that focuses in on diasporic Somali communities in transition. Emerging scholar Ismail Ahmed offers an ethnographic analysis of leadership in the Lewiston Somali community that creates a fascinating "insider" view of the same cultural contact and change that Nadeau addresses from City Hall. Ahmed describes how Somalis have responded to the transition to Lewiston, and he calls for new models of leadership and civic participation. A different Somali community in transition, the Dadaab refugee camp in Kenya, is the subject of Nasra Mohamed's essay. A founding student member of the Somali Narrative Project, Mohamed's family spent ten years in Dadaab following their exodus from Somalia. The poignant narrative of her return is woven with stories she transcribed of Somali youth still living in Dadaab with the hope of resettlement and the dream of education. Higher education experiences and issues for Somalis are the topic of the last essay in this section, by Ismail Warsame, another founding student member of the collaborative, as he describes cultural challenges for himself and other Somalis in schools and colleges.

Part III features interactions that show identities as mutually formative: How is Maine shaping what it means to be Somali? How are Somalis shaping Maine? "Caaliya's Storytelling," by narrative scholar Kristin M. Langellier, asserts the strong sense of identity characteristic of Somalis in Caaliya's statement, "wherever I go I know who I am." Caaliya creates her protean identity in an intricate conversation with Somali and non-Somali listeners as she tells stories of Somali ethnicity and Islamic religion in the context of changing notions of gender, race, and class in Maine and "the West." Then historians Mazie Hough and Carol Nordstron Toner feature Somalis at work in Maine: in the distribution centers of Maine icon L.L. Bean, in community gardens in Lewiston-Auburn, and within the cultural spaces of their own economies ordered by *biil,* a Somali form of capital. Their essay highlights some innovative and reciprocal adaptations between Somalis and Maine employers and economies.

The quotation heading Part IV, "Anything to Help," was spoken by a student member of the Somali Narrative Project (SNP) and highlights its collaborative spirit. The essays in this section describe efforts to forge knowledge and deepen understanding about Somalis in Maine through storytelling and dialogue. The brief essay by Kristin M. Langellier shows some intercultural challenges and lessons learned as the SNP was established to connect with Somali community members in Lewiston. The second essay, by Carol Nordstrom Toner, features the engaged learning and creative contributions of Somali students in the collaboration as they pushed the project forward and into new dimensions. The third essay, by Kimberly A. Huisman, presents an outreach dimension of the SNP in the form of readers theater as public pedagogy. It traces and illustrates the process of collaboratively creating texts to perform for community audiences, the performances themselves, and the dialogues they spawned.

Part V, titled "Don't You Know? I'm Somali!" responds to Somali community members' request to create a "library of real stories" to document and preserve their immigration experience for themselves, their children, and the next generations. These oral narratives from interviews with Somalis in Maine provide an addition to and extension of the stories by young Somali Americans throughout the volume. However, as oral rather than written storytelling they bear the marks of encounters within complex cultural currents. To read them is more like overhearing a conversation, sometimes with background noise, than listening to an uninterrupted story. They come with gaps and breaks and tacit assumptions, but they are rich with the cultural style and substance of their Somali speakers. The chapter presents Somali voices organized as a collective narrative of their journey from Somalia to Maine and their current negotiations of identity as Somali Americans. We hear the voices of ordinary citizens—neither victims nor social problems—talking against the backdrop of their extraordinary experiences. In these voices and stories throughout the volume, Somalis make and remake themselves in America, and simultaneously, we remake who we are as Americans.

Ahmed Samatar calls this process in which generations of Somalis are making a new narrative a "critical adaptation" to the challenges they face in the global and American milieu. The book closes with an afterword by Samatar, endowed professor at Macalester College, founding editor in chief of *Bildhaan: An International Journal of Somali Studies,* and author/editor of five books on Somalia. His epilogue is a commanding, aching, and concise retelling of the historical moment of catastrophe that resulted in the Somali diaspora. About the critical adaptation of Somalis to the United States he writes, "while gains in their endeavor require a genuine welcome, durable sympathy, and deep investment by the American people and institutions, the bulk of responsibility for adjustment lies with the new arrivals." As he outlines the formidable obstacles Somalis face, we listen with hope for what comes next in our cross-cultural story.

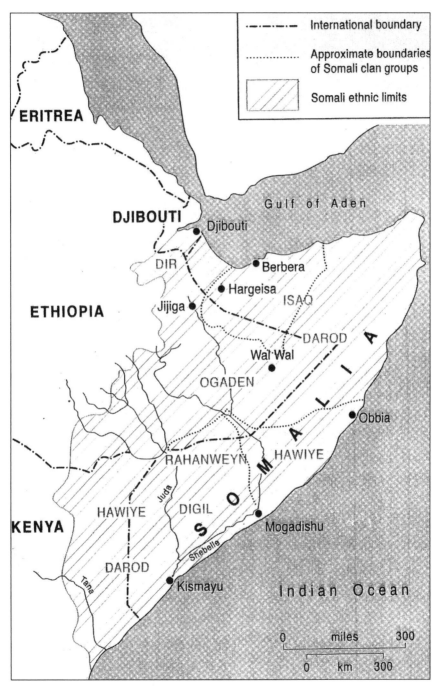

FIGURE 1. Map of ethnic Somalia

FIGURE 2. Map of Islam in Africa

Chronology of Events in Somali History and the Diaspora

900   Through long contact with Arab Muslims, Somalis convert en masse to Islam.

1869   Suez Canal built, opening eastern Africa to Europe and colonization.

1860–   European colonizers partition Somali territory and people into
1897   British Somaliland in the north, Italian Somalia in the south, and French Somaliland on the Gulf of Aden coast. Ethiopia claims the Ogaden and the Haud territories of Somalia.

1890s–   Sayyid Muhammad Abdille Hassan* (called the "Mad Mullah" by
1920   the British) leads the anti-colonial struggle against "infidels"— Ethiopians, British, and Italians.

1948   Somali nation re-partitioned after Italy's defeat in World War II.

Independence

1960   British Somaliland and Italian Somalia become independent. They merge to form the Democratic Republic of Somalia.

1969   President Abdinashiid Ali Shermaarke assassinated. Army commander General Mohamed Siyad Barre leads the military coup to overthrow the democratically elected government. State becomes the Somali Democratic Republic.

1970   Barre declares Somalia a socialist state and nationalizes most of the economy.

1974   Barre establishes a standard Latin script for the Somali language and commissions a national literacy campaign.

International Women's Day launched.

Somalia joins the Arab League.

* There are no standard transliterations for Somali names, and readers may encounter slight variations throughout the essays.

1974– 1975 Catastrophic drought and famine in northern Somalia lead to internal displacement of nomads.

1977 France grants independence to French Somaliland, which becomes the Republic of Djibouti.

1977– 1978 Somalia invades Somali-inhabited Ogaden region of Ethiopia. With the help of Soviet advisers and Cuban soldiers, Ethiopia defeats Somali forces. When USSR changes sides to aid Ethiopia, Barre expels Soviet advisers and gains the support of the United States. When Somalia fails to regain the Ogaden, hundreds of thousands of Ethiopians of Somali descent flee to Somalia.

Drought and Civil War

1979 Severe drought, famine, and poverty intensify dissatisfaction with Barre regime.

1979– 1989 Various guerrilla forces form to overthrow the Barre regime. A first wave of Somalis begins to leave the country, fleeing political oppression and seeking political asylum.

1991 Oppositional forces overthrow Barre and force him from Mogadishu. Civil war breaks out.

Disintegration and Diaspora

1991 The Somaliland Republic in the north declares its independence from Somalia.

A second wave of Somalis, vastly more numerous than the first, flees to seek refuge worldwide, including the United States.

UN sets up refugee camps, such as Dadaab and Kakuma in Kenya, for Somalis.

Civil war in Somalia continues to present day. With no recognized government, country slides into chaos and armed violence.

1992 Drought in central and southern Somalia leads to 25 percent of population in danger of starvation. Thousands die daily.

George H. W. Bush announces U.S.–led and UN–sanctioned peacekeeping forces, Operation Restore Hope.

1993   UN sends troops for peacekeeping and humanitarian roles as fighting continues in Mogadishu.

Guerrilla forces shoot down several Black Hawk helicopters and humiliate survivors (subject of American book and film).

1994   U.S. President Clinton withdraws all troops from Somalia.

Islamist Advance, Retreat, and Rivalry

1995   UN peacekeepers leave Somalia, their mission a failure.

1998   Puntland region declares itself semi-autonomous from Somalia.

2000–   Repeated efforts to elect new president, establish transitional
2004   parliament, and restore a central government.

2003   Anti-terrorism coalition formed to pave way for revolution against warlords in control of Southern Somalia.

2004   Transitional Federal Government formed, internationally recognized and backed by the United Nations, African Union, and United States.

2005   Fighters loyal to the Union of Islamic Courts (UIC) defeat U.S.–backed leaders and warlords to take control of Mogadishu.

2006   Mogadishu opens airports and seaports for first time since 1995.

UN reports that about 35,000 Somalis flee to escape drought, continuing rivalry, and war.

United States backs joint Ethiopian and Somali government forces to capture Mogadishu.

2007   Pitched battles between insurgents and government forces lead to worst fighting in fifteen years. Hundreds of thousands of refugees flee amid upsurge in violence.

Humanitarian Crisis

2007 UN declares Somalia as the worst humanitarian crisis in Africa. The number of Somali refugees hits one million, UN reports.

2007– 2008 Piracy along Somali coasts leads to international crackdown.

2008 International concern for radical Islamist-led insurgency grows.

2009 Radical Islamist al-Shabab advances in southern and central Somalia.

2010 Somali government is widely recognized (by UN, Arab League, African Union, etc.), but it is too weak to govern nation.

Diaspora in Maine

2001 Somali migration to Lewiston begins in February.

After 9/11, Canada, Australia, and the United States admit significantly fewer Somali refugees.

2002 Lewiston mayor writes a letter to the Somali community, asking them to stop coming.

2003 Simultaneous rallies by a white supremacist organization and counter pro-diversity coalition staged in Lewiston.

2004 Somali Bantu migration to Lewiston begins.

2010 Somalis continue to come to Maine for family unification and as secondary migrants.

PART I

"The Water in Maine Is Sweet": Contexts of Cultural Contact

Editors' Note: *Stories of young Somalis alternate with each chapter in this book. Like all storytellers, the young Somalis in this book make their stories from the fragments of memory of their homeland, other homes, and home in Maine. Most of the stories in the book had their origins in two student workshops, one with young Somali women and one with young Somali men. Each narrator considered what story she or he wanted to tell about her or his diasporic experience, why to tell it, and how to shape its arc, images, and emotions.[1] Honoring the roots of Somali oral traditions, the students told their stories aloud to each other, receiving encouragement and animated feedback from their audience of peers. Next the oral stories were transformed into writing; and then faculty and students edited and polished them for publication here.*

How We Left Mogadishu

Gulaid

This was the most striking night of my life.

It was 1991, a few days after the civil war started. Our family had already moved from our home in the part of Mogadishu where the government stronghold was very close because we could not tolerate the constant shelling from the government army. My father stayed behind in our neighborhood to protect our house. I was living with my mother, my brothers, and my sisters in our aunt's place, a little farther north in Mogadishu.

My aunt's house was very close to the ocean. There was a road there—not the main road, but people could escape from the city by it. We were thinking that if worse comes to worst for us in Somalia, then we would flee by that road. So that's why we moved to live with my aunt. They had a three-bedroom apartment in a house. My aunt, her husband, and their children didn't have much room for us—or for anybody—but in times of war people can live in very crowded areas. It was a little better than our house in Mogadishu because there were no bullets or rockets falling around us every day. It was fine, until that night. All of a sudden—around three o'clock in the morning—there was a big explosion that shook the entire building, shook the entire ground.

When I woke up, everyone was crying. My mom was crying, and she was shouting that my sister had died. And nobody really knew what was happening. I was very young at the time, but I remember vividly that I was wearing my *macawiis*, Somali pajamas that circle around your waist. It was burning; my *macawiis* was burning. I must have torn it off. I had to get out of the burning building. I had to walk outside through somewhere that was not the door, because the door had been destroyed by a missile. Later on my uncle, who had been in the army, told us that we had been hit by a very destructive weapon called a BM 21. It is about nine feet long and weighs about sixty or seventy pounds, roughly thirty kilograms. When we came outside, we saw that not only had it destroyed our house but it had also struck the neighbor's house. It killed my aunt's neighbor. I saw another woman outside who was bleeding, too. As we all came out, everybody was crying and everybody was bleeding. There were shrapnel wounds on our hands and feet, and all over people's bodies. We were terrified; it was the worst night I have ever had.

Everyone in the neighborhood was terrified. And people were telling us, "There could be another one coming, so you might want to leave here, you might want to go." We did not even have clothes. Our entire house was burning, and there were no firefighters or anyone to call for help. So you could just leave—that's the best you could do. We all evacuated except for my sister Leyla, who had a really bad wound on her hand or on her arm—we couldn't really tell. She was bleeding badly. Recently I called her in Portland, where she now lives, and asked about that night. We were talking in Somali, and Leyla told me this:

"I felt something heavy fall on my hand. I couldn't get up. I couldn't lift my arm at all. And I was very thirsty, and I realized I was bleeding heavily. Then I heard my mother asking, 'Who is dead?' My cousin responded, 'I am dead.' He was almost losing his mind because his clothes were burning on him. Then I got up and told my mother that I had lost my hand. And she shouted my name out loud: 'Leyla is dead,' and she kept repeating that many times. I was asking for water but nobody answered me. Finally somebody brought me a glass of water. My mouth was full of dust but I just drank the water anyway, without even washing out my mouth. I was so very thirsty."

Except for Leyla, the rest of us had only minor injuries, but we were told that if we didn't take her to a hospital somewhere, she might bleed to death. So my neighbors who had a car took her to the nearest hospital, which was itself under fire from rockets and shells. Even that hospital was taking a lot of hits from the government army. It was a really, really difficult situation in Mogadishu. My sister Leyla told me, "When we arrived at the hospital, we were met by rebel soldiers instead of doctors. They drew their guns on us, telling us to back away. But we told them that we were victims of the government shelling, and they let us in. I remember one of the aid workers was trying to help me. He probably had never had medical training, because he was bandaging my arm by the elbow when I was bleeding from the shoulder. Later on someone with more experience came and took off the bandage and put it back on correctly."

That night we stayed with my aunt's neighbors for a couple hours, but my mother was saying, "That's it, we have to leave, we cannot stay here anymore." My father was not with us because he was staying with our house in our old neighborhood, but we could not call him; there was no phone communication. He was miles and miles away, and nobody could walk because of the dangerous situation.

My uncle had an army truck; he had been in the army, but he deserted because of what the government was doing. The truck was huge, because it was what they used to transport soldiers. My uncle said, "I could take the whole family somewhere that's safer." So my uncle took our family and all of his family in the army truck.

We stopped by the house where my father was, and we told him what had happened. My father was also frightened, and even he did not know what to do. He told us, "We can just stay here in my house," because he did not think that we could make it through. If we tried to flee, he didn't know how we could survive outside of Mogadishu. Our family had never been outside of the city, and we could bring almost nothing with us. So he said, "If anything is going to happen to us, it's going to happen to us in our house. At least we have food, we have everything, we live here. So we should unload the truck and stay here until we see what happens."

But then my sister Leyla and my other sisters were crying so hard with fear. They were saying, "After what has happened last night, we cannot possibly stay here. We are going to have nightmares." Everyone, including my

FIGURE 3. Young Somali men at the Islamic Center in Orono, Maine

mother and my aunt, everyone in the neighborhood was talking my father into letting us leave. Finally he had to say okay; he could not resist everyone.

That's how we ended up taking the road out of the city to escape the war in Somalia. My father came with us not knowing where we were headed, what our destination was, or how our future would be. We literally fled with nothing, not even clothes. Some people had maybe one or two pairs of shoes—and some of us did not even have shoes. We were just fleeing with our lives. The only thing of value we took with us was my mother's gold, which my father had bought for her. I left our house, everything intact but left behind, because the one truck could carry just us. That's how we left Mogadishu, and now we are in Maine.

1   Why Now? A Brief History of Somalia

Mazie Hough

In 1991 the increasingly authoritarian military rule of Siyad Barre collapsed and the country of Somalia descended into "turmoil, factional fighting, and anarchy." In spite of nearly a dozen attempts to create peace since then, Somalia has remained the "only independent country without a national government in modern times" and a failed state. Continuous fighting in the south has led to over one million refugees dispersed around the globe. An estimated three hundred thousand of them remain in the closed refugee camps in Dadaab, Kenya, where many have been waiting to return to their homeland for almost two decades. Meanwhile, Somali pirates continue to patrol the Somali coast endangering lives and cargo.[1]

The civil disruption has been so great that Ahmed I. Samatar calls this the age of *qaxootin* or desperate exodus for Somalis—one that is unprecedented in Somalia's history in a number of ways.

> First, the intensity of the internal institutional crises is of such magnitude that, a decade ago, I termed the condition a "catastrophe." Second, the rupture in the collective identity is so severe that Somalis have taken almost *any* road out of the country. Third, the numbers are so large, perhaps in the millions. Fourth, those in flight come in almost all categories—men and women, uneducated, urban and rural. Fifth, while longing for a better Somalia, many are so disheartened that a return in the short term is a forlorn hope . . . and finally, many of these dispersed Somalis carry with them trauma, venom, and guilt to an extent that enervates any attempt, thus far, at sustainable inclusive dialogue, never mind collective effort towards reconstitutions.[2]

It is the voices of the Somalis in this desperate exodus that are included in this book.

Contemporary Somalia is in striking contrast to the nation that European powers had once identified as "the only true nation state in Africa."[3] Explanations for the failure of Somalis to reconstitute their state often resort to identifying the clan system and its role in creating conflict. Anthropologist I. M. Lewis, widely regarded for his extensive research in Somalia, has emphasized the determining and enduring influence of clan in his latest book. But, as Samatar notes, this explanation of Somalia's collapse is seductively simple. Most importantly, a singular lens on clanism obscures change over time and "completely underplays the crueler and costlier colonial conquests."[4] Furthermore, as anthropologist Catherine Besteman notes, "a unitary focus on clan rivalry as the destructive force fueling genocidal conflict and state disintegration ... fails to explain why clan tensions should suddenly erupt on so grand a scale and with such brutal devastation, apparently for the first time in history."[5] Only by understanding the past can we who are all now implicated in the Somali crisis understand the forces that brought the Somalis into our midst.

This brief history of Somalia sketches some of the ways in which Somalia's strategic geographic location on a major trade route connecting Africa, Asia, and the Middle East opened Somalis to currents of international trade and politics. In many cases, what has happened in Somalia was determined by global politics and the Somalis' response to forces outside of their control. To understand Somalia's current history one must consider the international relations that framed it. Arabic trade pulled Somalia into the Muslim community; European colonial regimes created boundaries that destroyed the ecological balance of the pastoral communities and violated Somalis' ethnic and cultural bonds; and during the Cold War the Soviet Union and the United States supplied Somalis with arms in such quantities that together they created "one of the largest armed forces in Black Africa."[6] At every stage, various groups emphasized and manipulated clan divisions for their own particular purposes.

Prior to the arrival of the European colonizers in the last quarter of the nineteenth century, Somalis lived in a complex society that was defined by its semi-arid landscape and its coastline in the center of world trade. Roughly the size of Texas, Somalia has only two rivers (the Juba and the Shabeelle), both in the south. The majority of Somalis, identified as ethnic Somalis, share a language, an ethnicity, and a commitment to Islam. They trace their lineage back to two brothers, Samaal and Sab, whom they claim are descendants of the Quraysh, members of the Prophet Mohammed's tribe. The majority of the ethnic Somalis are Samaal—pastoralists who travel as much as one hundred miles seasonally to move their herds of camels, sheep, and goats in search of grazing lands and water. The minority Sab reside primarily in the south and are more sedentary, engaging in trade and herding and drawing on the agricultural labor of non-ethnic Somalis.[7]

Abdullah A. Mohamoud describes the socio-political organization of pre-colonial Somalia as "kinship associated with communalism."[8] It was a society in which kinship, social contract, and religion united to give the "stateless Somalis a rightful political center of gravity," according to Samatar.[9] The institutions of those earlier times have changed, but they remain.

Each of the six major clans is divided into a number of subclans known by the name of the common male ancestor. As one Somali woman observed, mothers teach their children their heritage: "Typically every child at an early age will learn his or her sub-clan kinship genealogy and will be able to name as many as twenty or thirty patrilineal ancestors."[10] Within the clan system, the most "meaningful and binding" social grouping is that defined by the *diya*, an "alliance formed by related lineages within a clan by means of a contract *(heer)*." Members of a *diya* group are responsible for supporting one another and providing compensation for the injuries or deaths of fellow members. Women are married at a young age out of the subclan. As a result—belonging to two subclans—they have a recognized role to play in peacekeeping. As one Somali scholar writes, "the clan is a protection, an insurance, and a means of survival for its members."[11]

Heer is a "secular and unwritten social contract" that maintains the social order at different political levels. This customary law ensures that "lineage segmented groups" will not make "use of each other's pasture zones and bore wells without prior permission," that neighboring clans will exist peacefully, and that the "tension (that) arises between groups and lineages for the access to meager resources such as water and pasture" will be settled peacefully.[12] Men make decisions collectively in the *shir* (council). In doing so, they are guided by both *heer* and the tenets of Islam.

In addition to the ethnic Somalis, three other ethnic groups are prominent in the history of Somalia. Arabs settled on the coast to form trading communities and remained there. Along the river valleys are descendants of the pre-Somali inhabitants and the Bantu. Many of the latter are descendants of slaves brought from the east coast of Africa during the coastal slave trade.

Both the pre-Somali inhabitants and the Bantu are agriculturalists and, as a result, are considered *habash*, or inferior, by the pastoralist ethnic Somalis.[13] Outside of the Somali clan system, they can be attached to the ethnic Somalis in a variety of ways: through adoption by a clan or through a client relationship in which they retain some rights within the clan but remain distinct. All Somalis, ethnic and non-ethnic alike, are united in their religion. Islam came to the Somali coast with the traders as early as the eighth century and now virtually all Somalis are Muslims.

As separate as the clans and subclans might be, a strong oral tradition[14] and the gathering of clans around wells have created a larger community in which a scattered people remain well informed of what is going on elsewhere. These gatherings often stir political discussions, leading observers to comment on the high level of Somali political involvement. As one commented in 1963, "Politics was at once the Somalis' most practiced art and favorite sport. A radio was the most desired possession of most nomads, not for its entertainment value but for news broadcasts. The level of political participation often surpassed that in many developed democracies."[15]

While practicing pastoralism over generations has enabled the Somalis to survive in a climate where water was always limited, Somali society has not been static. Early records suggest that Phoenicians, Egyptians, Greeks, and Romans all engaged in trade for incense and myrrh with Somalis. Beginning in the seventh century, with the growth of Islam, Arab and Persian traders began to establish communities on the coast and to engage in extensive trade in gold, livestock, leather, ivory, amber, and slaves. These coastal traders brought Islam with them and thus brought the Somalis into the wider Islamic world. Not only did Islam encourage Somalis as Muslims to travel to Mecca at least once in their lives, but it also welcomed them as members of an expanding international Muslim community or *umma*. As Lee Cassanelli observes, members of the Sufi community settled among the clans and "these Muslim intellectuals . . . provided conceptual maps to help members of those societies navigate changing social, political, and religious relations." The local sheikhs were the first to put in writing the genealogies that ultimately "connected virtually all Somalis in the Horn to one of two common ancestors." Throughout the colonial era their discourses offered "an alternative voice on governance and public morality."[16]

The traders also brought with them the opportunity to travel. "The relatively high degree of political sophistication in the otherwise primitive environment," one observer commented in the 1960s, "stems in part from the Somalis' fondness of foreign travel and adventure. It is not uncommon to encounter Somalis who have seen much of Europe and America traveling as seamen, and who have lived in Marseilles, London, or New York for a few years before returning to their tribes in the interior." The strong connection among clan members meant that this experience of travel was shared with others in the hinterland.[17]

The delicate ecological balance maintained within Somalia's pastoral and agricultural system was disrupted with the arrival of the British, French, and Italians in the last quarter of the nineteenth century. The extent to which each colonizer involved itself in Somalia depended in large part on what it hoped to gain from its territory. Drawn primarily by the desire to protect and serve their trade routes to their colonies (a desire which increased with the opening of the Suez Canal in 1869), the British and the French interfered little with Somalis in the hinterland. The French established a trading center and a coaling station in Djibouti; the British turned to the Somali herders in the north of the Somali territory to supply meat to their military depot in Aden, right across the Gulf. Only Italy, coming late to the division of Africa, aimed to establish a colony of settlers in the south and develop commercial enterprises along the Juba and Shabeelle Rivers. The arrival of the Europeans coincided with the growing strength of Ethiopia, which, under the imperial reign of Menelik II, had begun to extend its authority over lands that Menelik claimed were once part of its empire. As a result, all three European colonizers found themselves negotiating with Ethiopia, the only Christian kingdom in Africa.[18]

"Among the most far-reaching consequences of colonialism in Africa," one political scientist states, "has been the partition of the continent into political units whose borders were determined largely on the basis of European rivalries and interests."[19] This notion was poignantly true in Somalia where the colonizers drew and redrew the boundaries according to their own interests, paying attention to the global balance of power more than to the needs of the pastoralists, "for whom there is one frontier only: the furthest limits to their pastures."[20] The Somalis responded with armed resistance. Both the creation of boundaries and the conflict that the boundaries introduced undermined the long tradition of pastoralism that had sustained the Somalis for centuries. By dividing the land and its people, the colonizers also created a desire for nationalism among the Somalis even as they fractured their common heritage.

In a series of negotiations amongst themselves, the colonizers established boundaries that divided the Somali territory into British Somaliland and Italian Somalia, Ethiopian controlled regions of the Ogaden (1896) and the Haud (1897), and the Northern Frontier of Kenya (1920). These new boundaries cut lines through traditional grazing lands and divided clans. Although the treaties that established them explicitly stipulated that pastoralists had the right to move freely, they nonetheless interfered with the pastoralists' lives. The Anglo-Ethiopian treaty of 1897, for example, stated that the tribes "occupying either side of the line shall have the right to use the grazing grounds on the other side" and that the Ethiopians were required to provide them with "good treatment." Nevertheless, the treaty gave Ethiopia the right to control the Somali communities within its border. Ethiopia sent military expeditions to collect taxes and to provide cattle and beasts of burden for its garrisons. The result was frequent clashes between Ethiopians and Somalis.[21]

The Somalis resisted interference from the colonizers in both the northern and southern territories and as a result "more punitive campaigns were carried against them than against any other people" in East Africa. While every clan family participated in at least one uprising over the century of colonial rule, the most noted resister was Muhammed Abdille Hassan, known by the British as a religious fanatic, the "Mad Mullah," and by the Somalis as the "Warrior Mullah." Regarded as a hero of Somali nationalism, he waged war against the British and Italians from 1899 to 1920, engaging in the longest armed resistance in Africa.[22]

Hassan was a disciple of Mohamed Salih, the founder of a mystical order of Islam. He called on Somalis to resist the colonizers in the name of Islam. "Do you not see the infidels have destroyed our religion and made our children their children?" he orated in 1899. Enraged by the availability of alcohol and the opening of a French-run Roman Catholic orphanage, he proclaimed a holy war for the purification of Islam, the expulsion of foreigners, and the unification of the Somali people. He called on the Somalis to drop their clan identities and become dervishes (members of a Muslim order of ascetics). At his height, he commanded ten thousand armed men. He was a brilliant poet whose polemics, according to Lewis, "immeasurably enriched the Somali poetic heritage."[23] "I, on my own volition," Hassan claimed in one poem, "chose to fight the infidels. / It was I who said to the filthy unbeliever: 'This land is not yours.' / It was I who sought and found the prophet's guidance. / It was I who rejected again and again the infidel's offer to buy me out,

/ It was I who refused to sell my faith to gain the gates of hell."[24] His words as well as his actions inspired succeeding generations of Somalis.

While Hassan's resistance invoked pride among many Somalis, it also caused devastation. Hassan threatened to kill those who chose not to join him, and he followed through on his threat. Furthermore, the fighting severely disrupted the nomadic lifestyle that was necessary for pastoralists' survival. Some estimate that a full one-third of the male population died during the lengthy insurrection.[25]

Colonial politics and wars left their mark on Somalia. Prior to the arrival of the British, French, and Italians, Somalia had been recognized for its ecological richness and diversity. As late as 1897 one British traveler observed that it was "one of the best hunting grounds to be found at present anywhere in the world." By 1943 another visitor remarked that Somalia had been transformed from a "park-like environment" into a "barren, dusty, windswept waste."[26]

Colonial practices threatened Somali unity as well. The fact that different European powers colonized different parts of Somalia for different purposes served to further divide the Somali population. The Italians under Italy's fascist regime developed southern Somalia's infrastructure and increased its exports.[27] At the same time, they also implemented "a complex body of discriminatory laws designed to uphold the racial status of the colonists." In addition, the Italians resorted to forced labor to run the new agricultural enterprises for cotton, sugar, and bananas.[28] The British meanwhile invested little in northern Somalia, leaving it to remain as a "backwater, little more than a supplier of meat to Aden."[29]

World War II both heightened Somalis' sense of their common destiny and frustrated their desire to be united. The war was fought in Somalia with the Italians invading British Somaliland and the British fighting to regain control. Eventually the British defeated the Italians and gained control of both British and Italian Somalia. With the British Military Administration now governing eastern Ethiopia, British Somaliland, and former Italian Somalia, nearly all Somalis were united under one rule.

This unified Somalia was quickly and disappointingly dismantled, however, in spite of formal requests by Somalis to keep the territory united. In 1948 Britain returned the Ogaden to Ethiopia; in 1949 the United Nations returned southern Somalia to Italy as a trusteeship with the understanding that Italy would prepare the territory for independence in ten years. In 1955, the British returned the rich grazing lands of the Haud in the north to Ethiopia. And finally in 1961, in spite of a government-appointed commission determining that a separation from Kenya was "almost unanimously supported by Somalis and their fellow nomadic pastoralists, the British left the Northern Frontier of Kenya under Kenyan rule."[30]

In 1960 Italian Somalia and British Somaliland gained independence and united to form an independent Republic of Somalia.[31] "Somalis wake up," their national anthem exhorted. "Wake up and lean on each other. And whoever is most in need of support, support them forever." The dream for a Somalia that included all Somalis was reflected in the very fabric of the new republic. The exact number of representatives in the National Assembly was not established by law so that the number could be expanded as other Somali territories joined the Republic. The national flag included a five-point star to represent the five areas claimed as part of the nation: the former Italian and British territories, French Djibouti, and the Somali territories in Ethiopia and Kenya. Most unambiguously, the constitution asserted: "The Somali Republic promotes by legal and peaceful means the union of the Somali territories," recognizing all ethnic Somalis, no matter where they lived, as citizens of the Republic. The new government did not claim the territories outside of the Republic, but asked that Somalis living in those areas be granted self-determination.[32]

According to the United States government, the new republic "remained a model of democratic governance" for its first nine years.[33] It guaranteed universal suffrage, freedom of speech and association, and the right to fair trial. Its first election, held in 1967, represented the first democratic change of regime in Africa.[34] The new republic, however, faced major challenges. On top of any earlier clan divisions and those between the non-ethnic and ethnic Somalis, there was now a division created by different colonial legacies. The north and south had different administrations, languages, educational systems, and legal systems, not to mention different police forces, taxes, and currencies.[35]

In 1969 Somali President Shermaarke was killed by one of his guards. Following a bloodless military coup, Siyad Barre took control of the government. Barre implemented a series of reforms that he termed "scientific socialism" and which he defined as a "commitment to equality, economic independence, and economic growth."[36] Calling for an end to tribalism, nepotism, and corruption, he dissolved the national assembly, suspended the constitution, and banned political parties. The country was now governed by the new Supreme Revolutionary Council.

One of Barre's first laws was to abolish "tribalism" by banning any recognition of clan or ethnic distinctions. He also instituted a legal system to formally replace the "blood payment" of the *diya* system (the contractual arrangement within clans). As part of a mass literacy campaign to promote unification and nationalism, he supported the development of a written Somali language and initiated an education program that brought civil servants, military personnel, and students into the rural areas to teach. In addition, he pushed for gender equality by creating a national organization for women's programs and implementing new laws governing marriage, divorce, and inheritance. He also outlawed infibulation (the most severe form of female genital cutting).[37] "The key," he noted,

> is to give everybody the opportunity to learn reading and writing.... It is imperative that we give our people modern revolutionary education ... to restructure their social existence ... It will be the weapon to eradicate social balkanization and fragmentation into tribes and sects. It will bring about an absolute unity and there will be no room for any negative foreign cultural influences.[38]

At the same time, Barre tightened his control of the country. In 1970 he introduced National Security Laws and a National Security Service to investigate all those suspected of disloyalty or treason. He opened detention centers for those being investigated and held public executions of those who resisted his new laws, including noted Islamic clerics.

Somalia gained its independence just as the Cold War was heating up. The Soviet Union and the United States both considered the Horn of Africa a strategic site. The United States first supported Ethiopia while the Soviet Union agreed to provide Somalia with military training and aid. The two superpowers switched sides when Barre invaded the Ogaden region of Ethiopia in 1977. Ethiopia had just experienced a revolution and the Soviet Union chose to support the new socialist-leaning state. Without support from the Soviet Union (and fighting Cuban soldiers who had come to aid Ethiopia), Somalia suffered a defeat. The campaign both drained the Somali economy and created a large number of ethnic Somali refugees who left the Ogaden to settle in the north of Somalia. In search of support, Barre turned to the United States. Between 1980 and 1988 the United States government poured $163.5

million in military technology into Somalia. This, on top of the military technology provided by the Soviet Union, left Somalia "rife with weapons." By the 1980s the Somali nation was "one of the most militarized in Africa."[39]

Anthropologist Catherine Besteman identifies two significant trends over the following two decades in Somalia: "a massive influx of foreign aid and ...a virtually complete disintegration of popular trust in the government as a result of flagrant human rights abuses, state-backed terror, unpredictable political appointments and demotions, and the increasing concentration of state power."[40] In an effort to regain control, Barre began to deliberately inflame the clan rivalries that he had earlier tried to abolish.

The war with Ethiopia ruined more than alliances. More than 2.5 million lost their lives and as many were displaced from both sides of the border as they fled from the fighting.[41] In the wake of the war, resistance to Barre's regime intensified first in the north but soon throughout the country. By 1990, his "control scarcely reached outside of Mogadishu."[42] In 1991 the United Somali Congress, an armed resistance group in the central area, overthrew Barre and soon thereafter split into two opposing parties. The city of Mogadishu descended into chaos as warlords drew upon clan identities to wage war over the spoils, disaffected and armed youth took the opportunity to engage in looting, and the armaments provided by the Soviets and the United States made killing easy.[43]

The fighting quickly spread as "waves of destruction and terror ... radiated outside of the city unpredictably." Various armed forces moved through the countryside and laid waste to the agricultural regions along the two rivers. With the destruction of livestock and agriculture, famine spread. By 1992, one diplomat estimated that one-quarter of the population was at risk of starvation.[44] Between 1993 and 1995 the United Nations made a humanitarian effort to stop the violence but withdrew after suffering significant casualties and without achieving any order.

As the fighting spread, Somalis from all walks of life moved to escape the violence. They took boats to Mombasa, flew by plane to Nairobi, and crowded into trucks or walked through semi-desert areas to reach the border with Kenya. Those who escaped were the lucky ones. As one refugee noted, "I can think of many who did not make it to the boats or could not afford the steep prices calculated in dollars and cash. Some drowned."[45]

With formal state government destroyed, clans became the only functioning social institutions. Militias relied on them to determine their support, and individual Somalis turned to clans for protection. The same clan lines also became sources of terror. Whether one left Mogadishu or stayed "depended on whether you were a member of a generic clan whose people felt safe only if they escaped, or of another generic clan, which stayed."[46]

Somali exile and novelist Nuruddin Farah, who interviewed Somalis who had fled, explored what the war and the flight meant to those who escaped. Drawing from the memoir of Hassan Osman Ahmed, he described the early months after Mogadishu's fall:

> So stifling was the fear, according to the author, and so generalized the violence that people did not know what to do. They worried about the basics, about water to drink, food to eat, they worried about the safety of their family and what to do if they were taken ill, because the hospital ceased functioning. If they had food in the house, they worried about the day when they might run out of it, they worried about their friends and family and whether these had any, or how they might get some to them if they did not. For it was foolhardy to remain indoors, and it was unwise to venture outside.[47]

Deciding to flee was a decision made in haste; to hesitate could mean death for the whole family. As one Somali commented, "I reckon it is wiser to join the masses of people fleeing, and then ask why they were escaping than to wait and then be robbed, raped, or left dead by the wayside, unburied. What's the point of remaining in Mogadiscio emptied of all one's people?" The once cosmopolitan city became a "ghost town in the clutch of insanity ... a city run by gunmen, a place ruled by murder, mayhem, a madness unleashed."[48]

Those who participated in this "desperate exodus" were those who were "unable to find a modicum of shelter and safety in [their] homeland" or who decided that what was available there was "so unappealing and unappetizing that becoming a brittle and, at times, unwanted foreigner [was] preferable."[49] They fled initially across the borders to Ethiopia, Djibouti, and Kenya. From there, the luckier ones moved on to countries around the world. Finding refuge did not necessarily mean the ability to create a new life in a new land. Only those who could convince the United Nations High Commissioner for Refugees (UNHCR) that they were political refugees were accepted into the camps. Those who found refuge in the camps had to wait for UNHCR approval and a willing country's acceptance in order to resettle in another country—a willingness that was jeopardized by the

2001 Muslim terrorist bombings in the United States. Out of the more than 400,000 who fled to Kenya at the height of the war, a UN survey in 2003 estimated, that 160,000 still remained in the camps there.[50]

This more recent wave of refugees joined earlier refugees who had escaped from the political oppression of Barre and the devastation of the Ethiopian war. These new refugees, two sociologists noted, "included those who experienced the greatest horrors and suffered the largest losses. They watched with disbelief as former neighbors and friends turned on each other. Many witnessed the murder and/or rape of close family members and the deaths of those who did not survive the harrowing treks to safety. Many fled with no more than the clothes on their backs."[51]

For almost a decade international efforts to help end the loss of life were limited to "meager humanitarian aid" while the Somalis tried and failed to create a national government a dozen times or more. Finally in 2002 the Intergovernmental Authority on Development (IGAD) initiated a two-year peace process. This led to the current Transitional Federal Government (TFG) with a president and a 275–member parliamentary body.[52] In December 2006 Ethiopia, backed by the United States, invaded Somalia. Ethiopia claimed that the growing power of the Islamic Courts Union was a threat to the country and that the purpose of the invasion was to support the Transitional Federal Government. The UN sponsored new talks between the TFG and the opposition alliance for the Re-Liberation of Somalia (ARS) in 2009 and the Ethiopian forces withdrew. The goals of the new, post-invasion parliament are to write a new constitution and to plan for a new representative government.[53]

Five months after the fall of Barre, northern Somalia declared itself an independent Republic of Somaliland. It has yet to be recognized by any government, but it has functioned effectively ever since. In 1998 Puntland, on the northern coast of the Indian Ocean, established its own semi-autonomous government. Meanwhile, in southern Somalia, especially in the cities, the looting and warfare continue and the disaster is compounded by famine. Millions of Somalis are now finding refuge around the globe.

For those who remain in war-torn Somalia as well as for those carving out new lives for themselves in foreign countries, clans continue to matter. "To be sure," anthropologist Catherine Besteman acknowledges:

> people living under the terror of a collapsing state sought refuge in social networks with great emotional bonds—ties of kinship ... It is

true that much of the recent fighting between the so-called warlords has taken place between groups pulled together on the basis of clan affiliations. Using the sentiment of clan (in addition to the promise of booty and food) to rally support has apparently been a useful strategy for Somalia's warring factions.[54]

Somalis remain in touch with each other across the diaspora, providing financial and emotional support to those near and far. Without money sent by kinsmen from abroad, the deprivation in Somalia itself would be far worse. The *biil*, as the Somalis define this support, "constitutes a lifeline without which dependence on international food aid—or starvation on a large scale—would be inevitable."[55]

It is not only Somalis, however, who reinforce clan divisions. Even external agencies have divided them along clan lines. Somali scholar Peter D. Little, for example, points out that clan identities were "strongly influenced by" the UN and other development agencies seeking to help Somalis:

> These held static, traditionalist definitions of clan and the necessary resources to reinforce the stereotypes. External agencies frequently worked within a clan idiom themselves, often insisting on proposals from clan "elders" even when some of these were covertly militia heads. The number of acknowledged clans quickly multiplied in response to such requests and opportunities.[56]

Those of us who now host Somali refugees must see their history as a history of change as well as continuity. Our interpretations of Somalis' past can cloud or enhance our understanding of their present challenges. As Edward Said has so famously asked, "What is another culture? Is the notion of distinct culture (or race, or religion, or civilization) a useful one or does it always get involved either in self congratulations (when one discusses one's own) or hostility and aggression (when one discusses the 'other')?" As Africans and as Muslims, the Somalis have been "blasted from one history to another."[57] Only by understanding the complexities of their past can we recognize our role in the catastrophe and welcome Somalis into our midst with appreciation. Their history in the diaspora is only just beginning. Understanding the currents that brought them to our shores should enrich the voices in this volume.

Moving Past

Kay Ahmed

My past seems to have a funny way of catching up with me. In the loud and busy cafeteria of the Memorial Union at the University of Maine, I was often the topic of choice when it came to speech patterns. "Ha ha ha *carrablaay*," my friends would say teasingly in Somali. In a literal English translation, this meant that I was missing my tongue. Strangely enough, I almost did lose mine.

In the breezy summer afternoons in Somalia, just after the sun went down a little, my sister, three of my friends, and I would run to the dusty yard on the side of my house and start our daily game of soccer. After seeing us run out, my mother would give us her daily dose of nagging: "Why are you girls always running out there? Why can't you just stay in the house like all the other girls in the neighborhood?" Being the fearless and talkative six-year-old that I was, I would always argue with her until she got tired and left us alone, which she did almost always. She would give me a stern look and say, "Be careful and take care of your sister—and we will definitely have a little talk later about your thick skull, young lady." This was her way of trying to scare me into giving up. But I never did, and she never gave me that talk.

There were five of us, which meant that we would have an odd amount of members on each team; so one of the girls decided to be score keeper. Rules were set in place, and with one toss of a coin the game started. Ten minutes into the game, it was still tied 0–0. "Kay, Kay, go left, go left," my friend was yelling excitedly as she kicked the ball far to the left. I ran as fast as I could, hoping that I would get to the ball before the opposing team got to it. I ran and ran and then—boom, I fell in a hole.

In Somalia, they make a toilet by digging a twenty-foot hole in the ground. At the bottom, they put blades like a garbage disposal to cut the waste. They cover this with cement, cut a hole in the cement, and put a hut over it all. So the hole I fell into was a new toilet under construction. In the United States yellow and black caution tape blocks off areas like this so kids don't fall in. But here, in Somalia, they only had a little sign and some wood blocking the hole—and someone had moved the wood.

Before I knew what was happening I was screaming and yelling. The sharp blades were cutting me left and right. I was screaming for help but there were no words leaving my mouth—only blood. My tongue was cut so deeply that only a little piece of skin was holding it together. With a thump and a bump came a blackout.

I remember two Caucasian doctors hovering over me with clipboards, looking at me and speaking a language I didn't know. I thought they were Italians because the only Caucasians I had ever seen were Italian. I dozed in and out under the medication; I had no sense of time. I remember one evening, my dad or my mom or both my parents—I am not really sure—asked, "Are you okay? Where does it hurt?" Trying to comfort me, they said, "It's going to be okay. We'll do everything we can for you." Later I think my dad had come in and asked, "Can you talk?" And I said, "Mmm." I couldn't. I could only make little movements. It was scary. I had gotten surgery; my tongue was put back together. But it wasn't moving. They were going to have to connect the nerves for me to be able to talk again. And my dad said, "We're going to have it fixed." I remember the doctors hovering over me again. I can't even figure out which parent—because it was just a blur—saying I was going to go into surgery again to take care of my tongue, make sure that it was functioning. After that I went into intensive speech therapy for at least two or three years.

Recently I went on a retreat with other Somali students to tell stories. I knew what story I wanted to tell, and so I did. I told the story of how I got my tongue cut off—or almost cut off. And as I was telling the story, people were asking me questions. "Where were you when this happened? Where did the Italian doctors come from—did you go to Italy? When did this happen? Wasn't Somalia in civil war then?" I realized that I didn't know the answers. And so I called my mother and asked her. And I was shocked to find out that it hadn't happened in Somalia at all. It had happened in Kenya, after we had escaped during the civil war. When my mom told me this, I began to remember in bits and pieces the story behind my story.

We left Somalia in a hurry. I remember my mom talking about so many of our things: "We left it in the house." All my childhood pictures, all the memories, are gone because we left so fast. I was probably four or five when we did the walk to Kenya. I remember we had one gallon of water for all ten of us. How are you going to survive on one gallon of water? I remember the truck, which we didn't even ride—we put the things we were carrying in the truck and we walked. Our parents wanted to make everything seem as normal as possible.

We went through the whole day walking while someone drove the truck. We kept walking and driving. I remember fainting a couple of times. I would wake up. "Where are we? What is all of this? Where are we going and why?" I was curious; I was just a kid and I didn't understand anything that was going on.

When we came to Kenya—the way that my parents talk about it—it was never our destination. It was just a pit stop that we made. We just had to get out of the danger zone, get out of Somalia, and get to a country that had an actual functioning embassy. I remember struggling in the refugee camps. I guess I don't remember the time between that and when we had our own home in Kenya with the new toilet in the sand. And then I almost lost my tongue and went into extensive speech therapy.

I was shocked with what I learned recently from my mother about having left Somalia so fast. My parents always tried to keep things calm and cool. I think that, as humans, that is what we all want to do—because there are some people who don't have that ability who spend their whole life in struggle, who can't move on. That causes more pain. You don't want that; we're not built to keep doing that. That's like carrying a whole planet on your back. You just can't do that; you wouldn't survive. You have to move forward. If nobody could move past things, humanity wouldn't exist.

I learned as a Somali the ability to move on, to move past things, and I think I will carry that throughout my whole life. And I think my kids will take that from me, if they take anything from me: to just move on.

My dad says, "The past is the past, let it go." It's funny how he says that, but he also always says, "Don't lose your culture. You are the ones who are going to keep the memories of my father and forefathers alive." And he jokes, "Isn't that what you children are for? To pass on our stories?" But it isn't a joke, it's the truth.

My story started out as a triumphant story about almost-but-not-quite losing my tongue. It turned out to be not only a story of my own survival but of human endurance and our ability and need to move past things.

Why Maine? Secondary Migration Decisions of Somalis in Maine

Kimberly A. Huisman

Maine is now home to more than 6,000 Somalis, at least 3,500 of whom live in Lewiston and neighboring Auburn.[1] Although their migratory paths are as varied and interconnected as the people that have traversed them, most Somalis share a common past of having lived in other places before relocating to Maine.[2] A small percentage of Somali refugees were resettled in Maine through refugee resettlement programs—mostly in Portland—however, the majority of Somalis in Maine chose it as their home. In fact, municipal officials in Lewiston, Maine, estimate that secondary migrants account for 95 percent of the city's Somali refugee population.[3]

Many ask, "But why Maine?" and "Why Lewiston?" At first glance, it is perplexing. After all, Maine is cold, it is overwhelmingly white, there are few Muslims, wages tend to fall below national averages, and the economy is struggling. But closer observation reveals many reasons for this secondary migration to Maine. This chapter addresses two central questions: First, why do Somalis move in and out of Maine? Second, in what ways are the secondary migration decisions embedded in culturally specific patterns of relations among Somalis?

Somali Resettlement in the United States

Since the passage of the Immigration and Naturalization Act in 1965 and the Refugee Act in 1980, African immigration to the United States has steadily increased. In the case of Somali immigration, this rise has its roots in the Somali civil war, which began in 1991. Given the continued violence and turmoil in Somalia and the tens of thousands of Somalis still residing in refugee

This chapter is adapted from Kimberly A. Huisman,"Why Maine? Secondary Migration Decisions of Somali Refugees," Ìrìnkèrindò: a Journal of African Migration (forthcoming, June 2011).

camps in Kenya, Somali immigration to the United States is expected to continue increasing. While many will arrive as refugees, increasing numbers of Somalis will arrive via family reunification programs, sponsored by relatives who have become permanent residents or U.S. citizens. Somali refugees have been resettled in every state except seven.[4] Somali settlement in the United States is characterized by both concentration and dispersion. The majority of Somalis are concentrated in large metropolitan areas such as Minneapolis, Minnesota; Atlanta, Georgia; and Columbus, Ohio, but they are also dispersed around the country.

However, Somalis seldom remain where they are resettled. Lidwien Kapteijns and Abukar Arman point out, "Even after resettlement Somalis do not sit still," and Oivind Fuglerud and Ada Engebrigtsen emphasize, "Somali migration should be understood within the larger context of nomadic traditions."[5] Since 2000, "A great deal of secondary and tertiary migration has occurred as Somalis relocate in search of various types of opportunities (e.g., affordable housing, employment, education, and health care)."[6] Indeed, many Somalis relocate to find jobs and refugee services.[7] Increasing numbers of Somalis have been drawn to meatpacking jobs in small cities and rural towns in the Midwest.[8] The estimated Somali population in Minnesota ranges from fifteen thousand to thirty thousand, and according to one study, 60 percent of Somalis living in Minneapolis-St. Paul moved there from elsewhere in the United States.[9]

Somalis have a tendency to settle in communities with other Somalis.[10] Some relocate to large metropolitan areas with established Somali communities, but others move to small metropolitan or rural areas whose populations are racially homogeneous and where the Somali refugees are often highly visible. For example, Somalis account for 10 percent of the population in Lewiston, Maine, and 13 percent of the population in Barron, Wisconsin.[11]

Somali Refugees in Lewiston, Maine

The research site of this study is Lewiston, Maine. As the largest state in New England with a population of 1.3 million, Maine is known for its long, cold winters and heavy snowfall. Maine's second-largest city, Lewiston, is located forty miles from the largest city, Portland. Lewiston is predominantly white, Roman Catholic, and Franco American, and has been dubbed "the most Franco city in the U.S." At the time of the 2000 census, 96 percent of Lewiston's 35,690 residents were white.[12] An estimated 28 percent of the population speaks a language other than English at home, and of those, the majority speak French.[13] The residents of Lewiston tend to lag behind the rest of the state in education and socioeconomic status. Lewiston contains two of the poorest census tracts in Maine; according to the Maine Department of Labor, the city's 15 percent poverty rate exceeds the statewide average; and the median household income falls below the statewide average.[14]

Somalis began relocating to Lewiston at a historical moment when population decline was at its most severe and the availability of housing was correspondingly high. In 2001, there was a newly established Somali population in Portland, but given that city's housing vacancy rate of less than 3 percent, Somali families were resettled instead to Lewiston, where the vacancy rate was then 20 percent (declining to 7 percent by 2008). Between 2001 and 2005, the majority of secondary migrants to Lewiston were ethnic Somalis, and in 2006 and 2007 Somali Bantus made up the majority of secondary migration relocations.[15]

Today, many of the city's formerly vacant apartments and stores are occupied by Somali families and Somali-run businesses and organizations. On Lisbon Street, the primary thoroughfare in downtown Lewiston, a storefront mosque is in the midst of retail shops selling Somali food, clothes, books, and videos. Somalis stroll along the street wearing traditional colorful *hijabs* ranging from the more conservative two-piece *jelaalbib* to the looser *maser*. Many of the men wear long, loose tunics *(ma'awis)* or embroidered caps called *kooiyad*. However unlikely, and perhaps to its surprise, Lewiston has become a Somali community.

The findings presented in this chapter are based on five years of data collection and observations. Data includes twenty-seven interviews with individuals (fifteen women and twelve men), eight focus groups comprising a total of thirty individuals (twenty-one women and nine men), and many hours of participant observation in Somali homes and neighborhoods, stores, cultural celebrations and festivals, school events, a wedding, and other public spaces.[16]

At the beginning of the interviews and focus groups, participants drew their migration histories on maps of the Horn of Africa and the United States. Participants were then asked to relate their decision to move to Lewiston, their experiences living in Maine, and if applicable, their explanation for now wanting to leave.[17] Participants in this study ranged in age from eighteen to seventy-one, had arrived in Maine between 2000 and 2008, and were interviewed between 2006 and 2009. Prior to moving to Lewiston, all of the participants lived elsewhere in the United States, and most had moved several times.[18]

Somalis on the Move: Coming to Maine

Migration is not a new phenomenon for Somalis. Participants in this study reported complex migration histories even before war prompted a mass exodus. For many, mobility with the changing seasons was a way of life. Most participants or their parents had moved within Somalia, typically from the north to the south in search of better economic opportunities after independence in 1960; across borders to neighboring Kenya, Ethiopia, or Djibouti to join extended family; to other countries, such as Yemen, Saudi Arabia, or Italy to work or go to school; or in with relatives in another area of Somalia to attend school or find work.

Movement within Somalia was common and elastic, taking place within dense kin and clan networks, with the orality of Somali culture and gender norms sustaining the connections and linking people together. Like Fuglerud and Engebrigtsen, who found among Somalis "a tendency towards dispersal and of managing tasks through long-distance networks,"[19] I discovered that relations among Somalis exist within a wide web of social connections spanning the United States and global diaspora. Almost every participant reported regular contact with immediate and extended family throughout the United States and the world, in places like Canada, Kenya, Ethiopia, England, Australia, Sweden, and the Netherlands. Somalis in this study migrated internally for a variety of reasons, but most actualized their move through their membership in social networks.

Initially, the bulk of Somali secondary migrants moved to Lewiston from Clarkston, Georgia, a city ten miles northeast of Atlanta,[20] but since that time, Somalis have been relocating to Lewiston from many different locations including Columbus, Ohio; Minneapolis, Minnesota; and Boston, Massachusetts. According to the City of Lewiston, Somalis who applied for public assistance between 2001 and 2007 came from thirty-five U.S. states, three countries, and one hundred cities, and many had lived in several different states. The paths of the following three men are typical. Mohammed moved to Maine in 2006 from Vermont, where he had lived for twenty months. Prior to that he had spent six months in Atlanta, where he was initially settled after eight years in two refugee camps in Kenya. As of 2008, Guleed had been in

Lewiston for eighteen months. Prior to that he lived in Chicago for eight months, where he was initially settled after eight years in the Kakuma refugee camp in Kenya. Khalid lived in Dallas, Texas for three years before moving to Maine.

Why Lewiston?

According to city officials, more Somalis are moving into Maine than are leaving. During an interview, one city official commented, "Since the end of 2001, I don't think we've ever seen a month where we haven't had an average of twenty-five to thirty relocations."

For Somalis in Lewiston, economic incentives cannot be the primary factor for secondary migration, given the extremely limited job opportunities there. Lewiston city official Phil Nadeau writes, "What confounded most refugee resettlement experts about Lewiston's secondary migration relocation activity was the absence of any resettlement activity or industry that might have influenced their relocation decisions to the city."[21] This economic reality has contributed to the widespread public perception that Somalis are moving to Maine to use welfare benefits. Rumors circulate that tax dollars are used to give Somalis large cash sums and free cars.[22]

Indeed, several of the participants in this study did mention welfare benefits as a reason for moving to Maine.[23] Sufia, who arrived in Lewiston with her family in 1992, said:

> I moved to Lewiston because in Atlanta, where I lived for about nine years, I had two jobs. I used to work at a factory and I owned a little store. One day my son was somewhere and I was looking for him when I fell and broke my leg. In Atlanta they don't give adults Medicare or any type of medical plan. So I moved to Maine because I was told that the adults get Medicare and medical expenses would be paid for.

Similarly, Cawo, a woman in her early twenties, reported that her large family moved from Decatur, Georgia, because her father heard that "there would be better assistance here."

The majority of Lewiston's early wave of secondary migrants left Georgia, which has one of the lowest levels of welfare benefits in the United States (ranked fortieth), to move to Maine, which is among the highest (ranked thirteenth).[24] Georgia also has one of the harshest lifetime limit policies on

FIGURE 4. Mogadishu store on Lisbon Street

FIGURE 5. Lisbon Street mosque, located in a nondescript storefront (typical of mosques throughout the United States)

welfare benefits in the United States at forty-eight months (a year less than the sixty-month limit established by the federal government in 1996).[25] In contrast, Maine has no lifetime limit and, unlike Georgia, allows benefits to continue to children when their parents are no longer receiving assistance.[26] One city official opined:

> Maine has a history of being more benevolent in the sense that ... It makes entry into those public assistance programs easier. There are no residency requirements in Maine ... [From the first day] you live here, as soon as you meet the [income] eligibility requirements, you're in. You go to Ohio [and] there you've got to wait thirty days ... The other thing is that Maine is one of only a handful of states in the country that allows people to remain on the federal programs beyond the five-year maximum ... We don't get reimbursed from the federal government, but states can continue to offer them as long as they pay for them, and Maine does.

However, while welfare benefits may be a factor for some Somalis' decision to relocate to Maine, this widespread perception appears to be exaggerated and other factors tend to be overlooked. Although many secondary migrants do come from states with middle or low-level benefits, such as Georgia and Texas, many others come from states that actually offer equal or higher benefits than Maine, including New York, Massachusetts, Vermont, and Minnesota.[27] Moreover, the data indicate that a significant number of Somalis leaving Lewiston are headed to states with either lower monthly benefits (Utah and Arizona) or harsher lifetime limits (Minnesota, Washington, and Utah) than Maine.[28]

Several participants pointed out that when people see Somalis congregating on Lisbon Street in Lewiston, they assume that they are on welfare. Omar, a Somali man in his thirties, challenged this. "If you see a Somali standing at Lisbon Street it doesn't mean that the Somali is idle. That Somali will be at Lisbon Street because that is the center of information for the community ... Maybe he came from night shift, passed through the *halal* [store] to pick his meat, he will pick up a calling card, and then go home and sleep for the rest of the day."

Closer examination indicates that while some Somalis may be attracted to the social services provided in Maine, they are not the primary motivating factor driving secondary migration. The most common reason given for moving to Maine was to improve quality of life. Although welfare is one aspect of such an improvement, more frequently cited aspects included safety and increased social control, good schools, and affordable housing. As Muna, a Somali woman in her twenties, put it, "Atlanta was hard, you know, a big family, it is really hard to raise kids in Atlanta." In these ways, Somalis resemble other secondary migrants who seek a better life for their families.

Safety and Increased Social Control

Many of the study participants were initially resettled in large, inner-city neighborhoods characterized by high crime, drugs, gang activity, substandard housing, and grossly underfunded schools. Some participants expressed dissatisfaction with the macro-level structures in these neighborhoods such as housing and schools, while others referred to the tensions and conflicts that occurred on the micro-level in these communities. Omar points out:

> Many . . . refugees are [resettled] in very deprived communities. So by the time you come and realize where you are, it is like, "Oh, my God. Where am I living in the U.S.? Is this the country I was coming to?". . . It's these very tough neighborhoods where even the front doors have gates and the whole night what you hear are police sirens and gunshots and murders.

Cawo's family moved to Maine from Atlanta because her kids were being bullied. "There was a lot of violence in the community I lived in." Similarly, Halima, a woman in her twenties, cited the conflicts that ensued between African Americans and Somali immigrants: "African Americans usually inhabit the dilapidated neighborhoods; like most people, they react to the new immigrants and therefore tensions begin." Halima's observations were echoed by several interviewees who described being harassed and beat up by African Americans at school.

Safety, especially for raising children, was the most persistent reason given for moving to Maine. To understand why safety is paramount, it is important to remember that unlike many immigrants who move to the United States for economic opportunities, Somalis were fleeing war and poverty in Somalia or harsh and unsafe conditions in refugee camps. One young woman stated, "My mom moved us [to Lewiston] since she was the only one with us . . . My father did not come with us—he is still in Kenya—so that's why we decided to come here because it's quiet and smaller, with less crime."

Some Somalis moved to Maine to have more social control over their children's religious and cultural behaviors and dress, as well as to keep closer tabs on their whereabouts. Some parents expressed heightened concern for teenage sons, whom they viewed as at higher risk than daughters for being drawn into oppositional cultures in inner cities. Many participants noted that it was easier to exert parental control over their children in Lewiston compared with other places they had lived. This was often attributed to the small size of the city as well as to more religious conservatism among Somalis in Lewiston than the Somali population in nearby Portland. One young woman, Aman, reported that, "We joke all the time when we see someone and say, 'how much do you want to bet that my mom's gonna call me knowing where I am right now?' . . . It's kind of a joke . . . They can keep a closer eye on us because it's a small town and everybody knows each other."

For some parents, the desire to have more control over their children was especially acute when their children were young and in school. Relative to other places they had lived, Somalis viewed Lewiston schools as safe places where their children could get a good education.

Good Schools

It is well documented that educational opportunities are a determinant of secondary migration for immigrants, and for the participants in this study, education was essential. This is not surprising since Somali culture tends to have "strong positive attitudes toward, and expectations of, modern education."[29] As one young woman stated, "School was definitely one of the biggest reasons why we moved here."

Most Somali families moved to Maine when their children were young, but two participants moved to Maine as adults because they had heard good things about Maine colleges. When describing the importance of education among Somalis, Halima explained, "One thing you need to understand is that, religious or not, . . . teaching [their children] and encouraging getting a higher education is one thing that is common for all parents." Most participants had positive things to say about the schools in Lewiston, especially compared to their experiences elsewhere. Eighteen-year-old Aman reported, "In contrast [to Boston] we definitely have gotten our education. I just graduated and we have been a lot safer here and the schools have been more structured, more serious, and more willing to help us . . . [Here] there are more caring people who want to see you succeed."

For many parents with young children, access to educational opportunities temporarily outweighed the availability of jobs. These parents regarded education as an investment in the future. From Khalid's perspective, "It is very hard to find a job in Lewiston but I think it is good place to get an education, for our children to go to school. When we get enough English we have to move out to find a good place to work." Similarly, Guleed, a father of five, stated, "That's why we moved to Lewiston. We wanted to improve our education. I think if we get a good education maybe we will move to another place where we can have a good job."

Housing

Many participants cited cheap, affordable housing as a factor in their decision to move to Lewiston. Because the vacancy rate hovered around 20 percent when Somalis first started arriving, rents were extremely low. A Lewiston city official reports, "The rents have increased ... [but] in Lewiston you can still have $350-a-month apartments ... The market will demand that that kind of price be in place because there are still landlords that are looking to fill the units." Caaliya, a woman in her twenties, puts this in perspective: "In California even though we had jobs they weren't able to sustain us ... Rent for a two-bedroom apartment was $1,200 ... here in Maine [it] was $462." Along these lines, Faadumo, another woman in her twenties, stated:

> We were in Atlanta for three years ... My mom was working at two jobs and my father was trying to get his degrees back and all of his papers, and he was also working. I was working, my sister was working, and still it wasn't enough because our rent was really really high ... We moved a lot ... And then finally my parents were like, "We have to go somewhere else because the housing here is really expensive."

Housing is further complicated by the size of Somali families. Most apartments in the United States are not designed to accommodate large families. In California, Caaliya's family of sixteen could not afford housing sufficient for all of them, so she and some of her siblings lived with other families. Such arrangements were common.

Some participants reported that federal Section 8 housing vouchers are more available in Maine.[30] One Somali caseworker observed, "There is no waiting line in getting subsidized housing or Section 8 in Lewiston ... The grapevine is that once most get their Section 8 vouchers they move out to other states. I know of five families that have moved to Arizona." While some of my participants did allow that they moved to Maine to obtain better public assistance benefits such as welfare and Section 8 housing, this reason by itself cannot explain the quality of life issues—safety, schools, housing—that drew Somalis to Maine. As noted earlier, many of those who are leaving Maine are moving to places that offer fewer welfare benefits.

Why Do Somalis Leave?

Participants cited a variety of reasons for leaving or wanting to leave Lewiston, including "the winter," "all the trees," "sometimes there's nothing to do," "we can't find housing to accommodate our growing family," and "[I'm] disappointed with the school system." Although many left or desired to leave because they were dissatisfied with life in Lewiston, many others spoke highly of living in Maine, and several of those who left reported that they missed Maine and hoped to move back one day. Farham, a fifty-five-year-old man who moved to the Southwest with his wife and seven children, expressed a strong desire to return. He said, "One leg of mine is still in Maine. I like Maine. It was the first place that gave me an opportunity to be where I am today. I have to pay that back and will return to Maine." When describing life in Maine, he said, "The water is very sweet in Maine. Once you taste it you'll never [want to] leave." Overall, three persistent and recurring themes about leaving Maine emerged from the data.

Lack of Economic Opportunities
The most commonly reported reason for leaving was joblessness. Many Somalis struggled to find full-time work, and those who graduated from college left for other states with stronger job markets. Halima's observations are echoed throughout the interviews: "I see the young college-educated leaving the state because of unemployment. I was talking to some of the students, and they are all planning to leave right after graduation."

Many adult participants who did find work reported working seasonal jobs or having to travel long distances to work. Guleed said, "It is very hard to work in Lewiston for the refugee migrants ... One day I applied for twenty jobs for different companies. No one called me." Another man stated, "[Somalis] go to work in Freeport, they go to work in Augusta, they go to work in another city, but not in Lewiston." Aman, whose family is in the process of relocating to the West Coast, said, "My family is leaving because there is not enough jobs here. There's not enough . . . I don't see that there are a lot of options for people like us [here]."

Many of the younger participants reported plans to leave Maine after college, in part because they have seen how hard it is to make a living in Maine. Omar reported, "I finished college. I stayed here but I could not get a job." A young woman reported, "Two of my siblings have graduated from college and they stayed here for a year just looking for a job and they can't find anything so they have to look outside the state." The following responses were typical among Somali college students: "I'm going to leave Maine as soon as I am done with college," "I'm planning on staying here until I graduate and get my master's degree," and "There is not much in Maine for me. As soon as I graduate I'm leaving. *Inshallah* (God willing)."

Libaan, who is pursuing his master's degree and hopes to stay in Maine, observed that the out-migration of Somalis is similar to the out-migration of other college-educated Mainers: "I mean it's well known that even Mainers, when they graduate from college, they leave." While this may be true, a key difference between native Mainers and Somalis is that among Somalis, the entire family tends to move, either in stages or all at once, whereas native Mainers are more likely to move on their own. This reflects a key difference between U.S. culture, which emphasizes individualism, and Somali culture, which places more value on the group over the individual.

The educational opportunities in Maine seemed to outweigh the lack of jobs, at least until family priorities shifted. Libaan noted that "When people with young kids move here, they don't worry about their kids getting jobs until they get to the point that they have to pursue jobs." Yet, even those who were quite satisfied with the educational opportunities in Maine also reported experiences of racism or expressed some dismay over the lack of racial and cultural diversity within the schools, the second most important reason given for leaving Maine among my participants.

Racism and Lack of Religious and Racial Diversity in Maine

Some participants reported coming to Maine either to escape racialized experiences in other urban areas or because they believed that the North would be more accepting of racial and religious diversity than the South. Several young Somalis reported being beat up or harassed by other racial minorities prior to moving to Maine. Thirty-four-year-old Omar reported: "I came [to

Lewiston] from the South which was totally a different world. When I arrived in Atlanta ... I saw all the big trucks with the Confederate flag on top of it, and I was like 'My God!'" He continued that Somalis "want to go places where they are no longer in the limelight, but once they arrive here they come to realize that you cannot take one step without being identified as a Somali ... Oh my God, this place is not even diverse!"

Some participants had only positive things to say about their experiences in Maine. Halima, reflecting about the Many and One rally that drew an estimated four thousand people,[31] stated:

> I love Maine ... I don't know if you remember January 11, 2003, but people from Lewiston clearly stated that they would not welcome racism in their communities. I remember going to the rally against my mother's will. There were so many people from all over Maine. I remember thinking, "Well, there you go, after all, we are welcomed here." I remember this one incident at a gas station where an old Caucasian woman walked up to me and said, "We love to have you here." It was early in the morning, like 4:00 a.m., and I was going to work in Freeport. Lewiston is a great city, and most of the Somalis there don't face racism. This does not mean that racism is not an issue. There is always that one person or group in every community in the United States.

Ladan, a woman in her late twenties, stated, "Here most of the people are white, so I thought they would discriminate because I'm wearing a headscarf or because I'm black, but actually it was different ... One day I went to Sam's Club and this lady was asking me about my *hijab* and she said, 'Oh, I like your scarf. I would like to have one like that, too, you know.'" And Farham stated, "I have not experienced discrimination on the basis of race or religion in Maine. Lewiston people are very polite and very respectful, but slow to open up to new immigrants. This is due to most of them having lived here since their birth. They already have all the friends they need."

More commonly, however, participants reported more nuanced and often negative experiences about being racially and culturally different. Living in Maine has taken a toll on Caaliya, a recent college graduate who is leaving Maine to attend graduate school in a large city:

> It's exhausting ... being Somali and living in Lewiston because it's not just limelight, it's kind of like a shining, beaming spotlight that goes

with you wherever you go ... because if I go to Boston [or] New York, people at most will go, "Oh, there goes an African American Muslim.". . . It's almost like a craving for invisibility.

For Hibo, a young woman in her early twenties, "The lack of diversity in Maine is mostly what I dislike about being here ... It sucks to be a minority in a state where almost 99 percent of the population is white."

After praising the education she received in Maine, Aman qualified her experience: "The racial and cultural tension are a major reason why I want to leave. I mean education-wise—books, studying, academics—it's been good but I think socially it hasn't been. People don't understand about our religion and our culture ... they kind of back away because they just don't understand." Thirty-four-year-old Ahmed, who moved to Lewiston in 2001, also described dealing with such misunderstandings:

> I was working in this company in Brunswick with this guy, and we were sitting down just talking back and forth, and he was like, "When Somalis come over here, they are paid by the taxes ... and Somali people just keep coming over here because they find free housing and food stamps ... They want to take over the whole Lewiston city." He hates Somalis so bad.

And for Rashid, a forty-year-old Somali man, "Many times what I find difficult is that even though Mainers are fairly nice people and down to earth, they also came from a small town [and] they have a small town mentality."

Experiences of racism and issues of diversity are complex and contextual. Some Somalis chose to relocate to Maine from larger, urban areas like Atlanta, in part, to escape the tensions and conflicts between themselves and other racial minorities.[32] Many participants reported that they had not experienced racism or identified as "black" prior to immigrating to the United States. Once here, they quickly learned that they were defined as "black" by others and what this meant, including the fact that African Americans are subject to racism and largely viewed as being at the bottom of the racial hierarchy in the United States. Moving to Maine was one way of simultaneously distancing themselves from the stigma of being labeled as African American and preserving *soomaalinimo*, or being Somali—something that is viewed as essential to live a "secure and dignified life."[33] However, some Somalis do leave Maine because of racism, and even more often, because of the state's lack of religious diversity.

Constricting Effects of Religious Conservatism and Social Control

Omar, who has a fairly liberal view of Islam, reported that the Somali community in Lewiston is "very conservative," explaining, "One woman told me that in Lewiston you have to toe the line or else you will be reprimanded and called names until you're driven out of town [by other Somalis]." He went on to say, "In some circles Somalis have been referred to by other Muslims as 'the Muslim police'" and have "behaved in ways like the Moral Police of Saudi Arabia and Afghanistan." Other interviewees stated that if a Somali woman walks down the street in Lewiston without a *hijab*, she will be repudiated by other Somali women.

Some participants were more subtle in their criticism of social control and pointed to generational tensions between parents and children. For example, Aman wanted more freedom and anonymity in her life:

> When I think about living here, I think of living under my mom's eyes, I guess. I just want to be able to go out somewhere without somebody judging me or giving me an eye. When somebody sees you somewhere they call your mom and they say, "Oh, I saw your daughter here." . . . I feel like in Seattle you could walk around all you want and nobody [would say] anything.

In sum, given the many and nuanced reasons why Somalis move in and out of Lewiston, it is clearly problematic to reduce secondary migration to economic factors alone. While some of the reasons for secondary migration among Somalis are consistent with existing scholarship, my research participants' explanations suggest greater complexities and require deeper cultural analysis of the migration experience.

Culturally Specific Relational Patterns

Perhaps most people living in poor urban areas are dissatisfied with their quality of life and the lack of economic opportunities available for them and their children. Hence, it is not enough to just point to the factors outlined above to explain secondary migration. Rather, to understand why Somalis are able to pick up and move out of such places while the native born tend to stay, it is necessary to probe more deeply into cultural dimensions.

A closer examination of the forces facilitating secondary migration among Somalis reveals that cultural patterns of relations within expanding social networks make this movement possible. Importantly, the Somali networks extend far beyond the impoverished areas of their primary settlement. This networking distinguishes Somalis from poor minorities living in inner cities, who tend to live in a more isolated context with highly localized social ties.[34] The movement of Somalis is thus actualized by their involvement in dispersed social networks tied by cultural relations. Whether Somalis move to or from Maine in search of jobs, education, or safety, the way they learn about new places and opportunities is through their expansive social networks. Furthermore, in most cases, the social networks facilitate and buffer the transition from one place to another. There are always people on the other end to provide food, shelter, and assistance once they arrive in a new place. As Caaliya elaborates, "You are given rides to where you need so you have all that social support so there is no real cost in your moving ... The only thing you are asked to do is pay it forward for the next family who comes." For many Americans moving from one place to another is a costly endeavor, financially and psychologically, but Somalis' social connections enable those with few resources to pick up and move, needing only the means to get there. Somali social networks are grounded in historic and cultural specificities including nomadism, closely knit and persistent kin and clan networks, the centrality of oral communication among Somalis, and a gendered tradition of scouting for new places to live.

Nomadicism and Meanings of Home

A common explanation of secondary migration is that Somalis are a nomadic people, accustomed to moving around. One interviewee stated, "Somalis love being American, especially in getting naturalized and getting a U.S. passport—which is a gateway to the rest of the world, satisfying their pastoralist mobile tendencies of moving from one place to another." Another had a similar story: "Every time my parents are in a place for a really long time they want to move ... They are like 'okay, we've got to move up to Bangor' because they've been in Lewiston too long and now they're feeling like, 'Oh, my God, we have to move' ... They don't care where they're moving to, and I'm like, 'You guys can't stay put in one place!'"

Many Somalis in Lewiston do have nomadic histories, suggesting that such an interpretation has some merit. However, Dianna Shandy views this perspective as problematic because it reduces secondary migration to a "genetically derived wanderlust" while overlooking the positive ways in which social organization and social ties help sustain mobility and secondary migration.[35] Focusing on nomadism can also lead to cultural misunderstandings. Shandy also points out that social service providers often assume that people who move frequently have weak social ties, placing them at risk for a wide range of social problems. Yet in her work with Nuer refugees, Shandy found the opposite to be true: "It is precisely because of the existence of enduring social ties that Nuer are able to migrate repeatedly within the United States. Mobility serves as a mechanism to maintain social connections for both present purposes and future contingencies."[36]

For Somalis, nomadism was facilitated by their dense social ties as well as their conceptions of home. While some participants viewed Somalia as their only real home and expressed a desire to return one day, many—especially younger Somalis in their early twenties—viewed home in a more fluid way. For them, the meaning of home transcended a physical location. Caaliya said, "My home is where the people I love are . . . A physical place doesn't matter if the people you love aren't there." Many participants shared Cawo's sentiment: "Home is where my family is. It has no name or address for it . . . just the feelings of my family being there and making me feel safe." For Rashid, "Home to me is everywhere . . . This [Lewiston] of course is my home but it's not 100 percent home. There is something missing." According to Galad, a man in his sixties, "Home depends on the situation you are in at that moment." These descriptions of home indicated the absence of a permanently fixed place. One woman's qualified statement, "*right now* Lewiston-Auburn is my home," exemplifies this temporal quality.

Reducing secondary migration to nomadism alone "misses the critical distinction between describing a form of social organization that has the capacity to absorb and sustain mobility."[37] The social organization of Somalis is rooted within cultural specificities of their changing history of homes. For participants in this study, nomadism as well as other culturally specific factors did help facilitate movement. Yet, that nomadism exists within a wide and complicated web of social networks, both in Somalia and the diaspora.

Structure of Kin and Clan: *Ilko wada jir bey wax ku gooyaan* ("Together the teeth can cut")

The Somali proverb "Together the teeth can cut" is about family unity and strength. As the cornerstone of Somali culture, family is broadly defined to include extended family and clan. For example, when discussing how her "uncle" will assist her when she moves to Minneapolis in the near future, Caaliya explained, "I only call him uncle because we're related in the fact that we're all Somalis in the same tribe, as opposed to actually being family members."

Somalis go to great lengths to help one another. There is a strong tradition of hospitality in Somali culture in which Somalis are obligated to host and help each other. Ladan, a twenty-nine-year-old woman, stated, "In Somalia, most of [our relatives] are nomadic, so when they come to your house, you give them food ... Hospitality over there is different; we like to receive guests, and that way you just feel happy that you have helped so many people." Grounded in deep historical traditions, social relations are embedded in a wide web of familial and clan ties. Somali families are large and complex, and for some, polygamous. Most Somalis know and can even verbally recite their family genealogy back fifteen to twenty generations, in many cases tracing their family tree back to Samaal, who is considered the founding father of Somali people.[38] Galad, a sixty-three-year-old man, stated, "I can count all my ancestors up to thirty generations ... Every day I tell my children ... First of all, they have to know their relatives, and second, they have to know that they are from a great country with great culture."

Although kin and clan continue to take precedence in the United States, Somali networks are expanding and transforming within the U.S. context where social exchange may be extended on the basis of national (Somali) or religious (Muslim) identity. When describing this process, Omar said often people initially help each other on the basis of their Somali identity, and once the newcomers have been properly received in the new setting (e.g., picked up at the airport, fed), phone calls are made to find a closer clan or kin match. He stated:

> The Somali coming into town, no worries. We'll go there to receive you, then once we've received you we take you home. Then you rest. Then after that we'll discuss where you are going ... then I hand you over ... The Somali mindset is [that] when somebody sees you, he sees you as a Somali. Then, of course, one or two days later he will have to pass you on to a closer, more immediate family member. It's a natural, right thing to do. We are all Somalis, but when it comes to a certain level of comfort or details you must have a name of a person ... That's

why genealogy works positively in terms of [how] you identify your-self—then people figure out who is your closest relative.

Caaliya stated, "My mom has always told me you're a Somali first, always. It doesn't matter … When you're in airports and you see another Somali person you won't pass them [without acknowledging them] because their clan at that point is irrelevant … We could be killing each other in Somalia, [but here] it really doesn't matter."

Robert Putnam's concepts of "bonding" and "bridging" social capital are useful in understanding the shifting identities and changing social relations among Somalis in the diaspora. "Social capital" in general refers to social networks that are based on mutual trust and reciprocity. One dimension of social capital, bonding social capital, connects people to their own social group in which social networks are built around homogeneity (e.g., within religion, race, class, ethnic group), and trust is limited to others within the group. Another dimension, bridging social capital, occurs when social networks extend outside one's primary group (e.g., outside of family, clan, religion, race) and trust is more general. This form of social capital can transcend group divisions and links people to the broader social structures in a particular society.[39] In the U.S. context, what characterizes bonding or bridging capital for Somalis is fluid and evolving. For instance, in one context relations among Somalis from different clans might be considered bridging capital, whereas in another, where identities are shifting and clan affiliations are fading with new generations, this very exchange could be viewed as a form of bonding capital, helping their "brothers" and "sisters." My findings indicate that in the Lewiston/United States context new identities and allegiances are being forged, particularly for the 1.5 and second generations of Somalis,[40] to create more levels of bonding and bridging capital that fall along lines of clan, family, religion, and ancestry (Somali or African).

The remaking of social networks is also related to shifting identities among Somalis. Somalis express who they are in numerous ways.[41] Some participants view themselves as Somali first, Muslim second. Others are very clan-identified and will only shop in stores owned by members of their clan. Still others prioritize their Islamic identity and align themselves with Muslims of other nationalities. Some see themselves aligned with other Africans, even those who are not Muslim. Regardless of how individuals self-identify, Somali identities are being transformed in the U.S. context, and with these changes, social networks are expanding in ways that include both bonding and bridging capital. Caaliya stated that Somalis "don't realize that once they get in the American culture they are African American."

As identity is changing in the U.S. context, social networks among Somalis are expanding. For example, Omar's cell phone contact list has grown tremendously in recent years to include people outside of his familial and clan relations. Glancing down at his cell phone, he observed, "I have three Omars here. I have Omar Maryland, Omar Virginia, and Omar Ohio." Another participant described how social networks grow via the process of receiving Somali truck drivers when they come to town:

> If a truck driver is coming to Maine for the first time . . . he will call me and say, "I'm a truck driver. I just entered Maine now . . . In two hours I should be in Lewiston" . . . So what we do—because we know as a truck driver he's been on the road for so long—[is] go and pick him [up] from the truck, bring him home. He will have to clean his clothes . . . They will [stay for] three to four hours, socialize, eat food—[we] take them to a Somali restaurant, take them around, then drop them back off, then they leave. So that's how we expand.

As Somali identities become more fluid, the radius of networks extends. For most, these networks are still confined to members of their own racial, ethnic, or religious group rather than bridging them to people who are not Somali, Muslim, or African, but with time and new generations this will continue to change.

Orality of Somali Culture: "We Mix Tradition and Technology"

Traditional Somali culture is oral. In fact, it wasn't until the early 1970s that a written language was formally adopted in Somalia. According to Cawo, "We share everything through stories passed down from generation to generation. We still know a lot about our culture—and it's alive, because we are not fully integrated . . . I have family in Ethiopia, Kenya, Somalia, the United States, the Middle East, and Europe . . . We keep in touch through other family members."

Information is shared in person through family and kin networks, and also via those who travel among locations. In Lewiston, many Somalis communicate with each other on Lisbon Street, in Somali stores, or at the mosque. Somali truck drivers passing through Lewiston are sources of information about places to live. In large cities, Somali taxi drivers play a key role in sharing information. Omar described how a connection with a truck driver influenced his decision to move to Maine:

> When I was trying to move from Georgia in 2001, I first heard about Lewiston from friends. Then a guy who was a truck driver working with my brother mentioned it, but at that point I was not even looking at Maine ... He said, "Well, when you are ready I will give you some names and contacts locally."

Participants in this study preferred oral over written communication, and most information was shared through word of mouth, either in person or over the phone. Even those who used email still preferred to communicate orally. Omar said, "We write emails, which are not very good, I don't think. Many Somalis, when I send them an email they call me back after they've received my email, immediately." This was echoed by Libaan, a young man in his mid-twenties, who said, "It takes so much time to write an email."

Cell phones are used widely among Somalis and play a vital role in disseminating information. When discussing cell phones and the orality of Somali culture, one participant observed, "We mix tradition and technology." Cell phones facilitate immediate person-to-person contact and networking as opposed to the place-to-place networking of land-based phones. According to Libaan, "If people want to know about some city there's an easy way to find out. Somalis are networking people and you can call somebody that you don't know and you say, 'Do you know anybody in Seattle?' and they will find somebody's number for you." Participants reported that even professionals and college-educated Somalis who were accustomed to using the internet often preferred the telephone. Libaan stated, "If I wanted to move to Columbus, Ohio, I could go the regular way and look things up on the internet but Somalis don't usually do that, even educated people don't do that. They will say, 'Why do you have to do that? All you have to do is just call this person.'" This often results in a flurry of phone calls because, as one participant put it, "You don't pass the buck and say, 'Oh, I'm not available' and just leave it at that ... you check and see who else is."

The downside to the use of cell phones in the context of Somali cultural expectations is noted by Omar: "You aren't going to get peace ... Your phones are never going to be quiet because you will get calls at night at home about somebody coming in. So it's very overwhelming." Caaliya called oral communication a "double-edged sword" because word of mouth can lead inadvertently to the spread of misinformation: "It's good in the sense that we network really well," but "as a community I don't think we source the information out the right way." As one Somali caseworker illustrated:

> The negative part of Somali networking occurs when I, as the caseworker, give Muna seventy dollars and Fatuma fifty dollars. Fatuma will say, "Huh, he gave Muna more." [Fatuma knows this] because they know each other or they are related. You see now? It backfires on you, because you will be questioned in terms of being just and fair, but they will not understand. And I will say, "Listen, I cannot discuss Muna's family." They [will] want a breakdown of why she got that, and I [will] say, "I cannot discuss my client's information with you. But you qualified for fifty, and that's what you got."

Thus, while the orality of Somali culture keeps Somalis connected in an immediate way, this bonding social capital can also pose risks if groups are "superglued" and isolated from the broader society.[42]

Processes of Scouting and Gender Relations

Men and women both play a role in sharing information about new locales, deciding when and where to move, and welcoming newcomers into the community. My data indicate that men's roles and responsibilities largely exist in the public realm while women's roles and responsibilities are relegated to the private realm. Generally, men's more expansive social networks include family, friends, and acquaintances, whereas women's strong female networks are more likely to be limited to family and friends. Men tend to fulfill the more visible roles of scouting and transporting people to and from places, sharing information in public settings, while women tend to connect with other female friends and relatives within the private space of the home or over the phone. As Omar stated, "Of course the men do the airport picking up, the finding of the addresses ... The men will do the logistics, the connections and everything."

Scouting is the process of sending family members to check out potential places to live. For example, two Lewiston families sent their older sons to live with another Somali family in Utah; they were to report back about whether or not the family should move there. Another participant reported, "My uncle who lived with us came here and stayed with someone just to check it out and see prices for things and stuff like that." When describing the process of scouting, one young woman reported, "If I was planning on moving, my dad would send out my older brothers to go check it out and actually have a firsthand experience."

Various factors, including violation of gender norms, make it unacceptable for a woman to travel to a new location to assess it. Caaliya stated, "As a woman, let's say I call someone in Boston and there was this guy who lives in Boston and I was going to stay with him . . . I wouldn't be able to because my mom would have a heart attack . . . you know what I mean, because that's just not done." One participant emphasized the impracticality of sending women, especially those with children, to do the scouting: "If I had two kids I can't go to an apartment where there are four other guys living in cramped quarters. But with guys as long as there is space on the floor it is easier for them, they are more mobile."

The research literature regarding who initiates scouting and secondary migration in the family is mixed. Some have concluded that men decide while others have found that women are more likely to influence relocation decisions. My research, however, suggests that among Somalis, both women and men have a role. Halima stated, "Most of the time women find out about a new place to move to from friends or neighbors. Since mothers are closer to the children, it is the mother that knows what the kids are up to. Therefore the mothers influence the decision making. Sometimes the father might go and visit another city or state and ask his family to move." Another young woman, Aman, stated, "In my family my mother and father discussed it and made the decision to move to Lewiston together." Some participants shared her experience: "It was a family decision. My dad told us about it and we took a vote and we all decided to move."

The concepts of bonding and bridging capital are also useful for understanding the gendered dimensions of social capital. The public and private distinctions between Somali men and women provide men with more opportunities to expand the bonding and bridging dimensions of their social networks. However, this may change as more and more Somali women obtain college degrees and lead increasingly public and professional lives in the U.S. context.

Conclusion

This chapter addressed two central questions: (1) why do Somalis move in and out of Lewiston, Maine? and (2) in what ways are the secondary migration decisions of Somalis embedded in culturally specific patterns of relations? I contend that in order to understand secondary migration decisions of Somalis, one must examine the culturally specific contextual and relational processes undergirding these social decisions.

The most important factor pulling Somalis to Lewiston was the opportunity to improve their quality of life (i.e., safety, good schools, housing, and public assistance) and live among family and kin in accordance with their religious and cultural beliefs. The small size of Lewiston was particularly attractive in that Somalis were able to live in close proximity with one another and keep a close watch on their children. In the aftermath of a brutal civil war and years living in the harsh conditions of refugee camps, Somalis' main priorities are safety and security. In this way, Somali refugees are unlike immigrants who come to the United States in search of economic opportunities: Somalis, at least in the short run, are concerned more about safety and quality of life issues.

However, the major factor pushing Somalis out of Lewiston is the lack of jobs. Finding a job was not a reason given for many Somalis who moved to Lewiston, but my data suggest that as Somalis acquire education and skills (i.e., human capital) and as children grow up, jobs and economic opportunities take on more importance. Two other push factors are the constricting effects of religious conservatism among Somalis themselves and the racism and lack of religious and racial diversity in the larger community.

My research revealed numerous and compelling ways in which the secondary migration decisions of Somalis are embedded in culturally specific patterns of relations. These included expanding kin and clan networks, extending the orality of Somali culture with new technologies, changing constructions of identity, and gendered roles around finding places to live. These cultural dimensions highlight the nuances and complexities of secondary migration decisions and call attention to broader structures as well as micro-level processes. Specifically, the broader social structures (e.g., U.S. refugee policy, welfare programs, schools, labor market) clearly influence Somalis' decisions to move from one place to another. Calling attention to the deficits within these larger structures reminds us that micro-level processes are best understood in relation to macro-level structures. For instance, if refugees are settled in safe areas with good schools and jobs, they may not want to move. When Somalis pick up and move away from their initial places of resettlement, they rely on culturally specific social networks (e.g., scouting and oral communication) when deciding when and where to move. Thus, the decision-making processes of Somalis are embedded within both structural and cultural domains.

In sum, the data suggest that Lewiston may be a stepping stone for Somalis, a safe place to raise children and accrue human capital through educational opportunities before pursuing better economic opportunities elsewhere. However, additional, longitudinal research is needed to explore this further and to study how secondary migration patterns are changing over time.

I've Never Seen Africa

Bashir Mohamed

Unlike many Somalis in Maine, I was born in America. I was born in Atlanta, Georgia, and I grew up there until my high school and college years in Maine. My mom had me at a very young age; she was nineteen years old. She came to America about six months before I was born. So she was new to the country, and my dad had only been here for a couple of years before her. There were only a handful of Somalis in Atlanta in the 1980s. It was before the civil war in Somalia, so there was peace at home. There was no need to come here as refugees, and Somalis migrated for education and other opportunities they wanted.

So growing up I was like any average American kid. I grew up with Cartoon Network, Tom and Jerry, and Super Nintendo. My parents spoke Somali to me at home, but English was the language I first spoke. Both my parents worked outside the home, so they took me to day care. I learned English there, and when I was a child the country of Somalia didn't exist. It was basically just America, even though I still knew there was a distinction in how things were when I was home and how I was in society. I remember when I was in kindergarten and first grade that when my mom came to the school to drop me off and to pick me up, she wore traditional Somali clothing. I would say, "Mom, why are you wearing this?" because all the other parents would wear regular American clothing. She would say, "Are you embarrassed by me?" and I said, "No, but that's not what you're supposed to be wearing."

In the mid-1990s, after the war broke out in Somalia, my grandparents and my cousin came from Africa. They were my first exposures to Africa. Everybody in the house was talking in Somali and eating Somali food. When I listened to their conversations, I realized that they were speaking a different language. I was curious and wanted to know what they were all talking about. But instead of learning more Somali and more about Somalia, I taught my cousin about American life. The cartoons, video games, card games, and all the accessories made it easy to do. Still, since that time I've been hooked on Somali food.

Our family moved around a lot in Atlanta, from apartment to apartment. We never had one home base with friends that we grew up with. Every year we would go to a different school and meet up with a totally new group of kids, some of whom were African American, some white, some mixed, some Hispanic. Because my name is Bashir, people would look at me like something was different or strange about me. As I was trying to assimilate and fit in, I started acting like the African American students at my school and going by a nickname—because I didn't know my true identity. I had so many unanswered questions. I wasn't around Somali people except for my family.

Then we moved out of the city of Atlanta. My dad bought a house in suburbia; he was trying to get our family away from the inner city, which had more Somalis (because the civil war had started) but was also growing in crime and gang violence. The house my parents bought was in Lawrenceville, Georgia. I started fifth grade and finished all of middle school there. We still had friends of different races, and we used to play basketball a lot, but we were more isolated from the Somali people and culture. We stayed connected with our religion, Islam. Our dad used to teach us the Qur'an, making us memorize parts of it by playing games. But all that connected us to being Somali was the religion. I couldn't have a conversation with another Somali person who wasn't part of my family because it was just too awkward. I could understand Somali but I was unable to speak it.

One summer my family decided to move to Maine. I was puzzled and asked, "Why do you want to move us there?" But my brothers, my cousins, and I thought, "All right, let's go. We will have more freedom." We wanted to leave the suburbs because we didn't have a car. We were just stuck in the house, and all we did was play basketball. We ended up going to Lewiston the summer of 2002.

At that time there were a lot of people moving into Lewiston. Lewiston, Maine, is a predominantly white city that hadn't seen this much diversity in a long time, probably since the French-Canadian migration. So they were surprised, especially because we're Somalis. You could tell right away from how they looked at us, wondering what's going on? I was about fifteen years old, and I had this kind of American mentality—all Americans are the same, and all Americans are the same as all the white people in Georgia—and we always clicked with white people in Atlanta and Lawrenceville. I came into the apartments in Lewiston and they were full of Somalis, and we clicked and had a good time. I was learning to speak Somali, and I started realizing how to enjoy the company of your own people, because you can understand each other in a different language. You grew up with the same morals and traditions.

My brothers, my cousins, and my new friends went to high school together, and there was racial tension there, especially during my first couple of years as a freshman and sophomore. The students weren't familiar with us; I remember I was almost the only person in every class who was Somali. People would ask me questions like, "Did you guys used to live in huts and stuff back home?" And I asked them, "What are you talking about?" And they would say, "Back in Africa?" like it was a normal, serious question. I said, "What would you do if I told you I've never seen Africa, and where I'm from there are buildings that you probably have never seen in your life? I'm from a city that's, like, a hundred times more crazy than Lewiston, Maine!" One girl didn't believe me, so I told her my story and she was surprised. In the lunchroom at school the Somalis would sit at one table and the whites at another. It was like segregation before the civil rights movement. There was tension and fighting, and so I just stayed with my people most of the time. The longer I was in Lewiston, the more I became connected to the Somali culture and language.

In my junior year, a couple of other young Somalis and I decided to join a varsity sports program—track and field. I remember at the first practice the team members were like, "What are you doing here?" They thought of us as a different race—the Somalis of Lewiston. When they heard me speaking perfect English, it was like a step across one barrier. We started talking and having conversations, and as the year went on I became very good at the sport. The better I got the more they accepted me. By the end of our senior year we ended up winning the state championship together in the spring for outdoor track and field. The other team members would invite us to their houses. Their parents knew us, and if we needed a ride they would pick us up. Today I go to the University of Maine, and the guys who were on that track team go here, too, and every time we see each other—it's like a brotherhood. We always show each other respect and remember each other.

For a year I went to a school at Youngstown State University in Ohio, where I was the only Somali person in the whole school. That was an eye-opener for me, because the longer I was there the more I was losing my identity. I wasn't hearing or speaking any Somali. After that I decided to do research on my own. I started going on Somali websites looking at projects, from myths to legends to history facts. I began following the civil war, and pretty soon I was listening to Somali music, too. It was like I was there. I'm actually planning to go back to Africa this summer for the first time to see how it is. A lot of people told me I would fit in there.

3 A Work in Progress: Lewiston Responds to the Rapid Migration of Somali Refugees

Phil Nadeau

Introduction

Given its distinction as the "nation's least racially diverse state,"[1] it is unlikely that anyone could have envisioned how the relocation of several Somali families to Lewiston in 2001 would trigger yet another historic cultural shift in Maine's second-largest city. Over the last nine years, several thousand refugees, predominantly Somali and Somali Bantu, have changed the cultural landscape of a city with deep Franco American roots. This latest cultural shift captured the attention of the public, news media, and academics from around the world.

Although Lewiston's community response to the rapid relocation of several thousand refugees has distinguished itself in many ways, issues associated with the ongoing employment needs of a growing refugee population have posed challenges for the city and for the many refugee residents who remain unemployed. Although some refugees have found employment or started small businesses in vacant downtown storefronts, local officials have recognized the significant weaknesses of a federal refugee resettlement policy that has largely failed to provide low literate, limited- to non-English-speaking refugees the required amounts of education and training to gain employment.

These policy shortcomings are in stark contrast to those of Australia, which has committed to resettlement humanitarian goals while also providing a baseline of resources to assist all refugees in attaining the very same economic self-sufficiency goals expressed by the Office of Refugee Resettlement. For refugees, this is not a matter of desire but rather one of reasonable accommodation for education and training. In the words of James Truslow Adams in *The Epic of America*, refugees want what all Americans want—to be given the opportunity to succeed "according to ability or achievement" and "to attain to the fullest stature of which they are innately capable."[2]

A City of Immigrants

Understanding the issues faced by refugees and immigrants in Lewiston today requires some knowledge of the city's immigrant history. Lewiston was founded in 1795 and incorporated as a city in 1863. The introduction of textile manufacturing in the mid-nineteenth century attracted thousands of immigrants to a community that had experienced unprecedented levels of population and economic growth throughout the last half of the nineteenth century.[3]

Lewiston experienced a large influx of Irish immigration during the 1840s. As their numbers increased, so did tensions, which occasionally escalated into violence between the new residents and native, largely Protestant, Lewistonians. In one instance, anti-Catholic Know-Nothing sympathizers participated in the burning of Lewiston's first Catholic church built by Irish immigrants in 1855. The Irish did not pose any real economic threat, as locals held most of the better jobs in the new mills. In fact, Irish workers often performed labor in which many residents preferred not to engage, such as digging canals for new mill construction. The lower wages paid to the new residents, however, contributed to levels of poverty and exposed natives to new social challenges such as mass sickness, slum housing, and public welfare.[4]

Lewiston experienced another wave of immigration beginning in the 1860s with only " a few hundred" French Canadians living in Lewiston by 1870[5]—all part of the mass migration of approximately 750,000 French Canadians who moved into New England between 1840 and 1930 to work in the woolen and cotton mills sprouting up throughout the region. The Franco relocations accelerated as the number of textile mills increased. By 1900, 23,761 people lived in Lewiston; 70 percent of the labor force worked in its mills, and 56 percent of the city's population was French Canadian with 64 percent identifying their origins as "French" (French Canadian or French).[6]

By the mid 1950s, Lewiston was the preeminent textile manufacturing center in Maine. One cotton mill operation, Bates Manufacturing of Maine, employed six thousand people, making it the state's largest employer. Additionally, its neighboring "sister city" of Auburn became the shoe manufacturing leader in Maine, producing four million pairs of shoes annually.[7]

Over the last thirty years, Lewiston's economic and cultural profile has shifted; 2000 Census data revealed that the total number of residents identifying themselves as French Canadian made up only 29 percent of the population, while those identifying themselves as French were approximately 48 percent. During this period, all of the textile mills and shoe manufacturing plants that supported the local economy closed. These closures fueled efforts to move the city from its manufacturing roots to a more diversified service and light industrial economy.

Although the 2008–2009 recession pushed unemployment to its highest level in some thirty years, unemployment rates through much of the last decade hovered at historically low levels,[8] with an overall poverty rate (15.5 percent) only slightly higher than that of Maine's largest city, Portland (14.1 percent).[9] The City of Lewiston reported that economic investment in Lewiston-Auburn between 2000 and 2009 exceeded $500 million.[10]

All of the economic and demographic data appeared to point to a true economic and social renaissance. The city was well on its way to redefining its economy and, with the arrival of several thousand refugees, reshaping the social landscape while also reversing thirty years of population decline. The real question for many adult refugees relocating to Lewiston was how low levels of native language literacy and English proficiency would hinder their ability to participate in the city's new economic renaissance.

A Community in Transition: The Early Years, 2001–2003

Somalis first arrived in the United States during the 1920s, attracted by employment in the steel mills, educational opportunities in American universities, and employment as merchant marines. As political unrest and civil war escalated in Somalia in the mid-1980s and early 1990s, many more Somalis arrived as refugees. Between the fiscal years of 1990 and 2003, over 45,000 Somalis resettled in this country.[11] The Catholic Charities Maine (CCM) Office of Refugee and Immigration Services resettled 315 Somalis and approximately 3,500 other refugees in the greater Portland area between 1982 and 2000.[12] The gradual resettlement of these few hundred Somalis most likely affected the decisions of an additional 1,000 or more secondary migrant Somalis to move to Portland between 2001 and 2002.[13]

There are a variety of reasons why secondary migrant populations move from their initial communities of resettlement. Perhaps the simple explanation offered by the Office of Refugee Resettlement (ORR) is the most reasonable: "better employment opportunities, the pull of an established ethnic community, more generous welfare benefits, better training opportunities, reunification with relatives, or a more congenial climate."[14] This quality-of-life theme was also communicated by Somali community representatives in an open letter to former Maine Governor Angus King in May 2002: "Given the possessive nature of Somali parents towards their families and children, [cities such as Atlanta, Nashville and Louisville] are seen as places where the potential for running into undesirable situations [is more likely]. These include drugs, guns, and related violence as well as other social problems such as homelessness."[15] Although media speculation suggested that more generous state welfare benefits significantly influenced some Somali relocation decisions, there was little evidence to support that notion in Maine.[16]

The arrival of large numbers of Somali secondary migrants in Portland from the greater Atlanta area continued to the end of 2000. These numbers and a 2.3 percent rental vacancy rate in Portland forced the Portland Department of Health and Human Services to house the new arrivals in municipally operated shelters and local hotels.[17] At Portland's request, municipal social service staff from both Portland and Lewiston worked to relocate several Somali families to Lewiston in February 2001.[18]

By April 2001, Lewiston's General Assistance Office (GAO) estimated that fewer than one hundred Somalis had relocated from Portland to Lewiston.[19] The subsequent arrival of families in Lewiston from outside Portland and Maine, however, signaled to GAO officials that Somali arrivals were no longer looking to Portland as the preferred city of relocation. Lewiston GAO applicant interviews revealed that Somalis were beginning to board busses from the DeKalb County area of Georgia bound directly for Lewiston. By August 2001, 260 Somalis had relocated to the city, although various media sources reported that up to 1,000 had taken up residency during this period.[20] Records show that the locations from which they arrived expanded over time: Columbus, Memphis, Minneapolis, Kansas City, New Orleans, and several other communities.[21]

The initial relocation of Somali families from Portland to Lewiston was often driven by family and friend reunification. The number and speed of Somali arrivals, however, was inconsistent with other typical relocation patterns of secondary migrant groups. Anecdotal evidence of other national relocations suggested that immigrants tended to resettle in areas populated by primary resettlement groups or in communities where employment opportunities existed.[22] For example, Minneapolis-area Somalis moved into the surrounding towns of Rochester, St. Cloud, and Owatonna to seek employment in meat processing industries.[23] Without similar employment opportunities, secondary migrant movement often appeared to require a certain "critical mass" of primary resettlements before a community became attractive as a secondary migrant relocation area.

The first Somali relocation movement to Maine suggested that the initial resettlement of 315 Somalis to the greater Portland area was of sufficient primary resettlement "critical mass" to encourage secondary migration to that city. What confounded most experts about Lewiston's influx was the absence of any primary resettlement activity or the presence of a single industry that might have influenced the relocation. Though many media reports on Lewiston's Somali relocations identified the same quality-of-life issues articulated by the Somalis to Governor King,[24] the city's livability could not fully explain the relocation phenomenon in Lewiston (see Huisman, chapter 2, this volume).

In the early years of the relocation, city officials had difficulty understanding the complexities of the Somali social and cultural structure. As they educated themselves about their new refugee residents, they found that one characteristic of the population became increasingly clear: there were precious few Somalis who could speak English fluently. City leaders made it a top priority to seek out Somali representatives who could communicate effectively.

Officials met with dozens of Somali men and women within a few months of the first relocations but had difficulty discerning who actually represented the Somali community. Although officials were aware of the important role of Somali "elders" within their culture, city officials soon learned that it was the ability to speak English, not cultural tradition, that often dictated which Somalis would represent their community at meetings with local, state, and federal officials and the media. There was often discussion among Somali residents about creating a single "formal" representative body, but a consensus was never reached on how this representation would be achieved (that has not changed as of 2010).

By January 2002, the city had developed several personal relationships with key Somali leaders. In addition to relationship building, it was becoming evident to city officials that they needed to do more in the area of cultural awareness as the refugee population had grown to 560.[25] With the assistance of community leaders, refugee representatives, Lewiston's GAO, school staff, elected officials, and a few state and nonprofit agencies, a series of meetings were organized to address ongoing social service needs and to create an information exchange network for agency professionals.

These meetings ultimately led to a May 2002 public "town hall meeting" in which refugee resettlement experts, city officials, and Somali representatives addressed numerous rumors (including one that all Somalis received free car vouchers upon arrival in Lewiston) and provided local citizens with an opportunity to ask questions about immigration policy, tax burdens, program costs, school policies, and competing resource concerns. Though the event was attended by some five hundred people, exit interviews suggested that the meeting did not do much to change attending resident opinions on refugee and immigration policy or the Somalis' decision to settle in Lewiston.

Opinions may not have been significantly influenced by the town hall meeting, but that meeting and a May 2002 refugee report sent by the city to Governor King generated more public interest about the new residents. The governor's office and the public around the state were now following the events in Lewiston much more closely, although many continued to remain disengaged from any direct involvement.

State government, however, did respond with a higher level of collaborative effort from its frontline state agencies, ultimately leading to the formation of the governor's immigrant/refugee task force, whose mission was to develop more comprehensive statewide immigrant/refugee service and programming strategies. The town hall meeting also generated more intensive media coverage of the Lewiston-Somali story. By June 2002, what had been a statewide story attracted the attention of Patrick Reardon of the *Chicago Tribune*. His story was immediately followed with national news coverage on Fox News, Public Radio International's *The World,* and *ABC World News Tonight.*[26]

As intensive as the national coverage was, the real media frenzy began after former Lewiston Mayor Laurier Raymond issued an open letter to the Somali community. Most of the national media outlets in the country covered the mayor's October 1, 2002 communication, including CBS News, NBC News, CNN, the *New York Times,* the *Los Angeles Times,* and the *Boston*

Globe. In "the letter,"[27] the mayor asked that local Somalis contact family and friends outside the city and request that they not relocate to the city. The mayor's action was driven by his concerns that the city's ability to staff and fund ongoing relocations was exceeding its capacity to meet service needs. Public opinion about the letter was divided: many local refugees and non-immigrants viewed the letter as a racist attempt to stop the relocations, while others agreed with the mayor's assessment of the local financial impacts of so many unprogrammed relocations.

On October 11, 2002, the city, in collaboration with Somali leadership, delivered a jointly crafted press statement that addressed the furor over the mayor's letter, assuring the refugees and the public of the city's resolve to embrace the refugees' decision to take up residence in the city. While this gesture diffused some Somali concern, public and media attention persisted. Telephone calls, emails, and letters poured into Lewiston City Hall from around the world. City staff estimated the number of public contacts at more than two thousand over a two-week period, well beyond anything Lewiston officials expected.[28]

The irony of the attention generated by the mayor's simple written communication was that it generated the first tangible community-wide response from agencies, churches, academic institutions, and civic groups who had previously articulated little public support for the refugees. The mayor's letter appeared to serve as the key catalyst for greater levels of civic involvement as many previously unengaged organizations and individuals became more responsive to issues of cultural diversity within the community. Bates College, Lewiston-Auburn College, and the Central Maine Community College (then Central Maine Technical College) responded almost immediately by hosting a social meet-and-greet function for the Somali community and the general public in October 2002. The Calvary United Methodist Church organized a public walk in support of Somali residents and a broad constituency of about two hundred individuals from a variety of local churches, civic and advocacy groups, elected officials, and concerned citizens (many of whom had not previously participated in any civic activity) formed the Many and One Coalition in protest of a November 16, 2002 recruiting meeting announcement from a white supremacist group. The Many and One's crowning achievement was a counter-rally to the white supremacist recruiting meeting held on January 11, 2003. The counter-rally attracted some 4,500 people and significant national attention.[29]

FIGURE 6. Citizens again rallied in 2006 to confirm their support of Somalis and diversity (Kennedy Park, Lewiston).

Over the following year, local post-secondary institutions took action to welcome their Somali neighbors. Bates College hosted a March 2003 event, "Toward Harmony," and provided a public forum to discuss cultural diversity and social/cultural change within the community. Both Bates College and Lewiston-Auburn College expressed interest in utilizing the resources of their respective institutions to gather data and generate better information about local immigrant populations.

Academic interest in the Somali population did not stop at Lewiston's borders. The events of 2002 led to a greater level of involvement by the Maine and greater New England academic community, which launched a number of academic initiatives aimed at gaining a better understanding of the refugee community and its needs. This work included: a Clark University effort involving some fifteen Clark students and professors who conducted a community assessment to help Somali residents better understand their community and express their needs; Lewiston's involvement with Brown

University's Center for the Study of Race and Ethnicity in America; and the city's numerous academic contacts and service learning initiatives with Bates College and the University of Southern Maine. Other initiatives followed beyond 2003: the preservation of Somali culture through the University of Maine's Somali Narrative Project; Colby College Professor Catherine Besteman and her work with Lewiston's Somali Bantu community; and Texas State University Professor Lawrence Estaville and University of Southern Florida Professor Fenda Akiwumi's published work on the Maine Somalis.

The overall community response to the refugee relocation in Lewiston also continued to evolve well after the January 2003 Many and One rally. While the city worked with a number of agencies to refine how services and programming could be improved for Maine's new refugees, a number of initiatives were launched that directly involved the Somali community. These included: the National Civic League's selection of Lewiston as a 2006 finalist and 2007 "All America City" award winner (for refugee resident participation programs such as the "New Mainers Partnership" refugee case management program and the "Lots to Gardens" urban garden and farmers' market programs);[30] the creation of the 2008 New Mainers Workforce Project; and the Lewiston-Auburn Public Health Committee, created in 2008, which grew out of 2007 discussions with Lewiston-Auburn public health leaders interested in developing an "International Clinic" to better serve immigrant health needs.[31]

Most notably for Lewiston, the initial secondary migrant case management partnership begun with the City of Portland in 2003 evolved into the New Mainers Partnership, a first-in-the-country, municipal/faith-based collaboration between the city and Catholic Charities Maine. The 2005 restructuring of this secondary migrant case management program, funded by the Office of Refugee Resettlement and Maine's Department of Health and Human Services, was a milestone moment for refugee services in the community and the state. This new partnership preserved desperately needed case management services for as many as four to five hundred new secondary migrant relocations each year (services typically provided privately by refugee resettlement agencies) and received national recognition from the National Civic Review.[32] This project continues to provide secondary migrant case services to this day.

Literacy and Refugee Employment Challenges

Over the next seven years, the community and its "new Mainers"[33] continued to show progress in the number of refugee-owned businesses and improvements in the area of local-state refugee services, programming, and policy, but concerns around refugee employment and workforce development persisted. Lewiston's new economy had shed many of the entry-level jobs that were once available in the textile mills and shoe shops—jobs that often did not require a high school education. The city recognized that many jobs in its new economy would require more education, marketable skills, and some reasonable level of English proficiency.

This new economy necessitated that refugees compete against more proficient English speakers, especially as the unemployment rate continued to rise after 2006.[34] The complexity of the situation became even greater as city and school staffs started to encounter high levels of native language illiteracy among many Somali and Somali Bantu. Local officials feared that the native language literacy/English proficiency issue would make the task of accessing jobs and training more challenging for many of these refugees.

The difficulty for local officials was that much of the information about the refugee population, particularly the employment data, was anecdotal. The city believed that it needed quality data to better understand refugee employment levels and how English proficiency and low native language literacy were impacting refugees seeking or attempting to retain employment. Such data would not only better inform local refugees but also provide city leaders with the critical information necessary when seeking more state and federal financial support to fill the academic and vocational ESL (English as a second language) service gap for many refugee residents.

Amanda Rector's 2008 refugee employment report for the Maine Department of Labor and the Maine State Planning Office was produced in response to the city's refugee employment and data concerns.[35] Rector's report was notable in several respects: it was the first attempt by the Maine Department of Labor (or any other local/state or academic organization) to gather meaningful and useful employment data on Lewiston's largest refugee population; it confirmed that levels of refugee employment were low and trending downward; and it provided validation for city officials who believed that low levels of native language literacy and non-English speaking were negatively impacting refugee employment levels.

Although Ryan Allen had conducted a similar study of Portland's refugee population two years earlier for the Maine Department of Labor,[36] local officials believed that another study was needed to verify Lewiston refugee employment levels and patterns, given the different economies of the two cities. Both reports noted that refugee employment decreases in both cities may have been driven by variables such as dependence on temporary employment services (according to Allen, "nearly half of the refugees who worked in Maine found their first job at a temporary help services business"[37]), and that native language literacy and English proficiency were significant contributing factors to refugee unemployment.

According to Rector, "[t]hese immigrants face some barriers to entering the workforce. First and foremost, there is a significant language barrier. Most Somali immigrants do not speak English, and the jobs open to non-English speakers are limited. Additionally, there are cultural barriers."[38] Ryan provided similar observations in his 2006 study, adding that "these refugees who are functionally illiterate in their own languages probably have little experience with working in an industrial economy. [As] [t]hey are unlikely to understand the importance of a variety of conventional expectations in the workplace ... [s]ervice providers should focus more intensely on refugees who are illiterate in their native languages when providing English language instruction and an introduction to working in Maine. These individuals may face the most challenges as they look for employment in Maine and work towards self-sufficiency."[39]

The special educational challenges associated with "low-literate adult" (LLA) refugees and the importance of ESL education are well documented.[40] For adults who have little to no formal education as children, Sandra Lee McKay and Gail Weinstein-Shr reported that "[s]tudents who have not had experience with print or with formal schooling are inevitably left behind as their classmates with histories of education benefit from classroom activities and homework assignments ... [that] tap their previous experiences. Weinstein postulates that the literate orientation of the typical ESL classroom denies certain learners the comprehensible input they need to make sense of the new language. Miller found that Hmong adults in southern California who were not literate ... either fell behind or dropped out of those programs where they were mixed with more highly literate peers."[41] Further, Susan Chou Allender found that "learners who have had limited previous experience of formal education have difficulties managing information input, organizing learning material, following verbal and written instructions, and processing large chunks of new language. They are distressed by error or by failure to recall learned language."[42]

The literature supported the city's concerns that high numbers of LLA refugees were going to pose unique programmatic and funding obstacles for the city. Furthermore, the fact that the refugee resettlemet money remained with the primary resettlement community and did not follow secondary migrants to their new locations would further limit funding options.

The volume and frequency of new secondary migrant arrivals was something that distinguished Lewiston's refugee experience when compared to that of many other communities in the United States (Lewiston Social Services Department data reflected that secondary migrants made up 95 percent of the refugee population in February 2008). The predominance of secondary migrants meant that no direct resettlement funding was available to area refugees—the kind of funding that could support some level of ESL education. The few ESL dollars that were coming into Lewiston from the Office of Refugee Resettlement were being directed to the Catholic Charities New Mainers secondary migrant case management program, which limited ESL funding to adult citizenship courses.

The insufficiency of ESL workforce funding was compounded by the growing numbers of Low Literate Adult (LLA) refugees. Data from the adult education ESL programs showed that a high percentage of secondary migrants still needed ESL services after having been in the country for two years or longer. Sue Martin, Director of the English Language Learners program in Lewiston's public schools, suggested that many of the secondary migrant adults had most likely arrived in Lewiston having received minimal educational opportunities given their brief amount of time in-country[43] (the ravages of an extended civil war and overcrowded refugee camps resulted in limiting educational services in the camps[44] and in their country of origin.) Lewiston Adult Education staff interviews supported Martin's report of low or limited English proficiency and native language literacy rates within the Somali community.[45] Local observations and data were consistent with studies showing literacy rates as low as 24 percent among the general Somali population.[46]

Further complicating the LLA ESL concerns was a population of more than five hundred Bantu who began to relocate to Lewiston in 2004.[47] In addition, most other refugees who relocated to the area after 2004 had been in country three years or less and many were also non or limited English speaking and either preliterate or low literate adults according to observations made by Lewiston Adult education staff.[48] The rising number of Bantu relocations only added to the already high numbers of LLA refugees living in the city and elevated the concerns of local officials who advocated for ESL becoming an immediate and pressing federal workforce funding priority.

The Lewiston Adult Education Center provided ESL enrollment information from 2002 to early 2008,[49] which showed evidence of low refugee literacy levels.[50] The data did not account for levels of native language literacy, the percentage of the total population that required ESL, or the success of enrollees completing a given level of ESL instruction. However, 62 percent of all enrollees entered the program at CASAS Student Performance Levels (SPL) 1 and 2, providing compelling evidence that a significant percentage of adults seeking ESL services had little to no English reading, writing, or speaking ability. Adult Education Director Ann Kemper also confirmed that almost all ethnic Somalis and Somali Bantu were enrolled in SPL 1 and 2 in 2007–2008 and, based on staff assessments, were determined to be non-literate in their own language when entering the program.[51]

According to Kemper, those who were enrolled in SPL 1 and 2 levels were unlikely to succeed in securing employment locally (with the exception of some seasonal work such as apple picking or working at a local wreath-making business) until they progressed sufficiently to move up to levels 3 and 4. Kemper also stated that English literacy had improved for all refugees who enrolled in SPL 3 and 4 levels (levels that indicate the ability to compete for entry-level jobs requiring a minimum level of English speaking and writing ability) over the last few years and that many of those students had moved into some form of employment, although many were seasonal employees and subject to periodic layoffs throughout the year.

Federal Refugee ESL and Employment Funding

The general public, and possibly many in Congress, believe that primary resettlement programming provides sufficient training, translation, and education services for all refugees to become economically self-sufficient. Though the current ESL model may have been sufficient for those refugee groups who came into this country with some education in their native language (and possibly some marketable skills), the science suggests that refugees with insufficient education in their own native language will require years of education to attain a basic level of English proficiency—something local officials argue is a necessity to even compete for basic entry-level positions in today's job market.

The Lewiston Adult Education program utilized every available resource to deliver needed ESL education and job training to every enrolled student, but its limited budget simply could not deliver the recommended levels of academic or vocational ESL instruction needed for many LLA refugees. According to Sue Martin, "research says it takes five to seven years for most people literate in another language to move through the five levels of language proficiency and be able to study content in English ... [T]he older the student, the longer it takes [to learn a second language as] the level of illiteracy in one's primary language [increases]."[52] More significantly, the inability to achieve a certain level of casual speaking ability in another language increases the difficulty in securing employment,[53] with "[English] literacy difficulties appear[ing] to increase with age (except for the 15–19-year-old age group), particularly for non-English speaking migrants."[54]

It is important to reiterate that the arrival of ethnic Somalis and Somali Bantu to Lewiston was the result of secondary migration and not primary resettlement. The funding that supported primary resettlement (reduced to eight months of funding from the original thirty-six months approved by Congress back in 1980)[55] was not available to the city for secondary migrant services. The significant majority of refugee resettlement funding is heavily weighted to support the resettlement agency (commonly referred to as a volunteer agency or "Volag") and the affiliated state organization to relocate refugees into their community of primary resettlement. The current funding model assumes that most of the resettlement needs of a refugee would be addressed within the first year of resettlement, with the financial support for that refugee individual/family remaining with the affiliate agency and its ability to leverage other funding (this assumes that the refugee and/or family does not leave the community of primary resettlement).

The choice of which community will serve as the resettlement community is completely within the control of the volunteer agency. But this does not prohibit the refugee from departing his or her resettlement community at any time. Typically, the volunteer agency makes an attempt to match the refugee to a community's ability to support the resettlement. According to the U.S. Committee for Refugees and Immigrants:

The (volunteer agency) organization must 'assure' the Department of State that it is prepared to receive each matched refugee. This 'assurance' is a written guarantee that various basic services will be provided to the refugee and any accompanying family members in the initial resettlement phase. At this time the resettlement organization determines where in the U.S. the refugee will be resettled. The availability of housing, employment, needed services, readiness of host community, and a variety of other factors determine exact placement.[56]

Although Lewiston's economic profile has been showing signs of dramatic improvement, it remains the least wealthy of Maine's large cities. Of the eight largest cities in Maine, the 2000 Census ranked Lewiston last in median household income and median family income, and first in the number of families receiving welfare payments.[57] Given that Lewiston did not have the profile elements consistent with most resettlement communities, the city was never selected as a primary resettlement site for Somalis. Consequently, the typical flow of refugee resettlement funding and service support simply never existed. Refugee movements into Lewiston were the product of secondary migration and necessitated that ESL education, workforce development, and training would be largely locally funded.

According to Kemper, the absence of federal ESL subsidies limited her program's ability to deliver higher level ESL education to all who needed it.[58] Though agencies such as Catholic Charities Maine provided some ESL funding for basic citizenship classes, much of the adult ESL program was almost exclusively funded by insufficient local dollars. The meager level of federal/state ESL commitment to Lewiston met only the minimum demand for both "survival" and basic ESL education.[59]

In Lewiston's case, estimates provided by Kemper indicated that approximately 55 to 65 percent of the total adult education budget was dedicated to basic ESL education.[60] Adult education contributions from the federal government, in the form of Workforce Investment Act-Adult Education and Family Literacy Act monies, provided only 24 percent of the total ESL funding—a commitment that would only cover a fraction of the intensive ESL needs for LLA refugees.

Consider the cost for only those ESL students, many of them LLA refugees, who enrolled in SPL 1 adult education courses during the 2005–2006 school year. Using the McHugh study cost estimates for providing a full 110 hours of study to successfully complete one level of literacy,[61] the cost of moving those students through only five CASAS levels of proficiency would be $2.2 million over five years (400 students x 550 hours instruction x $10 per hour = $2.2 million). The first year of this investment would have added $440,000 per year or 116 percent to the adult education Fiscal Year 2008 ESL expenditures of $378,746—and would only fund SPL 1 students for 110 hours. What is alarming about this estimate is the likelihood that many LLA refugees would require a far greater number of hours of ESL education given their native language literacy levels.

A wider view of how refugee funding flows from the federal government to the state government and ultimately to the community agencies is critical to fully understand the scope of the refugee workforce funding deficiency in Lewiston. A review of the ORR 2005 fiscal year budget shows that the total employment dollars available to states and communities came from a blend of program accounts including both formula and competitive discretionary funds within the Social Services and Targeted Assistance budgets.[62] The combined total of these budgets was approximately $200 million—much of it set aside for primary resettlement and significantly less than what is actually needed to minimally support basic ESL workforce training nationally. The scope of the shortfall is striking considering that SPL 1 needs for four hundred Lewiston students totaled $440,000 for only one course per year, which would translate to $440,000,000 for four hundred thousand refugees (estimated legal permanent residents in the McHugh, Gelatt, Fix 2007 study)[63] nationally or more than all the ORR employment services appropriations.

Lewiston researched Targeted Assistance grants but was ineligible for this best opportunity for employment funding. Though Lewiston could not qualify for Targeted Assistance funding, a review of the ORR program language is revealing. The regulations state that "[s]ervices funded through the targeted assistance program are required to focus primarily on those refugees who, either because of their protracted use of public assistance or because of difficulty in securing employment, continue to need services beyond the initial years of resettlement. This funding requirement also promotes the provision of services to refugees who are ('hard to reach') and thus finding greater difficulty integrating. Refugees residing in the U.S. longer than five years, refugee women who are not literate in their native language, as well as the elderly are some of the special populations served by this discretionary grant program."[64]

The ORR goes on to say that "[a]ctivities under this program are for the purpose of supplementing and/or complementing existing employment services to help refugees achieve economic self-sufficiency."[65] Although the city did not qualify for Targeted Assistance funding, the agency's Targeted Assistance criteria did underscore the federal government's difficulty in understanding that fiscally challenged communities like Lewiston did not have access to the supplemental funding needed for refugees who were experiencing "difficulty in securing employment."

Once the city understood that ORR job training funding was not available, the city turned to Workforce Investment Act (WIA) Title One (which "provides job training and related services to unemployed or underemployed individuals")[66] and Title Two funds of the Adult Education and Family Literacy Act[67] as potential sources of ESL support. The city discovered that neither of these funds provided much support for the growing LLA refugee population in Lewiston or Portland. The total of all Title Two funding for adult literacy for the Lewiston Adult Education Center's 2008 fiscal school year was limited to $89,805 for an adult education program that was dedicating 55 to 65 percent of its $583,000 budget to provide ESL basic education, survival skills, and some modest support around vocational training.[68]

Lewiston's disappointment with WIA funding was shared by other agencies. According to the National Immigration Law Center, "[a]lthough the WIA's goal is to 'improve the quality of the workforce,' the law has been ineffective in serving immigrants and LEP (limited English proficient) persons. Most job seekers have been prevented from participating in training programs under the WIA because of the 'work-first' mentality.... Even when immigrants are given the opportunity to enroll in training programs, there is a dearth of programs that meet their training needs."[69]

Local officials were now confronted with the knowledge that refugee workforce training funds were in limited supply not only in Lewiston but throughout the entire state. Lewiston's inability to provide sufficient LLA refugee workforce training was directly related to two basic facts: Maine's commitment to refugee workforce development funding had come largely from inadequate state Workforce Investment Act Title One and Two funds;[70] and the ORR's limited employment program funds largely excluded Lewiston's refugees from accessing what few job training dollars were available.

The scarcity of meaningful LLA refugee workforce ESL training, and of any prospect of having programming that would meet even basic workforce development objectives for most LLA refugees in Lewiston, appears to under-cut the refugee workforce policy goals expressed by the Office of Refugee Resettlement. Much of the data discussed in this chapter demonstrates that the ESL needs of many Lewiston LLA refugees would not have been met even if the city had received some level of Targeted Assistance funding from the Office of Refugee Resettlement. Congress' reluctance to appropriate a rea-sonable level of adult refugee job education funding left Lewiston's new Mainers with few options. Unless the federal government reexamines its pri-orities and policies around refugee workforce development, it is unlikely that the situation in Lewiston will change in the foreseeable future.

LLA Refugee Workforce Development Alternatives

Lewiston's experience and the failure of U.S. refugee policy to adequately address the educational and vocational needs of LLA refugees raises an important question. Are there examples anywhere in the world where the ESL needs of LLA refugees (and possibly all refugees) are considered to be part of a national labor strategy which enhances the employment prospects for those unable to speak or read in their new country's language?

One of the best examples of developing a more focused national approach can be found in Australia. Australian refugee workforce development has been part of a well-defined national labor strategy that begins with manda-tory (with some limited exceptions) registration for ESL and a federal com-mitment to provide funding for ESL education and vocational training. According to Susan Chou Allender, "[t]he Australian Government estab-lished the Adult Migrant English Program (AMEP) as an integral part of its postwar immigration strategy to facilitate the settlement process."[71] AMEP is "the only language program of its kind in the world. [I]t is hailed interna-tionally for its contribution towards the successful settlement of migrants. More than 1.5 million migrants and refugees have learn[ed] English and received settlement assistance under the AMEP."[72]

The 1991 policy transferred a substantial portion of funding for English language and literacy from the migrant settlement program to mainstream vocational education and training. Under the National Training Reform Agenda, government and industry initiated a major program of reforms, to ensure the immediate relevance of vocational education and training to the needs of industry. These reforms provide the current policy for the provision of English language teaching."[73] AMEP "provides funding for 510 hours of ESL tuition for newly arrived adult migrants with English language proficiency below functional level."... Students must "register with the program within 3 months of arrival, start their tuition within 1 year and complete within 3 years."[74]

"Participants under 25 years of age with low levels of schooling ... [receive] 910 hours of tuition (and) over 25 years of age ... up to 610 hours of tuition."[75] In the workplace, refugees may receive additional ESL training if the employer chooses to participate in a competitive grant process for on-the-job training. The Workplace English Language and Literacy Program provides financial support to businesses that support language, literacy, and numeracy training in the workplace and contribute 25 percent matching funds in the first year and 50 percent funding in the second and third year.[76]

Although the Australian approach to ESL was known to some locally, it was understood that the prospects for a commitment similar to Australia's was unlikely in the near future. The absence of a meaningful workforce funding commitment did not hamper the desire of local and state agencies to assemble a modest comprehensive workforce training program for LLA refugees, although the numbers served would meet only a fraction of the need. In Lewiston, plans were developed in mid-2008 for a workforce preparedness project that would deliver 120 hours of training "specifically oriented towards participants with limited English proficiency, little or no work history, ... targeted at clients that have high beginning ESL skills (SPL 2-3)."[77]

The New Mainers Work Ready pilot project was developed as "a gateway for participants into the world of work" with pre/post mentoring, child care and transportation services.[78] The six-week program was modeled around the very successful Central/Western Maine Workforce Investment Board "WorkReady" workforce preparedness curriculum. While the original "WorkReady" program required that applicants have an eighth grade education or the equivalent CASAS average score of 220,[79] the New Mainers Work Ready project was developed to allow refugee applicants entry at the SPL 2 level of literacy which, according to National Reporting System standards,[80] equates to a first grade education. The New Mainers program was also promoted by the coalition partners as a credentialed program and endorsed by local businesses—something that would help level the playing field for prospective refugee job seekers. On October 22, 2008, thirteen new

Mainers successfully completed the 120 hours of training and received certificates acknowledging their accomplishments.[81]

The small but impressive successes of the New Mainers Work Ready project and a somewhat similar New Mainers Workforce Alliance project in Portland, Maine, was communicated to Maine's congressional delegation, which supported a $500,000 special appropriation from the U.S. Department of Labor for a larger Lewiston-Portland LLA refugee workforce demonstration project in 2009.[82] Following the Senate Appropriations Committee approval of the proposal in May 2008, the bill authorizing a reduced final appropriation of $330,000 was signed by President Barack Obama in April 2009. In June 2010, the Lewiston City Administrator's Office signed the final agreement from the U.S. Department of Labor, and the expanded refugee workforce pilot program was launched in September 2010.

Conclusion

Lewiston's creativity and commitment positioned the community to address the dramatic and rapid cultural changes that followed the historic relocation of several thousand secondary migrants to the city. The city's response resulted in significant and notable improvements for many "new Mainers" at the service, program and quality-of-life levels. However, for many of those same refugees, the matter of simply finding a job has become much more problematic. Though U.S. federal refugee policy directs the ORR to make refugee economic self-sufficiency a key component of its mission, Congress has failed to support either the ORR or the U.S. Department of Labor with the ESL funding needed to support refugees with low levels of native language literacy who enter this country as legally documented residents. The evidence shows that significantly increased levels of ESL education funding are needed for LLA refugees to compete in the broader and increasingly complex U.S. English-speaking job market. If U.S. policy makers continue to see refugee resettlement in this country as an important humanitarian and foreign policy commitment, the necessity for adopting a comprehensive, national labor strategy for LLA refugee workforce development, similar to that of Australia, is an imperative driven by the desire of refugees to become gainfully employed, the need to provide support to financially challenged communities, and the need to mitigate the potential social and economic costs associated with chronic, long-term unemployment.

Kidnapped

Faiza Ahmed

As I was looking at my beautiful country for the last time through the window of the plane, questions rushed through my head. Why do we have to leave our country? How are we going to survive in a new land whose language we cannot speak? Am I ever going to see my best friend, Nasteho, again? Didn't my dad think about us when making the decision to move? Didn't he care about us? I was lost in my mind, browsing through questions without answers while looking down at the priceless view fading away.

My name is Faiza, and I was born March 21, 1990, in a small country in the east of Africa called Djibouti. I was raised there by my beautiful parents, and I am one of nine children. Back in Africa, we were in the upper-middle class and had a stable life. Our family owned two houses: One was located in an amazing getaway city, where the weather was fair and the air so refreshing that we spent every summer there for vacation. The other house was in the downtown of the capital of Djibouti, where I grew up and went to school.

Since our country was colonized by the French people, they left us their language to learn in school. When I was six years old, I started going to a French school where I learned that language and Arabic; and then, starting in ninth grade, I learned English. Prior to that, at the age of three, my parents had enrolled me in an Islamic school called *dugsi* to learn about my religion. I remember that I made tons of friends in Djibouti, met close and distant cousins, and did a whole lot more.

When I could not think that my life could get any better—because I had turned fifteen at that time and was thinking about living it up with my closest friends, just like a regular teenager—my dad delivered the saddest and most stunning news ever: we would be leaving for America in a few days. It felt like someone had stabbed me with a knife through my heart. I was in such shock that I stopped doing anything. My dad didn't tell us why we had to leave or give us any other option—besides staying in Djibouti without parents or a house or anything else! We had to go with them to the United States. And, apparently, my dad had already taken care of everything on the down low without warning us: telling our school that we were leaving and getting our transcripts; telling the housemaids to pack our stuff and who to give our furniture to. He did not even give us enough time to see our friends, our cousins, or anyone else. It felt like we had been kidnapped on a dark night without saying good-bye to our loved ones.

I remember being on that plane with my siblings sitting right by my side, all asking ourselves why we had to leave. None of us could come up with a good answer, since we had such a good life over there in Djibouti. We promised each other to despise our dad for putting us through that pain. I remember like it was yesterday: we gave him the dirtiest look ever to show him how much we resented him. My dad knew what he was doing all along, and he even packed jackets in our suitcases—which seemed really weird to us, since we were from a country where the heat and humidity were really high.

So after taking one plane after another, we finally landed in the Boston airport. Before stepping outside, my dad got the jackets from our luggage. My siblings and I looked at each other and started talking to him sarcastically.

"What's that?" we said.

"Your jackets," he said.

"Yes, we know they are jackets, but why did you get them out of the luggage?" we said.

"Because it is cold outside and they are going to protect you from it," he said.

We just laughed and started walking. As soon as we stepped outside, the cold, windy weather hit our faces and made us run back inside to put on those big, ugly jackets. Oh, it felt so good wearing those jackets outside because it was so snowy and windy, nothing like I'd ever seen or felt.

It was now nighttime on April 6, and our uncles who came to get us from Maine brought us to Burger King in Boston to eat. At first, my siblings and I were so excited to be eating the food that we had seen on TV back in Africa: Burger King burgers! However, after tasting the fries and the burger, we immediately ran to the bathroom and threw up. It was the nastiest, saltiest food we had ever tasted. So then we left Boston and drove with our uncles back to Maine. On my way, all I kept seeing were trees and no buildings at all.

So I said, "Uncle Abdi, are you taking us to a place full of trees?"

He laughed. "No, sweetie. It is not like that. We are not even there yet. This is just the highway." After an hour we got to my auntie's house, and she cooked some Somali food for us. We ate and slept.

We stayed for a week. It was hard for my siblings and I to get used to the time over here. We went to sleep early and woke up in the middle of the night, not knowing what to do and where to go. We could not watch TV because we did not understand enough English. We did not know what to eat because the foods that were in the fridge were so different. But after time went by, we somehow got used to it.

We started school. They put us into different grades based on our ages. We were put into an ESL class full of Somali and Chinese students. We felt like we were lost in a class full of Somalis because the Somali dialect in Djibouti is different, and this created problems in communication. So we isolated ourselves and did not talk to any of the Somali kids. By not talking to them, they thought we were too good for them. We talked differently and we dressed differently. Even though we are Djiboutian-Somalis, we still felt like we were different from them. They assumed that we had an attitude. Luckily, our ESL teacher was Franco American and knew French. So out of everyone, we felt like she was the only one who could understand us.

So our teacher worked with us through our hard times and made it easier for us by providing French-English dictionaries and meeting with us one by one to improve our English. My dad was a big help too, even though we did not like him for bringing us to America. He helped us by talking in English at home more often. English was his second language, since he had worked at the U.S. embassy in Djibouti for more than twenty-five years. It was really hard adapting to the new lifestyle, learning another language all over again, and trying to fit in with the Somali crowd in Maine—we felt like outcasts, since we were the only Somali kids wearing Western clothes and not wearing the headscarf. Overall, we worked our hardest, took summer classes to improve our English, and got used to a life without the housemaids and other nice things we had in Djibouti.

We had been living in the United States for more than a year, and we still didn't know the reason why we had to leave our beloved home back in Africa. We finally got a chance to let go of the anger that we had against my father, and we decided to ask him why we had left everything behind. We sat around in the living room, everyone quiet, and stared right in his eyes, waiting for an answer from him. He looked up and looked down. He looked at my mom, and she nodded her head. He looked straight in our eyes and said, "So you guys knew that I was retiring in 2005 and that your mom doesn't have a job?"

We looked at each other and said, "Yes, we knew that."

"Well, since I knew I was retiring in 2005, in 2003 I asked the U.S. ambassador for visas for my family to come here, and he gave them to us. I knew that after I retired we would not be living in the same condition as we were before. I was trying to be a good father, and did not want my children to go through a rough life in our own country." He added, "I know that Djibouti has a good education system, but no jobs that are guaranteed for you guys after graduation. So I asked for visas while I had the chance so that my children could have a better life and not suffer like some kids do in our country."

We looked at each other with tears in our eyes, and I knew then that we had been wrong all along, because our father had acted for the sake of his children. Without his wisdom and his care and skills, I would not be here in the University of Maine; I would not have accomplished as much as I did; I would not have the great new friends I have now; I would not be the responsible and hardworking girl that I am today; I would not have the prospect of a job in the future. And I would not have the chance to tell this story.

FIGURE 7. Editors with young Somali women (Northport, Maine)

PART II

"We Are Not Under the Tree": Somali Communities in Transition

FIGURE 8. Young Somali woman (Northport, Maine)

My First Glimpse

Aisha Mohamed

In America, the beauty ideal for a girl is to look slim and tall, while in Somalia being a thick girl is considered beautiful. Looks aren't what is most revered in Somalia because of the *hijab*, which covers our body, protecting us from having our outer beauty revealed. Girls in Somalia can't play soccer or go to the café and just chill out, while boys and men can go anywhere without having any guardian. The way a female presents her personality and her talents is what is most important. The real beauty of a Somali woman is determined by her cooking skills, maternal instincts, and the tone of her voice.

I was born in Mogadishu, Somalia, May 9, 1990. One Friday afternoon, when I was four years old, while I was playing with my youngest brother Mohamed Deeq (who was six years old), I had my first glimpse into the different realities of life for boys and girls.

Mohamed Deeq and I went everywhere together. I dressed like him; I wanted to pronounce things like him. If he was still sleeping when I would wake up, I would curl up next to him, pretending to sleep while waiting for him to awaken. We no longer had our favorite, traditional toys because they had been thrown away during the constant migrating caused by the civil war. So we started using a *gumbar* (short chair), which was made from dried cow's skin, to play with. We took turns carrying the chair on our backs, pretending it was our child.

On this particular Friday afternoon my mom walked in and handed my brother clean *khamiis* (traditional long clothing worn by Muslim men). I was jealous and wanted to wear these clothes, too, but my mom refused to let me. I went to our room and took a set of my brother's clothing and put it on. I saw Mohamed Deeq, my father, and oldest brother walking to the *masjid* (mosque) and I started following them. My dad turned and told me to go back home. I became stubborn and continued to walk behind my brothers and him. My dad threatened me and said that he would hit me if I didn't go back home. But I didn't take his threat seriously, as he had never hit me before. As soon as I saw my dad turn back around, I continued to follow them all to the *masjid*.

Once we arrived and my dad saw me again, he said, "You're still following us?" He told me to go back home.

I said, "No, I want to go inside. My brothers are going. Why can't I?"

My dad said, "Let's go home."

I said "No."

He took a little stick from the ground and tapped on my finger. I started crying. Then my dad took my hand and walked me home. I was waiting for my mom to say I could go back to the mosque, but she thought I was crying for attention and ignored me. My other siblings were playing *gariir* (marbles) and not paying any attention to me either. I moved into a corner to wait for my dad and brothers to return from the mosque. When they returned my dad gave me a piece of candy, as he always did.

When I was five years old, we migrated again, this time to Kenya. There my dad worked, my older brother played soccer, and my mom and sisters stayed home preparing meals and cleaning the house. Mohamed Deeq, though, stayed and helped me with my chores. I rebelled against everything girls were supposed to do. I didn't want to do dishes. I didn't want long hair. I didn't want to cook. Mohamed Deeq and I would stand on chairs side by side doing the dishes. He would wash and I would rinse. Washing the dishes wasn't part of my daily chores then but rather a punishment for me. He was my protector.

Mohamed Deeq and I would play Power Rangers while my older sisters were tending to the household duties. My brother always insisted that he would be the red Power Ranger while delegating me to be the pink Power Ranger. I had no choice. I had to be the pink Power Ranger or I would be left out of the game entirely. My brother would say, "I am the guy, so that means that I will take all of the responsibilities; therefore, I am red."

When we moved to America, my mom worked full-time while my older sister replaced her at home, preparing all our meals and driving us to school and appointments. My oldest sister was the first to learn English and trans-lated for the rest of us. My second-oldest sister also helped with the cooking, cleaning, and caring for Mohamed Deeq and me. My oldest brother Ahmed wasn't responsible for any of the household duties. At that time his only worry appeared to be playing soccer, just like it had been in Kenya. However, life for him changed when my oldest sister decided to quit school, marry, and have a family of her own. He took on the role of both the dominant male and a part-time household caregiver.

Elementary school began for each of us not too long after arriving in Portland, Maine, and we moved quickly from Reiche Elementary in Portland to Riverton on another side of town. This move introduced me to my new best friend, Suad, who today is like a sister to me. I remember the day I first met her as though it were yesterday. She was wearing blue overalls with a red and blue striped shirt. Her hair was braided in a style which reminded me and the other children of Medusa, a name she didn't find offensive. I was dressed in typical Somali girly garb, consisting of a long brown skirt, a brightly colored shirt, and black *hijab*. My only deviation from the girly garb was the sneakers on my feet. I remember that the boys in the classroom compared the way Suad and I were dressed, referring to me as a "good Muslim girl" while calling her a "bad Muslim girl."

Later that day, I went to Suad's house to meet her family. Her mom and sisters continually complimented me on the way I was dressed. In their eyes my style of dress represented my moral character. The following day Suad arrived at school wearing a white *hijab*, a long skirt, and a colorful top. She walked up to me, and I sensed her anger immediately as she stated, "Thank you very much for making me have to wear this." I apologized and explained that I didn't dress like this to show off, but rather to be more in line with our religious beliefs. She understood, and neither of us has ever looked back on that day with negative feelings. We became closer with our newfound ability to talk things out rather than jumping to conclusions or making judgments.

A few days after that incident I decided to begin dressing like the American kids, but especially like the American boys. I wore baggy pants, a bandana, and sneakers. I would punch the other boys in a friendly gesture rather than using a friendly hello. As I moved into middle school my mom began to realize that my feminine characteristics were being dissolved by the ways I was behaving and dressing. Plus I wasn't doing the same work at home that my sisters were doing. My mom said it wasn't fair to my other sisters, who had begun cooking at the age of nine. She herself was the eldest of thirteen children and had begun the transition into homecare at the young age of six. But this was a practice I wanted nothing to do with. I felt that if the boys and men didn't need to do work then I wouldn't need to do it either. Equality needed to exist in my eyes, and I said so. But my mom didn't agree, and I was forced to quit playing sports and assigned regular household chores.

I never did all the chores assigned to me, as I refused to do the bathroom and the refrigerator. I agreed only to do the living room and dishes—after they had been rinsed by my siblings. When I reached high school, my mom said that in order to maintain the tomboy image I had fought so hard to achieve, I must go further in my education, as no man would live in a house with a woman who can't cook or clean. This was something I welcomed wholeheartedly. I had witnessed how difficult it was for my mother to become the primary breadwinner, and I knew that a better education would protect me from falling into my mother's struggles. I knew that I didn't want to be dependent upon a man to provide for me as an adult. But I also knew that I would always be a daddy's girl, and he would always be there for me if I were ever to need him.

I continue to have a strong connection with both my youngest brother, Mohamed Deeq, and with my oldest brother, Ahmed. Ahmed is my go-to guy for money to have my hair done rather than having my sister yanking at it for me. While he would give me advice about boys and how to dress as well as inspire me to take on the crafts of cooking and cleaning, my sister would tell me "stay away from the boys" stories. I still lean toward my masculine side, but underneath it all I always remember that I am ultimately a young woman and revel in knowing so. These tensions about gender run through both Somali and American societies.

Fragmented and Collaborative Leadership in a Changing Somali Community[1]

Ismail Ahmed

Somalis crossed continents and cultures to settle in the small city of Lewiston, Maine. This transition results in many changes in the lives of immigrants. Two processes take place: desocialization, in the course of which groups often feel invested in preserving their own identities and old roles; and resocialization, during which groups gradually develop new, bicultural identities. Protecting the old while searching for the new, as one generation subsequently follows another, is likely to produce stress and conflict. Leadership plays an important role in such transitions and can either mitigate or exacerbate the strains for both new residents and the host community, depending upon its appropriateness to the particular situation. For many local non-Somali observers, leadership constitutes the foremost cause for the fragmentation of Lewiston's Somali immigrants and should therefore be the focal point of social and cultural analysis. Not many Lewiston Somalis, however, recognize that their new context requires a more adaptive leadership approach; hence, they continue to experience leadership and contextual confusion.

This ethnographic study describes the dominant concepts of leadership among the Somalis in Lewiston, Maine. Based on interviews, interactions, and observations, I argue that the "walk and the talk" of Lewiston Somali leaders is not entirely successful in the Somalis' new cultural context. Nor does the social capital that the Somali community wields—the resources and information exchanged through social networks based on mutual trust and reciprocity—succeed in meeting its complex needs.[2] Furthermore, my study suggests that the gender, ethnicity, social position, culture, and/or religion of the traditional and fragmented cadre of leaders may present barriers to emergent leadership practices. My discussion also provides insight into capacities that are most relevant for the emergence of a different type of leadership emphasizing collaboration and partnerships that mobilize new forms of social capital. My study concludes with ways in which the capacity to adapt among the current Somali diaspora in Lewiston can be deliberately and intentionally cultivated as an asset that Somali leaders will need if they are to help their followers negotiate their complex acculturation process. My analysis is intended to be helpful to both Somalis and non-Somalis in understanding the root causes of the current power struggles within diasporic Somali communities.

Studying Leadership in Lewiston

Lewiston Somalis left Somalia and passed through other countries before resettling in the United States. Upon arrival in the United States, some relocated to Maine from other states as secondary immigrants.[3] Through all these movements in search of a new home, Lewiston Somalis brought with them a bag full of culture. Culture, in its broadest ethnographic concept, is the sum of a social group's observable patterns of behavior and way of life.[4] In the past, Somali pastoral society had very limited centralized traditional government, few centralized leaders, and no permanently constituted formal social institutions. As there were no definitive political leaders even during the advent of the modern nation-state after independence, pockets of cultural hierarchical structures were present to organize social life. Thus, social organization was fragmented within and between ethnic identities, and alliances among identity groups were formed to create subgroups of mutual governance.

According to Somali oral traditional culture, the recognition of the tribal leaders is based on hospitality, praise, and fame.[5] Personality and character also play a role in leadership. There is no continuity of power, only an honorific and respected title among the Somali leaders. Nor is there continuity of centralized authority in such a system, as a section of the members can disband at anytime to form another decentralized subunit. These cultural leaders have no traditional functions as office-holders, per se. They are mostly married and senior in age and lineage. The one who is the most influential becomes the permanent head of the ad hoc council (a structural oxymoron in European thinking). As cultural leaders, these men are listened to and their proposals carry weight. Their influence tends to vary from situation to situation and individual to individual; however, they generally command respect and authority through their perceived wisdom, skill in talking (oratory), or other personal qualities. Lewiston Somali leaders have also shown leadership tendencies similar to this historical profile of traits.

Traditional Somali leadership is structured within a council of elders. In the *guudiga* (ad hoc council of elders), adult males contribute and participate equally, although their contributions may be characterized by cultural members as "arm-twisting" and "back-stabbing," resulting in the development of splinter groups and factions as well as clan re-alliances.[6] The force of character of one of the members may sway the council's decisions and deliberations. Interestingly, outside the council—where community leadership is invisible—very rarely are all those eligible to speak able to attend or even get the chance to air their views. Upon arrival in Lewiston, for example, Somalis had several internal meetings to address issues that affected the community. Most of these meetings were held behind closed doors, and they involved an element of deception, such as pre-selecting participants and convening before sunrise or late at night in the mosque. The majority of the "other" participants would show up after morning prayers only to find issues deliberated and decisions already made.

Decisions that affect the followers' interests may thus be made in the absence of some members; however, sometimes decision making avoids dissenters' views. Deliberations are ad hoc, and councils are summoned by mutual agreement as need arises, depending on the mood and self-interest of the most charismatic leader. Alternatively, if an issue involves the group, clan, or subclan, the Somali elders representing the group are bound by custom, consensus agreement, or contract to punish anyone who fails to accept or implement the decision. A ready example of these dynamics in the Lewiston context is the overwhelming public response to the mayor's letter requesting Somalis to slow their migration to the city in 2002. When the Somali elders in Lewiston issued their response to the mayor's letter (see appendix A and appendix B for letters), they prohibited any other Somali member from commenting or speaking about the issue without the elders' approval.[7] The elders claim that their consensus is the majority's decision and that conformity serves the general interest of the Somalis. Members tend to acquiesce; and if they withhold their assent, they cannot get support when they need assistance, resulting in the loss of protection provided by the clan and its elders.

Lewiston Somalis are struggling with a division within their leadership ranks due to the various interpretations of their cultural and traditional perspectives, while at the same time trying to adjust to new leadership in their current context. Cultural values or beliefs can unite or divide a group, but in either case they create a commonly shared focal point.[8] For example, among Lewiston Somalis, each subclan has a specific kinship structure, as well as specific religious and economic practices. These differences are evidenced by the mushrooming of a variety of Somali ethnic-based stores in Lewiston to "serve our people" and cater to their economic interests. Even as different subgroups may have widely disparate attitudes on the surface level of their kinship, religious, and economic systems, they generally share a common belief in the deeper, often subconscious meaning behind these cultural elements. It is little surprise that the Lewiston Somali community is robust with clan-based mutual assistance associations that manifest ways for clan leaders to control and shape the power structure among Somalis in the city.[9] Clan-based leaders are also identified as quasi-religious leaders in that they use the power of Islam and the mosque to advance their clan biases, authority, and control over others.

Apart from the need to adapt a new leadership paradigm in their diasporic home, the transition to Lewiston challenges Somalis to partner and collaborate with the wider community, including other immigrant groups. Partnering would enable Somalis to consolidate their cultural, traditional, and religious beliefs with new ways and means of surviving in a sharply different culture and environment. Already their children are agents of change and are bringing these ways right into their homes. Unfortunately, the children import norms of individualism and consumerism that counter the beneficial traditional collective social support of mutually sharing meager pastoral resources. What Lewiston currently lacks is the combination of systems that could sustain a community that has undergone great diasporic cultural shock.

The complex, multilayered, and shifting nature of Somali social institutions is not immediately obvious and can only be elucidated by systematic study. My ethnography of Lewiston, Maine, focuses on Somalis who, like myself, have settled and worked there since 2001. For this research, I frequented "joints" (an Anglicism readily adopted by Somalis) like the local mosque, Somali *halal* stores, Somali ethnic restaurants, and some homes for a period of twelve months in order to observe informants. I participated in community dialogue forums, workshops organized for Somali leaders by mainstream service providers, task forces to discuss issues of the new immigrants, and platforms where new immigrant needs were raised. I observed some participants while they worked in the community providing services to the Somalis, and other participants at community events surrounding a death or a wedding. To widen my interactions with community members, I attended religious and non-religious ceremonies such as Eid ul-Fitr and Somali Independence Day. I also volunteered in the community, offering tutoring, mentoring, and advising services as I encouraged informants to share their experiences of leadership.

To identify informants to interview for my study, I used the criteria of people who have labeled themselves as leaders, based on my participant observations and extended through snowball sampling.[10] In total, I interviewed twenty people based on two ways the informants self-identified as leaders. Ten leaders who perceived themselves as such had positions in the community. They were eight men and two women who were leading organizations which dealt with decisions and advocacy around particular issues.[11] Ten more participants were men who considered themselves elders.[12] All interviews were administered by the researcher and were audiotaped with

FIGURE 9. Red Sea Restaurant, Lisbon Street (Lewiston, Maine)

prior permission from the interviewees. Each interview lasted about an hour. The same standard instructions and questions, both in Somali and English, were asked of each participant to assess his or her involvement in leadership and its meanings.[13] The interviews were transcribed, and, while still in the field, I went back to the informants to elucidate any ambiguities requiring clarification.

These interviews were of an intensive and serial sort, accomplished in natural settings and usually accompanied by close observation, if not participation, in the settings (street corners, restaurants, and the mosque). I often got close to the informants as a cultural insider/outsider. This dialectic of simultaneously being an insider and outsider is a familiar situation for the native researcher.[14] My holding some insider status offered important additional benefits and possibilities, most notably with respect to generating a relaxed atmosphere conducive to open conversation and willingness to disclose. In one of the interviews, for example, a Somali respondent interpreting my appearance expressed relief about my not being some scary academic. At the same time, I experienced difficulties that those perceived as outsiders might face, exemplified when one interviewee provided a series of highly defensive responses, including "if you were one of us, you would not need to ask." The ability to share subcultural gossip, anecdotes, and observations with informants further enhanced initial rapport, as well as offering an invaluable and effective stimulus for conversation during the interviews themselves. While care was taken to avoid leading informants toward particular answers through such contributions, the ability to sometimes move interviews toward a two-way exchange rather than the usual question-and-answer format can offer substantial advantages in terms of trust and conversational flow.

Continuities and Conflicts in Leadership

To the question, "What is leadership?" almost everyone answered immediately with language about "representing the community and leading others." Many participants shared similar responses, such as, "A leader is a person who is God-fearing and follows the example of the Holy Prophet." According to one of the informants, a leader is "a figurehead who leads and gives direction to others." An elder commented that leadership is "the experience in leading others gathered for many years." Another participant summarized his leadership philosophy as "the desire to guide the people and willingness to exert authority and power." One of the two female informants used the similes, "Leadership is like mother earth; it nurtures and does not expect to be compensated. It is like a river . . . [that] stays on course and keeps going." Many personal examples, most derived from Islamic scripture, were expressed in the interviews: "We are Muslims. The Somali culture and tradition forms our leadership philosophy."

Through these explanations, the Lewiston Somali concepts of leadership can be seen to be based primarily on the cultural value of having a "head"— usually a man—leading people like a pastoralist herding unruly camels through the desert. In this metaphor, the socioeconomic dynamic of pastoral Somalis depended on the male lineage owning herds of camel that they passed on as wealth and used as a means to gain leadership status. This tradition is no longer viable in the Lewiston leadership context, and, as I will suggest in subsequent themes, it is becoming problematic to reconcile it with newly emerging leadership roles.

According to the elders, another overwhelming personal leadership trait is "to be able to communicate with the people." Presumably this communication is mostly in the Somali language since there was no mention of communication with non-Somalis. When I noted to informants that the ability to communicate seemed to define the audience and language as Somali, they responded that they were in Lewiston as individual nuclear families, having left behind their extended families, and therefore needed to communicate among themselves first, in order to create a big family, before reaching out to others. One participant claimed, "If our children do not learn Somali language and culture, our Somali heritage will be lost."

Other personal leadership philosophies expressed are more pragmatic ones, such as "to lead is to earn a living . . . the leader lives well and takes care of his people." Some of the informants believe that American society is more complicated than Somali society, especially in respect to multiculturalism and social mobility. Therefore, they express that it is important that Lewiston Somalis should not be wary of acculturation, but at the same time they should not be disrespectful of their elders and tradition. Informants voice a fear of their children not accomplishing both of these objectives, but rather becoming fully Americanized.

Many respondents cast the influences on their leadership philosophy in religious terms. As almost 99.9 percent of Lewiston Somalis are Muslim,

Somali tradition and Islamic tradition are intertwined. When I questioned a respondent's statement about leadership being a mixture of Islamic and non-Islamic practices, he said, "Those who propagate Somali traditional leadership are still in the dark ages. In this context, a strong Islamic belief is the only cure of the ills and dangers of Western way of life," suggesting that only Islam can counter Euro-Christian and other alien forms of leadership in the diaspora. One informant noted that he draws from his family's strong Islamic upbringing and always refers to the Qur'an and the teachings of the Holy Prophet. When I brought to his attention that certain Islamic traditions were not practiced in the part of Somalia from which he comes, he quickly quipped, "That is why I am here. If the folks adhered to Islamic teaching back home, I will not be here." He then quoted a famous Muslim *hadith* (saying of the Prophet) to express his view of leadership: "If there were three people who came together, then choose one to be a leader."

The informants agreed that they had Somali traditional tendencies and that these especially influenced their leadership beliefs. One of the young informants confided to me that the leaders in Lewiston are influenced by their traditional Somali beliefs more than anything else, but they tried to camouflage these beliefs with Islam. The two women I interviewed vehemently swore to me that the leaders were "a bunch of tribalists." When I noted the fact that women were considered leaders too, they shyly looked down and said, "Yes, we are also inflicted with the clan disease," continuing in unison, "Who is not?" This statement suggests that personal leadership ignorance is associated with inherent traditional tribalism.

Informants agreed that whoever leads them needs to help them make an easier transition into American society and that the issues are not simply ones of tradition and culture. They shared their perception of many positive changes in their traditional values. They have noticed and learned most of these new values from their children. For example, one informant explained how his children are proud to be Americans, which has built their self-esteem and confidence. Some of the informants agreed that their traditional values still affected their leadership. One informant said, "Tradition is like hunchback—it is a hard to get rid of." The informants defended their traditional values, but at times explained how frustrating it is to be different from the Anglo-Christian mainstream. The young informants maintained that "the old guards" were propagating traditional values that are not relevant to the current Somali context.

Whereas the "old guard" insisted on the preservation of traditional values, young leaders wondered about their relevance to leadership in the current Somali context. One informant said, "Listen Ismail, there are no camels here. Everything is structured ... ABCD ... We are not under the tree." One of the female informants said, "Tradition has its place only in our bedrooms ... out there we need to come up with values that can work here." Another participant commented that her daughter was proud of embracing the good values from two cultural systems: she knows how to save some money to use for her own needs like an American, but she also knows how to assist extended relatives like a Somali. In sum, from the female and younger informants' perspectives, choosing relevant traditional values and rejecting irrelevant ones should be an important part of the leader's role in the immigrants' acculturation process, intellectual development, and cultural identity confirmation. Unfortunately, this was more easily expressed verbally than practiced by the Lewiston Somali leadership.[15]

Some of the participants agreed that the current community leadership was not fully developed nor experienced enough to assist the Somalis in this transition in the current context. Some Somalis living in Lewiston had never interacted with other Somali clans, let alone the Euro Americans with whom they now work. While their children attend school and meet Somalis and non-Somalis, the parents still live in their tribal enclaves—at least physically, mentally, emotionally, and socially. This segregation may have some effects on community leadership, as suggested by the incident one informant narrated to me: a mother reprimanded her children for playing with children from the "wrong" clan. Informants often attribute such incidents to the lack of cohesive leadership that embraces a heterogeneous Somali community.

Aware of these tensions, the leaders interviewed felt that they have not done enough to bring the Lewiston Somali leaders to the table to discuss how they are perceived by the Somali followers. One emerging Somali leader explained to me that the hours wasted on trying to reconcile the differing leaders were taking a toll on the community. A female informant said, "I hope these men could iron out their differences ... amongst themselves. There are no Togolese or Sudanese among them. ... just Somalis fighting and fighting."

Lewiston Somalis do not find a support system in the existing leadership, according to one informant, a college student: "Nothing is being done on uniting the Somalis. The leadership is a big barrier ... they are always dividing the people along tribal lines. This one is this, that one is that." When I asked her what she will do about this situation she answered laughing, "God willing, one day all these men will be dead and the new generation will bring the change." This notion of generational takeover as a solution to the wide leadership disparity was echoed by some other informants, too.

The interviews included anecdotes of how ordinary community members perceived Somali leaders. The leaders I interviewed did not surprise me with what they had to say about the existing traditional Lewiston Somali leaders. They all had constructive suggestions, such as one informant's recommendation to call a general meeting involving all the leaders. Another said, "We need to reject leaders who divide people." Leaders also criticized themselves by saying that the state of the existing leadership was pathetic, and something needed to be done about it. I often heard the informants discuss how the existing Somalis leaders need to adjust to the American context.

Many Somalis feel isolated, even though they have been living in the United States for at least five years and many have become American citizens. As one parent put it, it is not enough that their children learn English because in America, Somalis must be bicultural as well as bilingual. Community leaders can help reach this goal, confirming the notion that Somalis cannot be isolated and excluded from mainstream leadership, as some informants hinted. One participant told me that his family has lived in three places in the United States: Atlanta, Columbus, and Lewiston. Every time they moved to a new place, they encountered a similar leadership problem of a fragmented community with individualist leaders running organizations and businesses, and serving their clan and allies. From this perspective, it appears that Somalis in Lewiston have replicated the roles of their villages in Somalia.

None of the informants considered Lewiston Somalis as part of the larger municipal community. Many reported that they could not identify themselves with the organizations in Lewiston because of language barriers and differences in social backgrounds. As one participant put it, "I don't feel part of Lewiston, mainly because I don't speak very good English." Another informant acknowledged the part played by informal leaders whom he described as "some God-fearing people out there who help although they are not leaders [in the traditional sense]. They go out of their way to help the disadvantaged ones." These "God-fearing," informal leaders take on roles of active, grassroots efforts. For example, an elderly woman in the community goes door to door every month to collect money that can be used in case of a death in the community. She accounts for this money and puts it to the good cause of funding funeral expenses. Although the informants acknowledged the benefits accomplished by informal leaders, they also saw them as a threat to the traditional figurehead leadership.

The emerging leadership consists of those who are uniting the community and asking for accountability within the existing leadership ranks. One informant, who is a member of a youth initiative, said, "When we came to America some of us said to ourselves, wait a minute, there is something wrong with our leadership style. We learned and adapted other styles that we now can use to assist others." The issue of emerging leadership generates a big debate among the Lewiston Somalis. An elder asked me in this regard, "What style? We have our tradition and ways of doing things. Let me see how far the emerging leaders will go." I took this to be a rhetorical question, but he was quite serious and went on to explain how he will fight the "young, reckless" emerging leaders. This response starkly illustrates the power struggle being waged in the Lewiston Somali community over styles of leadership. From this informant's perspective, being an older Somali and a practicing Muslim qualified him to lead the Lewiston Somali community.

Informants thus differentiated two leadership styles along a continuum: a more formal traditional leader and a more informal contemporary leader. The informal leadership was more voluntary, while the traditional leadership exercised a more culture-based patron-client form of interaction. The traditional leaders tended to isolate Lewiston Somalis from the rest of the community, whereas the informal leadership encouraged interaction with the larger American society. In placing considerable emphasis on their ability to honor obligations to ethnic affiliates, traditional leaders sometimes denied unaffiliated others to an extent which caused conflict. This preferential dynamic is contrary to African traditional settings whereby leaders are not expected to exclude part of their followers.[16]

In how they focused on internal relations, traditional leaders emphasized bonding capital—limiting the exchange of resources and information within one's group; whereas by encouraging both internal and external interactions, contemporary leaders promoted the value of both bonding and bridging social capital.[17] Unlike bonding capital, which is exclusive and inward-looking, bridging capital is inclusive and outward-looking in order to build social networks outside of one's group. Thus, the contemporary leadership style stresses the importance of working within and outside of the community to establish trust and strengthen relationships and ties. Contemporary leaders, for example, sought to promote collective participation in town meetings that gather Somalis and non-Somalis. These kinds of meetings are akin to those of the dominant New England society but which in fact do not differ significantly from the traditional "under the tree" deliberations of Somali society. Traditional leadership appealed to older immigrants; the informal leadership was advocated by young immigrants, some women, or those who had taken the pains to learn leadership in their new context. Because of the perceived differences in linguistic proficiency, adaptation magnitude, educational knowledge, and socioeconomic backgrounds, traditional leadership has lost its attraction for many adaptive immigrants. The emerging leadership has the potential for meeting the needs of new immigrants in a new context. This alternative form of leadership does not entirely replace traditional leadership, but exists simultaneously within the adaptability of the Lewiston Somalis with more diverse, professional, knowledgeable backgrounds who are conversant with the English language and Western ways of thinking. The approach to working within and outside the community aligns contemporary leaders with strategies that Robert Putman argues are essential for developing a strong civic society.[18]

Despite the benefits of moving toward a new, more inclusive model of leadership, at least on the surface, the followers in the Somali community in Lewiston do not appear to want the newer emergent leadership. Instead, they seem to prefer a leader who does not expect much active interaction from them, even if that leader might be unkind and inconsiderate. Alternatively, followers may embrace a docile mosque committee leader who is not vibrant and does not stay on top of issues afflicting the Somali community. Ironically, the emergent leaders who are more compassionate and dynamic tend to be discounted by the followers because they expect too much time-consuming participation from them. Furthermore, emergent leaders tend to burn out from meetings that do not produce results.

The foregoing analysis suggests that the traditional Somali leaders in Lewiston value social relations within one's group and practice authoritarian more than authoritative leadership; that is, leaders seem to possess genuine authority but fall below expectations in misusing it in inhumane and inconsiderate ways.[19] Informants talked about the dictatorial tendencies of the traditional leaders in silencing the emerging leaders and using religion as a weapon to discredit social organizing that came from the "young Turks." Momadou Dia confirmed this notion by stating that "*self-reliance and self-interest* [emphasis mine] tend to take a back seat to ethnicity and group loyality."[20] This study suggests that Somali leadership and community members have a considerable distance to go in order to address the complex social and cultural dynamics that can achieve greater self-reliance, self-sufficiency, and self-rule in the changing arena of the Lewiston diaspora.

Continuing Challenges in Leadership: Collaboration and Community Partnerships

Numerous studies have highlighted the importance of community empowerment to create an informed leadership. These studies stress the centrality of engaging local communities in collaboration, of offering real stakes in the change process, and of the difficulties associated with achieving local participation in partnerships.[21] As I interviewed and observed Somali leaders in Lewiston, the community partnership issue came up both explicitly and implicitly.[22] Participation by new immigrants in partnerships can have ambivalent effects on community partners.[23] Mostly, the Euro American partners of Lewiston have attributed the lack of community participation to disinterest among Somali leadership or often blamed it more generally on Somali traditional culture.

As suggested in the previous discussion, many Somali community members prefer a traditional leadership style that is more exclusive, inward looking, and does not require much active participation from them. This style has strengthened trusting relationships within some segments the community, but it has failed to develop trusting relations with the larger society. Based on interviews and observations it was apparent to participants that the Somalis in Lewiston possess social networks essential to developing social capital; however, in addition to the networks being limited to the Somali community, these networks are typically fragmented. A number of social networks may occur in the community, but they are often only shallowly connected to each other. Community leaders, therefore, are typically only central to particular social clusters within the community.

Innovative leaders have to act as "brokers," making connections between these competing networks within the community.[24] This study suggests that the Somali emergent leader may be a key agent in change. Apart from contributing to the resources the community badly needs, the entrepreneurial side of the emergent leaders includes the ability to cope with risk and uncertainty; creativity in solving problems through divergent thinking; and more competitive yet collaborative efficiency in use of available resources.[25] Yet emergent leaders must secure the trust of others to be effective. Such leaders must win confidence through their reputation for competence in the acquisition and management of resources, and they must enact goodwill by their personal attributes of vision, commitment, and energy. Leaders prove their competencies by meeting their obligations to the community, however conceived, and they gain goodwill towards their innovative undertakings by reciprocating goodwill. These leadership dynamics involve creating new norms, including norms governing collaboration with the larger Lewiston local authorities and local businesses.

Three aspects of emergent Somali community leaders' behavior mark them as what I refer to as a "leader-collaborator": their vision, however skewed; their sense of vocation; and their transactional role as resource "managers" despite their illiteracy or limited English proficiency, poverty level, and the limitations of time and money. Such traits in leadership are relatively rare in the regeneration world of the global diaspora but almost certainly nonexistent within the traditional Somali leaders in Lewiston. All leaders in this study were good learners, quick to spot an opportunity (however selfish it was) to turn contingencies to their advantage. They did integrate new ideas into their thinking and did try them out. All had a sense of mission, even if vague, and were horrendously overworked—they "ate and slept" community. They acknowledged themselves as community representatives and gave many hours a week to fulfilling their social capital obligations. Some who felt compelled to participate in partnerships described it as a "full-time job"; for others involved, burnouts and total withdrawal were the inevitable result. However, their willingness to work within the available meager conditions also included taking advantage of the social opportunity structure or personal career development or connections with the community networks. Somali leaders in Lewiston were not good collaborators in that they did not pursue their sectional goals with a competitive vigor, but also they did not have a wider vision that included a sense of justice that allowed them to cooperate with others. It was apparent that some of the leaders even lacked vision and had become dependent on partnerships for their identity and status as community leaders. These leaders often acted as gate-keepers for sectional interests.

Traditionally, leadership in the Somali community has been dominated by alliances of loyal tribal/ethnic men. Historically, they have led community institutions like the mosque, Islamic schools, businesses, mutual assistance associations, and social and civic networks. This model of leadership has predisposed the Somali diaspora to autocratic, antidemocratic, and egotis-tical tendencies. As a consequence, the first generation within the new Somali community have experienced a monolithic leadership paradigm that often validates notions of elite, tribal, sexist, hierarchical, and more extreme Islamic command-and-control relationships between leaders and followers. Entrenched in Somali leadership culture and traditional behavior, this model is frequently but not always internalized and replicated by some Somali women and youth.

Emerging Somali leadership will inextricably be linked to the social cap-ital and civic infrastructure of the resourceful working-class women and youth who are struggling to break the welfare dependency cycle in order to gain economic and social independence. Unfortunately, the nostalgia for messianic, charismatic male leadership has significantly warped the community's perception and understanding of its potential. In this sense, the heroic mythology of the "great man" has in the post-civil war and post-resettlement era paralyzed the development of a full new Somali leadership paradigm.[26] Again, the responses to the mayor's letter by the Somalis in Lewiston demonstrate the emphasis on this patriarchal mythology, as women and youth took the backstage to male leaders. In the month of planning the pro-diversity rally responding to the mayor's letter, it was no accident that Somali male organizers chose not to actively include Somali women and youth in meetings. The elders and religious leaders also discouraged Lewiston Somalis from coming out the day of the rally. They deemed themselves as the sole powers to settle the conflict and absolve the mayor from any wrong-doing in the name of "elders talking to wronged elder." More than anything else, the poor attendance and participation of Somalis in the Lewiston rally was testimony to the underutilized social capital and the inadequate leader-ship in the Somali community.

Leadership status seemed to have influenced almost every aspect of the lives of informants, including the degree to which they were able to request and accept outside help; this bears close resemblance to what is discussed by scholars of civic engagement.[27] Numerous studies have shown that the deteriorating community leadership may be the single most significant factor in not utilizing social capital. Notwithstanding major life events, family support among the Somalis seemed to have conferred protection against the breakdown of social capital. Thus, social capital and support, particularly in the form of available community resources, may protect people from becoming overdependent on social service providers and services in the face of displacement and resettlement.

The experiences of Somalis reveal that, despite some sense of achievement, unresolved conflicts pertaining to their expectations of leaders seem to deepen with advancing years. Divided by the competition over scarce resources, a history and tradition of mistrust, multiple migrations, and the inability to communicate with each other, the Somali leaders in Lewiston have yet to recognize their common challenges or work together to find solutions. Yet their ability to find ways to communicate, build trust, and work together is critical to the health of their neighborhoods within the larger community. The housing complexes in which the Somalis live are integrated with Euro Americans and African Americans, Latinos and Asians, and other new African immigrants living next door to each other and using the same social amenities. In order, for example, to form a neighborhood watch over their homes and children, Somali families will need to be able to count on their ethnically diverse neighbors. In other words, Somalis will need to work on developing bridging social capital by establishing networks and trusting relationships with people outside of their community. Tackling even larger issues such as the lack of jobs, poor transportation, dilapidated housing, educational programs which do not meet their special needs, and the absence of youth development programs requires more clout than any single group or individual possesses. The need for members of different ethnic groups and even countries of origin to recognize their interdependence is especially obvious at the local level. The future of these communities depends upon different groups learning to collaborate with one another and on leaders' success in building relationships and social networks both within and outside of the Somali community.

The validity of this analysis of leadership together with its important component of social capital is complicated by the lack of a single word in Somali that translates literally to "leadership." Added to this is low knowledge of concepts of Euro American leadership and a lack of familiarity with bridging social capital, as well as a low level of literacy in English and illiteracy in their own language for many. Most of the informants tended to use a restricted vocabulary to express their understanding of leadership, whereas they spoke eloquently on the virtues of bonding social capital and its importance to the community. That Somalia is a relatively homogenous society in terms of language, religion, and ethnicity may explain this lack of familiarity with bridging capital. Despite the cultural complexities surrounding informants' interpretations of these concepts, however, attempts to relate their self conceptions of leadership to overall adjustment with life based on views of social capital showed low overlap between Somalis' and the wider community's constructs that contribute to mistrust and misunderstandings.

It should be pointed out that Somali social service providers in Lewiston, including some of the leaders interviewed, have assimilated some Euro American values and acquired organizational skills. These informants acknowledge that the concept of leadership is extraneous to the Somali culture but also that Somalis, including elders, are eager to learn about the subject. The discussions touched on regrets by Somalis for not seeking education sooner after arriving, but older people may feel less assertive, uninterested, or inclined to seek further training. Such difficulties in educating the old as well as the young members of the Somali community indicate a widespread need for education on the subjects of leadership, bridging social capital, and civic engagement. Further studies may be useful in exploring the extent of denial of poor leadership in older Somalis stemming from traditional and religious motives and the potentials for new developments in their understanding of what leadership might be used for. Other studies need to consider and compare the social situation of youth and women refugee leaders in Lewiston with other Somali enclaves in the United States such as Minneapolis, Minnesota, and Columbus, Ohio.

The complexity of resettlement and life problems calls for considerable human and financial resources beyond orientation lessons and ESL classes for refugees in order to prevent the obvious deleterious effects of social stressors, communication barriers, poor health, and poverty level of the new immigrants. The evidence of unmatched expectations about access to external and internal sources of social support needs to be considered within the context of insufficiency of community services in Lewiston (and many communities across the world) in order to deal with the distinctiveness in cultural perceptions and leadership acculturation. There is no doubt that Lewiston Somalis need new forms of support in order to assert themselves in their new context, but the sooner they move from welfare to self-reliance and mobilize their abilities in the form of social restructuring and regeneration, the better it will be for the community's survival and prosperity in this highly competitive Euro American context. The new context compels Lewiston Somalis to adapt new ways of enhancing and bettering their leadership and development of bridging social capital.

Civic Engagement: A Call for Community-Based Citizenship

Transforming Lewiston Somali leadership requires new vision, new strategies, and a new leadership paradigm for the twenty-first century. Practicing public leadership in a new manner requires significant community and organizational change. A Lewiston Somali leadership paradigm must consider several important points:

- The values of participatory methods and processes
- The acceptance of diverse points of view within the Somali community
- The need to systematically develop leadership among Somali women and youth
- The need to focus on developing trusting social relationships within the Somali community and between the Somali community and the larger community
- The need to view the leadership contributions of "elders" as equal and in partnership with those of ordinary citizens (followers)
- The belief that ordinary people in local communities *can* solve their problems and build community capacity with the support of the elders, religious leaders, youth, women, and private enterprise

Increasingly, public life and civic engagement require Lewiston Somali leaders to hear, understand, and consider the views of frustrated, marginalized followers—especially Somali women and youth. It is through collaborative processes that ordinary citizens begin to catalyze, energize, and include their neighbors (Somali and non-Somali) in community problem solving. Through this process they can create new associations, networks, organizations, alliances, partnerships, and forums. They can build relationships and trust to create a new and shared vision for their lives through engagement with diverse community members. Aspects of traditional leadership style, namely those of collectivism, can be re-emphasized and proudly acknowledged as derived from their positive cultural history.

Lewiston Somalis must invest in leadership development. Building viable social capital involves cultivating people who have the skills and capacity to promote and support the implementation of democracy, diversity, and leadership. While it is important to recognize and appreciate a wide range of leadership styles and approaches, people who are effective in diverse settings tend to share a number of similar qualities. These qualities include a solid understanding of how one's individual and group identity may positively and negatively shape one's worldview and behavior; and an understanding of the impact of ethnic, caste, racial, linguistic, gender, class, and cultural oppression on communities, families, and individuals. Sustained by their vision and deeply held belief that ordinary people have the capacity to create their own visions and solve their own problems, collaborative leaders with a commitment to participatory democracy will renew Lewiston Somali community life and build a new kind of civic participation infrastructure that takes full advantage of the abundant social capital within the Somali community and with the larger Lewiston community.

The responsibility of Lewiston Somali leaders for cultivating skills, knowledge, social capital, and leadership is a shared one. It is a challenge that must be met by the variety of individuals, associations, and organizations that play a significant role in nurturing the development of the youth as well as adults. Renewing Lewiston Somali public life is a necessary prerequisite for restoring both the health of Maine's rural communities and the civic engagement and participation of the new immigrants through citizen education. Through citizen education, Lewiston Somali leadership must review civic discourse deeply grounded in the culture, traditions, and ways of life of the ordinary Lewiston Somalis who ultimately must rebuild their communities.

The future of Lewiston Somali public life is therefore dependent upon community-based citizenship initiatives that emphasize civic literacy, leadership development and training, and community participation and engagement. Unfortunately, revival of popular civic education alone will not rehabilitate Somali public life. Although it is necessary condition, it is not sufficient for fundamental social change. Additionally, a major paradigmatic shift must occur within the Lewiston Somali community public life, coupled with a renewed focus on civic engagement at the grassroots level. This fundamental shift is necessary for restoring the capacity of the

Lewiston Somali post-civil war, post-refugee, post-resettlement, and post-secondary migration community to effect leadership change. Without a major transformation of the leadership paradigm that currently guides and dominates the Lewiston Somalis' traditional political, social, religious, culture, and public life and its civic infrastructure, the community will not recover from the late-twentieth-century leadership and social capital crisis that afflicts these new Americans.

Zest

Fartuna Hussein

I was five years old the day I finally met my father. A few months before I was born, on March 1, 1988, my father left the country to come to America to find a job and a house, to get settled, and to bring us over. I lived in Somalia until I was three. Then, because of the war, we moved to a refugee camp in Kenya, where we lived for two years, until I was five. During those years, my uncle—my dad's brother—served as my father figure.

In the summer of 1993 my father sponsored us to migrate to America. When most people leave refugee camps to go to America, their thoughts are about starting a new life full of hope and of opportunity and rebuilding their lives that were crushed by war and poverty. But all my excited thoughts were about meeting my father. Would he be the man I saw in my dreams? Would he be tall? Would he be short? Light? Bald? Would he be the nice, handsome man my mother described to me?

On the plane I was trying to make sure everything was perfect—my hair, my clothes—I even sat a certain way so that everything would be perfect when I met my father. We arrived in New York City. When we exited the plane, three men were waiting for us. Which one was my father? My brother and sister raced to my father and hugged and kissed him. It was the first time I had seen my father, and he was everything I had dreamed about. He was happy, excited, and very handsome.

I stood in the background watching and waiting. He was a stranger to me. I didn't know how to approach this stranger, even though he was my father. Then he came to me, where I was standing in the corner. He picked me up. *Aabbo* (my father) said, "My beautiful daughter, Fartuna." He hugged me and held me tight. It was like the hug babies get when they emerge from the womb. The warmth of his hug made me feel like nothing would go wrong. I knew everything would be good from now on.

After this meeting and greeting, we drove through New York City. Everyone else was dazzled by the city—the buildings, the lights, the people—but I couldn't take my eyes off my father. We finally arrived in Jersey City, our home. My father had a five-bedroom house; each one of us had our own room! Every room was full of toys. He knew what we liked and had prepared everything for us. He bought me Barbie dolls, but he knew I was a tomboy so he also bought me trucks.

Then he cooked for us. My mother had always done the cooking in Somalia. She had done everything by herself for the last five years. But now she just relaxed and smiled, happy to have him sharing the work again. He cooked a lot of food. He made Somali rice, lasagna, *hilib ari* (lamb). He prepared a feast for us! Our first family dinner in America! Before we ate, we thanked God for the food, and gave special thanks for being together as a family, safe at last.

After dinner, he gave me a shower. We were together, and I asked him many questions about his life here. He answered all my questions. He washed me with Zest soap. And even today when I smell Zest, it takes me back to that special day.

Later that evening, we went for a walk around Jersey City. It was a breezy summer day in June, with perfect weather for an evening walk. My dad showed us the school we would be going to, and he introduced us to the neighborhood. As we walked around, I felt so proud to be walking with my father, whom everyone seemed to know. I wanted everyone to know how proud I was. My mother had always been my hero; but now, in the few hours since I had known him, he had become my new hero. The way he talked to people, the way he embraced people—he had this glow about him, because he was so happy. He shared that moment with everyone. He shared his happiness with everyone. He said, "This is my family—they're here!"

Here we were, having such a happy day, when I noticed a man lying on the street corner. He was an older man with gray hair. He looked like he hadn't had a shower for days, his clothes were ripped and dirty, he had a dirty face, and he looked exhausted. He was lying on a cardboard box. Beside his box, he had a shopping cart full of cans and dirty blankets—like something you might see in a dump. He was just lying there. I kept staring at him. Why was he lying on the street corner? Was he doing this for fun? Was he waiting for someone? Was he tired from work? Why was this guy lying there?

"Dad, Dad! There's a guy lying on the street. Why is he lying on the street? Do people like to lie on the street? Is this where people lie down when they're tired? Maybe we should do that. But he needs to take a shower."

My dad said, "He's a homeless man."

"Why is he homeless? There are so many homes here."

"He doesn't have a home."

"Why doesn't he have a home?"

My father explained that he was homeless, that he had nothing. There were homeless shelters, but he probably didn't want to go there. As we walked away, I kept looking at the man. I was still puzzled—maybe because I had come from the refugee camp just yesterday, and already I had a home. Even in the refugee camp, I had a home. Even in war-torn Somalia, I had a home. I just could not understand why this man was homeless in a land of opportunity. Back home, people talked as though America had the answers for everything. I kept looking at the man. Did he have a family? Where were they? It was shocking to me. I had come to this country, and the place was beautiful. The people seemed nice. But here was this man sleeping on the street, homeless. My family moved around a lot, but we always had a home.

5 Dadaab Dreams

Nasra Mohamed

Editors' Note: *Most of the Somalis who are living in Maine came through the refugee camps in Kenya and most of these came from the three refugee camps in Dadaab. Once a sparsely populated village in the Northeast of Kenya, Dadaab now is home to three refugee camps: Ifo, Hagardhere, and Dagahley. Each camp is distinct and is separated from the others by eight to ten miles of desert.*

The United Nations High Commissioner for Refugees (UNHCR) estimates that there are approximately three hundred thousand refugees in the three camps. While there are a few Ethiopians and Sudanese, the vast majority are Somali and most of them will never leave the camps until there is peace in Somalia. While the UNHCR tries to resettle political refugees, the process is slow and those placed make up only a small portion of those in need. Noting that the United States is now accepting only a few hundred refugees a year, Doug Rutledge concludes, "The stark reality is that most people will never leave the camps until the UNHCR determines that Somalia is a safe place for the refugees to return to."[1]

The humanitarian organization CARE provides bimonthly food rations, but by all accounts these are inadequate and high rates of malnutrition are found among women and children. A survey conducted for the UNHCR in 2006 found that almost one-quarter of the refugees in Dadaab suffered acute malnutrition.[2] As one refugee commented, "In Dadaab, God help you."

In 2009, Nasra Mohamed returned to the camps where she had spent ten years of her childhood. "It has always been my dream," she said, "to go back to the camps to see what I can do to help." She took with her a camera, paper, pencils, and a few questions. Eager to bring the refugee voices to our project, she invited the high school students she met to write down the answers to her questions. Below, the students' responses are interwoven with her own story and identified with indentations.

We left Mogadishu when I was seven or eight. My father worked for the government, and we lived in a neighborhood with other government workers. At first the government sent soldiers to protect us, but even that was not enough. My uncle had a bus, and he came to our house and asked us to come with him to Kismayo before things got out of hand. My father didn't believe the government would fall, but my mother insisted that we leave. First we went to the small town of Afgoia and then to Kismayo, where my mother's family lived.

It took us seven days to travel from Afgoia to Kismayo because we had to take a back road to avoid any trouble with the rebels. There were twenty of us in two small cars: my mom, my brothers and sisters, and my aunts. My aunt had just had a baby. When the fighting reached Kismayo my mother insisted again that we leave, this time for Kenya. Now we were in a Land Rover with little to eat or drink. At one point my mother and the other mothers with little children drove to the border. I stayed with the men, and my father carried me most of the way. We crossed the border into Kenya in the middle of the night.

When we reached Kenya, we found different Somali clans gathered under different trees. Later the Dadaab refugee camps would provide wooden huts, but at this time, when refugees were just arriving, they provided us only with large plastic sheets. My father and the other men went into the woods to get sticks to build houses with. They had never built anything like this before. We were city people and we had nothing—not even tools.

We were luckier than most. My family was in a fairly secure compound with a fence around it. My father and the others didn't have guns, but people thought they did, and so they left us alone. My father taught school, my mother had a store, and my sister served as an interpreter, so we had pretty much what we needed. We did not have to go without as others did. After ten years in the camp we received our papers and were approved for resettlement in the United States: in Albuquerque, New Mexico.

On my first day of school in Albuquerque the teacher gave me *To Kill a Mockingbird*. She had only wanted me to read a few chapters, but I didn't understand and read the whole book in one night. Immediately I began to worry about this new country. Was it like the society in *To Kill a Mockingbird*? I was afraid to go outdoors. Then I met another Somali, who reassured me that the United States was not like that anymore. Six months later we moved to Maine, where I completed elementary school, high school, and college. In

2009 I achieved my long-time dream—I was able to return to the refugee camps in Dadaab, this time as a visitor. While I was there, I visited the schools. I spoke to a few of the students and asked them about their experiences in the camp, their educational problems, and their ambitions and potential careers. A few of them wrote me essays about their lives in the refugee camps.

Going back to the Dadaab refugee camps was a dream come true. On my way I stayed in Nairobi for about a week, and the whole time I was longing to visit the camps. I was so excited to finally be going home to see my family. I was born in Somalia, but I had lived in Kenya for more than half of my life, and it had been seven years since I lived there.

My heart was pounding as I took the nonstop bus from Nairobi to Dadaab at 6:00 a.m. This bus was not like the Greyhound or Concord Trailways. It was crowded with people, suitcases, and bags full of vegetables. There were people standing in between the seats. I wanted to take pictures, but I could not move. Despite the smell and temperature I had a smile on my face. The woman who was sitting next to me asked if I was from somewhere else or I was going abroad. I asked her why and she said, "You look so happy; it is so strange." I smiled and informed the woman that I was visiting my family after being away for a long time.

When the bus finally stopped at Hagardhere refugee camp there were many people there to greet it. The bus brings food supplements to the camps. I was not surprised that no taxis or cars waited; instead there were men with wheelbarrows and donkeys with carts. This is the form of transportation used in the camps. The bus stopped at the corner of the market, making it easier for people to transport their goods to their stores.

It had been a long day, but I was not tired. The weather was so hot you would think the sun was on your head. I had been to Hagardhere a couple of times before, and I remembered that I had never liked it. The entire area is full of sand. It is like a beach, but the sand is red, and when the weather is hot it is very difficult to walk. This time I was happy to be there: so happy I wanted to say hi to everyone around the bus. My sister's friend and my uncle were waiting for me. I handed my suitcase through the window to my sister's friend. When I stepped down from the bus a man with a wheelbarrow asked me, "Which block are you going to?" I just smiled at him, and asked, "Could you please wait?" He was in a hurry because he wanted to take me where I was going to and come back to get another customer. I was not in a hurry. Like a tourist, I was calm and kept on looking at the people and my surroundings. But I was not a tourist; I grew up in Dagahley camp, just an hour away.

I was so thirsty, but I knew better than to ask for a glass of cold water. When I lived at the camps there were no refrigerators and people drank water from containers in the shade. But then we walked into the market and stopped by a restaurant where there was a fridge. Deep down I thought, "Thank you, God!" My aunt offered me a cold glass of water and I immediately accepted. When I asked her where they got the electricity, she answered, "Things have changed. We use generators now."

Half an hour later we left the restaurant and started walking to Block C5, where my uncle and aunt and their children have lived for a long time. As I mentioned, it is very difficult to walk and their block is far away from the market. As we were walking, I kept looking at the man pushing the wheelbarrow. He was sweating a lot and I wanted to help, but then I could hardly walk. When we finally got to the house he put the wheelbarrow in front, ran to the shade, and asked for a glass of water. My uncle was not home and the children were all at school. My aunt offered to pay the man but I insisted on paying him myself. It was only one U.S. dollar.

I spent the night in Hagardhere, and it was one of the best nights of my life. I spent time with my cousins, three of whom were born after we had immigrated to the United States. Life was simple; people in the camp didn't have a lot, yet they were happy. We all laughed and talked. I had a torch the whole night, and I was a little jumpy because there are scorpions that come out at night.

A lot of things have changed since I was living in the camps. For example, the security is better. There are no armed men who break into homes to rob people at night or rape women. However, there are gangs that will stop you outside and take your watch or anything you have. For this reason, most women stay inside at night and the men arm themselves with sticks for protection. But there is no fear of bandits trying to come into your house. Families will stay up after dinner and laugh out loud without fear of who might come knocking. I enjoyed that freedom. In my time there was fear, and no one dared to speak loud at night, especially girls.

Mahad (male, twenty, 1992)

When we came to the refugee camp I was fourteen years old and the second oldest. We were three boys and a girl, the oldest being the girl. Currently we are a family of six members; three more were born in the refugee camp, but unfortunately our father and one of my brothers died. Our father died in 2005 in Somalia. He went back to visit some relatives who were by then in Kismayo. Days after his arrival he was shot dead by armed militiamen.

We have experienced various difficulties in the camp as far as our living standard is concerned. Our father was a blacksmith who earned little, not enough for the family; my mother had no skills and one income was not enough. When we lost our father, who was our only breadwinner, our living standard fell drastically. Currently we depend completely on food relief distributed by CARE. Bandits in the bush attacked our mother as she went to collect firewood. She was raped and humiliated. We were also attacked by bandits one night. They collected all we had and beat my mother seriously. All these difficulties have worsened the life in the camp. When it comes to bandits, things are getting better; however, everything else is still the same.

I have strong ambitions of having a better life than the one I am currently living. This is because I am hoping to be educated enough to improve my living standard. In the future I would like to be an accountant in an organization or a financial institution. I chose to be an accountant since I perform well in mathematics and in business study. I believe this would only be possible if I got an opportunity to advance my education by getting resettlement in a peaceful country.

I was awake very early the next morning, ready to talk to students and check out the schools. Mohamed, my sister's friend, came to get me. We walked to a center near the hospital, where we met with some of his friends and drove to Dadaab. From there we took a taxi to the Ifo refugee camp. It is practical for people to take taxis to go from one place to another, but there had been no taxis when I was there. I was shocked and excited at the same time; I could see the changes that had occurred in seven years. Mohamed explained to me that with improved security, people can now travel from one refugee camp

FIGURE 10. Ifo refugee camp, Dadaab, Kenya

to the next. I was so happy. There were no police to escort us. In the taxi the driver was listening to Somali music; everything was perfect. It took us less than twenty minutes to get to Ifo.

The taxi dropped us off near the Ifo market, and we walked from there to the secondary school. It had rained the night before, so the roads were muddy; people were walking in the mud. Mohamed looked at me and said, "Let's find a shortcut," so we started walking through the blocks. In one hand I was holding my digital camera and in the other I was holding my skirt, trying not to get it dirty. I saw two young girls and a man driving a donkey-cart full of containers with water. I could not resist taking a picture. One of the young girls looked at me and smiled. I smiled back and she confidently said, "You can take more pictures if you want." Mohamed, on the other hand, was standing on the other side of the muddy road chiding me. "Stop taking pictures of people, they might not like it." We kept on walking.

It was morning, but the sun was already out and it was very hot. When we got to the school I was tired and thirsty, but I didn't ask for water. I wanted to fit in and be just like the refugees living in the camp; no one else was running to drink water. Everything was quiet. The students were in the middle of their midterm exams. Ifo Secondary School is one of the biggest secondary schools in the camps. The classrooms were made of used tin cans, some of which had U.S.A. stamped on them. It was very hot, and the trees could not provide enough shade for everyone. Some of the students were sitting on school desks outside of the classroom.

I was so happy to be there. I walked toward the classrooms and started talking to some of the boys outside. The girls were all inside, making their own little group. I greeted the boys, smiling, but I didn't get the welcome I was expecting. Mohamed reminded me that I was lifting my *hijab*—trying to cool myself off in the heat—and he told me I should push it down. "We don't want to talk to a naked lady," they said. I adjusted my *hijab* immediately and asked some of the boys if they would let me ask them a few questions about the school. We agreed to meet shortly after their next exam. I then entered the classroom to say hello to the girls. They looked shy and were not interested in talking to me. I had to think about a way to get these girls to trust me too.

Raaliyo (female, nineteen, 1994)

I am Raaliyo, age nineteen, living in Hargardhere, Block L1. I first arrived in a refugee camp in Kenya—which was still in Nairobi in 1987—with my family members, including my father, mother, four sisters, and one brother. In the year 1994 we were transferred to a refugee camp in Dadaab. I started school in the year 1996, and now I am in form four. In my family my father is the breadwinner because he is working as a school headmaster.

In the refugee camp every child is entitled to a free education. Although education is available, the conditions we learn in are very bad. First of all there is the climate. Almost all months of the year it is very hot. We learn in classes with iron sheets on top and tins on the sides. It is very hot during class hours, making it hard for students to concentrate. If fans were provided, then I think students would tend to concentrate more, and at the end of the day they would have reached their ultimate goal, which is learning. The other problem is that school starts at 6:40 a.m. As a student who comes from a long distance away, I am not able to come to school that early. The leaving hour, 4:00 p.m., is okay. I can walk back home and help with the housework.

There is also a scarcity of qualified teachers. Students who finish form four are recruited as teachers without going to teachers' training college. If only they were taken to those colleges then I am sure there would be better performance in our school. In addition, the number of subjects taught in form one—twelve—is too much. As a student I can't concentrate on all twelve subjects. In form three we study either eight or seven, which is better. Additional subjects like music must be taught, because school is where we determine our talents and ambitions. The sad thing is music is not taught in school.

If I were able to get a scholarship, I would like to be a surgeon. This field is always left to the men, but I want to break into it. If I am lucky enough to get a scholarship to further my studies, then my dream of becoming a surgeon will come to pass.

While I waited for the students to finish their exams, I started talking to three adults who were in training at the school. Theta, from Ethiopia, looked like any regular twenty-four-year-old American; he was wearing jeans and a T-shirt. He is unemployed, not because he doesn't want to work but because there are so few jobs in the camps. Some of the young men I met had temporary jobs as translators and community advocates. When these jobs end, sometimes they do construction work so they can get money to buy clothing and food. Theta said, "I once had a dream of going to college and becoming a teacher. That dream is long gone." These young men don't have families here in the camp. They attend every training that the international agencies provide. "It is better than doing nothing. At least they provide tea and cold drinks." Theta lives off the food CARE provides for the refugees. He told me that the amount CARE provided was not enough. "We only receive three kilograms of maize, three kilograms of wheat flour, one cup of oil, and a little bit of salt for fifteen days," the three told me. When I asked how they managed, Theta said, "I live with a group of five people; we add our food and cook together."

Asad (male, twenty, 2004)

I am the firstborn of my family. My mother was killed in Somalia. It is our father who generates the daily bread for the family. Sometimes I support my father by providing water to the rest of the family, since I am the oldest. I also go to the forest on the weekends to collect firewood for my family. Life is very difficult in the refugee camps, and we all need to work together to survive.

As many of the students in the camp work at home, domestic labor upsets their focus on education. Most of the time I choose housework over schoolwork. Helping the family is a responsibility that most of the children in the refugee camps have put on them at an early age.

Many refugees suffer from a lack of medical assistance. It's my personal ambition to be a doctor if opportunity prevails for me. It is my dream to give back to refugees in the world as a doctor, so I can alleviate their suffering.

After the interviews we walked to the CARE camp, where I met Isniino, a female camp leader. Every block has a camp leader. They are elected for two years and can be re-elected once. These camp leaders negotiate with the World Food Program (WFP), CARE, Deutsche Gesellschaft für Technische Zusammenarbeit (GTZ), and other international agencies. They report problems to the agencies, request non-food materials, and negotiate about food packages. Isniino also advocates for women and talks about female genital mutilation (FGM). She came to Ifo in 1992 and become a camp leader in 2006. I asked Isniino about the girls' education in the camps. "Girls are the housekeepers—you know that—but we try to send them to school." They also, she said, face FGM and early marriage. "We try to educate the community about FGM, and it is not the same now."

Farido (female, eighteen, 1992)

In 1992 I arrived in the refugee camp with my parents and brothers. We were ten people. I, the third born, was two years old at the time. My mother is the leader of our family and the breadwinner. She is too old to manage such an extended family. My beloved father, who used to take care of us while we were young, was shot dead in front of our house by armed men in 1997. We became orphans—a vulnerable family with no support. When I was in class six in primary school, my uncle forced me to marry an old man who was his best friend at that time. The marriage was totally against my will. Later the man divorced me while I was six months pregnant, and he did not give me any support. In 2004, my last year in primary school, I gave birth to a baby boy and passed the exam to secondary school with flying colors. Now, in secondary school, I face discrimination and have become a social reject because I am a divorced student with a baby. I am in my last year in secondary school. All I want is to pass the exam and hopefully get a scholarship to study abroad.

To be in a refugee camp is the worst thing a human being can suffer. I learn at school in a harsh climate with a cruel sun; our learning hours are throughout the day and we don't have time to rest at night because then we are supposed to review what we were taught during the day. I learn seven subjects: English, Kiswahili, chemistry, biology, math, Islamic religion, and history.

Girls have the most problems in the refugee camps because boys review their books at night at the school, but girls do not have full security to go to school at night; they might be raped or tortured by unknown men.

If my education style changes and I get to a good place for my studies, I want to become a politician in my home country and worldwide. The world suffers from political problems. The only subject that I like and that has shaped my life is history. Because I like history I got myself involved in politics and wish to become a lawyer. I want to be a good leader who can rule a whole nation honestly and wisely without corruption. Corruption is a big problem in my country.

As we were talking, Isniino saw an older Somali man and took me over to meet him. He was Mr. Ahmed, the chairman of Ifo Refugee Camp. "Though life is very difficult in the camps," he said, "many people here have an insatiable hunger for knowledge." Though they have high hopes and big dreams, the students are lucky if they can get a seat in the secondary schools. Only 485 who pass the qualifying exams are able to go on. To ensure that even that many can go on, the refugees have raised money by selling food provided for them by World Food Program (WFP). "We don't get enough food," he acknowledged. "However, school is very important to us." Isniino, who has nine children, agreed. "By sending our children to school we see that they get an education instead of going on the streets. Parents do everything they can to help their children stay in school. When the children graduate from middle school, parents have to stand aside and hope that their children get enough points to pass to secondary school, but their power is limited. If their children don't get a passing grade, parents will have to let their fourteen- or fifteen-year-olds stay at home and do nothing. That is the hardest thing for parents to do."

But even admission to secondary school is not enough. Most students in the United States graduate from high school and look forward to college. In Dadaab there are no options for students who have graduated from secondary school. Sometimes international agencies give a few of the graduates jobs as teachers and social workers, but the pay is quite low. With few good options some students go to the streets to do drugs *(qat)*, while others go back to war-torn Somalia. It is hopeless to go on a road that leads to nowhere. Most of these students have hope, though their hopes may be crushed by the time they graduate.

We walked back to the school; the students were done with their exams. Abshir is a form four student. He was tired and sweating. The sun was very hot and he had just gotten out of an exam. He was dressed in his school uniform, blue pants and a white shirt. He walks to school forty minutes every day. "I don't go home for lunch," he told me. "I would not have enough time to get back, and it's not worth it." There is only one secondary school in every camp; schools don't have a cafeteria or vending machines. Abshir would love to own a bicycle, but here in the camps they cost at least $100.

FIGURE 11. Author with students at a refugee camp in Dadaab, Kenya

FIGURE 12. Dadaab refugee camp, Kenya

Abshir (male, eighteen, 1992)

My family consists of six members: my mother, my four younger brothers, and I, the first born. My mother is the breadwinner of the family. She collects firewood from the bush, brings it to camp through human portage, and then takes it from one block to another looking for buyers. My father died earlier, in the camp. Life in the camp deteriorates day after day, from bad to worse. People are very destitute, and security is not tightly kept. You hear gunshots fired in the middle of the night by unknown bandits, who rape mothers and young girls and take everything they see. There are also harmful cultural practices, such as forced early marriages that prevent girls from being actively involved in the community.

In addition to the living conditions in the camp, many other problems contribute to the educational problems. For example, the camp lies in the northeastern part of Kenya, which has a harsh and horrible climate with little or no rain. The classrooms are very congested. Sixty students will learn in one room, which is impossible in a normal situation. Besides that, there is the quality of the teachers. Hagadera Secondary has only ten teachers who are fully trained. The others are refugee "incentives" who only finished high school in the camps. In addition, there are only limited scholarships and training, [as well as] drug abuse among the youth.

My ambition is to become a doctor by getting a scholarship to [a university in] one of the European countries or America. There I could learn medicine and save the lives of many people in Africa who are dying from tropical diseases that can be treated, thus improving health standards and the economy as well. I pray to my Lord to make my dream true.

While we were still talking, one of the students mentioned that it was prayer time, and I asked them to show me where the girls' mosque was so I could pray, too. I got ready to pray and walked to the school mosque, where three girls were praying. I prayed next to them. This was finally my chance to talk with them without any disturbance; we sat outside where it was quiet and private. They looked shy but firm at the same time. They were dressed in their school uniforms, blue skirts with white *hijabs*. Before asking them questions I introduced myself. I mentioned to them that I was once a refugee and lived in Dagahley Block C3. I was trying to assure them that I just wanted to know what had changed while I was gone and that I was not in any way trying to interfere with their private lives. They agreed to talk to me and we finally had a great conversation.

I first asked why the girls' performance was so low. Halima, who is nineteen years old and in form three, said, "It is not that girls are not smart but [that] we work at home. Students here share their books, and it is very difficult to set a time to study together during the day. At night we fear." These were very dedicated young ladies. They all wanted to do something with their lives to break the cycle and become educated, unlike their mothers. Luul also goes to Ifo Secondary School; she has dreams but fears they might not come true. She wants to go to college. She pointed out that there are only "nineteen girls out of two hundred students in form three, and twenty-four girls in form two." The number of girls going to school gets smaller at each level. Some are forced to marry and cannot continue their education. I asked them if girls continue school while they are married. "That is impossible," they told me. "Husbands will be ashamed to see their wives going to school. However, it is okay for married men to go to school."

Basra (female, no additional information)

In the refugee camp I live a miserable life. I cannot get three meals a day. I live hand to mouth. My father died in the civil war and my mother is an old woman. She is the one who takes care of me. She goes to the bush every day and collects firewood on her back; she takes the firewood to the market and sells it at a low cost. At the end of the day she arrives home with a quarter cup of sugar and a glass of milk.

In fact, life stretches meaningless and joyless in front of me. I don't sleep at night because of hunger and overthinking, I keep tossing and turning on the rough mat I sleep on. People despise me because of the poor situation I live in.

I have experienced so many problems [in my education], including not having money to buy pens and books. In fact, it is so hard for me to get the exercise books, pens, and reference books that are required for the learning process that I even failed class eight and had to repeat it.

Also, I have domestic problems that hinder my learning. When my mother becomes sick I have to go to the bush and collect firewood for selling. On such occasions I miss many lessons. Consequently, the students discriminate against me; they know I hail from a very poor family and they will not get anything from me. Since I live a harsh life, my ambition is to live in a better place where my mother and I will not work so hard.

The last camp I visited was my favorite refugee camp, Dagahley. This was my second home. It is the place I think of when people ask me about where I went to middle school or where I grew up. I was so excited to finally visit there. When we stopped at the secondary school, classes had just ended and students were going home. I didn't ask anyone permission to take pictures; after all, this was home. But everything had changed. I was surprised to see that the seniors at the secondary school were the students who had been in elementary school when I was there. They were all grown, and I didn't recognize most of them.

We then went to the blocks. I told the driver I knew where we were going, but I was wrong. The roads had become smaller since I was there, because the number of refugees has grown and therefore more houses have been built. Luckily my friend knew where my former block—C3—was, but when we got there I got lost again. I was looking around when my former neighbor saw me and started screaming. She took me to where our house used to be. All my neighbors' children came to me, and I was happy, yet sad. They live in the same place they have lived for eighteen years; nothing has changed and nothing will. They deserve so much better. These fifteen- and seventeen-year-olds were born in the refugee camp. They never had the chance to see what city life is; they never got to play with toys, sleep in a bed, or use a clean bathroom. There were children playing soccer outside—just regular kids having fun and not knowing that they deserve more. To them, this is it.

The international organizations try to do what they can; however, the Somali refugees in Kenya have outstayed their welcome. It has been twenty years since civil war broke out in Somalia. The first influx of refugees arrived in Kenya in 1991, and Somalia is still in chaos. This year there were more people who fled Somalia and came to Dadaab. I could not believe my eyes; it was like 1991 all over again. These people chose Dadaab not because it is their dream place to live but because it is better than what is happening in Mogadishu. They left their homes and joined their fellow Somalis to live in huts made of sticks and mud covered with plastic. What many once thought was a temporary relocation has become their permanent home.

Many of these new refugees show signs of mental health problems and malnutrition. I walked by a group of the new refugees in front of the UNHCR office. This was like taking a journey down memory lane, only the number of refugees has increased significantly and this adds to the problems. The reduction in the food basket gives rise to widespread malnutrition for the elderly and children. In addition there is a water shortage and an increase of youth violence and drugs. The increasing numbers of students add to the existing problems of schools not having enough trained teachers and text-books to share. Hospitals are overcrowded with people who must share the already limited services. So many people have come from a war zone, and yet there are no psychologists to diagnose and help mentally ill persons. Many of the new refugees require urgent medical care, but the number of people referred to bigger hospitals in Garrisa and Nairobi is limited due to UNHCR and GTZ policies to restrict refugees to the camps.

The hospitals have a pediatric unit, a maternity unit, and a TB unit, to mention a few. These are all services that the refugees need, but there are not enough doctors to provide the services. After talking to middle school students I noticed that some of them had lost their teeth. There is almost no dental care. People who get a tooth removed have it removed with a tool that is shared by the three camps, making patients suffer with pain for months at a time. With the number of girls that go through female genital mutilations and marry early, sometimes getting sexually transmitted diseases, gynecological services are needed. Many deserving cases lack medical attention.

New or old refugees—they all call Dadaab home, these dusty little towns in northeastern Kenya. They don't have a better place to go; they are not allowed to travel within Kenya. The camp is like a prison, one that I remember clearly. Somali refugees all have one dream, one way out: to resettle in a peaceful country.

The Journey to Who I Am

Nawal Wali

I was in the living room in our three-bedroom apartment in Lewiston, Maine, checking my email and watching TV at the same time, when my father walked in. From the look on his face, I knew I was in for one of his long lectures. "Oh, here we go again," I thought. My father always went on and on about how at age fourteen he was living on his own, supporting himself and his family—how he was the perfect Muslim and never missed a prayer, never gave in to peer pressure (what he called *dhalinyaro* [teenagers]), and never became a *ciyaal suuq* (delinquent).

"It's important not to forget who you are. Don't lose your language and your religion." He always added this advice. I had heard this so many times. Then, right before I slipped into a daydream, as I normally did at this point, I heard, "Did you know that I suffered from PTSD?"

I stared at my father for a few minutes. He was sitting on the bright salmon-colored *fadhi carbeed* (Arabic-style couch) with one leg in front of the other. He had on his beige hat with a dress shirt and khakis. He had just come from the mosque, which was like a second home for him. He was leaning on his cane today.

All of a sudden the house became quiet. I answered, "No. When?"

He explained how when we first arrived in the United States, his life and his personality changed. He went from being someone who never gave in to the pressures of this world and was always working for the next world to someone who didn't have the same drive. I was amazed. My father had never talked about this sort of thing before. Then he started to tell me about all that he had gone through in Ethiopia.

"At that time, your mother and I struggled to put food on the table. We had no money, no property, and there were no jobs. Life was hard, but we had faith. One day I came home, and found you sleeping. My heart stopped." I thought to myself, "why would that cause his heart to stop?" He went on, "I didn't know if you were just resting, or dead of starvation. I had to check your pulse to see if you were alive." Hearing this story triggered my memory.

It was a dark night and very dry. There was nothing but a dirt road in front and behind, and nothing but flat grassland as far as we could see. We walked for days, and every minute of that walk felt like an eternity. I was only five years old. I felt my legs giving out on me; I could no longer walk. My father saw how tired I was and put me on his shoulders, even though there wasn't much life left in him. His mouth was very dry, and he looked exhausted. My mother was also suffering because she was pregnant with my brother Hamza and carrying Abdullahi on her back. My two other brothers, Ahmed and Mohamed, were walking between my parents.

After what seemed like years, we reached our destination, the Ogaden region in Ethiopia, where some of my family members resided. We settled near them in a hut surrounded by a community of about ten other huts. I remember playing, carefree, with my cousins, just having fun as kids. We ran around playing games, spending all our time outside, until nightfall. In bed, I could often hear the howling hyenas running past the hut, and I couldn't sleep. But when I felt afraid, I remembered my parents were close by.

I had everything I needed: I had food and clothes, I had friends, and my brothers and I were the best kind of friends. I had a great childhood. Little did I know that my parents were starving themselves to feed us. Now when I look at pictures of that time, I realize how thin they were. Now I know why. They protected us from hunger, fear, violence, and war, and they carried us through life making sure we had everything we needed. As we were so happily playing, our parents were shielding us from dangers and stress, from worry and harm.

I looked at my father now and thought of all the times I had shut the door in his face, not wanting to hear another lecture, not wanting him to tell me what to do and where to go, not wanting him to run my life. But this story showed me what he had given up and all that he and my mother had done so that I could live my own life. I now know why I should remember who I am and where I come from.

6 Challenges and Support for Somali Students in Higher Education[1]

Ismail Warsame

For centuries—or even millennia—people have migrated from one place to another for various reasons. Even though Somalis are known to be nomads who are always on the move, their nomadic instincts did not take them on intercontinental journeys in large numbers until recently. When the civil war broke out in the early 1990s, thousands of families—including my own—fled Somalia. These displaced people face many serious challenges as they adjust to life in a new country. This chapter examines how Somali refugees are responding to the challenges of higher education in the United States. I will share my own personal experiences in secondary and higher education, explore some of the social, cultural, and academic barriers that hinder the success of Somalis in higher education, and make some recommendations to better facilitate access to and success in higher education for Somali students.

My Personal Journey to Higher Education

I come from a family that values education. Like many Somali families, my parents were married at a young age. Due to my mother's back-to-back pregnancies and the necessity of raising her children, she never pursued a post-secondary education. Fortunately, though, with the help of my grandmother, she was able to let my father complete his secondary education in Italy followed by post-secondary education in Germany. Trained as an electrician, my father returned to work for the government until the 1980s, when he resigned from his post as the chief executive of mechanics at a plastics manufacturing factory in southeastern Somalia.

After years of turbulence brought on by the war, we were fortunate to resettle in Portland, Maine, in 2001. I am one of seven children, all grown now. My father, currently living in Portland with three of my younger siblings, never imagined reaching this age anywhere but in his native Somalia.

He became a naturalized U.S. citizen in 2006, the same year that my mother passed away after a short period of illness. Despite the inevitable psychological effects and difficult adjustments to the unfamiliar culture and environment, my father is in good health. He has extensive knowledge and experience as an electrician, but the language barrier has ended his thirty-year-long career.

Education has always been the core value in our household. Acting upon their firm belief in educational values, my parents instilled in their children the necessity to work hard in school and overcome every challenge along the way. Even as young children we were expected to excel in school. My three older sisters and my older brother provided me with the role models I needed for inspiration. My siblings used to tease me that I was the "mother's boy," always being spoiled by her. But even she was hard on me when it came to education. She made sure that everybody clearly understood the expectations. She was a very intelligent woman and an avid reader of history, literature, and poetry. I admired my mother's amazing memorization skills—she needed to hear a poem or story only once to memorize it. When she died, we lost not only the central pillar of our family but also our human library.

Despite the family support, I was not always particularly enthusiastic about school in my early years. While I could memorize and think critically, I struggled with organizing and communicating my thoughts. Further, we were always on the move, making it hard for me to focus in school. Growing up, we spoke Somali at home and Arabic in school, so I became fluent in both languages. As a refugee in Kenya I learned to speak Swahili. Despite my lack of enthusiasm for school, I always maintained excellent grades throughout my early childhood education.

It was later, when we arrived in the United States, that I began to struggle with school. At Portland (Maine) High School, I was put in English as a Second Language (ESL) classes along with other immigrants and refugees. The ESL program really slowed my learning progress, both in English and in other subjects. I had always learned languages in a "complete immersion" style and had never had any trouble. But at Portland High, I was in classes with other students who struggled with English, so I could not learn from them. In my opinion, students learn as much from fellow students as they do from teachers. Lack of extensive contact with native speakers added to the already difficult challenge of learning English. Further, I was deeply discouraged by the seemingly unintentional segregation that was prevalent in the school.[2] As a result of these challenges, I doubted my own abilities. Not in my wildest dreams did I think I would ever attend a four-year college after high school.

The turning point came in the summer of 2002, when I attended the Upward Bound Program at the University of Maine.[3] For six weeks I lived in a residential hall, participated in rigorous college-level research projects, attended presentations, and worked one-on-one with University of Maine faculty members. At the end of this program, my language skills had improved, my accent had softened up, and my confidence level had increased tremendously—I think of the experience as one that increased my cultural capital. It is fair to say that, besides my family, the Upward Bound program was the single most important influence leading me toward higher education.

Convinced that I could indeed pursue a college education, I returned to Portland High determined to achieve good grades in college prep courses. Against my guidance counselor's advice I signed up for challenging courses in my junior year—two science courses (one of them with a lab), two math classes, college-prep English, and a history course. In my senior year, I again took a full load of college-prep courses. Those two difficult years eventually paid off well. My English skills improved and, despite my relatively weak SAT scores, I was accepted to all the colleges I applied to in my senior year.

As my high school graduation approached, my excitement for the educational journey ahead of me increased. Colorful college brochures and campus invitation letters from all over the country started to find their way into my home mailbox. Some appealed to me more than others. "Bowdoin will teach you how to read and write," read one pamphlet. As a student still struggling with English yet very committed to attending college, I was thrilled with Bowdoin's message. Bowdoin invited me to their open house for minority students. I spent three days at Bowdoin College, where I ate in the college's dining facilities, stayed in the residential halls, attended three classes, watched a hypnotist show, and took several college tours. This experience propelled me to apply to Bowdoin, even though I thought a larger school might be better for me. When I was not considered for the full-tuition diversity scholarship, I quietly scratched Bowdoin off my list, knowing I could not afford it.

As I thought more about it, my choice to attend the University of Maine was an easy one. The university offers a wide array of majors, and as the state's major research institution, it enjoys a respectable national and international reputation. I was also drawn to the large selection of sports and other student activities, not to mention the affordable tuition. And thanks to my Upward Bound experiences, I already knew my way around the campus, I already knew many faculty members, and I had already made important contacts in the financial aid office. I also liked the "undecided" program for first-year students, because back then I had so many interests that it was impossible to narrow them all down into one major.

But even with all these positive factors, my transition to higher education was far from smooth. During the very first semester, I faced anxiety, loneliness, financial difficulty, and other unexpected challenges. I remembered my parents' advice that "with perseverance and persistence comes success." I remembered the many challenges I had faced in high school and felt that in time I could manage college successfully. In the end I was right. There had been a large Somali population in my high school, and some teachers saw all Somalis as at-risk students. But at the University of Maine, I was one out of only five Somali students. Hence, I could just be myself without constantly needing to prove myself. Instead of lumping me with a group of people, others judged me on my own merit. I could have a fresh start.

During my sophomore year, it occurred to me that I faced not only a language barrier but also a cultural barrier. My roommate was a big fan of Larry the Cable Guy. I tried so hard to understand the jokes made in his act; but no matter how hard I listened to the words, I was unable to grasp the real meaning and humor in those jokes. Sometimes I was frustrated and I almost gave up on the whole show. How could it be that I could understand the lectures given by the professors but I could not understand the simple jokes made by someone on Comedy Central? This was a mystery to me. My roommate had an explanation. "If you do not know the context of these jokes, you cannot get their actual meanings," he said. As the saying goes, knowing the disease is half of the treatment. Soon afterwards, I decided to immerse myself in local life and culture. I started attending campus events, reading the local newspaper, eating at the local diners, and having lengthy conversations with anybody who would listen to me, students or otherwise. My roommate's advice paid off. I grew more tolerant toward people with different views and lifestyles. I felt less homesick, uncomfortable, and lost around unfamiliar environments. But above all, Larry the Cable Guy was slowly but surely becoming one of my favorite comedians. This experience taught me that the cultural challenge is part of my education—actually a very important part. I told my younger brother, who was a senior in high school at the time, that college life is full of energy, challenges, and opportunities to grow both academically and socially; you have to embrace all the positive aspects of it to live up to your full potential.

Somali Americans in Higher Education

In contrast to my own experience, many Somali students aspiring to higher education find the challenges too great and the support systems too weak, leaving many falling through the cracks. In her research on immigrant education, Sonia Nieto found that immigrants have historically done poorly in U.S. schools.[4] Today the overall picture of Somali students in higher education is equally discouraging. According to Abdirizak Mohamed, the number of Somali graduates in the United States with four-year degrees in 2006 was so low as to be statistically insignificant. This shocking fact is true even in metropolitan areas where Somalis are concentrated, such as Minneapolis-St. Paul, San Diego, and Seattle. As Mohamed rightly points out, Somalis are intelligent and hard working, so their absence in higher education is, as he says, "wasted talent."[5] It is important to look at the major underlying factors that explain this disturbing trend that results in such a waste of talent. I consider both internal and external factors that undermine educational success for Somalis. Internal factors are those found within Somali culture, within the family and the community. External factors are those embedded in educational and social institutions in the United States. For the ease of argument I separate the two factors; however, it is important to note that in practice they are intertwined.

Internal Barriers to Higher Education

Many Somali parents who migrate to North America have had little or no formal education prior to their arrival in the new land, and even those who did have some prior education are generally unfamiliar with the American higher education system and unprepared to deal with the details of the college application process. As a consequence, the children of these parents face financial, academic, and social challenges in getting into higher education. Lidwien Kapteijns and Abukar Arman point to several strengths and liabilities that Somali parents contend with in educating their children.[6] On the positive side, Somalis' strong sense of communal identity and pride, general resistance to U.S. racism, and positive attitude toward modern education can help Somali youth succeed in school. However, the liabilities that many Somali parents face—lack of financial and cultural capital, generational conflicts, authoritarian parenting styles, and fractured families and identities—can hinder opportunities for parents to develop the bicultural competence needed to help their children succeed in school.

Cross-cultural misunderstanding on the part of their parents can add to the many challenges that Somali students face. The father of a bright young student who graduated from a reputable private liberal arts college recently shared his concerns: "She is planning to attend law school, and I am not sure if that is a good idea." Because he was reluctant to let his daughter pursue her law degree, I felt an obligation to be her advocate: "That is very good news, and you should stand behind her," I advised him. The father, who usually takes pride in being supportive of his children's pursuit of higher education, seemed unimpressed with his daughter's educational goals. I expect that most American-born fathers would be thrilled to see their children study law. In the case of this Somali father, his opposition to law school may have grown out of Somalis' general skepticism of government and law enforcement because of the corruption that has characterized Somalia. Some Somalis associate lawyers with lies and deception, putting the profession in conflict with Islamic values. As a result, many Somalis do counsel young students to avoid law school, though this attitude may be changing with younger generations. Ironically, this negativity toward lawyers is at odds with the great need for legal expertise within the Somali community.

These stories of cross-cultural misunderstanding are endless. Ahmad, a Somali university student, once told me, "My mother thinks I am lazy because I do not go to school until 10:00 a.m." Ahmad's classes did not start until 11:00 a.m., so he was actually getting to school in plenty of time. However, his mother thought that he was getting to classes very late and that he was becoming lazy. A female student told me that her parents—especially her mother—insisted that she enroll in a pre-med program. Although she was not interested in becoming a doctor, to please her parents she applied for and was accepted into the pre-med program. After three years in the program, she could not take it any longer and finally changed her major. Some Somali parents are unfamiliar with the range of career opportunities available for their children, while many insist on majors that are readily practical, such as engineering or nursing. Such parental attitudes could undermine the wider range of goals in higher education that young Somalis have.

Female students sometimes encounter additional challenges due to cultural norms and expectations for women. For example, it is not uncommon for female Somali students to go home most weekends to help the family with cooking, cleaning, and caring for children and the elderly. However, despite these challenges, many immigrant girls are outperforming boys. A growing body of research indicates that there is a gender gap in educational attainment in the United States and within immigrant communities.[7]

Societal and Institutional Barriers to Higher Education that Affect Somali Students

Numerous studies examine the complex social forces that can impede the educational goals of black immigrants. Explanations for below-average educational achievement of black immigrants include socioeconomic status, segmented assimilation, lack of social capital, contact with oppositional cultures (marginalized groups that reject mainstream values and norms), and the impact of stereotypes on achievement.[8] Somalis—and other American minorities—face many challenges in the American educational system, from systemic racial discrimination to poorly funded schools to social isolation.

Coming from a homogeneous society, many Somalis are not prepared for America's hodgepodge of unfamiliar cultures and social norms. And as if such culture shock were not enough for the Somalis to bear, post-9/11 anti-Muslim sentiments have alienated the Somalis even further. But Somalis enrolled in institutions of higher education face even more challenges.

Many Somalis are unfamiliar with bureaucratic processes within U.S. institutions, and likewise, many of the institutions fail to realize that Somali students may need assistance in navigating these bureaucratic requirements. Simple things like filling out the Free Application for Federal Student Aid (FAFSA) form can turn a Somali student away from pursuing a post-secondary education. Many FAFSA–eligible high school seniors are either unaware of the FAFSA form or simply unable to gather the required information to fill out the form, and hence do not apply for financial aid for college. Because I was lucky to have attended Upward Bound, where I learned about the FAFSA forms and filling them out online, I try to make sure that my friends and younger brothers know about these forms and deadlines.

Low test scores on standardized exams such as the SATs also discourage many students from pursuing higher education. These students do not realize that standardized test scores are only one factor in college admissions and that colleges will often consider a student with low scores if the rest of the application is strong. In many Somali families the parents are ill-equipped to assist with the application process—mostly because of their lack of familiarity with the system, but also possibly because "in Somalia, parents did not need to involve themselves with their children's education. This was completely the domain of the schools and the teachers."[9] If high schools and colleges provided more assistance for students and families, this institutional barrier could be addressed.

For those students who are able to successfully navigate the application process, once they get to college they often encounter many first-year adjustment issues and cross-cultural misunderstandings. One example of this is when administrators rely on Arthur W. Chickering and Linda Reisser's "seven vectors of student development" to evaluate identity formation and students' development.[10] This assessment measures seven areas, including developing competence, managing emotions, moving through autonomy toward interdependence, developing mature interpersonal relationships, establishing identity, developing purpose, and developing integrity. While these vectors are useful in the American social context, employing them to assess or advise Somali students transitioning between secondary to postsecondary education might lead to catastrophic results. For example, while individual autonomy is viewed as a sign of success in this particular model, in the Somali family structure "it clashes with parents' expectation to remain indefinitely in a position of mutual interdependence with family members."[11] Despite the shortcomings, Chickering and Reisser's theory actually remains useful to a certain degree, especially if the student-affairs professional takes cultural background into consideration. This psychosocial development theory can be useful for Somali students who are experiencing identity crises. The hardest part for Somali youngsters is the vector of "establishing identity," because even answering simple questions like "where are you from?" might be tedious and need a lot of rehearsal and follow-up questions. A usual first encounter for a Somali student might proceed as follows:

> Joe: So, where are you from, Ishmael? Did I say your name right?
> Ismail: I am from Portland. No worries about my name—most
> people mispronounce it!

Joe: Oh, cool. But what is your nationality?

Ismail: I am a United States citizen.

Joe: Oh, really; my bad. I was just wondering … hmm …
never mind.

Ismail: Well, now that you are interested in the whole story, I was born in
Somalia, lived in Kenya for a while, then moved to the United States with
my family. A few years later I was naturalized as a U.S. citizen, and now I
will probably be living here for good, like your grandparents did.

While Joe's rather strange questioning might arguably be motivated by
honest curiosity, it frustrates Somali students to explain their identity repeatedly, not just to strangers but also to their colleagues and sometimes even to
their professors and advisors. My personal experience in the Political Science
department demonstrated that a normal political discussion could quickly
result in a heated debate, and any political disagreement with someone could
lead to my being labeled as anti-American or as a terrorist sympathizer. Anyone
with a "foreign" sounding name like mine is probably familiar with the comment, "If you don't like it here, then why don't you go back to your country?"

The post-9/11 anti-Muslim context has made Somalis even more vulnerable to discrimination and exacerbated relations in the academy for
Somali students. As visible minorities—especially in Maine—Somali students are subject to discrimination on the basis of both race and religion.
Although there is some evidence that Somalis' strong and positive sense
of Somaliness—*soomaalinimo*—can help them resist negative stereotypes,
institutional barriers and stereotypes do affect their educational experiences.[12] The media tends to overlook positive contributions Somalis are making to the world and instead focuses on Somalis' links to terrorist activities.
Every time a ship is hijacked off the coast of East Africa or someone attempts
to blow up a jetliner halfway across the world, Somali Americans are scrutinized by the media and even sometimes by their neighbors. These tensions
have serious implications for students who are striving to pursue their educational dreams. I know of many Somali parents who are reluctant to send
their children to faraway campuses because of security reasons. By "faraway,"
I do not mean only out-of-state institutions—even state universities that
may be only one hundred miles away from the closest Somali communities
may seem too distant for some Somali parents and their children.

Recommendations for Educators

Somali students who manage to enroll in universities have already beaten extreme odds. They might have been or perhaps still are exposed to a plethora of obstacles that range from linguistic barriers and social isolation to dealing with parents who may be unfamiliar with the American education system. Like all students, they need and deserve the full support of their professors and student affairs professionals. Multicultural educator Sonia Nieto advises to "meet our students where they are and take them somewhere else."[13] Educators need to know where their students are in order to adequately support them. And those educators need to remember that they might be the sole support for a particular student in a seemingly hostile world.[14]

Students need support not only from faculty but from other areas of the university as well. The financial aid office is also critical to the success of most immigrant students. I was fortunate to have had a financial aid advisor who knew my financial situation from start to finish so that I did not have to explain my needs at every meeting. During my summers with Upward Bound, I met people from financial aid who advised me all through my undergraduate and graduate years. I cannot stress enough the need for a compassionate, consistent, and knowledgeable financial aid advisor if colleges are to be successful in student retention. Institutions that work with immigrants from disadvantaged backgrounds must pay special attention to these students' financial needs. Immigrant parents in general and Somali parents in particular are skeptical about the U.S. financial system and are reluctant to cosign loans for their children, subsidized loans or otherwise. Financial aid advisors should be aware of that fact and explore ways to overcome that obstacle.

Admissions and community outreach are equally important to recruiting and retaining Somali students. The University of Maine's director of admissions and staff work tirelessly to reach out to the Somali community. They utilize all aspects of community channels, including schools, community organizations, and at least three mosques where Somali families often gather. In return, these *masaajid* (mosques) have opened their doors for the admissions team to do presentations about the University of Maine. On one occasion at the end of Friday prayers, the admissions team presented their program and then took questions from interested parents and youth.

Finally, I cannot emphasize enough the need for open communication with the Somali community, especially to reach out to bicultural community members who are well versed in both Somali and American cultures, such as community organizers or recent college graduates. When appropriate, it is crucial to seek Somali-speaking professionals who can motivate Somali students to perform well in schools and serve as real role models. Providing such Somali professionals would also reassure Somali parents that their children will have the support they need on campus. With the combination of parental support, elevated educational awareness, and institutional commitments to recruiting and retaining disadvantaged students, Somali students could overcome major obstacles, strive for upward mobility, and thus avoid "wasting their talents."

A Bullet and a Snake, but I Kept Pushing

Liban Abu

I was born in Somalia. I'm the seventh boy in my family, and I have four sisters. My mom, my dad, and my brothers all lived in Mogadishu, the capital, but I always used to stay with my grandmother and grandfather down in Barawa, which was close to the ocean.

I liked growing up in Barawa. My grandfather worked in a utility company that provided electricity for the whole town. I used to go hang out with him. When he wasn't there I would go mess around with the power and shut off the electricity, and he would have to come and reboot the whole system again. When I wasn't hanging out with him, I used to go to my uncle's store and eat sugar. I would go in the back room and steal the sugar and eat it. After that I used to go to the ocean. The ocean was really beautiful. Every time I went to the ocean, I wondered what was beyond it and beyond Barawa. I used to wonder what it would take me to get beyond the ocean shores. I always used to wonder, what is the world like outside Barawa?

I found all that out when the war happened. The civil war in Somalia started in the early 1990s, I believe. Militants came and raided the towns. One particular evening I was sitting on the porch watching some Western movies. (My favorite movie back then was *The Good, the Bad, and the Ugly*.) While I was sitting there, someone shot a bullet through the wall, and it passed by my eyes. I remember that I saw my life flash in front of me. Then the same night they came again. It was heavy this time, and they sprayed bullets right into our house. Luckily, no one in my family got injured that day.

There and then we had to make a decision. We got out of Somalia and went to our neighboring country, Kenya. In Kenya we were in a refugee camp where we moved in with lots of other Somali people who fled the war. We all lived there. The refugee camp was a really nice community, a friendly environment. I loved Kenya. I already spoke the language, which was close to Barawan. It was easy for me to interact with the Kenyans, and we understood what each other was saying.

After a month in the refugee camp, I got really sick. I had malaria. I was close to dying, and so I was lying in my bed outside, underneath a mango tree. It was a nice breezy afternoon. Then a snake fell out of the mango tree and landed on my chest. I just sat there and made eye contact with the snake. I was ready to die. It was the second time I had given up on life. (The first time was when a bullet almost killed me.) As soon as I had lost hope, my life was saved again. We used to have a cat, and at that moment it came. The cat and the snake fought, tangled, and fought some more. The cat killed the snake, but the snake bit the cat before it died. My cat's name was Chino. He was a beautiful cat; I still have a picture of him. A few weeks later, my cat died. It was a sad moment for me.

We stayed in Kenya for three years, from 1991 to 1993. My family remained there, but I had to move with my dad's friend to a different country. We moved to London, England. I stayed in London for four or five years. I went to school there and learned the language. That's when I learned about my religion, too; I went to Muslim school there. During those years I lost contact with my family, but my mom and my dad trusted this man who was a close friend of the family, and so I stayed with him. Then my family got sponsorship to go from Kenya to America, and they came and stayed in Maine. I hadn't seen them for the longest time—since 1993. I saw my dad for the first time since I had left Kenya when he picked me up and brought me to America in early 2000.

America was a whole different culture again. I spoke English, but not the same English that Americans speak. I was speaking with a British accent, pronouncing the words differently. I went to a middle school in Portland, Maine, where I was put in an ESL class. Kids were making fun of my accent. I'm like, "Yo, at least I speak English; you guys are just learning English." I only stayed in ESL for one year. I got out of there, and I was taking regular classes with American kids. I was competing on their level. But the teachers still thought that I didn't speak English. I finished middle school early.

Then I went to high school in Portland. The high school was really big, and it was a whole culture shock for me again. I saw all kinds of faces. I saw Asians. The only time I had ever seen an Asian in my life was in Bruce Lee movies, which I used to love watching. I liked my high school. It was full of different cultures. I remember one time in early 2001—that was my freshman year of high school—I was in geometry class, and the school was put on lockdown. All the teachers were scared and running around. I asked them what was going on, and someone said, "Some guy has a gun outside." After a few minutes went by, they informed us that the World Trade Center [had been destroyed]. I didn't even know what the World Trade Center was until 9/11.

A lot of people got blown up, a lot of people died. I really felt bad for people that died, but I didn't know what had happened or how or why.

Even though the whole high school was full of black kids, somehow I always found myself being the only black kid in class. That was because I was in college-preparation classes, and the African kids or immigrant kids were in ESL classes. I didn't have a group of friends in my class because my classmates were always Americans; they understood each other, so they were always hanging out with each other. It didn't bother me too much. I didn't want to go back to ESL classes just to have friends. So I kept pushing myself. My bookwork was spectacular; I was working my hardest. But still, one of my teachers would look at me really weird, like I was a gangster. She was always picking on me because I would always show up a few minutes late for class. She always picked on me, but I didn't really care. I kept pushing myself in college-prep classes and, a couple of years later, in honors classes. Again, I was the only black kid in there, but I didn't care. I kept pushing myself.

I remember applying for colleges. I wanted to study auto mechanics, because my dad was an auto mechanic. My teacher said, "Oh, auto mechanics involve a lot of math, and I don't think you're really good at math." I was thinking, "What are you talking about? I'm taking Physics, Algebra II—I'm in the same classes with all these American kids." But I didn't want to say that to him, because I had too much respect for my teachers. African people always teach you about having respect for older people. So I just looked at it as motivation. I applied to Southern Maine, Orono, and Farmington. I got rejected by Farmington. When I got the rejection letter I just laughed. I got into Orono and a school in Massachusetts. I came down to the University of Maine because I wanted to be an engineer.

My natural choice was to become an electrical engineer, since my grandfather was one, but I wanted to be different. I didn't want to follow his footsteps, even though he was a great man and I love him. I chose mechanical engineering and technology. I was the only black kid in there, again. It didn't really bother me at this point; I had gotten used to being the only black person in my environment. The first semester I had to go to this class on machine tools. I'd never seen a class like that; I had no experience with machines like that. I walked in fresh off the boat. I remember that in the first class they put us in a lab, and the teacher was talking about all kinds of machines. I didn't really pay attention. The second day of class I remember messing up my piece of equipment. There was a TA (teaching assistant) in there, and he just started yelling at me. I had never felt so little in my whole life. He yelled at me and kicked me out of the lab because I had broken a five-dollar aluminum bar. I thought I was about to get expelled. I went back to my dorm. I was crying. I had never cried about anything in my life. I came back after the class was over and started apologizing to the TA. I told him about my lack of experience. But he said, "It doesn't matter," and he made me feel like an idiot. So I worked really hard in the class, and I became really good with machines.

I kept excelling in my mechanical engineering classes, and then I had to take an electrical class. I really enjoyed the electrical class and I thought, "You know what? I'm also going to study electrical like my grandfather." I chose electrical engineering as my second major. As I look back to where I came from, right now, it was all about hard work and dedication. I love going to the University of Maine and studying electrical and mechanical engineering. If I went back to my old high school and showed my college diploma to my teacher, he would probably have a heart attack. If I showed it to my TA he wouldn't believe it, because he thought I was an idiot.

College has given me the best moments of my life, and I have made a lot of friends. I met some kids from Somalia. They called themselves the "goon squad." These guys were really smart guys, and they wanted the same thing out of life as I do, so I naturally clicked with them. I always think back to that moment when the first bullet flew by my eyes and to the second moment when the snake almost killed me. These were life-changing moments for me, and I have never taken anything for granted since then.

PART III

"Wherever I Go I Know Who I Am": Cultural Interactions

It's Difficult to Be Me

Ubah Bashir

I have this feeling that I am constantly being watched. I feel like people are counting my mistakes and waiting for me to fail. Somalis by nature are competitive people. Everyone wants to know what the other person is doing so that they always remain at the top. The majority of people are looking for ways to outscore the rival. Very few people look out for each other. It's difficult to be yourself because you're constantly being judged and compared to the next girl.

Mothers are concerned that their daughters are going to embarrass them. There are family expectations that are very difficult to meet. There are social expectations not to embarrass the family. There is a constant need to be perfect. Even if you're not perfect, you put a smile on and act like everything is perfect. It's difficult to be me. I have so many expectations and demands to meet. At times I feel burnt out, like I have no more to give, but people still insist that I give more. Regardless of what I value, it seems like others come first. In Somali culture parents always come first. To them internal happiness means making others happy, not yourself.

I want to shout! I have my own ideas, my own passions, my own mind, my own talents, and my own value system. I want to live according to what I believe, not according to what my community or society thinks is good for me. Why are people so concerned with whether or not I wear a *hijab?* Everyone should be left alone to do as they please. Why do people care so much about what I do? Ultimately, I am the one that will have to answer to God.

There is self-hate, ignorance, and lack of freedom to be an individual in this culture. My dark skin bothers some people. I receive comments that I would be more attractive had I been born light-skinned. I ask, "Why? This is the way God made me. What makes light skin better than dark skin?" I'll tell you that there is a great deal of self-hate among my people. But the grass is not always greener on the other side. I know Somali girls who tried to bleach their skin. What did they get out of it? Absolutely nothing but more acne, redness, and dry skin.

See, you have to be a tough person to be a part of this culture, because this culture will insult and verbally abuse you. If you're not tough then you will not survive. I am who I am. I can't change how I was created, nor do I want to change how I was created. I just desire some peace and quiet. I want to be left alone to be me.

7   Caaliya's Storytelling[1]

Kristin M. Langellier

> My departure from cultural Islam is saying, "is it possible that I thought about why I choose to dress the way I dress?" It's not a sign of oppression to me, if you ask.
>
> Caaliya

This statement is part of a narrative interview with Caaliya (a pseudonym), a Somali woman in her early twenties who lives in Lewiston, Maine.[2] Caaliya is dressed in a long, thick dress of one color that flows past her knees, and a matching veil covers her head and shoulders, exposing only her face and hands. Her dress announces her identity as Muslim and (to some Western observers) presents a hypervisible icon of women's oppression. Caaliya does not disclose the specific meanings this dress has for her and why she chooses it. But she asks if it's possible she has thought about it and answers her own question immediately with, "It's not a sign of oppression to me," followed by an aside to the listeners, "if you ask." In fact, we had not expressly asked about her dress—but more importantly, we did not need to, as wearing the *hijab* can itself be seen as a speech act. The "you" implied in "if you ask" includes those present in the room and the Western discourses that Caaliya recognizes us to be a part of. She preemptively offers a response to this unspoken question.

I examine Caaliya's interview because of its power to simultaneously clarify and complicate Somali identity in the diaspora. The field notes I wrote immediately after the interview reflect that I thought it had been an "excellent interview"—that Caaliya had openly and insightfully talked about the complexities of identity as a refugee and a secondary migrant to Maine. And yet when I returned to the interview, I was equally struck by how cloaked, multilayered, and strategic Caaliya's performance of identity had been. I call Caaliya's storytelling a performance not because it is in any sense false or deceptive but because it exceeds what a text says. Performance makes a text say more and do more than it seems, so that it eludes the reader's attempt to fix its meaning.[3] The trickiness of Caaliya's performance mirrors the power of the veil itself: to be recognizable but not to be read. Transparent and opaque, straightforward and strategic, responsive and resistant, the dress-text and performance turn themselves inside out but without final disclosure.[4] In this moment of performance, Caaliya speaks and is visible but remains enfolded in covering; we researchers do not speak but we are exposed. For Caaliya is as actively reading us as we are reading her; and she engages both Muslim and Western discourses to form and perform her identity.

Somalis' orientation to strangers is characterized as simultaneously generous and suspicious, as they guard and share secrets on their own terms with adept oral and improvisational skills.[5] This analysis will not uncover Caaliya's identity—even if that were possible—but rather will follow her storytelling as it unfolds in a specific time and place as an embodied dialogue with others, situated within the context of existing discourses about refugees, Somalis, and Muslims. Analysis of Caaliya's narrative performance contributes to a small but newly emerging scholarship that inserts the story of Somali identity into North American narratives. It is a story already underway, and it is a story entrenched in the emotional and political minefields of what it means to become Somali American. In the face of a national climate hostile to immigration and of resettlement communities' question of "why can't they be more like us?" Somalis retain a strong sense of ethnic pride: a "sense of self that runs like a thick current" through their conversations.[6] The taken-for-grantedness of identity is precisely what is called into question in the diaspora, where Somalis are remaking themselves as Americans and are remaking Lewiston and Maine.

Somali refugees have experienced so much loss—their homeland, loved ones, ways of living, and means of livelihood. They struggle for both survival and a sense of identity as they tell the stories of their tumultuous journey to bureaucrats in refugee organizations, to their new neighbors in communities of resettlement, and to researchers such as us, as well as to themselves. Identities are stories we tell ourselves and others about "who we are" and "who we are not."[7] One risk for narrators is being locked into the identity position of the "refugee," the role of a victim bound to them and limiting their capacity to redefine and transform who they are in their new national and local settings.[8]

In presenting Caaliya's story, I try to disrupt the refugee-as-victim narrative to instead highlight her tactics to redefine and transform identity, including her readings of us, the interviewers. I eschew the "plight and flight" tale of her refugee journey to Maine in order to focus on moments that open up, contest, and complicate cultural identity in the Somali diaspora in Maine. To preserve the anonymity Caaliya requested, I minimize and generalize autobiographical details of her story. In brief, her family fled Somalia when she was twelve years old, spending eight years as refugees in Kenya where Caaliya learned English, perfecting it by watching American television. After a short time on the West Coast, she moved to Lewiston at the invitation of a family friend. At the time of the interview she was in her early twenties and had been in Lewiston approximately two years, where she worked in the service sector and was attending a local college to study leadership, with aspirations for a career to combat poverty. Her story fleshes out the outlines of Somali migration and movement: their diasporic dispersion as a people, her family's travels across countries and continents, and her own transition to college as a young woman.

Caaliya's interview was conducted on the campus of the small college she attends. Five others were present: three project researchers who are white,

FIGURE 13. Residents at an apartment complex in Lewiston, Maine

female, and middle-aged; the family friend who invited Caaliya to Lewiston, a Somali male whom she calls a mentor; and a young Somali female student from Lewiston, also wearing *hijab,* who attends a different university and is also a member of the project.[9] Caaliya's narrative of cultural identity is "a story co-produced in a complex choreography" of bodies, circumstances, cultures, and histories.[10] I follow Caaliya's unfolding narrative dance within the confluence of gazes that are both present in the room and within discourses that regulate meaning as they co-construct the possibilities of her identity. From her unfolding story, I identify and examine key moments when she engages with existing and evolving definitions of what it means to be Somali, female, black, and Muslim.

Throughout I consider how Caaliya is reading her listeners and talking back to regulating discourses, while also striving to question my own assumptions about identity and meaning and my own complicity in dominant designs. I argue that her storytelling performance circulates within the two most dominant narratives used to explain Somalis—identity-as-culture and identity-as-religion—and reworks them as they are fleshed out and localized by gender and race in the diaspora. In order to invite the reader into the dialogic spaces of performance possibilities that may challenge my readings, I present Caaliya's stories before offering my analyses of how identity is being co-constituted and performed.

"Wherever I Go I Know Who I Am": Enfolding Culture-as-Identity

I begin with one lengthy excerpt that occurs early in the interview. For the purposes of analysis, I segment it into four sequential narrative moves that are consequential for Caaliya's performance of identity, titling each story with a key phrase she speaks. In order to capture performance, the transcriptions are segmented into lines that suggest how the story was told as well as what Caaliya said.[11] These performance transcriptions suggest the rhythm, sound, and "feel" of the storytelling as it emerged in the interview. In the transcripts, "C" refers to Caaliya; "M" refers to the interviewer; and "K" refers to the author.

The first excerpt occurs after Caaliya locates her home on a map of Somalia provided by the interviewers.

"Wherever I go I know who I am"

M: and what was that town like, do you remember?
C: it was pretty nice [pause] it was actually very nice
and most of the people who lived there belonged to the same tribe I do
and it's—it was interesting because it's one of the things
    that's given me my grounding
    in my ethnicity
    in that sense that wherever I go I know who I am
and I have a strong [pause] ethnic identity, so to speak
as opposed to identifying as being a Somali or just being an African
those are labels that come from being in the United States
    or being in areas where Somalis are not the majority

Caaliya states with pride and clarity: "wherever I go I know who I am." A strong communal sense of identity comes from living in a Somali town among others in "the same tribe."[12] This claim is an embodied claim, coming from within, and it is not easily expressible to nor read by cultural outsiders. Caaliya's alignment with a community reflects how Somali immigrants continue to go out of their way to live together in the same towns, neighborhoods, and buildings; and Lewiston is no exception. She pauses before naming this embodied connection "ethnicity," distinguishing it from the national borders of Somalia or continental Africa as identity categories that she calls out as "labels" that come from the outside. These disidentifications with existing categories seem to be addressed particularly to the interviewers who, presumably, might misrecognize her. Their precision is perhaps a refinement based on the numerous occasions—bureaucratic, social, and educational—when refugees are asked to identify themselves and tell their story; or it may suggest a rejection of colonial names.[13] To this extent, her narrative is designed for an audience who does not know the ethnic identity that she and other Somalis in the room can distinguish, giving an inkling as to what, from the storyteller's perspective, can be taken for granted, what has to be pointed out, and what needs to be explained to listeners. In a sense, Caaliya instructs the non-Somali listeners about her identity using dominant codes while simultaneously alerting us to tribal differences which are local and indigenous to Somalia, and whose specifics she guards. Declining to disclose her tribe to non-Somalis may also function to mark us as Other and outsiders who cannot know the "I" of "wherever I go I know who I am."

In narrative terms, Caaliya's reference to "tribe" may be resisting mythic narratives of Somali homogeneity. That is, Somalis are unique in the African context in that they comprise one ethnic group (Somali), one language (Somali), and one religion (Muslim). This singularity of identity confers an aura of "specialness" within Africa and "superiority" within East Africa that intimates the complex history of northeast African cultural prejudice toward other Africans.[14] Somalis are, as a people, proud to be Somali, despite their country's long history of poverty. In a performance act that recites a previous performance, Caaliya quotes her parents as saying, "you're Somali, this is who you are and these are who your ancestors [are]." The narrative of Somalis as special draws on a related creation myth. Two clans trace a genealogical connection to one of Mohammed's early followers.[15] This lineage accounts for how Somalis claim Arabic heritage to distinguish themselves from non-Muslim Africans. Although this genealogy has not been historically verified, the narrative recited through the potent oral tradition of Somalis creates a powerful creation myth that overlays Islam onto Somali customs and culture. Lidwien Kapteijns and Abukar Arman argue that pride in Somali cultural authenticity *(soomaalinimo)* is in crisis because of the ravages wrought by the civil war, and under duress due to challenges in the diaspora.[16]

"But you still need to know"
Immediately following the preceding segment, Caaliya takes a narrative turn that reflects on African American history:

> I watched a documentary once where there were
> > African American people going back to—
> > I think it was Ghana—
> to look for their roots and Ivory Coast
> > and they were trying to trace that—[pause]
> and it was forced when you're a child
> > you can count like twenty grandparents
> > that you're never gonna meet
> > who are long gone but you still need to know

Among Somalis, genealogy functions as an ethnic identity card, naming and counting grandparents in a patrilineal descent to a founding ancestor. Whereas previously Caaliya differentiated Somalis from a generalized African identity, here she distinguishes Somalis from African Americans who, unlike

Somalis, do not know who their ancestors are. It may be helpful to recall that she is a recent immigrant to the United States and a secondary migrant to Maine. Notably, her storytelling enacts a brief detour through the discourse of race that further specifies Somali identity. This move responds not to an interview question (although it may preempt one) but to the dominant discourses of black-white relations in U.S. history. Like other immigrants and refugees, she has quickly learned the racial hierarchy whose public gaze already reads her body as black mapped against hegemonic whiteness. Reading the United States and the interviewers, she again offers a counternarrative: she is not a black subject whose ancestors underwent the Middle Passage.[17] Her storytelling looks backward to remember her own ethnic history. Somalis are not black in Africa in the sense that "race is not 'the' defining social identity except in South Africa"—although racial strata are not absent in Somalia.[18] But as importantly, the storytelling looks forward, to the present and future, warding off a potential misrecognition by non-Somali listeners and simultaneously asserting a Somali uniqueness. Caaliya's narrative detour to distinguish her history from African American history multiplies blackness in the United States and opens a possible space for Somali identity: a resistance to race-as-identity when race is understood as skin color. Caaliya returns to this complicated racial thread at a later point in the narrative.

"We look homogenous but we really aren't"

An interviewer question asking Caaliya to talk about the meanings of being Somali prompts the next story:

> M: but when your parents would say,
>   "this is who you are, you're Somali"
> what do you think that, y' know, when you say that to us—
>   I'm not sure what you mean
>   what did they um assume when they would say "you're Somali"?
> C: it means that um
> with you being a Somali comes a set of morals, of values, of cultural ideals
>   and "this is who you are and this is who you should live up to"
>   And with Somalis being [longer pause]
> We look homogenous but we really aren't
> it's very—the difference from me and her it can be very huge at times

                in terms of our culture and the way we do things
        so [pause] some Somali cultures are more restrictive than others
            and it depends on what is okay for a certain tribe
            is not okay for another tribe

Caaliya continues to talk back to assumptions about Somali-ness based on continental, national, and racial constructions addressed in the "but you still need to know" story; but in this excerpt she also offers significant, positive assertions of ethnicity that link to the "wherever I go" story. Tribal affiliations mark internal differences among Somalis. Caaliya's storytelling in this moment mobilizes two potentially contradictory narratives that underwrite Somali identity. One draws again on the mythic homogeneity of Somalis based in their history, heritage, and communal culture described above. The set of morals, values, and cultural ideals asserted at this point are listed by Caaliya as respect for elders, how to be kind, the importance of family, and obligations to others. At a later point in the interview Caaliya illustrates an example of Somali youths' respect for elders by telling a story about a young American daughter shouting at her mother while they are using the photocopier in the public library. Caaliya concludes the story with this cultural point about being Somali: "there is no way you would yell at someone who is older than you, much less someone who brought you into this world." Cultural ideals such as respect for elders are shared among Somalis.

But Caaliya quickly interrupts the homogeneity narrative with a contradictory one: Somalis are a divided people. Tribal differences, anchored in genealogy and accentuated in the civil war, are certainly a divisive, difficult, and sensitive identity issue among Somalis; and how they play out in relations to Somalia and to each other in the diaspora, such as in Lewiston, is not clear. Relations among tribes have been elaborated and analyzed in decades of academic study as Somali clanism and reiterated in the last twenty years to explain the civil war as among tribal warlords.[19] In the range of interviews conducted by our project, Caaliya's reference to tribal differences is unusual because Somalis in the diaspora submerge clan identities, complying with a communication taboo. At a later point in the interview she remarks that "I usually don't like talking about my ethnicity because it's part of the reason why Somalia is the way it is today, because of adhering to ethnic identity and ethnic pride that's exclusive."[20]

If Caaliya's disidentifications with generalized labels of "Somali" and "African" and "African American" were directed primarily to the interviewers, her talk of clan more directly implicated the other two Somalis in the room. Perhaps their presence required this marking of identity; perhaps Caaliya's relatively short residence in the United States has not yet suppressed clan talk; or perhaps the interview setting overrode the taboo.[21] When Caaliya says, "the difference between her and me can be huge sometimes," she refers to the other Somali woman present. Her characterization of tribal difference as "the way we do things" seems to invoke a discourse of multicultural understanding rather than of political conflict. Caaliya affiliates with the older Somali man in the room, who is "the reason why I'm in Maine," referring to him as "a family friend and we have a tribal relation." He made only one brief comment in the interview, and it is not possible to completely specify his co-production of the narrative. But his presence was an occasion for Caaliya to talk at some length about Somali tribal rituals and relations, making explicit the intercultural limits that we, as non-Somalis, meet. She notes, for example, that she seeks him out to tell a joke to because "he'll get what I mean but someone else wouldn't." Midway through the interview, she performs a tribal joke they have shared. Its performance intimates the nature and importance of humor in Somali oral traditions as well as their rules for telling ethnic jokes, an identity theme she will elaborate below to criticize "political correctness" in the United States.

"You're a girl"

Immediately following Caaliya's statements on shared Somali cultural and tribal differences, we ask her to talk more about the Somali values she has invoked.

> K: so what are some of those [Somali] ideals?
> C: well, my least favorite one is
>   "you're a girl [group begins to laugh together]
>   so do not ride that bicycle"
> because apparently my hymen is going to go to hell
>   or like something's going to happen to my uterus [group laugh dying out]

In performance terms, Caaliya's response is a highly dramatized moment, done as a joke on Somali culture, and it evokes group laughter. It makes gender explicit and portends its troubles. Like all humor, the joke has multiple and complex functions for participants. It displays Caaliya's storytelling skill and use of humor. That the first Somali ideal named by Caaliya addresses gender norms, framed as "my least favorite," is perhaps no surprise, given the presence of three female professors and the visibility and authority of feminist discourse. The shared laughter appears to bond the group, at least momentarily, across genders as the male Somali joins in; and across tribal, Somali, and American cultures. In a distinctly dialogic moment, Caaliya embeds and performs the disciplining speech of Somalis: "you're a girl, so do not ride that bicycle," marking her cultural criticism with an altered voice and positioning herself as a character in the story and the object of social control by the linguistic shift to "you." This use of reported speech to comment on Somali culture functions to distance her from a patriarchal view of gender and to render it a target of criticism. Caaliya then switches back to the first person (I/my): "because apparently my hymen is going to go to hell or something's going to happen to my uterus." The incongruous mix of more formal and clinical language ("hymen" and "uterus") with colloquial swearing ("go to hell") contributes to the humor, signals the multiple audiences of the story, and displays Caaliya's linguistic repertoire.

This intensely performative moment also portends the trouble about gender that weaves through the remaining narrative. In Caaliya's disidentification with Somali culture, she appears to reject its patriarchal investments, the sexist values identified in scholarship and activism that reverberate through family, clan, and tradition.[22] Caaliya gives a nod to feminism and rejects the control of women's bodies and sexuality symbolized by the injunction against riding a bicycle.[23] The moment witnesses an ethnic woman who critically and constructively engages with her own heritage in the presence of a Somali male. It is nonetheless fraught with some peril both for Caaliya and for the listeners. Situated in the West, Caaliya and other Somalis are challenged to sort out what to reject and what to preserve of their culture. As a researcher equally embedded in the structures of global power, I must question to what extent I may reinscribe colonialism by calling for ethnic women to abandon their culture where it collides with Western feminism. Postcolonial theorists have warned feminists not to clothe the old story about the inferiority of traditional cultures in a new guise of liberating women from their own culture. As Leila Ahmed argues, "we need a feminism that is vigilantly self-critical and aware of its historical and political situatedness if we are to avoid becoming unwitting collaborators in racist ideologies whose costs to humanity have been no less brutal than those of sexism."[24] The Somali story is always told and heard within a history of colonialism.

"I can call you 'white' but you can't call me 'black'"

I conclude this section on culture-as-identity with a story that Caaliya says she has "told over and over," its reiteration suggesting not only its significance to her but also how she is repeatedly called to respond to race in the United States and Maine. As is already evident, Caaliya jokes and appreciates humor in both Somali and English. In the following story she discusses what makes appropriate cultural humor. She says, "like with American history, it's not appropriate to make an ethnic joke," but "I can diss his [her male mentor's] tribe any day of the week as long as I don't say anything about him as a person." This cultural difference leads to the story Caaliya introduces as about "political correctness and how it's becoming ridiculous":

> so I was like telling her [friend]
> "I can call you 'white' but you can't call me 'black'"
> and she was like "well, I'll just call you puddin' 'cause you look like chocolate"
> I told another friend of mine that, and she thought that that was a racial slur
> and I was like "no, she didn't mean it like that
>   'cause it depends on the context in which it was said"
>   'cause we were bantering at that point and I'm okay with that

I note first the performance features that mark the economy and polish of multiple tellings of this story. The story dramatizes dialogue among three friends in two closely yoked scenes that tie together Caaliya's critical point. In each scene she negotiates the black-white binary of U.S. race relations to defuse potential interpersonal conflict about race. Although the target of the earlier "you're a girl" story was Somali culture, this story criticizes the American culture of "political correctness." In the storytelling, Caaliya expressly challenges language policies that define race-as-color by emphasizing the terms "white," "black," and "chocolate." Like the "but you still need to know story" above, it distinguishes Somali from African American history. Caaliya displays her knowledge of American rules for ethnic humor but resists them: first by performing the "inappropriate" language within the story, and second by the evaluative point of the story. She invokes the conventional defense of individual intent ("she didn't mean it like that") and eschews the charge of oversensitivity ("I'm okay with that"). Linked with the earlier story on African American history, Caaliya's dramatized narrative on the excesses of political correctness in multicultural America can be read to say, "although you see me as black, race-as-color is not my/our story."

One way to take Caaliya's criticism of political correctness is to analyze how it itself risks reproducing racism; however, my purpose here is to explore how she is working to create and transform Somali identity in her storytelling performance. Caaliya's "it depends on the context in which it was said" functions to specify that race is a cultural and historical construct. Her consistent use of "ethnicity" instead of "race" to name Somali identity (she attributes the words "racial slur" to the other friend) can be read to interrogate blackness in the U.S. context at the same time that it reiterates the black-white binary.[25] The disidentification with African Americans that links Caaliya's two stories on racial difference suggests that she recognizes the risks of racialization wherein the host country and local conditions in Maine may overdetermine and reify Somali identity. Notably, Lewiston was a site of international media attention in 2002 when its then-mayor wrote a letter asking Somalis to stop their migration to the city because its social services were overwhelmed. This letter generated a small white supremacist rally simultaneously countered by a large rally supporting the Somalis as new Mainers.[26] Considering the local conditions of Caaliya's storytelling raises further questions about how the Somali resistance to American racism (in talk and possibly by locating in predominantly white Maine) may make visible institutional racism as well as render Somalis particularly vulnerable to it.[27]

At least initially, diasporic Somalis to the United States resist identification with race and racist oppression. However, recent researchers ask if Somalis in the North American context, in Awad Ibrahim's phrase, are "becoming black."[28] Murray Forman argues that Somali youths gradually adopt the mantle of blackness, consciously and unconsciously mimicking and adapting the codes of hegemonic American hip-hop dress, music, and slang in the formation of their own evolving teen identities.[29] However, the general focus on youth culture in these studies may obscure the interaction of race with gender. For example, Somali boys and men often present themselves in dress as not-that-different and thereby may be mistaken for African Americans; whereas most girls and women wear the *hijab* that pronounces a visible difference.[30] Although parental fears for their children by Somalis in Maine converge on the loss of culture and religion, they diverge by gender. Fears for sons that helped propel Somalis from larger urban areas in the United States to more rural Maine focus on gangs, drugs, and alcohol, whereas fears for daughters center on their sexuality. Caaliya introduced the gender troubles of Somalis in the diaspora in the "you're a girl" story, an identity theme she elaborates further in the latter half of the interview. To this point, her stories suggest how the strong sense of Somali identity based in culture is being altered in the diaspora. Western narratives of modernity define Somalia as "less progressive" for its views of tribal identity and of women, threatening to trap Caaliya in a struggle with her own culture. However, she navigates a liminal identity in the spaces between, using Somali culture to rework dominant narratives of race and gender. And as her narrative continues to unfold, gender and its relations to Islamic religion become more thematic and more complex.

"It's Possible I've Thought about the Way I Dress": Enfolding Religion-as-Identity

Caaliya's work to anchor Somali identity in culture is challenged by damages from the ongoing civil war at home and by the discursive constraints, particularly race and gender, of her new home in the United States. In the face of so many losses and so much change, Islam provides the single most stable source of strength and public communal identity for Somalis in the diaspora. Being Muslim transcends clan divisions; and Somali cultural authenticity is perceived to be largely coterminous with practicing Islam. In this section I follow Caaliya's storytelling through its construction of religion-as-identity, including conflicts over the definition of Islam that gender raises.

The following narrative reintroduces the theme of gender trouble and occurs midway through the interview in Caaliya's protest of "pigeonholing":

"You're a woman, you're supposed to be subservient to a man"

 one of the things—one thing that uh
 it's like someone would ask me
 "you're going to school
 is that okay as part of being a Somali
  because you're a woman
  you're supposed to be uh subservient to a man?"
 and I'm like "where are you getting this?"
 because that might be a reality for some Somalis
  and I acknowledge that reality is true
 but it's not *my* reality

The narrative "you're a woman" recalls the "you're a girl" story directed at sexism in Somali culture; however, it is now U.S. assumptions about Somali culture that Caaliya targets in her counternarrative. The two stories are structurally similar in their use of reported speech to enact the storyteller's evaluation of the narrative event. Again Caaliya's performance of the quoted voice marks her criticism: she is neither "some Somalis who are subservient" nor some "pigeonholing" Americans. Her brief narrative suggests again how the U.S. context challenges gender meanings of Somali cultural and religious background. Notably, Caaliya's response uses terms that define her identity as individual rather than collective—"it's not *my* reality." This defiance may appear to contrast with the communal and tribal terms expressed in the "I know who I am" story, but it also expresses the "sturdy individualistic independence" of Somali character.[31] In addition, Caaliya's defiance may mark the youthful rebelliousness of college-aged women. As she resists the colonialist assumptions about gender in Western discourses, Caaliya explains her gender behavior by drawing on the (also Western) vocabulary of individualism.

"Like female circumcision [pause] would be culture, not religion"

The interviewer (M) introduces the relation of culture and religion: "Well, some people talk about being Muslim as well as being Somali, and are those the same thing?" Caaliya responds, "not in my mind. Uh, a lot of Somalis tend to be cultural Muslims, and some of the things that Somalis tend to think are Islamic are actually just their own cultural manifestations or distortion of the religion. For me the two identities are very separate." I follow up Caaliya's distinction with this question:

> K: can you give us an example of what would be culture versus religion
> give us—what would be an example of separating those out?
> C: like female circumcision [pause] would be culture, not religion
> Uh [pause] I know that we don't have to be circumcised or uh
>   do the FGM thing as far as religion is concerned if it caus–
>   um I actually read up on that and was like, if it causes–
>   if it's proven to cause harm you're actually not supposed to do it
> but it's just that–it wasn't something that–
> it's not a religious value and a lot of people–
> in my case it was it was or where I grew it was almost a purification process

which is retarded, if you ask me
   in the way that you don't have to mutilate someone
     to purify them for whatever reason
 and [longer pause] it wasn't done to me
   but it was done to a friend of mine
and I watched when it was being done and it was not pretty [long pause]

Pauses, false starts, and repairs mark this topic as a treacherous area. Presumably, there are several ways to separate out Somali culture and Islamic religion. Caaliya's example of female genital cutting[32] suggests again how Somalis speak in a field already marked with the topics and designs of colonialism that frame traditional practices as barbaric, a field perhaps augmented by an interview setting with three female professors associated with women's studies. Caaliya's example echoes the gender theme weaving throughout the entire interview, and she takes up the narrative line initiated by the bicycle story. Perhaps this subsequent gender story offers an interpretive context for Caaliya's seemingly incongruous use of the words "hymen" and "uterus" in the bicycle story, focusing as they do on women's sexuality and reproduction. In any case, her example seems to be overdetermined by the discursive context, despite female genital cutting not being part of the interview protocol or probes.

Caaliya first names the practice "female circumcision," drawing on religious systems of meanings, and then she shifts to the acronym "FGM" (female genital mutilation), the vocabulary of the West and of feminism. Both labels are laden with assumptions from which Caaliya distances herself. She rejects the justification of female genital cutting as "almost a purification process," describing it as "retarded"; and, in a move anticipating her talk that follows about wearing *hijab,* tacks on "if you ask me" although she has not been asked. "If you ask *me*" seems to mark "which is retarded" as merely her opinion, softening it or mitigating her accountability. The use of "retarded" may also draw on peer slang, in which Caaliya is fluent, and it is perhaps another instance of "political incorrectness" within the U.S. multicultural context. However, it may be more interesting for its semantics and logic about modernity. To mutilate in order to purify contrasts a "retarded" Somalia with a progressive United States. Caaliya's position separating the identities of culture and religion sets into motion a series of spaces: between circumcision and mutilation, between "a lot of Somalis" and "for me," between "what was done to a friend of mine" and what "wasn't done to me."

For some Somalis, the separation of culture *(dhagan)* from religion *(dinn)* is a way to emphasize membership in the modern, global Muslim community, a membership that supercedes national or ethnic groups.[33] Caaliya explicitly and forcefully disidentifies as a "cultural Muslim," the term that she uses to describe both some Somalis and some Muslims. Elsewhere in the interview she explains that "my Somali identity was something that was drilled into me ... I don't have to wonder where I come from. My Islamic identity is something I had to learn, I had to relearn it actually." Being Muslim has not been verbally thematic to this point more than halfway through the interview, although its embodied current has flowed beneath the previous stories about Somali culture. Now Caaliya treats being Muslim explicitly, and what is crucial to her narrative is learning and relearning Islam. Only recently and in the diaspora have Somali women read the Qur'an on circumcision and learned that it is not an Islamic requirement. In Somalia, female genital cutting and infibulation are still widely practiced. When Islam was adopted en masse around the year 800, Somali patriarchal values echoed, maintained, and reinforced female genital cutting.[34] Women and men learned Islam, like Somali values, through oral traditions that mapped Islam onto Somali traditions. Somalia has a history of low female literacy, with no or little schooling for girls until the 1950s, coupled with a tradition of girls' participation in education diminishing even further when they approach marriageable age in their teens.

But both literacy and female education slowly began to improve after Somali independence in 1960 and through the Barre dictatorship of the 1970s and 1980s, continuing in the exodus from civil war through the 1990s and into the twenty-first-century diaspora. Caaliya is clearly a beneficiary of growing literacy and female education, including health education in the West and religious education within global Islam. She emphasizes the value of "relearning" her Islamic identity as well as the high premium she places on education and her current college experience. "Read[ing] up on it" provides the basis for her rejection of female genital cutting as "a religious value." Notably, Caaliya is part of a new generation of Somali women who can access the Qur'an on their own rather than exclusively through male religious leaders and female oral traditions. Although the Islamic position is divided on the practice of female circumcision, almost all progress made to extinguish it has been made by religious leaders who denounce it because Somalis tend to distrust both foreign and medical discourse on the subject.

Caaliya's separation of culture and religion exonerates Islam as the justification for female genital cutting, although it does not resolve tensions among Islam, Somali culture, and gender.

My question on how Caaliya separates culture and religion is revelatory of her position on female genital cutting and discloses her own bodily experience ("it wasn't done to me"). Possibly she would not have offered it as an example had she undergone circumcision. But however disclosive, Caaliya stops well short of telling a cultural or personal story, whether her own or her friend's. The events were witnessed ("I watched") and evaluated ("it wasn't pretty") but are not told in detail nor with the reported speech that characterizes her other stories. In narrative terms, this couplet of lines constitutes an opening that gestures to a story but closes off access. In the silence that travels across the listeners, Caaliya refuses to become a spectacle for colonial consumption and resists the scrutinizing gaze. Her storytelling aligns with feminism but simultaneously protects a cultural and personal space from intrusion. The aside to listeners, "if you ask," exposes the Western obsession with cultural practices such as female genital mutilation that reinscribe the colonial narrative. Caaliya's critical reading of us in this statement links to her storytelling on wearing the *hijab* and moves further into the folds of Islam in her identity performance.

"It *is* possible I have thought about why I choose to dress the way I dress"

After the lengthy pause, the interviewer (M) asks Caaliya what she would like to tell people about being Muslim. She first responds with broad descriptions: "it's a beautiful religion," "it's not synonymous with acts of terror," and "I guess my biggest thing would be living in America is [pause] the freedom for a Muslim to be a Muslim in any environment." In this way Caaliya shifts from the more embodied particularities invoked by her brief narrative about female genital cutting to a more collective Muslim voice. Her concern is that "Muslims are becoming apologists," which she specifies as "you have to apologize for why you believe or what you believe." This more general, plural, and impersonal "you" is prelude to her statements about Islamic dress with which I opened this essay and which I quote here at greater length:

> one of the things I find [pause] I find [pause] um difficult
> is for you to be a Muslim and say
>> "I believe in this thing because I am a Muslim"

I don't–"I'm not Muslim because I was" –
which is *my* departure from cultural Islam is saying that
   "is it possible that I thought about why I choose to dress the way I dress?"
   it's not a sign of oppression to me, if you ask
it may be oppression to someone else
   some people might have an objection to it
it *is* possible I have thought about why I'm dressed this way
it is also possible I have made a conscious *choice* to dress the way I dress
   or to behave the way I behave
it might not be for you but I reserve–
I have the right to be respected for my choices

In this shift from "you" to "I," Caaliya moves from "Muslims are becoming apologists" to the gendered specifics of her own dress, adroitly addressing the embodied and situated setting of the interview as well as the discursive demands of the performance. To whom do Muslims feel compelled to apologize? To Westerners, Christians, feminists, and us, the interviewers, even if "it might not be [oppression] for you." Beginning with punctuated pauses and followed by repetitions and re-starts, the storytelling builds to a more rapid pace—all signaling that Caaliya is delicately piloting through the dangerous tides of feminist, Islamic, and Somali identities. In the "you're a girl" and "you're a woman" stories, she has aligned with Western feminisms to criticize and rework gender in Somali culture. However, gender now takes a different turn in that here Caaliya associates gender inequality not with traditional Somali culture but with "cultural Islam," with which she crisply disidentified in the "culture, not religion" story. Her "departure from cultural Islam" is textualized in the unfinished "I'm not Muslim because I was"— the implied "forced to cover" is unspoken as the subject position from which she departs. Recall that "cultural Muslims" in Caaliya's narrative, whether they are Somali or Arabic or other ethnicities, conflate culture and religion and do not question either of them. What Caaliya appears to oppose with "it's not a sign of oppression" is the general disapproval of Islam in the West. Her counternarrative is embedded where colonialist and Orientalist discourses intersect: the veiled woman is seen as backwards and oppressed by religion, needing the benevolent gesture of the West to bring her into the twenty-first century. Caaliya's storytelling places Islam and the West, Somali women and feminists, herself and us as interviewers, and her dress and speech in a performative tension. Her mobilizing of "the right to be respected for my choices" links to the vocabulary of democracy and individual rights introduced in the "you're a woman" story above.

Perhaps the most striking performance features of Caaliya's storytelling are the four repetitions of "it is possible," their echoes forming a border of silence around her meanings for being covered, keeping its ambiguity suspended in time and the spaces between Islam and the United States, her homeland and diasporic home in Maine, and the multiple participants in the narrative event. What might her covering mean in this intensely local interview setting? How does it implicate a more global context? What does it "do" as a speech act, as a performance of Somali identity? The debates on the meaning of the veil in the Somali diaspora explore both the dominant narrative of women's oppression and the counternarrative of covering as a form of resistance to Western domination.[35]

Rather than attempt to uncover her meanings by fixing an interpretation of the dress-text and storytelling performance, I follow Caaliya's unfolding story and honor its indeterminacies. Her repetitions of "it is possible that I thought" create a subjunctive mood that defers the specific act of "why I choose." Her dress-text and storytelling performance create a space of conjecture and provisionality about Somali identity. The veil that rejects and inverts determinate meanings calls attention to itself, and it calls attention to assumptions about how we make meanings out of a text. In this place of possibility, where performance exceeds the text, the veil can also surpass its existing meanings. Caaliya's "it is possible that I thought" insists, similar to Linda Duits and Liesbet van Zoonen's study of girls' wearing the veil in multicultural Europe, on considering young women "as capable and responsible agents who produce 'speech acts' with their choice of clothing."[36] As these researchers caution, claims of choice and autonomy must always be contextualized within the social pressures and discursive forces regulating women's sexuality. These pressures and forces constrain the veil as sign and the woman who wears it, the text and the performer of the text. Nonetheless, performance exceeds and can transform the meanings of a text. Taking seriously the voices and choices in Caaliya's narrative marks a space of possibility for Somali agency in performing the veil differently in the diaspora.[37] Caaliya's storytelling skillfully navigates the liminal spaces of being Somali, feminist, and Muslim.

Conclusion: "My Ethnic Identity Anchors Me Wherever I Go"

Near the interview's end, Caaliya returns to the ethnic identity with which she started the interview, saying, "my ethnic identity anchors me wherever I go." This statement harkens back to the opening salvo of the interview, "wherever I go I know who I am." Indeed, the structure of Caaliya's story-telling enacts how Somalis organize speech and argument: they begin with a conclusion, follow with an introduction, and end with the main point.[38] Caaliya's story of identity presents a sequence of linked interpersonal encounters that embody "who I am" and "who I am not" in the Somali diaspora. Throughout the storytelling Caaliya strategically engages discourses and dominant narratives, arguing and entertaining with her stories to an audience who might misrecognize or misinterpret her. She is Somali but retains tribal distinctiveness, she is black but is neither African nor African American, she is an ethnic woman but rejects sexism in traditional Somali culture, she is Muslim and covered but she contests the veil as a sign of women's oppression. If Caaliya has lost her Somali homeland, she retains a vigorous anchor of ethnic identity. By the narrative's end, it is a Somali ethnicity fleshed out, critically informed, and creatively nuanced by the diaspora to Maine. We follow the unfolding of Caaliya's story to discover yet more folds in its links, folds that layer difference and possibility. And like the veil which folded over her reasons for wearing it, the anchor of ethnicity hides depths and details that, as cultural Others, we have not uncovered, and indeed, cannot.

This anchor of identity is not a culturally pure "inside," whether located in Somali traditions or the Qur'an, but an anchor that travels with and against the narratives that would inscribe her as a Somali Muslim woman. Like a sea anchor, Caaliya attaches identity not to a fixed point on the sea floor, such as culture or religion, but to the water itself as a way to maintain headway in her movements across borders. Her embodied narrative challenges definitions of Somali-ness, of feminism, of blackness, and of Islam. She travels with her Somali culture and Islamic religion—they are the moorings of her possibilities—but she simultaneously critiques and contests them. Caaliya cannot be reduced to culture-as-identity because Somali culture cannot be understood without consideration of the race and gender in which it is embodied in the diaspora. Nor can Caaliya be reduced to religion-as-

identity because Islamic religion cannot be understood without consideration of culture and gender as they are lived in new spaces. Although Caaliya's
narrative suggests that gender is more troubling than race in performing cultural identity, racialization—particularly as Somalis live longer in the North
American diaspora—cannot be dismissed nor minimalized.

Caaliya's story is part of an emerging Somali story in the diaspora in
Maine and North America, a narrative whose end is not yet knowable for
her nor for Somalis or their host country and community. Under formation
and vulnerable to change, the story of "who I am" is told within the evolving
constraints of performance: when, where, with whom, and how the story
can be told, heard, understood, and used. With both voice and visibility,
Caaliya's storytelling imagines possibilities for Somali Muslim women in a
new homeland. Who "she" is as well as who "we" are depends upon relations
of identity, difference, and power as we co-construct our intertwined stories.
In discursive terms, we as researchers are part of the field and must strive to
be accountable for our participation in the making of stories and meanings.
As Caaliya shows with her aside "if you ask," we are also vulnerable to being
read and criticized for our complicities with dominant narratives of colonialism, feminism, and Islam. In the joint improvisation of dialogue across
cultures, we need each other's criticisms and creative possibilities.[39] How we
live our lives better and together is a serious question for all of us.

FIGURE 14. Young Somali women
(Northport, Maine)

Nothing to Cry About

Elham Salah

My mother was with me. She said, "Sit right here on the step below the woman. Sit between her legs." The Somali woman was tilting my head, stroking my hair. As she was talking to my mother, she was threading the needle. I didn't know what was going on. I was just sitting there, doing what my mom told me to do.

I was three years old, and I was living in Sudan with my mom, my dad, and my brother. My mom was pregnant with my other brother. On this morning my mom woke me up early and she told me to get dressed. She put a jacket on me because it was early and it was freezing cold outside. After I got dressed we had breakfast. And then we—my mom and me, it was just us—started walking down the dirt road, past all these houses that looked just like our own stone house. After a while we arrived at a house where the doorway was open, and sitting in the doorway was a woman with a colorful *shaash* (headscarf) and *baati,* which is a long dress that Somali women wear. I don't remember her face, just her colorful scarf and colorful dress. I knew she was Somali because of the clothes, and she was speaking to my mother in Somali. Sudanese clothes are kind of like ours—but they're not. We can just tell who others are, even in tribes.

My mom told me to go up to the woman and sit. And so I did that. The woman moved my hair behind my ears. She was looking at my face and my ears. I saw that she had a needle and lots of white string. She put the string through the needle and wound it around two or three times to make it thick so it wouldn't break. She tilted my head and looked at my ear. She told me, "Sit still," and she just jabbed the needle through my earlobe. I didn't see that coming at all. It was a moment of shock at first but it wasn't so much the needle but the threading of the yarn through the rest of the needle that hurt so much. I was crying and bawling, but my mom held me still. I think my mom knew the woman, and she knew that the woman knew how to pierce ears. My mom must have trusted her. I think she was trying to calm me down, but I don't think it was working at all. It was too painful. I didn't want to hear anything. How long was the string? I felt it was like a mile long, but it was maybe fifteen inches. She kept pulling it through like it was a yarn earring. That was the longest day of my life. I could see the string as she was pulling it through. I could see as the blood was drying from bright red to yellow to brown.

And it wasn't over. She had another ear to fix. The second one took even longer. It's not all that obvious, but in my second ear the hole is a little bit off from the middle. I think I was squirming around so much that the hole in the second ear isn't in the same place as in the first ear. By that time I was exhausted from that whole process. I just wanted to get out of there. I didn't know why this was happening. I went home and slept through the whole day and the next day.

My cousin got it done in Somalia, and they used a gun. When my baby sister was born a year later, we took her to get her ears pierced, and she got the gun as well. She was crying. Even though she was an infant I was thinking—I just couldn't help but think—"That's nothing to cry about. You have it easy. Stop sobbing. If you were only two years older you probably would have done what I did." Later on we had my sister, who was born in Georgia, and then we had my other sister, who was born in Maine—both of them had their ears pierced in a Walmart. It was like *boom-boom*. Twenty seconds.

Many years later I went to the mall with my friends. One of my girlfriends was getting her ears pierced. It didn't look painful, the way she had it done. So I decided to get a second piercing done in my second ear. It was a quick process and virtually pain-free.

After I got this second piercing, I went back to my mom and she asked when I'd had it done. I told her doing my second ear was so easy, and I asked her, "How come I couldn't have had it done that way the first time?"

"You remember that?"

"Yes, of course I remember that. I had this one done thirty minutes ago. It was so much easier than the way I did it when I was little in Sudan, and you took me to that woman and she sewed my ear with a string."

My mom was completely shocked that I remembered. I wonder if she would have it done the same way today if we were still in Sudan. In America we still keep the traditional piercing of little girls' ears, but not done in the way the Somali woman did it.

Growing up in the States you do adapt and you do pick up American culture—their music, their slang, their clothes. A lot of Somali kids go to school and they speak English. They go home and they speak Somali. They go to Somali weddings and they wear traditional clothing, but then they go to

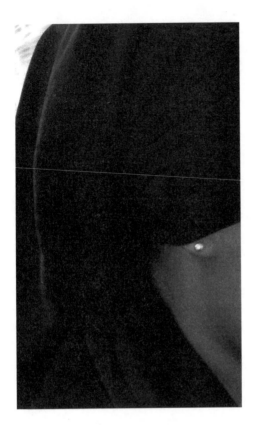

FIGURE 15. Young Somali woman

school and wear what everyone else wears. You have the culture that's pushed upon you, that you see every day at school and on the streets and on television. But then you also have the culture that your parents raised you with: the religion, the food, the language, the heritage and background. They teach you not to forget where you were born and where they were raised. It is hard to have two cultures. The American one is nice; you have some good things. But you also have the strong background of your parents. You know where you come from; you know who your ancestors are, who your people are.

I'm grateful that I had my ears pierced when I did, because I have something to remember Sudan by—because I only have flashes of certain things that happened there. It was easier for my younger sisters to get their ears pierced here, but at least I have that moment in Africa.

8 L.L. Bean, Community Gardens, and Biil: Somalis Working in Maine

Mazie Hough and Carol Nordstrom Toner

Work is central to the history of immigration and to the immigrant experience. Historically, immigrants experienced "push" factors that motivated them to leave their homeland, and "pull" factors that drew them to new places with better opportunities. Nineteenth-century immigrants in Maine followed this pattern. For example, the potato famine pushed many Irish farmers from their land in the 1840s while jobs building roads, railroads, and mills pulled them to Maine. Similarly, in the 1870s and 1880s, depleted soils pushed the French Canadians from their farms, while at the same time jobs in textile mills and shoe shops pulled them across the border to Maine. Unfavorable conditions in the homeland caused people to move out, while jobs created by the emerging industrial system in places like Lewiston, Maine, afforded the immigrants an opportunity to improve their economic situation.[1]

Likewise, Somalis have historically migrated to take advantage of economic opportunity, from their nomadic tradition to seek nearby "greener pastures" to their worldwide movement in search of a better life. Said one Somali man, "It is in keeping with our nomadic traditions to scout around for green pastures." Even before the start of the Somali civil war in 1991, Somali people had migrated to other areas of Africa as well as Europe, Asia, and North and South America. And similar to French Canadian migration patterns in the nineteenth century, their migration strategy usually involved making enough money to allow them to return and live comfortably in their homeland.[2]

In contrast to these migration patterns, however, Somali refugees coming to Maine in the twenty-first century left their homes involuntarily. They were not motivated by economic gain. Instead, the violence of civil war pushed the current Somali refugees from their homeland, while the promise of safe haven pulled them, eventually, to Lewiston. If we are to understand fully why

Somali refugees have chosen to live in Maine, we must understand their desire to raise their families in safety. Although it is clear that other places offer greater job opportunities, Somali refugees see Maine as a safe place. One Somali resident in Maine said,

> I was not thinking [of coming] to Maine. But in Atlanta the drugs, alcohol, and gangs were too much. Where we were living there were many gangs and many drugs. The Somalis are used to living in small cities. Some Somalis moved to Maine and said that Maine was very good—small cities, no crime. Everyone said, "Come here, come here." So my wife and I said, "We have to move there."... I never thought that in the United States there existed a state where the crime was almost zero.... In Maine you can leave your car downtown, parked anywhere, and no once comes [to steal it].[3]

But once their safety is assured, the new Mainers face the harsh economic reality of this place: most of the mills and shoe shops that drew previous immigrants are now shuttered, and the region has few low-skilled jobs that immigrants in other areas have taken advantage of, such as driving taxis, cleaning hotel rooms, and packing meat. For example, one Lewiston Somali identified taxi driving in San Diego as "one of the gateway occupations that are readily available, and people definitely have the skills to apply to get that job. In San Diego, a lot of Somalis, especially the men, the first job that they get is taxi driver, and they also make quite a bit of money at it."[4] However, in Maine the lack of such entry-level work contributes to the high unemployment rate. According to a Maine Department of Labor Report on Somali employment published in 2008, unemployment among Lewiston Somalis was about 51 percent.[5] Why is the unemployment rate for Somalis so high? And how are Somalis getting by?

Drawing on a variety of sources including interviews with Somalis and those who work with them, Maine Department of Labor reports and other government documents, newspaper articles, and Somali-related program descriptions, this chapter examines some of the perceived barriers to Somali employment in Maine and explores strategies that some Somali workers and their employers utilize to overcome these barriers. Concerned employers and determined Somali refugees are finding creative ways to work together, using strategies that require adaptation on both sides and that draw on the traditions of Maine and of Somalia. While L.L. Bean, community agriculture, and

Somali-owned small businesses offer a means of support, for those without work, the traditional Somali practice of giving *biil*, mutual support among friends and family, helps to make ends meet during hard times.

Perhaps one of the most obvious and difficult barriers to Somalis seeking work in Maine is the lack of English skills. One Somali job seeker stated succinctly, "Without English, no job."[6] Several studies on refugee employment point to low English language skills as the most important factor related to refugee unemployment in Maine.[7] For those Somalis who do not speak English, finding work is difficult across the spectrum, from unskilled to professional workers. Lewiston is attempting to provide English instruction (English as a Second Language, or ESL classes) for the refugees, but such programs are expensive and the federal government has not adequately funded the city's efforts (see Nadeau, chapter 3, this volume). Further, the Somali language was unwritten prior to the early 1970s, so many Somalis are preliterate in their own language, making learning English that much more difficult for them. For their part, many Somali refugees do attend ESL classes, though they often face a variety of challenges such as finding the necessary time, transportation, and child care. Despite the difficulties on both sides, the city hopes to increase refugee employability by making ESL classes mandatory for those accepting general assistance.

In addition to the language barrier, religious considerations such as prayer and traditional clothing also pose potential problems for Somalis in the workplace. Virtually all of Lewiston's Somali population is Muslim, and Islam requires believers to pray five times a day at designated times, with prayers preceded by ritual foot washing. Because prayer times are scheduled throughout the day, workers must take a break from work to pray. Further, most Muslim women prefer to wear the *hijab* (headscarf) and *goono* (long skirts). In some situations, the flowing skirts and long sleeves present a safety hazard, especially around machinery. Some employers require workers to wear pants as a safety precaution, but most Somali women prefer not to take jobs that require them to wear pants. Said one, "A lady told me she applied to that company and she got the job. They said, 'Our policy is that you have to wear pants.' She said, 'No, I can't wear pants because of my religion.'" One young woman explained that potential employers often reject traditionally dressed Somali women "without even giving them a chance." Some workplaces also prohibit the *hijab*. Depending on the situation, this prohibition might reflect discrimination rather than safety considerations.[8] In any case, most Somali women in Lewiston would not take a job that required removing the *hijab*, but would instead insist on dressing according to their beliefs.

Religious holidays can also pose a point of conflict between Somalis and their employers. One interviewee reflected on his attempts to persuade his employer to allow Somali workers a day off for Eid, an important Muslim holiday celebrating the end of Ramadan, a month of fasting. He and his coworkers were hired to clean a local office building. He commented,

> I used to work cleaning offices after work hours and there were a number of Somalis working with me, especially Somali women. Most of them didn't speak English, so I was the only person that could be the interpreter for those women. The Muslim holiday of Eid [was] coming in about a week so they wanted to have that day off to celebrate. They asked me during our break time to talk to the supervisor and request that day off. When I did, he told me that it was impossible because the entire workforce was composed of Somalis. He said, "If we do that, we would have to cancel an entire day of work." I explained to him that this is the only day that they celebrate, maybe two days in the entire year, and it's very important to them. He refused, and the women were really angry. Some of them said they would not show up anyway, they would take the day off whether he allowed it or not. He thought I was encouraging them in their demand. So I told him ... I myself also celebrate that holiday, and I want that day off. Eventually, he said he would give me the day off, but he wanted me to convince everyone else to work. He was trying to make a deal with me. I told him that wouldn't be fair. He said, "Well, you can take the day off if you want."[9]

In the end, some workers did take the day off, but the supervisor responded by undermining their ability to do their jobs and making false accusations about their work performance until some of them quit. This example serves to illustrate the workplace tensions that can emerge around religious and cultural issues. Another religious consideration for workers is the Islamic prohibition against pork and alcohol, a restriction that prevents many Muslims from taking jobs in grocery stores or restaurants where they could be required to handle these products. Such agency in job selection is a testament to the strength of the Somalis' religious convictions and their desire to participate in the work culture of the United States without losing their own cultural traditions, but it also helps explain some of the difficulties Somalis encounter in finding employment.[10]

Despite these perceived barriers to employment, some employers are motivated to work with the Somalis and find ways to accommodate the refugees' religious and cultural needs. L.L. Bean, the iconic Maine outdoor outfitter, is located in Freeport, an easy commute from Lewiston. This large company, currently worth $1.4 billion in sales revenue, faces a seasonal need for more workers each year when the company gears up for the holiday season.[11] From June through December, L.L. Bean hires hundreds of workers to supplement their regular employment force, but it has not always been easy for the company to find enough seasonal workers to meet its needs. When the Somalis arrived in Lewiston, the company saw an opportunity to fill its seasonal employment needs, and they proceeded to find ways to overcome the language, religious, and cultural challenges so many other employers found daunting.

We interviewed L.L. Bean human resources personnel Bob Schmidt and Sharon Parrit as well as team leader and translator Omar Mahamoud about various L.L. Bean policies used to attract some four hundred Somali seasonal workers every year. According to Schmidt, the company does not view the Somalis' religious needs as a barrier to employment. He explained, "We've been able to accommodate the need for prayer at work. We have break rooms and other areas that we've made available for prayer, and we've made sure during training that all employees know that if a break room door is shut and it's dark, don't be

FIGURE 16. Somali employees at an L.L. Bean warehouse, Freeport, Maine.

surprised if somebody's in there praying." It was after an employee was endangered while praying on a busy loading dock area that the company moved quickly to provide break rooms and other spaces for prayer. As for the time the prayers take, the Somalis pray in lieu of their break time. Says Parrit, "We work with the employees to find a time that works for our break schedule and for their prayer schedule. It's a win-win situation." In response to the necessary pre-prayer foot washing, a ritual that can leave floors a watery mess, again L.L. Bean has a practical approach to an issue that has become contentious at so many other workplaces. Schmidt says, "We use signage in our lavatories that says, 'Please make sure that the floor is kept dry,' because a wet floor can be a safety issue. In areas where it makes sense, we've directed folks to our fitness facilities where there are locker rooms and showers."[12]

Bob Schmidt argues that at L.L. Bean they treat all workers with respect and integrity, but he also admits that in responding to Somalis, they are "making it up" as they go along. When the company began hiring Somalis, Schmidt first learned about Ramadan, the month when Muslims fast from sun up to sun down. He noted,

> We had employees come in working the second shift and they hadn't eaten all day. And our shift work is generally 4:00 to midnight. So when you come in at 4:00, you really don't get a break until 6:00 or 6:30. I think during that first time Ramadan was during November, so sun down was not long after they started work and they needed to eat. Well, that wasn't break time. But we learned that actually we could accommodate that pretty easily.... It doesn't make sense [not to eat for two hours after fasting] ... so we've been able to accommodate that.[13]

This demonstration of cultural sensitivity also extends to clothing choices, as long as the clothing does not pose a safety issue. Although Somali women can wear the *hijab*, there are rules prohibiting loose clothing around machinery. But these rules are not for Somalis only. Sharron Parrit explains,

> People need to be safe, but we don't just focus on the Somali women. We focus on long dangly earrings, long hair, big chamois shirts, or flannel shirts that some younger people wear. Working around some conveyor systems, everyone needs to be safe; so you need to make sure that you are safe. We don't just say that to Somali women; we focus on everyone.[14]

The L.L. Bean response to another perceived barrier, the lack of English skills, has been to utilize iPods in training Somalis with low English language ability. Seasonal workers are employed primarily for "picking" (picking merchandise off the shelves in the half-mile long warehouse) and "packing" (packing the merchandise for shipment to customers). Workers with low English skills go through training for these jobs using an iPod that represents graphically the necessary movements and provides instructions in both English and Somali. Designed

FIGURE 17. Woman working at L.L. Bean warehouse, Freeport, Maine

FIGURE 18. L.L. Bean warehouse, Freeport, Maine

originally for non-English speakers, now all trainees use the technology. Said Parrit,

> So everyone who we train in distribution to be a material handler uses iPod technology, whether you're English speaking or you speak Somali. They sign out their little iPod and they plug it in. There's a learning specialist there to help, but employees can go on at their own pace and choose the modules that they want, either in English or in Somali. They can do it in their own language at their own pace.[15]

In a further effort to overcome the language barrier, the company offered—until recently—ESL language classes for their employees right on the L.L. Bean "campus." They also offered Somali language classes for English-speaking employees, and many employees carried a little card with key Somali phrases printed on it, that they could take out and use to greet Somalis. Said employee Omar Mahamoud, "If someone says good morning to you in Somali, you know, a lot of Somalis love that. It makes them feel welcome and comfortable."[16]

Mahamoud is one of several Somali employees that the company calls upon to translate when necessary. He helped program the iPods by recording instructions in Somali, and he provides translation when and where it is needed. He explained,

> I go around to the departments and go to the Somalis and ask them if they have questions, because a lot of Somalis are more afraid to actually face leadership, so they hide [their questions]. But I will go to the leadership and say, for example, "Aisha had a question; she asked me, when would you have time so you could sit with her and myself?" So we sit together, and Aisha can go through her questions ... I usually tell Somalis that we're going to go together and make sure to ask those questions and translate for you.

Mahamoud pointed out that many Somalis learn English on the job: "A lot of Somalis learn language here at L.L. Bean; I mean, that's how people do learn language."[17]

L.L. Bean tries to foster cross-cultural understanding at many levels. Human resources administrator Bob Schmidt praised the example of employees who "attended a class on Somali culture [at the University of Southern Maine] so that they could better understand the culture and be able to interact and relate with Somalis better." Schmidt went on, "Over the years, folks in my area have gone to Catholic Charities, to career centers, we've met with various Somali leaders . . . so we could better understand the culture and make sure that we can do our jobs better."[18] As part of diversity training, the company shows a video on Somali culture to all non-Somalis. They also invite Somalis to talk with the non-Somali workers about Somali culture and experiences. Parrit explained,

> [We asked them] to tell their story, what it was like to live in a refugee camp, what it was like to come to this country from Somalia . . . winter in Maine, driving in Maine, warm clothing when they're used to living in a desert culture. Or the people that are from Mogadishu, they're used to having big, elaborate houses where many members of the family live together; when they come here they usually go to the low-income housing where many people are cramped into an apartment. And just what was it like for them to go through that experience?[19]

For its efforts in promoting diversity and multicultural appreciation at the workplace, L.L. Bean has received numerous awards including the NAACP Excellence in Diversity Leadership Award in 2007. The company is also a member of the Diversity Hiring Coalition of Maine, a statewide group that promotes diversity at the workplace. Such awards and associations reflect the company's goals and achievements in workplace diversity. Bob Schmidt is quick to point out that L.L. Bean's focus on diversity is good for the employees, but that the practice is also good business. He sees the company's seasonal personnel needs, and he sees the Somalis as hard workers that the company wants to attract. "We're trying to create that [welcoming] environment because we need employees. If we don't have a welcoming environment, we won't get employees . . . and they work hard."[20]

The Somali response to L.L. Bean has been positive. Somalis who have worked there seem to agree that the company shows great respect for Somali workers and their culture, and they express appreciation for the many ways in which the company has accommodated their needs. For example, one Somali worker at L.L. Bean said, "The L.L. Bean people are very respectful. The team leaders . . . very respectful. They're respectful of your religion and also they respect your color. Yes, very respectful people. When you want to go to pray, you just tell your team leader."[21] The Somali workers share their experiences with others, so that recruiting is done by word of mouth. Most are hired for seasonal work, but there are about thirty or forty Somalis working at L.L. Bean year-round. Omar Mahamoud, who has worked there for six years, appreciates that the company gives Somalis opportunities for advancement. "What I like about L.L. Bean, they will give you the opportunity . . . they will say, 'Okay, we have this for you, can you handle it?' I never thought about applying for a leadership position, and my supervisor pushed me and said, 'Omar, I know you can do it. Just try it. Go ahead.' And I did."[22]

Despite these Somali employment successes revealed in the L.L. Bean example, high unemployment levels among Somalis persist. In examining refugee unemployment in Portland, Maine, one study suggested that the state and local governments should do more to utilize refugee skills and integrate those skills into the state's labor market.[23] For example, many Somalis are highly trained professionals whose skills are wasted because their credentials were left behind in Somalia or because their licenses are not recognized in the United States. Many of our interviews revealed stories of teachers, doctors, nurses, and engineers who are prohibited from working in their professions because their certification is not recognized. One interviewee tells the story of her father, who left his educational credentials behind when he fled Somalia. After his arrival in the U.S., he sent to Italy for his credentials, but when they came Maine local schools did not recognize them. At the time of the interview, he was taking classes at a community college while working part-time as a tutor in the local middle school.[24] In this example, the family experienced the downward mobility that many refugees face when they leave their homes and jobs abruptly. The brutality of war forces refugees to leave and re-establish themselves in a new country where they have no credentials, low or no language skills, and little or no finances of their own.

Of course not all Somali skills require certification. A minority group within Somalia, the Somali Bantu, are skillful farmers who need only the opportunity to put their knowledge and skills to practical use. While L.L. Bean adjusted its work culture to adapt to Somalis and thus attract a seasonal labor force, two programs in Lewiston assist the Bantu in adapting their agricultural skills to an American market.

While the ethnic Somalis have faced numerous challenges in obtaining work and becoming self sufficient, the Somali Bantu face even greater challenges. The term identifies Somali agriculturalists, descendants of slaves from Bantu-speaking tribes, who settled in the Juba Valley.[25] In contrast to the majority of Somalis who "considered clan affiliation and tribal identification sacrosanct and critical to survival," most Somali Bantu identify themselves by their place of residence. Racially and culturally distinct from the majority pastoralist population, in an occupation disdained by the others, the Somali Bantu have experienced centuries of discrimination and marginalization.[26]

The Italian colonizers conscripted the Bantu into forced labor on their plantations and into the army. Under Siyad Barre's Somali Republic, the government expropriated their lands for state irrigation schemes and for political supporters of the regime. During the civil war various militias "pillaged and brutalized them." Without affiliation with other Somali clans they were not part of the clans' protective support system and were thus particularly vulnerable.[27]

In 2002 the United States recognized them as a "special interest group" and approved twelve thousand Bantu refugees in Kenya for resettlement. In 2003 the first arrivals were dispersed across the United States to Houston, Nashville, Concord (NH), Phoenix, and Salt Lake City. As the editor of *Refugee Reports* noted at the time, "With the low literacy and English levels, large families, no United States support system, and an almost total lack of exposure to technology and urban life, the Somali Bantus will struggle to gain self-sufficiency and a foothold in U.S. society." In addition, as a persecuted minority, the "culture of subjection under which most of them lived may present special challenges to their American resettlement caseworkers."[28]

The Somali Bantu were resettled in communities across the country. As with so many of the other Somalis in Lewiston, they chose to come to Maine as secondary migrants looking to find a more "livable city." In November 2004 the first Bantu—approximately forty of them—arrived by bus from Irving, Texas. As predicted by those contemplating their resettlement, they were hampered in their ability to find work. While L.L. Bean made adaptations to its workplace for English and religious requirements, the work often required familiarity or comfort with technology—either the iPods used in training or the computers used to track orders. Not only, however, did the Bantu often lack experience with technology, they also lacked the experience that would enable them to interview successfully for a job. L.L. Bean requires an application interview and tests, but, as the International Organization for Migration noted in 2002,

> The Somali Bantus of Dadaab are not accustomed to being interviewed and answering questions in a linear sequential way. Often seemingly simple questions such as, "How old are you?" or "When

did you come here?" ... would be met by an inadequate response. Trying to obtain basic information could be frustrating ... Simply put, most of these Bantus have no exposure to interviews and are unaccustomed to responding to questions in a manner that results in proper identification. [29]

The Somali Bantu's isolation has further hampered them in their search for work. Unlike most of the other resettled Somalis, they often lack the support networks that provide them with access to jobs through friends and relatives who have arrived earlier. Furthermore, while many of the other Somalis come from urban environments where they have had access to a variety of jobs, the discrimination faced by the Somali Bantu has limited almost all of their prior work experience to agricultural work and manual labor.[30]

As different as they are from the other Somalis, Somali Bantu share a commitment to Islam and face similar workplace challenges as a result. Like ethnic Somali women, Bantu Somali women wear modest dress. Maine is a rural state and seasonal agricultural work is available,[31] but, as one interviewee suggested, Muslim women might have a hard time finding employers who would hire them:

> One month ago, a company [said], "We need people." They are hiring people and these people—the refugees, the Somali immigrants—they need jobs. They are hungry for jobs. They need to work. And [the company says], "We are hiring. We need fifty people. We need the refugee immigrant." ... They say they are hiring women and they say ... every single person has to wear ... pants [when] they're harvesting apples. So how do [the women] work? Well, the first time they went to their training and [heard] every person has to wear pants, they [said], "No," because it's not [accepted in our] religion for a woman to wear pants. So they fired the people. Now no one works there. So we have a hard time. It's a battle of religion, a battle of culture."[32]

As anthropologist Catherine Besteman notes, many of the Bantu families that have arrived in Lewiston are single-parent families headed by women. The Bantu, like other Somalis, often practice polygamy. Both United States refugee policy, which does not recognize families with multiple wives, and the devastation of war have worked to tear many families apart. "You have to be incredibly strong and resourceful," Besteman points out, "to support a family without a husband and without a co-wife."[33] You must also find a way to have the children cared for while working.

In spite of all the obstacles they have faced finding work in Lewiston, the Somali Bantu have a major advantage emerging from their traditional agricultural practices. Both men and women are excellent farmers. As Daniel Ungier of the New American Sustainable Agricultural Project (NASAP) notes, "It is clear that working outside and working the land is a huge part of their identity. It is what they have always done and what their families have always done. They have a familiarity with the land that is so satisfying and ingrained ... the challenge is to help them connect to the U.S. environment."[34] Two urban gardening programs have worked together to enable them to do just that.

Urban gardens have a long history in the United States. The earliest effort to provide garden plots in the city began as a form of relief for the poor in Detroit in 1893. The city-sponsored program helped those hardest hit by the economic depression by enabling them to grow their own fruit and vegetables. It provided a model that was soon adopted in other large cities including New York, Philadelphia, Chicago, and Baltimore. When the economic crisis was over, government support for the gardens disappeared.

The idea of turning urban plots into gardens reappeared periodically after that, particularly in times of crisis: during World War I and World War II when Americans were exhorted to grow food for victory and during the Depression, again to provide support for the poor. Since the 1960s, however, the community garden movement has been transformed. "Generally referred to as 'community gardens,'" Hilda Kurtz notes, "today's urban vacant lot gardens are motivated by neighborhood improvement and empowerment, as well as self-sufficiency and a desire to bring nature into the city."[35] In 1996 a community garden survey identified over six thousand garden projects and concluded that the number was growing rapidly.

The refugee garden program is one of the most recent incarnations of urban gardens. Across the country, those concerned with immigrants and refugees have found that being able to garden has multiple benefits for those torn from their home countries. Gardens provide a social space, a spiritual retreat from a confusing world, an opportunity to teach children about cultural heritage, and a way to supplement a meager budget.

The urban garden movement has been sustained by and has helped to develop a local foods movement. Consumer interest in and demand for organic and locally grown produce has exploded in the last few decades, and consumer demand has led to the development of farmers' markets throughout the country. While the local foods and sustainable agriculture movements are nationwide, they have a particular resonance in Maine where there is a strong connection between community gardens, sustainable agricultural production, and the local community. Like L.L. Bean, sustainable agriculture has a long, almost iconic, history in Maine.

Maine Organic Farmers and Gardeners Association (MOFGA), founded in 1971, is the oldest organic association in the country. It currently has the largest membership and budget of all organic associations and is known nationally for its Common Ground Fair. The Fair, first organized in 1977, emphasizes environmental protection, ecological farming, and local produce. One of its major purposes is education. People come to see and to learn. Last year the fair offered over nine hundred educational opportunities. MOFGA staff continue their educational efforts throughout the year, reaching out to gardeners and farmers alike.[36]

Educational Programs Director Andrew Marshall attributes the enduring success of MOFGA to Maine's agricultural and regional history. Maine's topography has never supported large corporate agriculture.[37] For this reason, when the disaffected young people of the 1970s looked for a way to return to the land (the back-to-the-landers) they found fairly cheap farmland in Maine. In addition they were inspired by Scott and Helen Nearing, who had settled in Maine and whose book, *The Good Life*, exhorted them to live simply off the land.

Small farms are able to survive in Maine because they have found community support that is steadily growing. The state nurtures the connection between farmers and consumers through such marketing programs as "Get Real, Get Maine." As Russell Libby, Executive Director of MOFGA, noted,

> We've gone from one farmers' market to, I think, eighty-five this year. We went from zero natural food stores to something like sixty-five. . . . There are restaurants all across the state where chefs are really focusing on local food. This year we certified about 400 . . . 385, I think, organic farms and processors.[38]

What all this organizing on the state level has meant is that farmers, even small farmers, are finding a way to support themselves. As one said of the farms in the Blue Hill Peninsula, "We're not big by any means, any stretch of the imagination, but it seems like there [are] enough people in this area … that want good, clean food, and local food, and are willing to pay a little bit more for it."[39]

A program called Lots to Gardens (now part of the Nutrition Center of Maine) introduced the Somali Bantu to the gardening movement and to the opportunity to farm. The program grew out of the experiential education project of a student at Bates College in Lewiston. In 1999 Kirsten Walter established a garden at Hillview, one of Lewiston's largest public housing complexes. She was committed to the principal that everybody deserves access to good food, everyone benefits from meaningful work, and that providing both builds individual and community capacity. She enlisted Hillview youth to build a garden. They in turn set up a vegetable stand to sell food at low costs to their neighbors and began a tradition of cooking a harvest dinner for the whole apartment complex.

When Kirsten Walter started Lots to Gardens there were very few Somalis in Lewiston. The Somali population began to arrive in 2001, however, and many of these newcomers settled in Hillview. Mumina was the first Somali to obtain a garden plot at Hillview. Having grown watermelons and tomatoes in Somalia, she was immediately attracted to the gardens, and has been volunteering and working with Walter ever since as community gardener, resident gardener coordinator, and community action researcher.[40]

Mumina is not a Bantu, but her grandfather was resettled on the Juba River under the Siyad Barre regime. Mumina speaks Maay Maay, the language spoken by many Bantu. She and Walter remember when the first Bantu woman arrived at Hillview. The woman surveyed the three gardens and asked, "Can I have the whole thing?" At the time of our interview, spring 2010, all the Somali gardeners in the three Hillview gardens, with the exception of Mumina, were Bantu.

The gardens provided by Lots to Gardens are intended to enable people to grow their own food. They are not designed to make money for those who garden them. Walter, however, has enabled the Somali Bantu who are eager to farm to connect to another agricultural project: the New American Sustainable Agriculture Project (NASAP). NASAP is a national farming program for immigrants and refugees whose Maine branch was established in 2002.

It now manages farms in Westbrook and Lewiston, Maine. "If you are new in Maine and want to farm, we can help you start," announces its web page. The primary goal of the project is to "deliver focused outreach and technical assistance, including educational programs, to limited-resources immigrant farmers, helping them to build successful Maine farms that are consistent with their cultural and lifestyle aspirations."[41]

The program provides garden plots on the Packard-Littlefield Farm in Lisbon, six miles from Lewiston Center. It is the only farm for refugees in the United States that is so close to a refugee population. The initial plot provided by NASAP is for training, but as gardeners show their commitment to and ability in farming, the program allows them to expand their plot. For Somalis, the training is in both English and Somali. Those who take a plot must also prepare a business plan and work with NASAP to find the resources to farm it. In addition, participants are eligible for individual development accounts—a program that matches dollar for dollar any savings that participants deposit on their own. In return, the individuals must attend workshops on personal financial management.[42]

Daniel Ungier noted that the program "is a very good fit for the Somali Bantu, but they have a lot to learn." While they have finely developed agricultural skills, they need assistance in adapting to the United States agricultural requirements. In both growing food and marketing it they need to develop new skills. Not only do Americans have different produce preferences, but even when they eat the same crops as Somalis, they have different ideas about product quality. "For example," Ungier pointed out, "we like zucchinis small, and they like them larger. These are details that are intuitive or even unconscious for Americans that the Bantu have to learn." While the immigrants he works with have "grown a lot of grain crops, grain crops are not good money makers here unless you have a large industrial farm. What you need is diversity."

In addition, the Bantu are used to having lots of space, but here they need to know how to make small plots cost-effective. "They are used to a lower yield per acre, which works where traditional land-use is practiced," Ungier said, "but it doesn't work here, where land is at a premium. For them, to have one or two acres seems very small. It is enough, but it requires different practices."

While these are major differences between farming in Somalia and in the United States, the most important differences are found in marketing. NASAP and Lots to Gardens have worked together to establish multiple farmers' markets in the city, but the venue is not all that is required. In most places in the world, Ungier commented, farmers only have to put out their produce in order to sell it. "Here, marketing is important. We invest a lot more energy into displaying the crops and luring people in," he said.

The NASAP garden training program offers advantages to the state. Nearly one-half of the farms in Maine are run by people who are sixty or older. Coastal Enterprises, supporters of NASAP, estimates that the state will need two hundred new farmers per year to maintain the seven thousand farms currently in production in the state. The Somali Bantu may be among this new wave of farmers who will help keep farming alive in Maine.[43]

But what are the advantages to the Bantu? Amy Carrington of Cultivating Community has worked with NASAP ever since its arrival in Maine. She notes that for some the farm provides their only income, while for others, it is supplemental. In reality, Carrington commented, farming barely pays for the gas necessary to get to the garden. Most of those who garden either work other jobs or collect public assistance. In addition, while the support that NASAP provides is intended to make the gardeners self-sufficient within five years, even once they have gained the necessary marketing and business skills "they have a whole new set of challenges," Ungier pointed out. The challenges are many. Farmers going on their own need to find land to purchase or lease and have to figure out how to provide the necessary infrastructure. "Any experienced American who is becoming a farmer would know who should drill a well, how much it costs, what your options might be." For those unused to American ways, that is really complicated, he concluded.

For these and other reasons, some argue that urban garden and farming programs are not in the refugees' best economic interests. Amy Stitely studied Bantu garden projects in Boise, Idaho, Utica, New York, and Lowell, Massachusetts as well as Lewiston, and she questions the value of training refugees to become farmers. "If small scale farming is no longer a viable vocation for Americans," she asks, "why are we encouraging new immigrants to enter this enterprise?" She adds, "Given that 85 percent of the graduates of Tufts (agricultural training program) have not achieved independence, it is clear that this is not economically sustainable." Nevertheless she concludes that the more modest social goals described by Amy Carrington may be possible. Carrington, she notes, rather than looking for the program to make the refugee farmers become independent, "accepts that the program might best act as a stepping stone toward a new life."[44]

And many argue that gardens offer numerous benefits that support the creation of a new life. As Deborah Giraud notes in her essay on the Hmong, a garden serves multiple purposes. Perhaps most importantly for those traumatized by war and relocation, it provides a "refuge from the stress of the changes in their lives." For those thrown into an environment dramatically different from their own, having lived through years of oppression, it also provides a social space where "no American verbal skills are needed . . . there are no pressures to understand, to translate, to feel judged." Gardens are "healing places; places where one is in control of what is planted and how it is cared for."[45]

For the Somali Bantu, who have been marked by centuries of discrimination and subjection, a garden project that builds on their knowledge may do even more than that. One evaluator of the Boise garden project commented that prior to the project, the Bantu were not proud of their agricultural heritage. For generations they were made to feel inferior for their agricultural skills; but now they take pride in them.

While L.L. Bean has adapted to Somali tradition and NASAP has taught Somalis how to adapt their traditional agricultural skills, urban Somalis have a long tradition of entrepreneurship with which they have created their own employment. In a recent published memo the current Lewiston Mayor, Larry Gilbert, cited the following Somali entrepreneurs:

> There are twelve store owners, eight truck drivers, three Somali restaurants and cafeterias, Somali home/health care (two of which subcontract a total of seventy-five employees), twelve who provide Somali interpreter services, and one [who] owns a cell phone company. There are between five and ten Somali property owners and five Somali owners of rental units.[46]

Author Doug Rutledge argues that Somalis' entrepreneurial interests derive from their history and geography, as Somalia's location is ideal for trade among Asians, Arabs, and Africans. He writes, "When Americans see Somalis starting businesses, this is not a skill that they are simply picking up from their new environment. It is an ancient aspect of their cultural tradition."[47]

In funding their new businesses, many Somali entrepreneurs rely on their tradition of *biil*, which is interest-free money that Somalis pay to family and friends in need, both in Africa and in the United States. *Biil* is provided not only to establish new Somali businesses, but also to pay for health care, rent, food, or other needs for those who are unemployed or simply needing help. Doug Rutledge describes this ethic of mutual support this way: "Normally, when a Somali person is out of a job, he can count on financial support from the community. If he is sick or hurt, the community will come together to help him. If he goes to the hospital without insurance, the community will collect money to pay the bill."[48] While most Somalis in the United States are far from wealthy, they are culturally obligated to share their money—as well as their house, food, and other necessities—with others. One Somali worker put it this way:

> We work hard because other people are depending on us. We have some people here with mothers living in Somalia, fathers living in Somalia, half the kids still in Somalia, uncles in Somalia, and they are all depending on you. The little money we send means a lot to them. Myself, I send $300 a month for my wife's family.[49]

Biil paid to overseas family members in the form of remittances constitutes an important contribution to Somalia's economy, both historically and in recent times. Author Jamshid Damooei argues that, "The remittances from Somali workers, traders, and seamen elsewhere have always been a traditional part of the Somali economy."[50] Since the upheaval caused by civil war, Somalia depends even more on money sent back from the diasporic working population. While estimates on the amount of money remitted vary, one study puts the figure at between $500 million and $1 billion sent to Somalia and Somaliland by Somali refugees in the year 2000.[51] Exact figures are difficult to compute, but Somalia may receive more remittances, per capita, than any other country in the world. Currently remittances are the "principal import" in Somalia, with remittance payments going to some 40 percent of Somalia's urban families.[52]

In her study of remittances paid by Lewiston Somalis, Laura Hammond points out that these remittances pose a "heavy burden" on Maine's Somali population. When newly arrived refugees find their first jobs (generally unskilled work with low wages), they quickly arrange to send remittances to Africa. Despite the financial burden, Hammond argues that these remittances play an important social role. The payments not only help families economically, but they are the "glue" that binds families together. Says Hammond,

Remittances help families to stay together not only through their economic power, but through the communication and sharing of affective ties that such exchanges make possible. Through remittances, existing social ties may be reinforced and new ties may be formed between people who come from the same clan or geographic area.[53]

One young Somali student explained that he often wanted to share his pay from his part-time job with his mother, to buy her new clothes or a nice dinner at a restaurant. But his mother always refused the money for herself, reminding him that the same money could feed family members in Somalia for a month.[54]

In this country, the payment of *biil* helps to explain how Somalis get by with high unemployment rates: one wage earner can support many friends and family members. This obligation to help others permeates the Somali culture and aids them in many ways. According to Rutledge, Somalis pool their money for a variety of purposes:

> The answer to the question of how Somalis get their money is that they earn it just like everyone else, but they also have creative ways of supporting each other, so when Americans see a Somali driving a car shortly after arriving in this country, they should not think that the government is in the habit of giving away automobiles to East Africans; instead, they should try to understand that ten people went in on the purchase of the vehicle, which takes five people to work during the day and another five to work in the evening.[55]

Paying *biil* falls not only to men, but also to women, and this suggests another adaptation that Somalis have made in order to survive. Employment at both L.L. Bean and in the NASAP gardens does not provide enough income for a family to live on. In fact, as Ungier has pointed out, while farming in Somalia was a family affair for the Bantu, in Lewiston the Bantu farmers tend to farm alone. The reason, he suggested, is that everyone within the family needs to work in order for the family to survive.

Women's greater participation in paying *biil* and performing waged work marks a significant change from their roles in pre-war Somalia, where most women performed unwaged work in the home. While some women in Somalia were involved in trade and small shops, most worked at home, cooking, cleaning, and rearing children. In the diaspora, by contrast, many Somali women are working outside the home, especially since so many men are unemployed. This greater participation in the workforce signals changing gender roles, a change that sometimes leads to conflict. In Maine, families are struggling to adjust to the new gender dynamics. One Somali woman commented on gender roles this way:

> For men, it's not a big difference. They have to work in Africa, they have to work here. But for women it's different. In Africa, they didn't really have to work [outside the house], but here they do. Women here are doing both the men's job and the women's job, which is to take care of the children and all that. That's the big difference for us. Somali women in America actually do the same thing that American women do: they work both in and out of the house.[56]

While Somalis are responding to the opportunities for work at L.L. Bean and other workplaces that have welcomed them, and they are responding to the chance to apply their traditional agricultural skills in community gardens, and they are supporting each other through paying *biil,* still many Somalis are leaving the state because there just aren't enough jobs for them in Maine. Somalis have exercised agency by seeking out places of work that fit with their religion and culture; likewise, leaving the state altogether is another form of agency.

Yet, clearly Maine benefits from the infusion Somalis give to the state's workforce. Maine is currently the "oldest" and "whitest" state in the United States. Some reports point out that Maine's aging population will eventually lead to a labor shortage in the state. Further, states lacking cultural diversity are the least likely to attract new businesses and new young people. Given these trends, some people are calling for greater efforts to accommodate Somali workers and other immigrants by stepping up the effort to offer English language training and by expanding agricultural opportunities.[57] With greater employment opportunities, Somalis can help themselves and help make Maine a better and more prosperous place.

Being a Muslim

Fathiya Sharif Mohamed

بِسْمِ ٱللّٰهِ ٱلرَّحْمَـٰنِ ٱلرَّحِيمِ

In the name of Allah, the Beneficent, the Merciful

When I was in the sixth grade I went on a field trip to Washington, DC with my classmates. On that trip I remember praying in the hotel as my classmates wondered what the heck I was doing—because they simply had never seen anything like it. I remember one of my classmates trying to find out why my forehead was on the ground and asking me, "What are you doing?" and

FIGURE 19. Islamic Center of Maine (Orono, Maine)

"Why are you whispering?" as I made different postures. When praying, our whole attention is focused, and we are not supposed to be distracted. But my classmate kept talking to me as I was praying. She wondered why I assumed different postures and why I did not speak to her while I was in prayer. When I finished praying I explained to her that as a Muslim, I pray five times a day, and when in prayer I do not talk to anyone but *Allah* (God). As for the postures, I explained to her that they are a part of performing the prayer. While her questions were an intrusion to my prayer, they also reminded me that many people do not know about Islam and being a Muslim.

Islam is my life. I am honored and fortunate to be a Muslim. Islam keeps me grounded and sane. Without sounding arrogant, I don't need anything from anyone except from Allah almighty. I believe everything happens for a reason and whatever happens is destined to happen. Islam gives Muslims meaning and purpose to life. I once asked a group of little boys and girls what Islam means to them. Each answered with a smile and without any hesitation, saying they were privileged and honored to be Muslims.

Being a Muslim means following the five pillars of Islam. One of the five pillars of Islam is profession of belief in the Oneness of God and the finality of the prophethood of Muhammad, Peace Be Upon Him (PBUH), which is called the *Shahadah*. The second pillar is the duty to pray five times a day, what is called *Salat*. The duty to pay charity is the third pillar, which is also called *Zakat*. The fourth pillar is to fast the month of Ramadhan *(Sawm)*; and last but not least is duty to perform pilgrimage to Mecca *(Hajj)*, if one has the means and is financially stable. The five pillars of Islam are the foundation for all Muslims across the world.

Being a Muslim comes before everything else in life. Putting Islam first means that the first thing I do when I wake up at dawn and the last thing I do when I lay down to sleep at night is to pray. Prayer is a big part of my life, and being a Muslim is not just something I do when I feel like it; being a Muslim is around the clock. Being a Muslim is as simple as what comes out of my mouth every day.

As a Muslim in Maine and the United States, I hear a lot of misinformation about Islam. To those interested in knowing about Islam, I advise talking with a sincere, practicing Muslim about his or her beliefs, values, and actions. If you yourself are also sincere, you will find answers to your questions about Islam. And, in the meantime, I suggest that you do not believe in everything you hear about Islam.

I would like to conclude by saying *Al-hamdulilah,* which means "thank you, Allah," and *Istakhfuru-Allah,* which means "I seek forgiveness." All praises are due to Allah and anything good I have said is from Allah. Anything false is from me, for as a human I am prone to make mistakes.

FIGURE 20. Men praying at Islamic Center of Maine

PART IV "Anything to Help": Cultural Collaborations

The Courage To Ask

Britney Harris

I am a white American-born woman from Maine married to a Somali man. I am light-skinned, but I wear the *hijab* (Islamic covering for women) and I speak Somali when I am with Somali friends and family. My appearance often causes confusion among both Somalis and non-Somalis.

One event that sticks out in my mind happened when I was in Minneapolis at the large Somali mall there. I walked into a small store where two older Somali women, the store clerks, were waiting on customers. As I browsed the colorful merchandise, one woman asked, "Somali Arab *miyaa?*" which means, "Is she an Arab-Somali?" I laughed inside and looked at her and said, *"Maya, American Waaye,"* which means, "No, I am an American." The women laughed and started speaking in Somali to the friend I was with, saying, "Wow, we thought she was half Somali, half Arab; she has the facial features of that combination." I was surprised by this comment, but it was funny at the same time.

FIGURE 21. Author with her husband

I was born in Brunswick, Maine on July 6, 1988, the first child to my young parents. When I was two and a half, my sister Bethany was born. At age seven, my mom, my little sister, and I were involved in a bad car accident. My mother was killed instantly; I was in a coma and was rushed to the hospital. Bethany was not hurt at all. I suffered seven skull fractures and also had to have my spleen removed. I recovered quickly and there was no lasting damage done. Years later my father remarried and had two more children with my stepmother. I have a good relationship with my parents, which has been beneficial throughout my life. My childhood was pretty typical of rural Maine. As a lower-middle-class family, we valued family time more than material things. My family means the world to me, and I remain close with all my siblings as well as my maternal grandmother.

When I was a senior at Bangor High School, I attended an event near the University of Maine. That evening I met Ismail Warsame, a Somali student attending the university. Meeting him was my first encounter with a Muslim, and we soon became good friends. I was very interested in his culture and religion, so I began researching and reading about Somalia and Islam. Through reading, online research, and talking with Ismail and other Mus-

FIGURE 22. Young women at Islamic Center of Maine (Orono, Maine)

lims, I decided that I wanted to become a Muslim, too. I believed in the core values of Islam, and I found that this religion filled a void in my life. Soon after I converted to Islam, Ismail left for Egypt to study abroad for a semester. While he was gone I realized that I loved him and wanted to spend the rest of my life with him.

Many people gave me a hard time about becoming Muslim and being with a Somali Muslim man. I faced many negative stereotypes. People even said things such as, "Oh, Somalis are dirty. They keep live chickens in their cupboards, and you should really stay away from him. If you marry him you will be one of ten wives and treated like trash." I didn't know where people got such crazy information, but I knew Ismail and I wanted to be with him.

Like the time I was at the Somali mall in Minneapolis, some people in Maine are thrown off by my wearing the *hijab*. One time I was working at Staples, an office supply store at the Bangor mall. I am a friendly, outgoing person, and while I was helping an older woman use the fax machine, I noticed she was puzzled as she looked at me. After I sent her fax through, I asked her to wait until her confirmation sheet printed out. She kept looking at me as if she were unsure of something. Suddenly she blurted out, "Are you the Qur'an?" I was shocked and didn't know what to say. I knew what she was trying to find out, but she just didn't have the vocabulary or knowledge to ask the right question. I responded, "No, Ma'am, I am not the Qur'an. That is the holy book that Muslims believe in. But I am a Muslim." I chuckled and smiled at her. She said, "Oh! Okay." I had been asked many questions regarding my religion and why I wore the *hijab*, but never before in that way! However, I was not offended by her question. I knew it was coming from her heart. I was glad she had the courage to at least ask.

9   Collaborating with the Community[1]

Kristin M. Langellier

The Somalis of Lewiston, Maine, came to the public's attention through the national and international media coverage of the event documented in the film *The Letter: An American Town and the "Somali Invasion."*[2] The documentary's title refers to the open letter written by former mayor Laurier T. Raymond on October 1, 2002, and addressed to Somali community leaders in Lewiston (see appendix A). The letter urged them to discourage the arrival of any more Somalis because the rapid influx of these secondary migrants was straining the small city's finances, social services, and schools. Somali leaders and supporters responded with a march of solidarity and the formation of the Many and One Coalition for "many people, many colors, one community" in Lewiston-Auburn (see appendix C). Subsequent media attention attracted a small rally by the white supremacist, anti-immigration World Church of the Creator to "save" Lewiston. Their January 11, 2003 rally of fewer than forty persons was parried by a counter-rally across town with an estimated four thousand participants.[3] The pro-diversity rally marked a turning point in support of the new Mainers, and Lewiston was recognized in 2010 as a leading city for embracing diversity.[4] Still, Somalis' resettlement in the United States is tinged by lingering tensions that surface in a struggling local economy, a national anti-immigration climate, and global tensions around Islam since September 11, 2001.[5]

The Somali Narrative Project (SNP) represents one among many responses of Maine people to embrace the diversity enhanced by the rapid migration of Somalis. It is an interdisciplinary, collaborative, and applied communication effort to document the experiences of Somali immigrants in Lewiston, Maine, to foster intercultural understanding between Somalis and non-Somalis, and to develop projects that address mutual interests of SNP members and Somali immigrants. Members of the collaborative include the four co-editors of this volume and student members (see Toner, chapter 10, this volume).

FIGURE 23. Readers theater performance, University of Maine's Hutchinson Center, Belfast, Maine

Because the SNP is inspired by feminist community-based models, we have been committed to conducting research that will benefit Maine communities as well as address our own questions (see Huisman, chapter 11, this volume). This chapter describes work in the first years of the project to collaborate with the Somali community in Lewiston in developing a narrative project to address our mutual interests. In these conversations, Somalis repeatedly identified a concern with the challenges of feeling "trapped between two cultures," Somali and American, particularly as their immigrant children come of age in Maine and the new generation is born in the United States. One participant expressed this as the need to create "a library of real stories" for themselves, their children, and grandchildren, stories told by Somalis who have experienced immigration and the struggle for a people and culture. As the four non-Somali members of the SNP, we entered cultural currents of interaction and interviews with Somalis and learned many lessons along the way.

Lessons in Crossing Cultural Currents

At the outset of our project, we were mindful that Lewiston Somalis were already subjected to state, national, and international media attention as well as scrutinized by other academic researchers, and so we tried to proceed with caution and care. For two years we met with three Somali students enrolled at the University of Maine to read texts on Somalia and the diaspora. During this time we also developed contacts in the Lewiston community, beginning with English-speaking social service providers in public offices. With the students we attended the Somali Independence Day, a Somali-organized celebration that invites the Lewiston public for an evening of speeches, traditional Somali food, and cultural music and dancing. We went to Somali restaurants and *halal* shops and visited Hillview, a public housing facility with sixty Somali households. As the narrative project was being shaped through our readings, relationships with students, and conversations with Somalis in Lewiston, we set a meeting in City Hall with two Somali caseworkers for Catholic Charities Maine Refugee and Immigration Services and with the director of the United Somali Women of Maine, a female-headed nonprofit refugee organization in New England. The purpose of this meeting was to collaboratively plan a community-wide discussion where the SNP could present our narrative project, solicit input on its design and implementation, and invite Somalis to tell their stories.

We learned an early lesson about language as we struggled to find a Somali word for "narrative." Somalis say, first, that they are not telling stories as much as they did in Somalia, and their greatest fear is that their children are losing their culture, history, and identity. For Somalis, storytelling denotes their rich oral traditions of folktales, poetry and history, and sayings; indeed, Somalia only acquired a written language in the early 1970s under Siyad Barre's two-decade dictatorship. Although the "official language" of our meeting was English, the Somali participants engaged in several intense conversations in Somali, to emerge at last with *dhaqan celin,* translated roughly as "preserving culture," to serve as a Somali title for our project. They identified generational differences (i.e., the elderly who speak Somali and remember the stories; the youth who speak English and do not know the stories). Where to hold the community discussion was also debated; and a Lewiston community center, because of its relative neutrality, was agreed upon.

Then gender norms came into focus as one of the refugee caseworkers, who is also head of the mosque, insisted that talk and storytelling would need to be sex-segregated. So we reserved two rooms, one for women and one for men, and discussed inviting an elder Somali male to facilitate the men's group. It was only long into the discussion of the snacks (samosas from the local Somali restaurant and bananas) for the community meeting that we realized that orthodox Muslim practice required that men and women eat separately, too, necessitating two setups for food and drinks. The discussion over place and rooms coded differences within the Somali community as well as between Islamic and western norms. Questions we would encounter again and again ask: What is traditional Somali culture and what is Islamic law? Which Islam? We noted that a good deal of storytelling about personal experiences was occurring in the mixed-sex community meeting with men and women, suggesting not only that the communication situation affects gender practices but also that Somalis talk in personal stories as well as the folktales, oral history, and poetry of traditional Somali culture. After the meeting we had lunch with two Somali women, where storytelling about their experiences with mothering, working, and living in Lewiston flourished.

The outcome of this small, cross-cultural group meeting at City Hall was a bilingual poster inviting Somalis to a community discussion on how to preserve its culture, history, and immigration experiences for future generations through storytelling. Our students translated the English version into Somali, and our contacts in public offices agreed to distribute the flyers throughout Lewiston. When we arrived at the appointed place in December 2005, the meeting time approached—and then passed. No one came, except the students who had accompanied us and a Somali couple from another Maine town, who migrated in the early 1980s before the civil war. We became reasonably and somewhat miserably sure that just one Somali came to the community meeting because of the posted flyer. Our mood was lifted when our energetic Somali students volunteered to go into action, plying the oral culture that bonds their people. They got out their cell phones, bundled up against the cold December wind, and went out walking to the *halal* store and other Somali downtown spots.

In the meantime, one local Somali, Ismail Ahmed, the first member of the Lewiston community to receive his master's degree, had read the flyer and came by the community center to talk. He was friendly, forthcoming, even frank. Trained in ethnographic methods and doing a study on leadership in the Lewiston Somali community, he told us the story of his research project (see Ahmed, chapter 4, this volume). He thought that as a cultural insider and a Lewiston Somali, he was uniquely positioned to study leadership in the community. Like a good ethnographer, he hung out among the Somalis at the restaurants, in streetside conversations, and entering or emerging from the mosque, where he was privy to storytelling and gossip. These were public settings with small groups of men, and they were marked by sociability and friendliness. However, he was increasingly frustrated in getting serious information for his research; until after a time, he became convinced that his position as a cultural insider was itself the problem. He suggested that as a web of connections amid internal distinctions, Somalis will not make themselves vulnerable in front of other Somalis, whether from fear of personal embarrassment, suspicion, or avoidance of confrontation. Furthermore, he suspected that they saw him as some sort of "stooge" of unnamed authorities on whose behalf he was gathering information. And so, in a protective gesture, they closed their internally conflicted ranks to him. Subsequently, he reversed his insider posture, positioning himself as a cultural outsider with an explicit research agenda. Instead of hanging out at the restaurants and mosques, he made appointments for interviews and began to be taken with more seriousness and into more confidences. In his more formal, expert, and outsider capacity he could also enter homes and talk with women without violating community gender norms, which yielded rich talk and insight. His moral to the interviewer's story: that our being clearly marked cultural and community outsiders might prove an advantage by garnering more respect and disclosure than a local Somali researcher is accorded.

Meanwhile, our intrepid students escorted about fifteen Somalis from the cold streets to the community center, and at last we had the makings of a community discussion! Among these were the female refugee caseworker and the female nonprofit director with whom we had met in City Hall earlier, although the male caseworker/mosque leader did not attend. Both young Somalis (college and high school age) and middle-aged Somalis (some of them their parents) attended. As they arrived, we talked about the two rooms for conversation, one for women and one for men, but everyone stated a preference to use the larger room downstairs together, which we did. The Somalis in attendance spoke English, although numerous side conversations in Somali accompanied all the "over the table" talk. Discussion emerged quite readily; indeed, the Somalis appeared less nervous than did we. Talk revolved around their concern for the children, sounding themes of how to promote their success in the United States while preserving their culture, religion, and language (see Hough and Toner, chapter 8, this volume). Participants helped shape the narrative project to create a "library of real stories" for themselves and their children "trapped between two cultures." They offered specific advice on how to engender storytelling. Among their suggestions were these:

(1) Work within Somali oral culture and through word of mouth to set up and conduct interviews. We had just witnessed how to invite Somali participation—via our students and their cell phones rather than bilingual, written flyers. Some Somalis are not literate in English or Somali (see Nadeau, chapter 3, this volume). We were alerted that due to fears of the United States Citizenship and Immigration Services and Patriot Act measures, as well as lingering distrust of authorities from two decades under dictatorship, Somalis of the first generation are wary of writing, and many may want anonymity. The young people in attendance, however, had few or no concerns about signing or publicizing their names.

(2) Conduct interviews individually to encourage more diversity of perspective. Individual interviews might also diminish the face-saving interactions that inhibited disclosure to the Somali researcher in his insider stance.

(3) Conduct the interviews in the Somali language and in participants' homes, although young Somalis and others with English may prefer to display their second language proficiency. We were also informed that talk in Somali homes would be interrupted and overheard by the continuous goings and comings of family and friends.

We have incorporated all of these lessons into the project design and implementation.

Near the end of the community meeting, the door opened and a respectful hush fell over us as one of our students ushered in her elderly father. She briefly introduced him to the group as he sat silently with his nineteen-year-old daughter. He does not speak English, and she informed us that he would just listen. In that cross-generational pair, we saw the site of our next lessons in the cross-cultural currents of storytelling with Somalis in Maine. We would continue, to paraphrase the poet Theodore Roethke, to "learn by going where [we] have to go."

FIGURE 24. Research assistants Muna Abdullahi and Emily Yearwood

That Day

Sadia

When we arrived at the airport in Syracuse, New York—my mother, brother, sisters, and I—we were met by two Caucasian men and a Somali woman. They were very helpful and very nice. They took us to our own apartment, our first one. They had toys waiting for us and chairs and everything, and every Christmas they would bring us toys. After about a year we moved to F Street, the housing project. You know, where there are those houses that all look the same, all in a straight line. We had one Somali neighbor who lived next door to us, and on the other side was an African American.

The Somali lady we first met introduced us to other Somalis so that we could talk to people. She introduced my mom to Roda, and they began to get close. Roda would come over to our house, and they would socialize for hours. They would cook together. Roda's kids would sleep over with us. Roda and my mom would go out for walks and go to weddings together. I was the oldest girl, so I would go babysit when they went out shopping and other places.

Roda began to tell my mom about her abusive relationship with her husband. That's when my mother said she ought to leave—for the sake of the children. Finally my mom convinced her, and Roda moved next door.

My mom had to get up at five in the morning and work all day. That's when Roda started to take us in. She was like a second mother to me. Every time my mother went to work she would call us over. She would cook for us, give us clothes, keep us until my mom came home. Roda had three kids. She had a son who was three, another who was eight, and her daughter was five or six.

In the housing project there was a mixture of people—Hispanic, Caucasian, and African American. But it was mostly African American and some white families. When I was living there I would only hang out with one African American girl; she was really nice to everyone. When I went to school I was sort of an outcast. I had one friend, a Jamaican. I also had a Bosnian friend because they were Muslims. I had to share a locker with one girl— I'm not sure if she was Hispanic or white. She brought a lock and she showed me how to use it, but I couldn't figure it out. She said, "You know what, just forget it," and went to class. I hated sharing that locker with her.

One time when I was in the fourth or fifth grade, a whole bunch of kids from the neighborhood came and started to throw rocks at us. I didn't know why. It was mostly boys with one or two girls. They were basically cussing and throwing rocks. We ran all the way home. I told my mother what had happened. Roda's kids were with us, too, and so my mom walked them home because they felt unsafe. After that I just stayed at home in the backyard, playing with my brothers and sisters. There were six of us at the time.

That day was just like a regular day. I woke up, went to the bathroom, and brushed my teeth. My mother called me: "Come on down. I want to braid your hair." While she was braiding my hair there was a knock at the door, and my brother answered it. At the door was Roda's daughter.

We asked her, "What are you doing here in the morning?" Her shirt was messy. There was stuff on her shirt that looked like ketchup.

"My mother's killing herself."

We said, "What are you talking about? You shouldn't kid about that."

"I'm not kidding." She said again, "My mom's trying to kill herself. I don't know what to do. She's throwing herself down the stairs and stabbing herself with knives."

We said, "Stop joking around."

She said, "I'm serious." The stuff on her shirt was really blood.

A few minutes after Roda's daughter came to our door, Roda's son also came to tell us what she was doing—how she was throwing herself down stairs and stabbing herself. The kids were crying really bad. They were saying, "What's going on?" They were really confused.

After that my mom started freaking out. She said, "Oh, my God!" and tried to run out of the house and go to Roda. But we all ran after her. "Don't go," we begged. My heart had nearly dropped. I was afraid we would lose my mother. I thought she might be stabbed, or she could be blamed. I didn't want my mother to be taken away. She was the only person I had here, because my father was still in Egypt and I thought everybody else here was racist. "Something bad might happen to you if you go over there," I said to her. "You should call somebody." So she called Roda's house.

The night before, Roda had called my mother and told her, "If something happens to me, make sure my kids are safe. Please be sure they live in a stable home." And my mother had said, "Why are you talking about that?"

On that day my mother called and called, but Roda didn't pick up the phone. We didn't know who else to call. We tried our neighbors, but no one answered. So my mom went next door to the Somali neighbor and told her what was happening. Our neighbor said, "I don't speak English. You should call 911, but I don't know what you should tell them. You should call somebody." We decided to call the lady we met when we first came to America. My mom told her what had happened over the phone, and the lady said, "I will be right there." She called 911 on her way to the house, but it took a while for her to get here. By the time the police came, Roda was already dead.

After the police came and after the ambulance took the body out, Roda's husband came. My mom said, "What are you doing here?" He said he wanted to know what was going on. She said, "You know what's going on, get out of here." She told the lady that he might be a suspect and they arrested him.

After the ambulance left, it was almost 7:00 a.m. and the school bus was going to come at 7:15 a.m. My mother told us all to get into the house. My mom started crying; we all started crying. She told us, "Forget about this. Erase it from your mind." She gave us our bags and said, "Go walk together to the bus." There were four of us who had to go to grade school together. My brother was in middle school, so he had to go alone. The rest of us all sat together, and we were all crying. The kids on the bus looked at us. "Why are they all crying?" they asked. "Your cries are irritating us. Why are you cry-ing?" They had seen the crime scene. They had seen all the cops there, and so they knew something bad had happened. But they didn't ask "how are you doing?" or "what's going on?" or even "are you okay?" They just said, "Shut up. Stop crying." I tried to stop crying. I was worried about my mother—the whole day I was at school, I was thinking about my mom. I couldn't concentrate, and I was crying the whole day. All I could think of was my mom, my mom, my mom.

When I got home I asked my mother, "Are you all right?" And then, "Where are Roda's kids?" The whole day I was at school they had stayed with my mom. She had cleaned them up and given them clothes to wear. And then the police had taken them away. My mom said, "They're not with us right now." My mom didn't know how to tell the kids that their mother was dead. They were all under ten. How can you tell someone their mother died?

Then Roda's kids were in the shelter—the orphanage. My mom would go to see them every chance she could get. She would take me with her, some-times. The orphanage was a good place, mostly: they were fed, they had toys, and they told me, "This is a really good place." But then the father took the kids to court and wanted full custody. My mother testified against him, but they let him have the kids for a month. When he failed to take care of them, the closest relatives were contacted. But they were really harsh, too. "We only want to take one," they said. So each relative took one kid, and Roda's children were scattered across the United States; I think the daughter was in Canada. My mom would talk to the relatives and ask her how the kids were doing. But then the phone calls stopped and we lost track of them.

After that happened I wanted to leave New York. But a year later it had faded away. I tried to erase it from my mind.

When my family and I decided to move to Maine, we took a family vote. My dad told us, "Do you want to move to Maine? Your cousins and family live there. You'll have people to play with." Everybody voted. We all voted to go. Some of my dad's relatives came to help us move. They were distant relatives, and I didn't know who they were at all. The guy who drove us took us to his house, where I could tell the lady had been cooking all day. We had a big dinner.

We moved to another housing project with all the houses all the same, all in a straight line. When we first moved there I stayed at home because I didn't know anybody. But my brothers went outside, and they met a lot of nice Somali boys. So I said, "Well, I might as well go outside." And I met some girls who were very nice.

On my first day of school, my dad dropped us off. When my dad had taken us to register for school, there was one teacher who had said to me, "When you come to school, come to me and I'll help you." She showed me where the office was, helped me find my classrooms, and took me to my ESL class. When I first came into the ESL room the teacher introduced me, and the girls all came up to me and surrounded me—mostly Somali kids. I felt more welcomed. Back in New York I didn't talk much to anyone at school. But after that first school day in Maine I sort of got comfortable. I started talking more; I didn't feel so awkward. I felt like I really knew these people. We had something in common.

In Syracuse I went to a mosque only for special occasions. We didn't know how to drive and we usually didn't have anyone to take us. I didn't know anyone in the mosque there, so I would just stay with my mom or the people who had brought us there. It was a big place, and there were all kinds of people: Sudanese, Somali, Arabic. In Lewiston, we can walk to the mosque. At Eid prayer, people come up to you and say, "Happy Eid." They give Eid money to kids. Lewiston is a small community, so all the families know each other.

Here in Lewiston, people in the Somali community are really helpful to each other. If one family is in trouble, they all pitch in and help each other. There was a family whose son went to jail. He was accused of something and it wasn't true. A Somali lady went around and collected money for his bail. So we really help each other out.

My family is thinking about moving again. They want to have a different place. And it is really hard to find a job in Lewiston.

10 Engaged Learning: Somali Student Initiatives

Carol Nordstrom Toner

I didn't know much about Somali history except through the stories from my grandmother. But as we heard the stories from people we interviewed, like my father and my neighbor who has been in the United States since the 1970s, I learned a lot I [hadn't known] about. Reading the books and hearing the stories was very educational for me.

Amina

Amina was one of the first Somali students to join the University of Maine's (UM) Somali Narrative Project (SNP), a collaboration that included UM Somali students, four UM faculty members, and some members of the Somali community in Lewiston. Her comment on what she learned from working with the SNP reveals an important element to that collaboration—that the project engaged the students in active learning. This chapter explores how the Somali students who initially joined the project provided essential cross-cultural connections that linked the research team to the Somali community. Further, this chapter argues that the students quickly moved beyond this key role when they saw the larger potential for leadership and education available to them through the project and through their own initiatives. With bold imagination, they seized the opportunity to become leaders in the project, shaping the materials and the directions our project took while also initiating a number of other programs on and off campus.

The Somali Narrative Project provides a creative model for active learning, whose goal is to move learning beyond the classroom and connect ideas to the larger community. As educator Martin Bickman puts it, active learning seeks to "relate the abstract to the concrete, contemplation to action."[1] Many educators today argue that involving students in active research is one of the most effective ways for students to learn. The many activities that characterize the Somali Narrative Project, including conducting oral interviews, performing before audiences large and small, presenting at national and international conferences, meeting Somali students from other communities, and working with the Admissions Office to recruit Somali students, exemplify active learning. Further, this project and the additional initiatives instituted by the Somali students reflect the ideas of Brazilian educator Paulo Freire, who believed that the most productive pedagogy includes supporting activism in education, giving voice to the oppressed, dialoguing with students, and incorporating students' lived experiences into education.[2]

The first meeting between the Somali Narrative Project and the University of Maine Somali students took place in the fall of 2004. We were all a little nervous but eager to make this cross-cultural group work. While we hoped the students would be interested in collaborating with our project, we worried that they might view us as hopeless outsiders or even interlopers. But when we explained the idea to collect Somali immigration stories and to facilitate cross-cultural dialogue in Maine, they responded enthusiastically. They expressed their concern that younger Somalis in Maine had already lost their Somali language skills and forgotten much about their homeland. They spoke also about their elders and the need to make them feel comfortable and respected. They themselves had already experienced the pain of cultural conflict, so they supported the goal to increase cross-cultural communication in Maine. They thought the project a good idea and stated they would do "anything to help."

Our first project together was to establish a reading group where faculty and Somali students could become familiar with Somali history and culture.[3] In this group of four faculty members and three Somali students, we focused first on a volume of Somali history, followed by the fiction of world-acclaimed Somali novelist Nuruddin Farah, and finally several accounts of the Somali civil war and the diaspora.[4] Because their own education had been interrupted by war and refugee camp life, the Somali students had read none of this history and literature; they were as enthusiastic to learn about their country as we were. In a spirit of collaborative learning, the students quickly became comfortable responding to and critiquing the readings and adding their own personal stories to the discussions.

This unique learning experience combined bright, enthusiastic students who were personally engaged with the readings, and instructors who were novices in the field but seeking to learn about Somali history and culture. The students initially chose *not* to participate for credit, which meant that we could do away with grades, thus freeing all of us to focus on learning without the onus of judging or being judged. We discussed the material in a non-hierarchical democratic manner, listening carefully and giving every voice equal consideration. The students seemed comfortable sharing their thoughts on how their own personal experiences were reflected (or not) in the readings. For example, when we read Somali poetry, one of the students shared the memory of his mother and grandmother reciting long poems that they had memorized. Another time, in reaction to reading a casual reference to a fictional female character who appeared in public without covering her head, the students protested with a discussion of head-covering protocols. The experience yielded mutual benefits: the Somali students were able to extend and criticize written texts by drawing on and using their strong oral traditions and personal experiences; the faculty were able to witness Somali verbal expression as it worked within and against the written texts.

The materials we read in this group were often quite moving, leading us to think of ways these readings might be used to educate others about Somali history and culture. Inspired by the notion of theater-based social transformation as articulated by Augusto Boal and his followers, we put together a readers theater script based on our readings. Our intention was to use readers theater to introduce Somali voices to audiences in various Maine communities, hoping that such performances would lead to dialogue and greater cross-cultural awareness and tolerance. (See Huisman, chapter 11, this volume.) With a book grant from the University of Maine's Women in the Curriculum and Women's Studies Program, we decided to focus our performance on Somali women's experiences. When we met to discuss which of the authors to include in the script, the students had strong opinions. While the faculty members were drawn to the novels of Nuruddin Farah, the students argued that the voices in this script should be those of real people, not fictional characters. We saw the wisdom in their argument, and we all agreed to drop the novels from the script.[5]

As the students' comfort level in this group grew, they even provided leadership in shaping the most sensitive material. The script begins with traditional Somali poems and songs that reveal women's work and roles in traditional Somali nomadic culture—cooking, child rearing, caring for animals, and loading the collapsible nomadic dwellings on camels. These topics

FIGURE 25. Readers theater performance, American Folk Festival (Bangor, Maine)

were straightforward enough, but we struggled with more sensitive issues such as female genital cutting (FGC), a topic addressed in several of our readings.[6] As cultural and religious outsiders, faculty members approached this difficult issue cautiously, but our female students felt strongly that we should include this topic in the script. In fact, they volunteered to read the Somali women's voices that describe both the process and some women's thoughts about the practice. The students were eager to challenge FGC in this public way, displaying their opposition to the practice while educating others about its dangers. They made especially clear their argument that FGC is not a religious requirement; rather it is a cultural tradition that they feel should be eliminated in all but a symbolic way. When we performed the readers theater in towns and on campuses throughout Maine, the audience often raised questions about FGC, which the students handled with conviction and grace.

We extended our performances of the readers theater out of Maine as well. In 2006 our group performed at the International Conference on Immigration in Halifax, Nova Scotia. This trip provided us the opportunity to experience the intellectual atmosphere of an international conference, to learn more about immigration issues in Canada and the United States, to tour Pier 21 (the old point of immigration in Canada), to educate another audience about Somali culture, and to cohere as a group. During the long drive from Orono, Maine to Halifax, the students told many personal stories ranging from their frightening experiences fleeing Somalia to their discouraging confrontations with discrimination in this country. With every story, we learned more about these students and their culture. One student explained that his father, a Somali-trained electrician without U.S. credentials, bagged clothes at the local thrift store but was buoyed by the fact that his children were doing well in U.S. schools. Others joked and laughed as they shared stories of life in Somalia—memories of the taste of camel's milk or the dances at wedding ceremonies. Others told sober stories of escaping Somalia—walking for hours, worrying about the dangers posed by both lions and armed militants. And we heard stories of cultural conflict in Maine— for example, one student lost a job over her decision to wear her *hijab* at work; another challenged his employer over working on Eid. The students used this unique time and space to listen to each other's stories.

Our readers theater performance took us to a Theatre of the Oppressed conference in Minneapolis, where the students experienced the Somali malls and restaurants in the largest Somali community in the United States. They led us to and through the Somali mall and then ordered up a feast at a Somali restaurant. When one of the students noticed an announcement about a fundraiser for Somalia that evening, we all decided to attend the event. Some of the students seated themselves next to the non-Somalis in our group and whispered translations so that the experience would be meaningful for all of us. During this Minnesota trip, we met with Professor Ahmed Samatar, the James Wallace Professor and Dean of the Institute for Global Citizenship at Macalester College. Three of our students were international affairs majors who were especially happy to meet and converse with this esteemed Somali professor of international studies. Before we left, Professor Samatar graciously offered copies of the journal *Bildhaan* to the group, as well as CDs from a recent international conference on Somalia. Meeting Professor Samatar expanded the students' ideas about themselves and encouraged them to think more about the possibilities of graduate study.

When we attended the National Women's Studies Association conference in Cincinnati to perform our readers theater piece, we shared in an impromptu late-night storytelling party with several of our Somali female students in their room. With only women present, they removed their *hijabs* and let down their hair as we all ate chocolate cake and listened to remarkable stories about life in refugee camps and in Lewiston. At that conference, an

African American educator from the University of Cleveland went out of her way to introduce herself to our group and to encourage our students to apply to graduate school, suggesting that financial aid would be available for such engaged students. Once again, the students experienced support for their stories as well as encouragement to continue their studies.

For a conference on immigrants and the meaning of home held in St. Cloud, Minnesota, part of our group traveled to St. Cloud while the rest participated from Maine via video conferencing. While sharing their stories, the students from both communities learned that they face similar challenges and hear similar stereotypes. Our students learned that American-born residents in St. Cloud circulate the same myths that are heard in Lewiston, myths that claim that Somalis do not pay taxes and the government gives Somalis new cars. During this discussion a remarkable thing happened when one of our Somali students realized that one of the St. Cloud students was a friend of his from his childhood in Somalia. That these two young men who had both been through so much and had traveled such great distances should meet again through technology for a discussion of "home" was deeply satisfying to us all.

In addition to performing the readers theater, the students were also instrumental in conducting the interviews with Somalis in Lewiston. Our first major introduction to the Lewiston community took place during the Somali Independence Day celebration, July 2005. The students introduced us to their families and friends and shared a Somali meal with us. The female students were beautifully attired in traditional dress—long flowing skirts and colorful headscarves—while our male students wore Western-style clothing. Obviously well-known and well-liked in their community, the students guided us through the day, explaining the cultural artifacts set out for visitors to inspect and admire. When the national anthem played, one student translated the message, which was something like, "Come, let us stay united; do not forget the poor and needy; you wonder why we are crying; it is because we have been oppressed by the colonizers and have not been able to speak ourselves." This celebration afforded us the opportunity to learn more about Somalia, to meet people in the community, and to see our students interacting with their friends and neighbors.

Over the next few years, we conducted more than thirty interviews and several focus groups with Somali refugees—men and women ranging in age from nineteen to sixty-something. The students contributed in many ways, making the initial contacts, scheduling the interviews, guiding us to various neighborhoods, and translating when necessary. We usually interviewed in teams of three—two faculty members and a student on each team. Faculty members led the interviews done in English; the students conducted the interviews done in Somali, stopping periodically to summarize or to exclaim to us that the person was telling a fascinating story. Time and again, the students negotiated cultural and language barriers; at the same time, they were learning more about their own history.

In a few instances, most notably with other young people, our students joined in the storytelling during the interviews. At such times some wonderful stories emerged. For example, one of the young interviewees explained that Somali parents are often anxious to have their daughters marry, prompting a discussion among the young women about their desire to attend college rather than get married. Another theme that emerged with the young people in discussion with our students was their desire to keep Somali traditions and language alive. They shared stories about local weddings and how some Somali traditions—such as wedding poetry recitations—are becoming rare.

The students shared their culture in other venues, too, as when one of our students invited us to his wedding in Lewiston. This joyful event featured the bride and groom in traditional Western wedding dress while the Somali women were dressed in their finest and most colorful silky *jilbab*. There were more women at the wedding than men, and the men were dressed in Western clothing and sat at tables separate from the women, including their wives. The guests stood and clapped and ululated to greet the bride and groom, who entered and sat solemnly at the head table. There followed dinner, singing and dancing. The photographer invited groups to be photographed with the bride and groom, including a large group of University of Maine students. Throughout this entire evening, various students would stop by our table to make sure we understood what was going on or to introduce their family members.

During a performance at the Franco-American Heritage Center in Lewiston, the students had the opportunity to consider their own immigrant experiences within the larger context of the city's immigrant history. For this event, five of our Somali students joined two French-speaking students from nearby Bates College to address a large audience of what appeared to be mostly retired Franco Americans. In this immigrant city where first English, then Irish, then French Canadian, and now Somalis have

FIGURE 26. Readers theater performance, Franco-American Heritage Center (Lewiston, Maine)

settled, it was striking to hear the Bates students speak in French about the history of the French Canadian immigrants in Lewiston while our students spoke in English about the Somali immigrant experience in Lewiston. Following their presentation, the students joined the audience for a French folk song performance. Both Franco Americans and Somali Americans have felt the sting of discrimination in Lewiston, and this event underscored the immigrant challenges that both groups have faced.

The Somali students have also shared their culture with the University of Maine community, as, for example, when they wrote and performed their own script during the university's Africa Week celebration. Their amusing short play focused on the generation gap in Somali communities, referencing differences between their parents' and their own ideas over issues such as dating, attendance at mosque, and dress style. The play was well-attended and allowed students of many cultures to enjoy the humor; generational humor, after all, resonates across cultures. Somali students also play active roles in the University's Muslim Student Association and the African Students Association, bringing their leadership skills and their culture to these organizations.

From the beginning of the project, the students demonstrated the value they placed on higher education. They were serious about their education, and they felt keenly the desire to persuade other young Somalis to attend college; but they knew all too well the barriers that young Somalis face in gaining entrance to college. (See Warsame, chapter 6, this volume.) It is daunting for many high school students to think about getting into college. It is even more difficult when the students' parents cannot read enough English to help fill out the entrance application or the financial aid application, or when parents fear the loss of cultural identity if their children leave home, or when teachers fail to encourage students to aspire to a college education. Our Somali students wanted to talk to high school students in Lewiston and Portland to encourage other Somalis to attend the University of Maine—or any university. They prepared a slide show about their lives on campus, and in collaboration with the University of Maine Admissions Office they traveled to Lewiston and Portland (the two cities in Maine with large Somali populations) to talk with high school students. They met with students individually and in groups to help complete applications and to talk about student life at the university. Their efforts took hold—by 2010 about twenty-five Somali students were enrolled at the University of Maine.

Our initial three students have graduated and moved on to other things: one is teaching school and applying for graduate school, one is currently attending graduate school at the University of Minnesota, and the third has just graduated from a masters program at the University of Maine and is now working at Oregon State University. One returned to Kenya in 2008 to visit the refugee camp in Dadaab where she had spent eight years before coming to the United States. While she was there she interviewed some of the students attending her old school in the camp. (See Mohamed, chapter 5, this volume.) Another of these original students recently addressed a University of Maine diversity workshop where he presented a paper on Somalis in higher education. All of these students stay in touch with the SNP.

The Somali Narrative Project has been an exciting research project and mutually beneficial for faculty and students. The effort to link the University of Maine with the state's newest immigrants is gratifying, and preserving stories of Somali immigrant experiences is essential to the historical record of these new Mainers. Moreover, the community-based project is consistent with the University of Maine's land grant mission to serve local communities. But the privilege of working closely with these talented students who are so skillful in negotiating boundaries—between Somalis and Maine people, between Muslims and non-Muslims, between adults and teens, between faculty and students, between men and women—has been most satisfying. Their contributions to the success of this project, with their translation skills, their humor, and their cross-cultural sensitivity and understanding, cannot be overstated.

Finally, the project demonstrates the methods and benefits of active learning as students learned so much outside of a traditional classroom while conducting interviews, performing the readers theater, meeting other Somalis and listening to their stories, and introducing the next generation of college students to the possibility of higher education. These Somali students took the opportunity to play leadership roles within the project and then developed their own initiatives. They learned about research, scholarship, and their own history while they taught others about their culture. What did the students mean when they pledged at the beginning to do "anything to help"? No doubt they were thinking of helping preserve their culture and improve cross-cultural dialogue between Somalis and non-Somalis. But they also helped the Somali Narrative Project, the University of Maine, young Somali students needing a bridge to higher education, and of course, they helped themselves by expanding their own horizons.

What I Didn't Know Before

Khalid Mohamed

One thing Somalis are known for is moving around. We are natural-born nomads. It doesn't matter if we're in Somalia or America—we're going to move around. I was born in 1986 in a small village in Somalia called Arabsiyo, and I came to America when I was eight years old. My uncle brought me to America, and his family brought me up in America. I had been through a lot in Africa that I didn't know about until recently.

The first place I came to was Atlanta, Georgia. I had never been out of Africa until my uncle brought me to Atlanta. I didn't speak any English, and they put me straight into a regular elementary school class. Maybe at that time they didn't have ESL, I don't know. I was in the same class as my cousin, who was born here. It was very tough for me, and I didn't know what was going on. One thing I remember to this day is that in elementary school, you do a lot of spelling in class, where the teacher says the word and you spell it out. Now, I didn't know any English, but I was sitting next to my cousin, and when we would have those tests I would copy from him! I remember another time I went to the cafeteria. My teacher's name was Miss Wood, but I didn't know how to say it. Now, in order for me to get some food, somebody kept asking me, "Who's your teacher?" and I kept answering, "Good."

We moved to Canada after that and lived in Ottawa for a year, and that's where I actually learned English. They had a phonics program there. Years later when I'd see the Hooked on Phonics commercial, I'd say, "Man, I learned it through Hooked on Phonics!" Then we came back to Atlanta, and after that I was excelling in school. The best way to learn a language is not through books, it's through being in the environment and interacting with the people. I was a kid, too, so it's a lot easier for a kid to absorb a new language than it is for somebody who is older who just came here. In Atlanta we moved between a lot of different apartments. I went to many different schools, until I came to Maine. My aunt was living in Maine, and she said, "It's better over here." Where we were living in a bigger city there was more crime, and my parents were scared we were going to get into gangs and go the wrong way; they figured that Maine has smaller cities, and it's not very dangerous.

I didn't even know where Maine was. When I heard it was in New England, I thought it was in London, but come to find out New England is like a couple of states put together—interesting! We came to Maine, predominantly white Maine. The only black people in my school were Somalis. There were probably about three black people, and they were confused because they didn't even know where to hang out! And I was paranoid because people were looking at me like I was an animal, like a creature on the Discovery Channel. People were looking at me differently, and right away they already had something formed in their heads about who I was.

The majority of the students were really cool and there were no troubles. But then you had those kids that were the "wanna-be gangsters." They probably listened to a lot of hip-hop or something. I remember one day some kid—I guess he was a "Blood," but I don't even know how a Blood gang comes to Maine—came to our school, and he was like, "I don't want to see you guys wearing a certain color." And all of us—we came from Atlanta, and we weren't going to have that! We would wear the colors on purpose; we were going to hold our ground. We weren't really instigating it, but if people were going to do racist and discriminatory things, we weren't going to let it go. There was a group that was passive, who didn't do anything. And then you had what I like to call the "soldiers"—they had a lot of pride.

So a lot of fights were happening in the school. Every day something happened over here or over there. A lot of my friends got into altercations. We had to keep our guard up. You really didn't know who was your friend or who was not, who was phony and who was fake. One time my car got surrounded by the whole school! There were four of us in the car. I was just trying to go home—I guess some kids were trying to act tough. The police didn't do anything. But another scene that was pretty horrific was when my friend's car got busted. They completely annihilated the car; they broke all the windows. It was a station wagon. I mean, it was ugly, but it was still a car! The car was messed up pretty good, so obviously my friend wasn't going to let that fly. So he went and—and the other kid, I felt bad for him, he had a nicer car, more expensive—did the same damage to his car. So that car got messed up, and it got crazier. We had monster trucks coming to our apartment—trucks with huge tires running through the parking lot and on the lawn, shouting, "Come out, niggers!" They had bats; they had all kinds of weapons. To tell the truth, I wasn't going to come out. I was looking through my window, and that's as far in the action I was going to get. I had school the next morning! They kept on coming back. It was a pretty dangerous time.

Right now I don't experience that much racism. It's not as prevalent as when we first came. Now you see kids that grew up here that went to middle school, elementary school, and even high school in a different environment, and they're like family members. When I came to high school we were foreigners, aliens. Now there's a bond, so Lewiston has changed a lot over time. Everything changes over time.

To tell the truth, when I lived in Atlanta there were not a lot of Somalis, so I didn't really know much about my culture. When I came to Maine, that's when my Somali got better. There are at least two different dialects of Somali: one from the north side and Somaliland, and one from the south side and Mogadishu. I'm from the Somaliland area. We Somalis make fun of each other because of our different dialects. If there's one thing I enjoyed about coming to Maine, it's that I got to learn about my culture. If I had stayed in Atlanta I would be different, because I would be totally Americanized. There is a balance here in Maine.

I was going to go to Africa because I hadn't seen my mom and dad for a very long time. My dad was really anxious for my visit, and I would hear stories about how he was setting up the house: "My son is coming back, my son is coming back, lalalalalalala!" But unfortunately, one or two months before I was going go to Africa, my dad passed away. So that's just how life goes: you can plan for things but you never actually know—you don't even know if you're going to live until tomorrow. So my dad passed away one or two months before my trip to Africa, and the ticket was already cut, and he was excited and so was I, but it was not meant to be.

Going over there was a good experience. I hadn't seen my mom since I was a little kid, since I was eight years old, and it was very emotional for everybody. I mean, I didn't really have a good connection with my parents, because I didn't grow up with them—my uncle and my aunt were my father and mother. A lot of my family members would make fun of me at times and ask me, "Why don't you say 'Mom'?" when we spoke on the telephone. In our culture you show a lot of respect by saying "Mom," but it was very hard for me to say that. And a lot of people were watching you, seeing how you're interacting with your mom. You know what I mean? It is obviously not a comfortable situation when you have alone time with your mother after so many years of being apart. And Somali people—they really love to pay attention to these things! They want all the details. They analyze it.

So, yes, when I got to Somaliland I got to know my mom a little bit better. And it was a lot easier for me to say "Mom" after that. And I really got into a good bond with my brothers and everyone over there. I'm the youngest out of ten children, and my mom would tell me stories that I never knew before, about me when I was little. Fortunately for me, it seems that I survived a lot of accidents. I was dropped a lot! That's why my memory is not very good from my childhood. My mom was telling me about when the war broke out and what it was like. There were guys who were raiding everybody's houses. They were killing people left and right, like you see on TV, exactly like those African genocides on the news. So my mom had me, and she was holding me in the traditional wrap. Somali mothers put the kids behind their back, and a scarf would be holding you so they could have both their hands free. I was tied behind her back, I was very little, I don't know how old. And they made everybody line up in the house in a row, like they were going to shoot us all down. But fortunately the guy who was supposed to kill all of us, well, some other guy called him and he left, and that's how I survived.

I had been in America for a long time, and I had never known about that part of my life. I had never known I'd been that close to dying. I remember watching movies about Africa and always thinking, "Wow, they've been through that." I was one of them, one of those statistics—I just never knew about it. We got lucky. We fled the place, my mother carrying me in a scarf on her back. There were a lot of people trying to help each other, getting cars, trying to survive by running away. We didn't eat food for a long time, because we were on the road just trying to get away, just trying to live another day, to escape from this whole insane thing. My sister also had a baby, only a couple of months old. He died of dehydration and lack of nourishment, and I never knew that either until I went over there. There were a lot of people killed over there, left and right. A truck driver who was trying to help people escape the police got shot down. It was horrific. Anything you see on the genocides in Africa is exactly what was happening to us over there.

Luckily, I survived, and when I went over there I learned the history that I hadn't known before. And it was very good for me to see how life is in

Somalia. There are no jobs. People are starving. There are people who don't have families in America to send them money. The one good thing is that Somalis who come here never forget about their family members in Somalia. Most Americans will go to work, and they'll have enough money to pay off their rent, their houses, get decent food, go on vacation—imagine getting a phone call saying, "We need a hundred dollars," or "we need two hundred dollars." You know that there are no jobs over there, and this is your family. So when you came over here, that was your whole mentality: to make a better life for yourself, but also to help your family members back home. One thing I'm really proud of with the Somali community is the support it gives to family members. It's all about family.

Now you have kids like me, who forgot about Somalia or don't really know what a struggle life is over there, or even that we had families back there. We have one of the greatest opportunities that those people in Africa don't have. We take it for granted. We try to live the regular American lifestyle. Most of us don't take advantage of the education program; we don't take advantage of anything. We've become those type of people that say, "We don't care about the family," and "we're just worried about taking care of ourselves." It's very sad. I'm not saying everybody is like this, but a lot of people are. When I went to Africa, I got back in touch with my family, and I got to know them and their lives. For the first couple of months after I got back to Maine, I was very motivated and I was trying to become the best I could be. There were times that I slipped, forgot about it and became selfish again, thinking about enjoying myself and just trying to have fun. But hopefully the experience has changed me for the good, and one day I would like to be able to do something for my people and my family back home.

11   Readers Theater as Public Pedagogy[1]

Kimberly A. Huisman

In early 2001, about seven months before the September 11 terrorist attacks, Lewiston, Maine, a predominantly white, Christian town in Southern Maine, experienced an unexpected influx of Somali refugees, catching many residents by surprise. The Somali Narrative Project (SNP), an interdisciplinary collaboration between faculty, students, and community members at the University of Maine, was established in 2004 to document the stories of immigration and to address the conflicts that emerged in response to the secondary migration of Somalis to Maine. Most of these conflicts have centered around religious and racial intolerance on a local level, but they are also intertwined with the anti-immigration rhetoric on national and global levels. This chapter examines how the Somali Narrative Project (SNP) strives to foster dialogue, democracy, and understanding about Somali immigrants in Maine. As a form of public pedagogy, the readers theater offers the best illustration of how the project aims to address issues of inequality and promote social justice in Maine communities.

The sociological imagination, a term coined by C. W. Mills,[2] refers to the quality of mind needed to understand the interaction between individuals' lives (biography) and larger social contexts in which they live (history). Mills argued that "Neither the life of an individual nor the history of a society can be understood without understanding both." With this in mind, we developed a readers theater script, which grew out of a year-long reading group consisting of four faculty members and three Somali students. The script was developed collaboratively and democratically, with both faculty and Somali students choosing texts, from which excerpts were scripted into "dialogic performances" about Somali history, culture, and experience. Initially, the script was based on published sources including oral traditions of poetry and lullaby, oral history, testimonies, and memoirs. After conducting twenty-five narrative interviews with Somali community members, we have been adding excerpts to include Somali voices in Maine. By including Maine Somali voices we aim to help audience members better understand the multitude of issues Somalis face in the United States and Maine—including issues of immigration and immigrant/refugee status; issues of health, work, and education; and inequalities of race, class, religion, and gender. A central goal is to encourage audience members to locate the private troubles of individual Somalis in Maine within a historical and cultural context, thus providing opportunities to put the sociological imagination to work and deepen their understanding about how the individual biographies of Somali immigrants are connected to larger social forces. As the script moves back and forth between macro-level issues of colonialism, war, and immigration and the micro-level stories of individuals, audience members begin to see how these two levels are inextricably connected—the seemingly personal troubles of individuals are related to the larger public issues.[3]

After the performance, audiences are invited to "talk back" about the issues and emotions raised by the stories. To date, we have performed the script ten times, including performances in seven Maine communities and three academic conferences. Audiences ranged from twenty to two hundred people and included Somali and non-Somali community members, students, academics, community activists, and practitioners such as nurses and social workers.

Development of the Readers Theater Script

The Somali Narrative Project grew out of our commitment to community-based research and our desire to develop a project that was mutually beneficial, one in which we could pursue our academic interests while working with community members to develop something that addressed their needs. Before developing any research plan we decided to first educate ourselves about Somali history and culture. We established a reading group and invited three Somali students to join us. The students were eager to read about their own history because they felt they had been robbed of this opportunity since they had to flee their homeland as young children before their education was completed. We obtained a grant to purchase books and met regularly over the course of one year.[4] During these biweekly meetings we discussed the readings, and our ideas for the readers theater evolved out of these meetings. During this year, we also met with Somali community members to solicit their suggestions for the development of our project and how our work might be of benefit to the Somali community.

The development of the readers theater script was an organic process. We realized that this approach of oral storytelling and performance was especially congruent with Somali culture. Somali culture is traditionally an oral culture; in fact, there was no written language until the early 1970s. Storytelling and poetry are highly valued and respected traditions that continue to infuse the daily lives of Somalis. Storytelling is an important part of Somali life in the United States, as stories are both created in the new context and transmitted between generations. Storytelling may take on greater meaning in the diaspora, as families struggle to retain their culture amidst the forces of assimilation. When discussing the readings with Somali students, it was sometimes hard to stay focused on the specific readings because the content would trigger stories that the students wanted to share. Initially, the faculty members resisted this approach and tried to pull the conversation back to the reading at hand. However, we quickly learned that the stories would come around to the readings and ultimately enrich our understanding of Somali history and culture far more so than had we strictly adhered to the readings.

Once the discussion morphed into storytelling the energy and enthusiasm in the room was heightened. Students excitedly told their stories, which inevitably led to more stories, which ultimately brought us back to the literature. Although they were eager to speak, they all listened attentively to each other. The organic process that we went through mirrored the "spiral of self-reflective cycles" that Stephen Kemmis and Robin McTaggart discuss when describing participatory action research—reflecting, planning, acting, and observing.[5] It also illustrated the democratization of learning which is central to critical pedagogy. The teaching method of the four faculty participants was also transformed. All of us were more accustomed to linear approaches (i.e., read the book, discuss its relevance and implications), and had to adjust to a more circular approach that the students espoused. Ultimately, this has affected our teaching in other courses as well. Moreover, as I discuss further in the next section, the boundaries between student and teacher often blurred during the class sessions.

After the SNP was invited to give a presentation at a local women's studies conference, we began to discuss what we wanted to do. How did we want to tell the stories? One of the four faculty members has worked extensively in the area of performance studies, and she introduced the idea of doing a performance based on the readings. At that point we divided up the readings and agreed to select excerpts that we found to be especially informative, moving, or powerful. We worked collaboratively over several meetings as the script evolved into four sections: early and colonial Somalia, the recent civil war, the diaspora, and Somalis in Maine.

Since that first performance the script has evolved and changed, depending on the audience and setting; thus, it is continually evolving. Audiences have included Somalis and non-Somali community members, students, academics, and practitioners. Settings have varied from informal, intimate rooms to a large and formal recital hall in a museum to an outdoor folk festival tent. The scripts range from a focus on gender and women's stories to a dialogue between Franco immigrants of the past and Somali immigrants of the present, highlighting various commonalities in their experiences. The various versions of the script address a multitude of issues—the effects of colonialism; the history and complexities of female genital cutting;[6] the impact of the civil war on individuals' lives; the experiences of immigration; the challenges to adapting to life in the diaspora. Infused throughout are poems and lullabies that provide an emotional reprieve from the more painful themes and also teach about Somali culture and traditions.

FIGURE 27. Readers theater performance, American Folk Festival (Bangor, Maine)

Readers Theater as Transformative, Public Pedagogy

A primary goal of the readers theater project is social change and transformation, and ultimately, working toward a more socially just world. This objective is primarily achieved through processes of democratization and dialogue that engage readers and audiences in experiencing Somali texts that focus on numerous dimensions of their experiences. I first explain how democratization and dialogue are central to making and performing readers theater. This will be followed by concrete examples of change and transformation resulting from the performances.

Democratization

The readers theater project involves the democratization of teaching, research, and performance in several ways. It challenges traditional hierarchies in teaching and research by altering the relations between teachers and students, researchers and researched, and performers and audience members to be more equal contributors to the learning process. This democratization of communication runs counter to traditional research, pedagogy, and performance in which research participants, students, and audience members

Figure 28. Readers theater performance (Portland, Maine)

do not play an active, equal role in the process. With the readers theater, traditional hierarchical arrangements of power and authority—in the classroom, in the field, and on the stage—are challenged. The readers theater first invites audience members to hear a multitude of subjugated voices while also examining structural contexts. In the classroom, the line between student and teacher is blurred and oftentimes reversed. In the field, the research process is collaborative in the way in which teachers, students, and community members each play a role in conducting the research and selecting excerpts from the narrative interviews for inclusion in the script.

In all three realms—teaching, research, and performance—there are opportunities to cross boundaries of race, religion, class, gender, and national identity. For instance, for many non-Somali audience members, the readers theater was their first opportunity to engage in a conversation with members of the Somali community. This face-to-face contact has the potential to counter the negative portrayals of Somalis, immigrants, and Muslims that are common in our society. This face-to-face contact stands in stark contrast to simplistic and faceless stereotypes about Muslims and immigrants, and thus has the potential to break down such stereotypes. Stereotypes are learned through primary (e.g., family, peers) and secondary (e.g., media) socialization, and thus, can be unlearned. The readers theater provides an opportunity to challenge stereotypes and aims to decrease prejudicial attitudes and discrimination. Readers theater brings people with diverse backgrounds into direct contact with one another. As symbolic interaction theories suggest, when people with different backgrounds interact with one another on equal terms, stereotypes can be challenged and prejudice decreased. This is because stereotypes are grounded in selective perception of groups and when evidence is presented that challenges these perceptions, people can begin to see that all members are not alike. Furthermore, when white audience members ask questions about things that they know little about (e.g., Somali culture), this places them in a position of being a learner and challenges racial and religious hegemony in U.S. culture.

The script challenges power relations and dominant cultural narratives about Somalis, refugees/immigrants, and Muslims. The counternarratives offered by the performance highlight the diversity within the Somali diaspora and community, while also revealing tensions and complexities of Somali cultural and religious identities. The richness and complexity of Somali culture and identity are reinforced through the readings, the variation of religious and cultural dress worn (embodied) by the Somali performers, and the diverse views expressed by the Somali performers during the dialogue following the performance. The inclusion of students and community members in conducting research and developing and performing the script challenges hierarchical notions of who can teach, who does research, and who can perform on stage.[7] The students' involvement at all levels challenges the traditional teacher-student relationship. As Carol Toner discusses in detail (chapter 10, this volume), the strong voices of the students shaped the script and performance in countless ways. For example, while the faculty—as white, Western women—were reluctant to include material on female genital cutting, the students were adamant that this material must be included and that in some contexts, we ought to use the term "female genital mutilation" rather than the more neutral "female genital cutting." Moreover, students' involvement also challenged traditional hierarchies within the Somali community; for example, when young female college students interviewed older Somali men with limited language proficiency, it opened up new ways of relating.[8]

Dialogue

Alice Mcintyre et al. point out that "dialogue comes from the Greek word "dialogos." *Logos* means "the word." *Dia* means "through." Dialogue, therefore, suggests a stream of meaning flowing among, through, and between us out of which may emerge some new understanding."[9] Dialogue has been a central component of the readers theater project at all stages, including the reading group, performances, dialogues with community, dialogues with other researchers, at conferences, and regular meetings among faculty. Paulo Freire states that "Only dialogue truly communicates."[10] He continues, "It is in speaking ... that people, by naming the world, transform it, dialogue imposes itself as the way by which they achieve significance as human beings. Dialogue is an existential necessity."[11]

In contrast to traditional research and traditionally staged theater, where the voices of participants are represented in text form with little opportunity for exchange and interaction, the readers theater performances go beyond representation and do more than give voice to participants. The performance is dialogic, providing a "way of having intimate conversation with other people and other cultures. Instead of speaking about them, one speaks to and with them."[12] Through making culture visible, the performance creates

FIGURES 29 AND 30: Readers theater performance, American Folk Festival (Bangor, Maine)

opportunities for speaking *and* listening, as well as opportunities for being seen *and* heard. Dialogue opens spaces for action and reflection and provides opportunities to engage with new perspectives.[13]

Dialogue has been central to the readers theater performances. The scripts have evolved through dialogue, and adaptations and adjustments to the script have come about through intense discussions with both students and audience members. We have found that dialogue can reveal both similarities and differences between Somalis and non-Somalis, which can lead to new insights and which can propel people to move forward and promote both social change and personal transformation.[14] Dialogue can lead to social change on the community level as well as on the personal level.

Social Change and Transformation

The readers theater performance and dialogue puts culture into motion and treats culture as a verb, as fluid and evolving rather than static and monolithic. Seeing culture as a verb challenges simplistic conceptions of what it means to be Somali—for both audience members and performers—and highlights how culture and identity are transforming in places such as Maine. We have observed some of the ways in which students' and community members' subjectivities are changing. For the students, this change is a complex process that cannot be attributed solely to their involvement in this project. Clearly, their shifting identities and viewpoints are informed by a multitude of forces as they interact within the U.S. and Maine contexts. However, we are convinced that their involvement in this project provides a space for reflection and dialogue about the ways in which they, as individuals, are evolving and changing. The project has assisted them in better understanding their individual and collective histories and helped them to contextualize their own experiences and life stories.

Students' participation in the reading group provided them with opportunities to connect their own personal experiences and subjectivities to larger social processes while also problematizing some of their tightly held assumptions about their history and culture. The students have all commented about how much they learned about their own history and culture from the readings, and many were inspired to read further and talk to their extended family members about what they were learning. For example, one student who came to the United States at a very young age with relatives returned to Ethiopia last summer to visit his mother. Before leaving he told us that he had very few memories of Somalia and barely remembered his parents. While visiting his mother, he thought of the interviews we had done and asked her to tell him her story of fleeing Somalia. For the first time he heard the dramatic story of his family fleeing with him as a baby on his mother's back. When he returned he told us that the story made all that we talked about in class more real, as he was able to relate his story to the larger social forces we had read about in our reading group. This story is a good example of the sociological imagination at work. After learning more about the history and culture of Somalia, he became more interested in connecting his own story to larger social forces. He was also able to recognize that his own private troubles were intertwined with larger social issues. This, in turn, deepened his awareness about how his own life had been impacted by forces external to him and outside of his and his parents' control.

During one of the performances, an audience member asked the students if their participation in the project changed them. Here are three of their responses:

I joined in 2004 after the professors asked me if I wanted to join a reading group about Somali history. I was interested. I grew up in Kenya, but all of my family is from Somalia, and part of my father's family still lives in refugee camps in Kenya. I never learned about Somali history except from what my grandmother taught me. I actually got a lot out of it, [learning] about Somali history and about the diaspora. Most of what I know about the refugee camps [comes] from the readings and stories I've been told. (female, senior)

I grew up in the States for fifteen years, since I was three. I [had never gone] back home before the class (I did go this past summer). Before I [couldn't have cared] less, [but] because of the class I learned about Somali history and culture. Now I care a lot. When I went back home I talked to people and listened to their stories. This class got me interested in my own culture. (female, sophomore)

I was actually born in America, so growing up I was Americanized. I know my language from my mom and a little bit of stuff about Somalia, but I haven't had that firsthand experience about how my people struggled and what they've been through. Since I joined this project, the readings [have] made me [realize that] . . . the things they went through were like ten times harder than I thought. It made me think twice about how I have family—like uncles and cousins—who are not as lucky as me, and to make every opportunity I have worthwhile. (male, freshman)

Most of the students involved in the project are committed to working toward social change through their desired careers in, for example, international relations and education. Though they brought this interest with them to the project, their commitment deepened as their sociological imagination developed. C. W. Mills argued that once people gain the ability to connect history and biography, they are able to recognize their own ability in affecting social change.[15] After graduating, one student went to Kenya to volunteer in the refugee camps where she had once lived (see Mohamed, chapter 5, this volume). She decided to bring a camera and notebooks along with her and ended up photographing and interviewing nineteen young men and women about their experiences in the camp and about their hopes and dreams. She contacted us upon her return to the United States and asked if we could help her do something with their stories. This student has also decided to get a master's degree in social work in the interest of continuing her commitment to improving the lives of Somalis.

Some of the readings challenged students' notions about Somali history and culture. For example, we read several books by Nuruddin Farah, a Somali author who came of age in Somalia during an era when it was not uncommon for women to wear Western clothing. Because this version of Somalia did not match their own experience and family narratives, initially, some of the students vehemently resisted this representation, and said Farah was wrong. Farah's representation of culture stood in stark contrast to their own identities and understandings of how to be Somali and Muslim. It was upon learning more about their own history that they were able to understand why these differences exist and how they came to be, which in turn helped them to better understand and contextualize their own experiences and family histories. The reading group, interviews, and performances provided opportunities for students to grapple with a multitude of Somali and Western views. And grapple they did (and so did we). They did not simply accept these alternative versions of Somali history and culture but questioned and challenged the ideas. This exposure to different viewpoints disrupted the students' own cultural narratives, while at the same time they challenged our own perceptions about social change. Their initial resistance gradually gave way to a more nuanced understanding of culture and identity, and they began to see their own constructions of culture as inextricably connected to the larger social contexts that have shaped their lives. The students engaged in a critical examination and discussion of the texts, demonstrating their expanding critical literacy. Brian Keith Alexander notes that "Culture operates both within the confines of its own constructions (power, social relations, time, history, and space) and under the forces of externalized pressure that affect the conditions of its operation."[16] Through reflection, the students have come to recognize some of the ways in which their own culture has been constructed and bound by internal and external forces. As a result, they developed a more critical perspective about the fluidity of their own culture and the complex ways in which it has been influenced by larger global processes. They began to do what Norman Denzin and Ronald Glass describe as understanding how people create history and culture while history and culture also produce them.[17]

The change and transformation of audience members through readers theater is less tangible because in most cases, we only have an opportunity to interact with them on one occasion, compared with our ongoing relationship with students and community members. Although we can't say with certainty, we are nonetheless convinced that the readers theater performance and dialogue constitute public pedagogy and has the potential to inform and engage audiences in transformative ways. Norman Denzin describes performance ethnography as "a form of public pedagogy" using "the aesthetic to foreground cultural meanings and to teach these meanings to performers and audience members alike."[18] Initially we had hoped to reach community members who held the more extreme stereotypes and hostilities toward immigrants in general and Somali refugees in particular. We soon learned that our audiences would consist mainly of curious and well-intentioned people who were interested in learning more about Maine's newcomers. Most of the people who attend our performances appear to be genuinely seeking a deeper understanding about Somali culture and how Maine is changing by the Somali presence. At first we were disappointed because it felt as though we were not reaching community members who held overtly racist views. However, the dialogue following the performance and the number of people who stayed even longer to ask questions revealed that learning was in fact taking place. Moreover, we realized that we were reaching a much broader audience in this format than had we published our research in more academic outlets. Although we cannot measure the actual effect our performance has had on social change, we are convinced that the performance has the potential to open "communicative space"[19] and "awaken moral sensibilities" which may lead to various forms of personal and social change.[20]

It is evident that many of the audience members were moved by the performance and dialogue and that the experience enhanced their compassion and empathy about the plight of refugees, in general, and Somalis in particular. In a socio-political environment where immigration is often discussed in a dehumanizing and disparaging manner, the personal stories of Somalis are at the very least, eye-opening, and at the most, transformative. During the performance, we make efforts to frame and mediate the meaning and significance of the stories within a historical and cultural context. We do this by distributing a handout with an overview of the script and bibliographic sources, by presenting a PowerPoint slide show with documentary photos in the background, and by having a display of books available about Somali history and culture. When responding to questions we strive to highlight the relationship between the stories and the larger structures and conditions that produced the individual stories, which we believe, in turn, promote a deeper understanding of Somalis in Maine: where they come from, why they are here, and what they experience.

Conclusion

Drawing from the work of C. W. Mills and reflecting about the current state of affairs in post 9/11 United States, Norman Denzin argues that "The need for a civic, participatory social science—a critical ethnography that moves back and forth among biography, history, and politics—has never been greater."[21] We agree with this perspective and contend that the readers theater performance is an effective means to achieve a civic, participatory social science that prioritizes democracy, dialogue, and social change. More specifically, the readers theater discussed in this chapter uses performance to address issues of paramount importance in the United States today, issues that tend to be divisive and oversimplified, including race, gender, immigration, and religion. By bridging theory and action, and knowledge and emotion, readers theater has the potential to reach large groups of people and to help foster awareness and understanding about complex social phenomena. The readers theater performance takes the stories of individuals and places them within a broader context with the hope of creating empathy and deepening understanding of controversial issues, such as those emerging from the Somali migration to Maine. Such an approach is a response to the call by scholars "to move beyond the purely representational and toward the presentational."[22] Through performance, readers theater puts culture into motion, creates new spaces for dialogue, and provides opportunities to expand consciousness and even compel people to act.

Memories

Kalteezy Kali

It's 2009: the year of laughter, tears, and memories. The year of pride and independence. The year of my graduation. In less than a month, I will enter the next chapter of my life. This year makes me wonder how I felt leaving my home in Kenya so many years ago. Kenya—memories of this place are engraved into my mind yet are as foggy as the day I left it. Did this really happen?

I was sitting in the dining room doing my American History homework. I blankly stared at the pages filled with facts and wondered if it was really worth reading history instead of being outside and enjoying the sunny day. Days like this were rare during the long Maine spring. The sun was shining beautifully—not a cloud in the sky—and the light was illuminating the window.

"What are you staring at?" I looked over to the person who interrupted my thoughts. It was my older sister Maariyah.

"Nothing. Just wondering how I'll be able to read about President Nixon's Watergate scandal when the weather feels and looks like this." I sighed, and looked down at the pages filled with words.

"Your solution is simple. Close the book, put it in your backpack, and go out. It's that simple. And I thought you were smart." She gave a chuckle and walked away. I looked over to her and saw that she was wearing a *bati,* a Somali dress worn around the house. She had her purse over her shoulders, keys in hand, and black flip-flops on her feet.

"Planning on going somewhere dressed like that?" I said to her back.

"Well, yeah. I'm going to the grocery store. Want to come?" She stopped and turned back around.

"Come with you dressed like that? Girl, you are out of your mind. Put something civilized on. You don't live in Africa anymore." I started laughing. She took a pillow and threw it at me. It went above my head and landed on the other side of the table. I got up and started walking toward her.

Maariyah said, "This is comfortable, my friend. I ain't tryin' to impress no one. And what do you know about Africa? You have no memories. Poor girl." She laughed and walked away.

"What? I have memories. More than you, anyway. Just because you're two years older doesn't necessarily mean you have more memories. And it's 'I'm not trying to impress anyone,'" I called after her.

The door opened and in came my mom. Great. My sister looked at me over her shoulder and smirked.

"Hey, Hoya," Marriyah said. "Your daughter thinks she has memories from Kenya. The only memory she has is of the time when she almost killed me with that rope that sliced my throat. And she only remembers that because I will never let her forget it."

My mom looked at my sister and said, "I'm sure she has memories. She was six. That's old enough to remember things."

I smiled and said, "I remember the morning we were leaving our home in Garissa." I paused. I looked at the window and could see that morning like it was yesterday. Some days I wondered if it was just a dream. A dream that was engraved in my mind. Maybe it was a dream that I cherished because I wanted it to be true. "That morning it was foggy. I was sitting on the ground a few feet outside our home . . ."

Our house was blue and very small. Only one bedroom. It was dawn. Throughout the neighborhood of our little town not far from Nairobi, you could hear the *Aadaan*, a recitation for the morning prayer. "*Allahu Akbar. Allahu Akbar. Allahu Akbar.*" Such a beautiful sound. Although I didn't know what it meant, it was beautiful. It moved me. I could feel the goose bumps on my shoulders and shivered a little. It was not cold. Mornings in Garissa were calm. It was foggy, but the orange-red sky was always there at dawn, rain or shine. I brought my knees to my chest and struggled to tie my shoes. They were pink and flashed when I stepped on them. They were new, and I was so excited to be wearing them. I heard footsteps and glanced up to find my mom walking toward me. She was carrying my six-month-old brother on her back and gracefully walked to me and kneeled down. She took my laces and tied them for me. I was six years old and didn't even know how to tie my shoelaces; most kids my age already knew how to tie their shoes. I was okay though. My mom promised she would teach me very soon.

She stood up, grabbed my hand, and pulled me up, too. She looked at me intently and said in our native Somali tongue, "*Maanto* (today) are you going to leave me?"

I smiled. I grabbed her hands. "Hoya, I'm going to America! America! Can you believe it!"

She smiled a thin smile. "America. Aren't you going to miss me? You're going to leave me?" Her voice cracked and her lips trembled.

"Hoya, don't worry. I'm going to see you soon! You will come to America too. Aren't you excited for me?" Excitement vibrated through my body. My dad came over, kissed my mom, and grabbed my hands. He was awfully quiet. We walked to the van and put our bags in. My older brother Hakeem and sister Maariyah boarded the van with other relatives. My mom came over, kissed us, and with tears running down her face turned around and walked away.

We came to the bus station a few hours later. There, we met the rest of the family. My little sister Aisha was there. Her face was streaked with tears. She was quietly crying and holding my father's hand. We had lunch at a smoothie shop. When a big bus came, we stood and started walking toward it. All of a sudden, there was a shrill, frantic cry. We looked back and saw my little sister on the ground, crying for my dad. He ran back to her and tried to calm her down. People were boarding the bus. My father soothed her with his beautiful words. I stood back and watched.

It wasn't fair. She was supposed to go to America. I looked at her and silently cried for her. Aisha. Sweet Aisha. The youngest girl of the family. My daddy had changed his mind at the last minute to take me instead of my little sister. "You're older. Aisha is too young to go," he had said. I would go to America, a great place. At least that's what they said. People glorified it for us. People made it sound like it was paradise. I knew I was going to America, but I didn't know what it was or why I was going. I knew, but I didn't know.

Now, my dad had Aisha in his lap. He held her until the bus driver impatiently beeped his horn. It was time to go. He slowly handed her to my aunt and kissed her. She saw my dad walking away toward the bus holding my hand with one of his hands while his other hand pressed his knee. My dad had polio and dragged his leg when he walked. Out of nowhere came Aisha again, crying hysterically. She grabbed onto my dad and held on. My dad almost lost his balance. My uncles ran to us and tried to get my sister off my dad's arm. It took three of them to get her off and bring her to my aunt. Aisha sobbed uncontrollably. I went onto the bus, scared to look back. At the very last minute, my father turned around and took a photo of Aisha, her face turned up to the sky, sobbing. Both her arms were held tightly by my aunt and uncle to keep her from running again.

In the airplane, I sat with Maariyah and Hakeem. They were asleep and I was just staring off into space. I didn't know where I was. I was scared. Where was my mom? I started crying and asking for my mom. My grandmother was with us, and she woke up at my crying and came to me. I asked her if I would see my mom tomorrow. She looked at me and whispered, "You will see your mom. You will see her." I suddenly had an urge to use the bathroom and got up and asked to go. A white person escorted me and locked the door behind me.

When I was alone, I pulled my dress up and pulled my underwear down and was going to sit when I caught a glimpse of the toilet. I looked and saw blue water that moved around in it. My eyes widened. Now I was really scared. What if I fell in? What if I fell into the ocean? I pulled my undies up, fixed my dress, and grasped the door handle. It wouldn't twist. I tried again. And again. Nothing happened. I started pounding on the door desperately. Loudly and roughly, I rapped my fist into the door over and over again. It felt like an eternity until the same white guy pushed the door open hard. I was suddenly sobbing. The guy was on his knees asking me questions. I didn't understand him and ran over to my dad, who was making his way down the aisle to me. My sister, brother, grandmother, and cousins had all woken up and looked at me with concern. I sat in my seat between Maariyah and Hakeem and sobbed quietly.

It was March of 1997. It was cold in Lynn, Massachusetts. I felt as though I was watching from a distance. Watching my dad struggle to walk the crowded sidewalks of Lynn. He was holding my hand. I had on a large yellow jacket. I watched from the other side of the street as Hakeem and Maariya held hands and walked in front my grandmother and cousins. It was silent. No one was talking. I would have thought that something was wrong, but it was a peaceful quietness. I don't know why we were walking. I don't know where we were going. I know that this is my first memory of coming to America.

It is six years before I finally see my mother again. She comes into the apartment and sits down on the kitchen chair. She calls me over and I stand between her legs. She just stares. I stare. She starts crying and I just stand there. I am thinking about the dream that I once had about leaving Kenya, when I wore pink shoes that flashed as I walked. A dream that has haunted me for almost a decade. A dream that makes me who I am today. A dream that my mother now tells me wasn't a dream but reality. In 2008 Aisha also came to America, just a summer ago. Who would I be now if my sister had come instead of me? Would I be complaining about reading about Nixon?

PART V

"Don't You Know? I'm Somali!": Somali Voices from Maine

Editors' Note: *Conviviality, friendliness, and generosity characterize Somali culture. Alongside the welcome they extended us as researchers, it is equally important to consider that the Somalis of Maine are often strangers to each other as well as to most Americans. Somalis are both internally diverse among clans, geography, and ethnicity and differentially integrated into American culture and Lewiston neighborhoods.*[1] *As I. M. Lewis describes it, they are simultaneously generous to and suspicious of guests, whether Somali or non-Somali: "They wish to guard the secrets of their culture, and only to share them on their own terms, as they choose."*[2]

The interviews we conducted with Somalis in Maine bear the marks of all cultural crossings—a layered text of saying and not saying, of offerings and of silences, of responsiveness and resistance. We understand these interviews as interpersonal interactions that are warm and immediate but also strategic communication by persons with agency and rhetorical skill (see Langellier, chapter 7, this volume). We took the stories offered by interviewees as a unique gift of the particular interaction and did not press for different items nor for more than was offered, beyond the request for clarifying remarks when we did not understand specific information. The excerpts below are not responses to structured, strict, and systematic questions but rather interesting moments in the currents of conversations dispersed across time and participants. Hence what follows is not comprehensive of all Somalis nor of all Somali culture. Nor does it expose the "hot topics" or exotic interests so often compelled and welcomed by United States mass media, such as clan conflict, female genital mutilation, Islamic intolerance of homosexuality, and the trauma of civil war and refugee camps.

The interview excerpts are drawn from five years of intercultural interactions compiled by the Somali Narrative Project (SNP).[3] *Most interviews were attended by at least one SNP Somali student and one faculty member. The interviews were as varied as the participants. Some interviewees took long narrative turns and spoke with little prompting. Some responded briefly and waited quietly for another question. In some of the interviews conducted in Somali our student members translated on the spot, whereas others were translated into English later, based on the audio record. Some were conducted in the quiet of a university office or a room in a community center, and others were dispersed within the hubbub of infants, children, and adults coming and going in the daily household routine, cell phone conversations, and the ubiquitous TV. Some Somali students knew the interviewees personally, but more often students were themselves meeting new Somalis and learning new immigration stories. Throughout we tried to be mindful that the notion of a scheduled interview or meeting at which one immediately opens up to answer a stranger's questions is a Western cultural form that clashes with the Somali cultural preference for a long period of pleasantries, food, and sweet tea before talk.*

Because the interviews were more like remnants of oral conversation than the whole cloth of individual life histories, we present the stories as collages of voices around common themes that emerged across the varying stories and participants. The excerpts thus create a collective history rather than tell individual stories. Many participants requested anonymity, and we purposely did not solicit identifying information unnecessary to the project. Hence we begin each excerpt with a pseudonym and note in parentheses the interviewee's sex, approximate age, language in which the interview was conducted, and approximate date of arrival in the United States.[4] This tactic preserves anonymity while suggesting a sense of the embodied narrator. At the same time it reminds us that there are diverse voices on a single theme.

The themes themselves follow a broad narrative structure of Somalis moving from their homeland to what "home" means to them now. Excerpts on the journey that brought them to Maine condense memories of Somalia and code the trauma of the civil war and refugee camps. As Somalis come to the United States and become American, they face challenges as their identities change and they change the face of Maine. Their ruminations on the meanings of "home" capture the poignancy of the ongoing diaspora. As the story unfolds, we offer additional Editors' Notes to contextualize themes that may aid the reader in situating their meanings historically and culturally. In these notes, we also provide sources for those who may want to read more on a particular topic.

Our transcriptions of the oral interviews try to retain the sound and "feel" of the storytelling, but we have edited them to promote readability.[5] We gently remind ourselves and readers of how challenging it is to speak and read across cultural and experiential differences. We encourage readers to use the technology of the ear as they engage the story excerpts: "that they must listen body to body, heart to heart, not so much recording as absorbing the other person's story."[6] The Somali story in Maine and the United States is just beginning to be told, and we invite readers to engage the "bits and pieces" of Somali stories by listening hard and by heart to voices that cross continents and chasms of cultural difference. Our hope was to approach interviewees as authors of their own lives and to frame storytelling as a vital history of change for Somalis and for Americans. To hear is to bear witness to the Somali diaspora and to participate in the cultural currents in which all of us mingle and flow.

Somalia Before the Civil War
Faadumo (female, twenties, English, 2003)

My father's mother and his grandma lived with us in a big house, and they used to always say, "Don't go outside. Let me tell you a story." I used to just go outside after school and play with the boys. My grandma didn't like that. She said, "Come, stay at home, let me tell you a story." They used to tell us folk stories, famous folk stories. One of my favorites was about a man whose mother asked him to go to the market and buy some eggs. He put the eggs in his pocket, and when he came home all of the eggs had broken. Then his mom said, "No, you have to put them in a bag." The next day she asked him to buy chicken. He went to the market and bought a live chicken and put it in a bag. By the time he brought it home it was dead. So the mother said, "No, you have to put a rope around it and bring it home." The next day she told him to buy a goat. He went outside, bought a goat, and strangled it dragging it home by a rope. By the end of the story he finally learned how to go to the market and do everything right. It's a good story. I used to like that story.

Cilmi (male, twenties, English, 2006)

What I miss most about Somalia is the air. The air, you know, feels fresh. I miss the kids I used to play with at home, and I also used to go to the coast. I can remember, so I am longing for those things and I wish I could see them again.

Ladan (female, twenties, English, 2004)

We had the time to just talk. As a kid, you would go [to your grandparents' house] and listen to them and get to know who they are, where they are from. They are the ones who actually know a lot, the generations before us. They know how to read poetry, and they remember so much.

Rashid (male, forties, English, 1985)

In Somalia, "family" means not only your brothers and sisters and father and mother—it means everybody that you live with. Sometimes our household would reach twenty people. We had many rooms in our house. We had cousins and other relatives that were related to my mother and my father. Everybody was treated equally. I think it was one of the good things in Somali culture, since we didn't have welfare or social services. In my immediate family, we had my brother and three sisters, my mother and my father, and also we had our cousins, who practically grew up with us. I considered them my sisters, you know. In Somali culture—it's funny, because it's almost like a communal lunch. Many people cooked the food together—mostly females, of course.

Hassan (male, sixties, Somali, 1997)

In Somali culture we respect women and neighbors. If somebody disrespected a woman—your sister, your mother, or your aunt—they had to pay a cow in punishment of what they had done.

Rashid (male, forties, English, 1985)

The Somalia I remember was a beautiful Somalia. Yes, there were tribalism and clanism and favoritism and all of that. But I left Somalia in 1983. When some of my friends tell me about what has happened over there since then, to me it is almost surreal. It is very hard for me to believe.

Many times I have talked to the young Somalis who live in Maine. I invited them to my house one day and I was telling them about Somalia. They asked how I came to the United States. I told them I had a Somali passport, and I had a visa to the United States. They couldn't believe it. They couldn't believe that at one time Somalia was a respected nation and that you could go to one of those embassies located in Mogadishu and apply for a visa. You could get a visa and travel with your Somali passport and people would look at you with respect. I remember coming to Texas as a teenager and going to a driver's license place and putting down a U.S. passport. They said, "No, no. Use the Somali passport." You know, how peaceful it was in those days.

I remember going to high school over there [in Somalia] and walking through school with my friends. I remember going to the movies every Thursday night—because Friday is our day off over there. I remember walking back from the movies at 11:00—sometimes 10:30—all the way back to my home. No one would even look at me. It was just like normal life. We would get up in the morning and go to school. Usually we walked. We had about six classes a day or something like that: Geography, English, Arabic, Islamic Studies, Math, Physics, depending on that year's classes. We came back in the afternoon, ate lunch, took a nap for half an hour or an hour.

Sometimes we preferred to go out and play soccer. At night we studied. And then Thursday night came: movie night. I remember my father giving me money so I could go to the movies with friends. Of course in Somali culture there was no segregation of males and females, and we would go together to the movies.

We had Chinese and Italian restaurants. My very favorite place was this Italian place where we used to eat Italian pastries. I still remember even the case where those items were. At the time I didn't know that cannoli was much better than the ones that we find here [in the United States]. The guy who owned the place was Italian, and he used this beautiful custard in those shells. I can still taste how sweet it was. Just walking through those beautiful avenues and streets, getting those desserts, going to the movies, and going back home at night happy. It was just a wonderful time, a wonderful time.

The Civil War

Galad (male, sixties, Somali/English, 1995)

When the war started I was told that leaving Mogadishu was impossible because there was no shopping, no water—everything was stopping. I sent my wife and daughter to Kismayo, and I remained in Mogadishu hoping that the war would stop. But the war became worse. Then after three weeks I left Mogadishu with friends, from Mogadishu to Kismayo. Even in Kismayo it was difficult, because Kismayo was not a big city. Yet the [entire] population left Mogadishu and went there. [Everyone] had guns; [they were from] different tribes, and they were shooting each other. I left after a few days and went with my family to the city of Madore. Then I went to Kenya.

Faadumo (female, twenties, English, 2003)

In Mogadishu it was weird because my mom would always say, "We have to move," and "We have to get out of here," but it never really happened. Then one day she said, "Go say good-bye to your friends." I just thought she was playing around. I went to my friends and said, "My mom is saying again that we have to move," but I didn't really take it too seriously. I didn't even say good-bye to all of my friends. Then we moved. It took me a long time to realize that we were not going back there.

Ahmed (male, thirties, English, 2000)

The fighting was mainly tribal fighting; two main tribes were fighting in the south. When one tribe was pushed back towards Mogadishu, then the other tribe had a chance to come out, because there is only one main road out of Mogadishu. Everybody was fleeing. Everybody was trying to run because the fighting was getting closer. There was heavy fighting going on, so everybody wanted to leave.

Halima (female, twenties, English, 2001)

I kind of remember the first day when everything started to happen. I remember the day because there were gunshots and machine guns and stuff like that. We didn't go to school. Then my dad found out the government was fighting. Then we moved, and in three days we left Somalia.

Ali (male, seventies, Somali, 1996)

My last day in Somalia was horrible. The militia confiscated everything that I owned. My house, my cars—everything that I had was taken away. So then we left, and my children and my wife and I went to Ethiopia. From there we went to Kenya, where life was kind of hard. We couldn't take it, so my wife took some of the kids and brought them back to Ethiopia. Seven other kids stayed with me. Those are the seven that are with me today.

Ebyan (female, thirties, Somali, 2005)

All of these people are dying, and the people are leaving. My mom [had] never seen dead people, but after a while she got used to it. My sister is older; I'm the youngest. She was about five [or] six years old, but she remembers. So I asked her, "Was it scary?" She said [that] at the beginning it was, but after a couple of days you [got] used to the gunshots and it [became familiar] because you'd been hearing them all day. . . . Dead people were everywhere. You [got] used to people dying in front of you.

Refugee Camps and Other Transitions
Ahmed (male, thirties, English, 2000)

When you come to the refugee camp, they give you a card to get food and other things, a blanket and a place to stay. If you had a family who was living

FIGURE 31. Dadaab refugee camp, Kenya

there before you came and they moved, they would give you their place to stay—you know, a shelter that they built. Luckily, we had family members who moved from the refugee camp to Nairobi, so we took their place. We stayed there about three years. I started learning English there, [in] grade three.

Halima (female, twenties, English, 2001)

Thousands of people ... left Somalia and came to a big lake. The people who live there told the people who came that it [was] not safe because there [were] lions around. These young kids wanted to go there to swim, so we did swim in the daytime. But at night, when we went to sleep, some of the men didn't sleep but stayed awake to protect the families from the lions. You could hear the lions roar.

Ahmed (male, thirties, English, 2000)

My aunt and uncle tried to get us passage to the United States, but we weren't successful. We moved from that camp to another. That's when we filed our own application to [come to] the U.S. You can apply for resettlement; then the United Nations takes a look at your application. If they find out that you don't have a chance to go back to Somalia or you would be killed, then they say, "Okay, this guy has a good argument not to go back to Somalia." Then they look for another place for you to live. We applied, and luckily we were given a chance to have an interview for [resettlment in] the United States, and we were accepted.

Bashir (male, fifties, Somali, 2004)

As a young person, I [had gone] to Italy—so I knew about Italy. When I was looking for a place to migrate to with my family, I was thinking about Italy. But then I learned about the United States and how people are treated in the United States, so I was very excited about coming here. As you know, people here probably have ancestors back somewhere outside of North America. So we thought if we moved to the United States we would fit in the society a lot easier than we would have in Europe. I also thought that as [people who have] parents or ancestors who are immigrants, people in the U.S. would understand my situation. They would understand that it's not good to persecute people. They would understand that people flee to other regions for good reasons. So that's another reason that we were considering the United States.

Ebyan (female, thirties, Somali, 2005)

When the war happened, in late 1991, we moved right away to a city called Beledweyne. I loved Beledweyne. I remember everything there, the way life used to be. In Beledweyne, that's where I learned life.

First of all, the whole country was in chaos, chaos that is still going on today. The reason we moved to Beledweyne from Mogadishu was [that] the situation in Beledweyne was a little bit better. There was peace and prosperity. We had no problems. 'Til the day I left it was a nice place to live. Beledweyne was in a strategic position—it had a connection with the northern part of the country and the western part of the country and the southern part. There was a lot of business going on and so many other things. The peace that was in Beledweyne wasn't a peace that was established by some sort of government or tribal leaders. It was a peace that was born within the people. People that needed peace gathered in that city; everybody was looking for peace, so peace came. Everybody wanted it.

Sahra (female, thirties, Somali/English, 1994)

In Kenya the living conditions were very harsh. We didn't have enough money. We couldn't even go outside and walk around. We were very scared of the police because we didn't have legal status to live there. We were refugees, but we were not recognized immediately. We were not supposed to leave or wander around the city. We were supposed to be in the camps. So it was very difficult to do anything. I did have my first baby there. There were midwives. Some of them didn't even have medical training, but they learned by practicing, helping people out with delivering babies.

Haweeya (female, teenager, English, 1992)

My parents didn't tell us stories 'cause they think I sort of remember, [but I think], "Did this ever happen or was it a dream?" I remember my dad had my brother on his back. I remember, when we were in Kenya, some soldier knocked on our door, and they made us all get out of the house—everyone who lived in the building. The soldiers were on the back of pickup trucks. Then we ended up going to another refugee camp, and we set up tents. I remember we met another family there, and we would get in line to get food.

Editors' Note: *Each year millions of people are displaced from their home countries and seek refuge in other nations throughout the world. According to the United Nations High Commissioner for Refugees (UNHCR), the global refugee population swelled to more than eleven million in 2007. The UNHCR encourages refugees to return to their homeland once conditions improve (voluntary repatriation) or to integrate into their host society (referred to as the country of first asylum). When these first two options are not feasible, the UNHCR encourages refugees to seek resettlement in a third country. The overwhelming majority of refugees remain within their region of origin while only a small fraction of refugees (1 percent) are resettled in one of the fourteen countries around the world that have resettlement programs.[7] According to the UNHCR, in 2007, 75,300 refugees were admitted to the fourteen resettlement countries, of which over half—48,300—were settled in the United States.*

In the United States, the majority of those seeking refuge from fear and persecution enter as government-sponsored refugees, and a minority are granted asylum after arriving in the United States.[8] Although only one in ten immigrants entering the United States annually are refugees, it is estimated that more than two million refugees have resettled in the United States since the passage of the Refugee Act of 1980 and that refugees and asylees comprise about 7 percent of all foreign-born persons living in the United States today.[9]

Between 2004 and 2007, most refugees in the United States came from Africa, with Somalis outnumbering all other African refugees.[10] In line with the federal government's policy of dispersion, these Somali refugees were resettled in forty-three states and the District of Columbia, with the largest number being settled in the metropolitan area of Minneapolis-St. Paul. A small fraction of the Somali refugees were resettled in Maine; yet, many more Somali refugees chose to leave their initial places of resettlement and move to Maine (see Huisman, chapter 2, this volume).

Immigration is a profoundly transformative process that alters landscapes and its inhabitants—both natives and newcomers—in complex, nuanced ways. Over time, many immigrants come to identify with their homeland and their adopted land, but in varying degrees. Some choose to resist the forces of assimilation and hold tight to their culture of origin while others readily adopt the ways of their new home.

Some immigrants see themselves as occupying a painful, liminal space in their adopted country where their identity is fractured and they don't feel anchored in their home culture or their adopted land. Others maintain ties to both cultures but are able to seamlessly move back and forth between them. Invariably, as their lives change over time, many immigrants move toward viewing themselves in a hyphenated way, as in the case of some Somali Americans. Yet, what does it mean to "become" Somali American? Is becoming Somali American an endpoint or a continually changing journey? And furthermore, what is an American in this increasingly diverse country?

There are no simple answers to these questions because the degree to which someone changes varies by a multitude of factors including time period, geographic location, and the background and characteristics of the people involved. At one time in United States history, newcomers were expected to shed their previous selves and fully embrace the culture of their new country. Those unwilling to do so were subject to harsh discrimination.

Today, there is more acceptance and awareness about the multiplicity of identities, yet discrimination toward newcomers still persists. In any case, "becoming" something is a complicated process that involves external and internal forces coming into contact with one another. Upon arrival, labels are imposed on newcomers by others. Few Somalis identify as "black" prior to coming to the United States, but through repeated experiences of being categorized as such, growing numbers may come to accept this categorization. At the same time, newcomers bring with them their own group identification and may resist categorization by others that does not mesh with their own group identity.[11]

As the following sections illustrate, for many Somalis, becoming American is also about staying Somali. Hyphenated identities are about both/and rather than either/or, and *becoming is an ongoing process of continuity and change, accommodation and resistance, gains and losses. The stories in these sections offer rich insights into how becoming American is not linear but is wrought with complexities, tensions, uncertainties, contradictions, hope, and fear. The stories are as much about struggle as they are about triumph. The voices that follow illuminate the "the millions of details of daily life that are the true separators between cultures,"[12] details that a native-born person tends to take for granted. As one Somali person put it, coming to the United States was "like being blind in the wilderness."*

Coming to the United States
Rashid (male, forties, English, 1985)

I remember my father giving me some advice. I remember going through what they call the check area. I remember boarding the plane. I [even] remember the seating: I was in the middle seat, and there were two guys sitting next to me. As soon as the plane started to fly they both started drinking alcohol. That was the first time I ever saw anybody drinking alcohol. I remembered the cowboy movies I used to watch, where cowboys got drunk and hit each other. The whole night I didn't sleep—I was watching out for myself. I thought, "Man, they are going to hit me." So the whole night I didn't sleep.

I remember taking the flight from New York and going to Dallas. A beautiful blonde woman in a tank top sat next to me. Here I am, a poor African guy that was in Saudi Arabia for a year and a half. I had never seen anything like this woman sitting next to me. I hadn't slept the night before, so I thought, "Am I dreaming? Is this a reality? Is this a joke?" I took naps in short fragments. It was the strangest feeling. It was almost surreal.

At McDonalds I remember looking for a place to wash my hands and I couldn't find it. Then I saw something that looked like a faucet and thought, "That must be it." I went over and pushed that thing—and ketchup came out! I remember hastily closing my hand and getting out of the restaurant before anybody could see me. When you come to a different culture you become almost paranoid at the beginning, because you think everyone is paying attention.

Hassan (male, sixties, Somali, 1997)

We left Kenya and moved to the United States with my children [on] March 25, 1997. We arrived in Massachusetts, specifically the greater Boston area. At that time we didn't really have any language skills; it was very difficult in the first few weeks, at least. You can imagine living in a place where you don't know the language people speak, the culture, or any of these things. It was very difficult, like being blind in the wilderness.

Sufia (female, forties, Somali, 1992)

At first, when we came, the U.S. government gave us $350. That $350 was only enough for the rent, and I had three children. My brother used to help us with other expenses—for example, paying for the telephone bill and shopping and things like that.

Haweeya (female, teenager, English, 1992)

After we came from New York we lived in Atlanta. We went to my uncle's house, where he had lived since the 1970s. I remember coming to his house ... the family was greeting us, and there was a TV. I had never seen a TV before ... and I got so scared. My little cousin [held] my hand and touched the TV. I [was thinking], "How is he doing that?" When my brother started preschool, I remember he was given a doll, and she had no headscarf on. He told the preschool teacher, "This grown woman is giving me a naked doll." He considered not having a headscarf [to be] naked. And he told my mom he didn't want to go back to preschool, so my mom kept him home. He ended up not going to preschool because this doll didn't have a headscarf on.

Ebyan (female, thirties, Somali, 2005)

We first came to New York and then ... to Hartford, Connecticut.... A Somali lady ... took us to the apartment that was arranged for us to live in. It was late at night. The kids were tired, and we were tired, so we just slept. There was no hot water or anything like that so we couldn't take showers and we slept. In the morning the same Somali lady came and brought us breakfast.

The place [where] we were living was [in] a bad neighborhood, [with] violence, drugs, [and] cops coming every day and arresting people right in front of our door. It was no place that we could live. Then my father and my brother and cousin came from Maine. They saw the situation in the neighborhood and how bad it was. They told us, "You cannot live here; you should come with us to Maine." That was why we stayed there for only two weeks.

Group interview (three males)

I got lost three times in Georgia. I took the train to find a job and I didn't know how to come back. I didn't know where my house was located. And I called the case manager: "I am in the bus station." "Which bus station are you in?" "I don't know." One day they called 911 and the police brought me home. Now we are in Lewiston, which is a small city. We can go from our house for food by walking or just riding a bike. We have a lot of people [around us] who are Somali, and we can help each other succeed and improve our English.

Finding Refuge in Maine

Galad (male, sixties, Somali/English, 1995)

Here in Maine, some things remind me of Somalia. For example, when I go outside of the city and see the green trees, I remember ... going out of the Somali cities and into the bush. And this street, Lisbon Street, in downtown [Lewiston], reminds me of a street in Mogadishu. Any time I pass that street, I remember.

Hassan (male, sixties, Somali, 1997)

I thought that my kids could only benefit from education, because I didn't have a lot of money. I wasn't able to work at that time, so I really thought about the only thing they could inherit from me [would be] my help in getting them educated. I didn't think they were getting the education that I envisioned for them in Massachusetts, at least not where we lived. So I traveled to Portland, Maine, and I looked into the education system there. People told me great things about Maine and about its education system. That's what prompted us to move to Maine—I was thinking about the education of my children. I also thought Maine was very safe. I looked at the kids playing outside in the playground without fear, and I thought this would really be a good place to raise kids.

FIGURE 32. Somali store on Lisbon Street (Lewiston, Maine)

Hassan (male, sixties, Somali, 1997)

I think the simple thing is to be nice to people and try to keep a positive attitude. There is a Somali saying that goes like this: "If a snake lives in a certain type of soil, it takes the color of that soil." And that means when you go to a different place, try to adjust to living there. While you're preserving your own culture, try to also make an effort to adjust and integrate into that society and be a productive member of that society. That's how you can easily make a transition from one place to another.

Faiza (female, fifties, Somali/English, before 1986)

I was laid off from my job in Atlanta, Georgia, and during that time I knew some families that moved to Maine from Georgia. I called and asked them about the situation in Maine. You can find jobs here, they said, and the school system was better here as well. People also told us that Maine was family-friendly and not as wild and as crazy as Georgia. When we moved to Maine, the biggest challenge we had was the housing situation. There were very old apartments that we first came to, and we were really disappointed because we came from a big city and housing was not that bad. But after a while we moved to a better apartment. Overall, people were friendly, but as you know there's no place where people will welcome you 100 percent. Even now there are people who shout at us when we are walking around or swear at us. It's understandable that some people will not be comfortable with us moving here. We expected something like that to happen. We learned to live with knowing that some people would be nice, [and] some people wouldn't be so nice.

Group interview (three young women)

We moved here because of safety. The environment we had lived in was pretty hard, and we had relatives here. My dad said that since we had no relatives in New York, we should move here, where there is more of our family.

Halima (female, twenties, English, 2001)

When I came [to school] I went to the guidance counselor's office. After I registered she showed me the list of classes that juniors [were taking] that year. She asked me what classes I wanted to take, so I chose the classes I wanted to take. She asked, "Are you sure you can handle it?" I said, "I think so." I took English 11, Algebra II, Anatomy, Physiology, and Sociology.

Bashir (male, fifties, Somali, 2004)

I tell my children that education is education. I explain that whether you learn something in the United States or in Europe or in Somalia, it's the same. For example, four times four is equal to sixteen whether you study math in America or elsewhere. I tell them everything will be useful. No matter where you learn, make sure you do well. That's how I encourage people, and that's how I encourage my own kids.

Sahra (female, thirties, Somali/English, 1994)

The school system is generally good. My kids have very good teachers and we're very happy with them. I also get good feedback from the teachers. They tell me that my children are doing a good job; they don't get into trouble; their progress is moving [well], so we are very grateful for that.

Group interview (three young women)

I don't really know why my mom came here. There is nothing appealing about this place, but they always speak of safety and stuff. But there are no jobs here, and it just doesn't make sense. I know she didn't come here because of Somali people, because there was a large Somali community where I was living. Maybe it was because she knew women from Maine through weddings and stuff. My mom knew other moms from here; maybe they told her it was a good place or something.

Rashid (male, forties, English, 1985)

Going to my first school, I remember taking the intensive English program with many classmates from all over the world. I remember the first experience I had with somebody who didn't believe in God. He ... was from Italy, and we were talking about religion and culture. He said he didn't believe [in] God, and I almost ran out of the class! I was in shock. And I remember my teacher at the time ... talking about his girlfriend—and he was like sixty years old. I remember saying, "Wow! So you can have a girlfriend when you are sixty years old!" Because in my culture, girlfriends are for young people—and you hide it. But this guy, he was so proud, talking about his girlfriend.

Bashir (male, fifties, Somali, 2004)

My perception of Lewiston was not very good before we came here. We were watching the event that took place in 2002 in Lewiston that highlighted the discrimination against Somali refugees. When we actually decided to move to Lewiston, we were very careful; we were really scared. But things were not as we thought. [People here] were very nice. [Bad] things happened, yes, but not nearly as much as the media was saying. Actually, I was pleased with the response that we got from other members of the community, the Jewish community and the Christians. They all rallied to our support. Recently, somebody threw a frozen pig head into the mosque while people were praying. We actually found a lot of people helping us, taking part in our outrage. The community in general, whether they are Muslims or non-Muslims, acted positively and showed solidarity in support for us. Everyone from the mayor to the governor—they all came to our support, and they all showed respect for our culture and for our religion.

Ali (male, seventies, Somali, 1996)

When we came to the United States, we were astonished at some of the things we saw. We cannot believe that we live in this place right now. I mean, the snow is something that I never thought I would be living with. The snow and the cold are something. And I'm still wondering, "Is it true that this is happening?" But in general, in the United States I found peace. I was safe. So I like it—other than the snow and cold!

Ahmed (male, thirties, English, 2000)

There are still some bad people over here who think Somalis live out of the taxes paid by the American people. I was working in this company in Brunswick, and one day this guy said, "Somalis come over here and live on our taxes." I told him [that on] the first day [I got a job], I started paying [taxes] like everybody else. He thought the only time we [had to] pay taxes was when we got our citizenship.

Bashir (male, fifties, Somali, 2004)

When we arrived in Maine we didn't really have that many problems. I had lived in Europe when I was younger, so I knew the Western lifestyle. And my kids went to English school in Kenya, so they helped me with translation, filling out forms, and all kinds of things like that. It was relatively easy for us to adjust to living in Maine.

Galad (male, sixties, Somali/English, 1995)

I worked in Lewiston High School for one year as a volunteer. After that year they gave me five hours a day, twenty-five hours a week, helping the international students in mathematics—some Somalis, some from other parts of Africa, and from China. Then after two years I went to the community college. With my degree and references, I was able to tutor. I tutored mathematics, algebra, pre-calculus, and calculus. Now I teach college algebra. I work five hours a week, but at least I am teaching. I know many people who are lawyers but don't have the opportunity to work [in their profession]. They work in Walmart or something like that. I know a doctor in medicine, but he [does not work as a doctor]. I am happy because I was a teacher, and here I am still teaching.

Group interview (three males)

It is very hard to get a job in this country if you don't have enough education and if you don't know how to speak the language. [English] is not our language, and it is very hard to understand. If you are young, you can go to school and it is easy to learn. But once you become an adult it is very hard to learn, because you have family and kids.

Group interview (three males)

In Lewiston, it is very hard for refugee migrants to find work, especially for Somalis.... We have some schools to go to, to improve our English, but it is very hard to work in Lewiston. When I first came to Lewiston I tried to get a job. One day I applied for twenty jobs at different companies. No one called me. But I think it is good to come here to go to school and learn some English, then move out to find a good place to work.

Bashir (male, fifties, Somali, 2004)

One of the things that we are currently responding to is the fact that the lunch menus in schools do not really abide by or help the students identify their *halal* [options], which is like the kosher diet. We want to make sure that the school workers understand that we have a different culture, we have a different religion, and there are certain foods we cannot eat. And young children ... cannot identify these [foods] on their own. We want to collaborate with school officials and let them know that parents have concerns regarding the food that is provided in the schools. Also, the Muslim prayer times are to be followed in a timely fashion. We want to make sure that schools understand that if students want to pray they should have a space or at least time to do that. So we are working on that as well. We are working with the high schools and middle schools.

Sahra (female, thirties, Somali/English, 1994)

In Atlanta, there was nobody that would help you out with the children or anything like that. There's also more networking and cooperation between Somali parents in Maine than there was in Georgia. If your kid, for example, is running down the street without anybody supervising [him or her], your neighbor might call you and let you know that your child is out there without anybody. So here things are possible because of the tight-knit community.

Hassan (male, sixties, Somali, 1997)

I would like to see Somalis in the school system, in the government, anything. I would like to see more Somalis enter those fields as professionals. Until we have a viable number or critical mass in those fields, we will have to rely on other people who are interested in Somalis, who want to know more about Somalis, who are sensitive, who are educating themselves about Somalis.

Haweeya (female, teenager, English, 1992)

Me, my friend, and her brother were the only Somali kids—the only black kids—in Lewiston Middle School, which was kind of weird. . . . I was expecting the worst, but as soon as I got on the [school] bus they were . . . so friendly. Then I went to school and everyone [was] like, "Hi. Sit with me." If I was lost in the hallway, people would help me out. It was really friendly when I first came.

Farham (male, fifties, English)

I didn't leave Maine forever. I left because I have a business in Arizona, but one leg of mine is still in Maine. I like Maine. It was the first place that gave me a good opportunity to be where I am today. I have to pay that back and will return to Maine. I will never forget the gratitude I have for Maine. Maine is the best place for the new immigrant compared to the rest of the United States of America. It's a small place. Most Somalis say this is the best place. Somalis say the water is very sweet in Maine; once you taste it, you'll lever leave. When I talk to people in Maine, they say, "Farham, you will be back one day."

Editors' Note: *What does it mean to be Somali and American? What forms identity is something like what is formed when one makes bread from flour, water, shortening or butter, a little sugar, a dash of salt, and any other ingredients that confer its unique flavor and texture. The bread made from a particular combination of ingredients, whether leavened or not, is something more than any one of its ingredients. And too, bread is only bread when the ingredients are so fused that they cannot be separated out again. Likewise with identity: We cannot understand it by focusing on only one of its facets; and we cannot separate out one facet from the others because they are interlocked. Facets such as gender, race, religion, language, and citizenship infuse the whole, and the infused whole becomes something different when parts are left out, forgotten, or unnamed.*[13] *Like a recipe, the list* of ingredients for being Somali is not the identity itself; however, the ordering of its elements can suggest some of the ways in which Somalis communicate who they are in the U.S. context.

Somalis in the diaspora retain a strong sense of ethnic pride called soomaalinimo.[14] This pride in Somali cultural authenticity is challenged in the diaspora: by the ravages of the continuing civil war; at the interface of Somali cultural norms with those of the global north and west; and in the displacements of their migration into new worlds, including their unlikely settlement in Maine. Likewise, living in the diaspora is altering the traditional foundations of Somali identity in clan differences.[15] Reciting one's genealogy operates as an "ID card" for Somalis, counting back generations to a founding ancestor that connects clan and kin. Clan divisions and divisiveness are also recited by Western media to explain the civil war as among tribal warlords.

For many Somalis, culture and religion are one: Somalis had converted en masse to Islam by AD 900, and nearly all identify as Muslim. Being Muslim transcends clan, kin, and country (Somalia, Ethiopia, Kenya, Djibouti) divisions, providing the most singular and stable source of strength and public identity for Somalis in the United States. Although we present a discrete set of excerpts that talk about Islam below, we more often had the sense that this facet is so infused in Somali identity that it is not marked as distinct. In that sense, when one is reading any of the excerpts, the current of Islam always flows beneath the talk. Beyond that suffusing quality, however, are many differentiations and nuances about how Somalis in the diaspora and Maine practice Islam. Some, for example, distinguish carefully between Somali culture and Islamic religion, particularly with regard to issues of gender.

As Caaliya's narrative of identity suggests, how Somalis are constructing and reconstructing the meanings and relations around gender is complex, multilayered, and varied. Gender issues pervade every aspect of traditional Somali life, the refugee experience, and the challenges of living in the diaspora—family and kin, education, work, religion, and more—whether or not they are specifically discussed in the selected excerpts. In traditional Somali culture, for example, men interact more in public spaces than do women; heritage is patrilineal; and kinship structures are patriarchal, including arranged marriages, polygamy, and the practice of female genital mutilation.[16] These patriarchal practices, coupled with the Western tendency to equate Islam with women's oppression, mark one arena of contested meanings as gender identity is negotiated in the spaces between traditional practices and Western feminisms.[17]

Family, understood within the structures of clan and kinship, is supremely important to Somalis. In the transition from Somalia, many women have entered the job market to support families, negotiating the daily challenges of getting housing, food, transportation, health care, and schooling in an environment where their language, religion, and culture differ from the mainstream (see Hough and Toner, chapter 8, this volume). Somali girls are responsible for care of the extended family. Girls may drop out of school due to the conflicting pressures of the Somali and American culture and turn to marriage as a solution. Wearing traditional Muslim dress makes girls and women highly visible in schools, on the streets of Lewiston, and in jobs in Maine. Somali boys' dress, however, frequently mirrors current Western youth fashion, such as hip-hop: dress that does not readily distinguish them from their American peers, black or white. Although Somalis do not consider themselves black, their bodies are racialized against hegemonic whiteness and African American history and popular culture.[18] Parental concerns for their children in the diaspora reflect the inextricable ingredients of identity as language, religion, gender, and race. Fears for sons that helped propel Somalis from larger urban areas in the United States to more rural Maine focus on gangs, drugs, and alcohol. Fears for daughters center more on their sexuality, dress, and dating. Fears for both boys and girls are fueled by the allures of American popular culture.

Family and Cultural Traditions
Rashid (male, forties, English, 1985)

As Somalis, we are basically nomads; that is in our blood. From a young age we are brought up to believe this world belongs to God. We are all children of Adam and Eve, and this land is for us. This is our mentality. Even if we don't [consciously] think like that, subconsciously that's how we think. And that's why we see so many Somali people going all over the place.

Ladan (female, twenties, English, 2004)

Most of our relatives were nomadic; when they came to us, to our house, we gave them food. Hospitality in Somalia was different. We liked to receive guests. We felt happy to have helped so many people we know.

Ebyan (female, thirties, Somali, 2005)

What I miss most about Somalia is that the time there was blessed. It just seems like the time here is so quick and the day goes by so quickly. In Somalia, I mean, you used to wake in the morning, go to school, eat lunch, and after a while you would go to sleep, take a nap, go to the market, buy stuff, visit families, visit people, come back. The day used to be long over there; here the day is just short.

Ladan (female, twenties, English, 2004)

[I worry about the loss of culture] especially for the youth. I would recommend [that] they go back and find out their history—their family history, their culture, the people and the food and everything—because I don't think there is time for that here. You get so busy with daily life. When we were back home, people would just sit down together and eat together and share a meal. There was no TV, there was no distraction. We would talk [for] hours and hours.... people were much closer there. Now everybody is scattered all around the globe. You know you don't have your family with you, so you just forget about everything.

Rashid (male, forties, English, 1985)

I have cousins who speak Chinese. I have cousins who speak Dutch. I have cousins who live in Australia, and, of course, they speak English. I have cousins who live in Saudi Arabia who speak fluent Arabic. But from people who have gone back to Northern Somalia for vacations, I [have] heard about cousins who did not understand each other because they all came from different cultures.

Faiza (female, fifties, Somali/English, before 1986)

My kids can understand Somali, but they have a hard time responding to it. They cannot speak that well. For the most part, I speak to them in Somali, and they understand everything I tell them. But they just cannot reply in Somali. That's the challenge. The reason for this is that I used to work twelve-hour shifts when I was in Atlanta, and that situation was difficult. [Everything else] around them was having a major influence on them, so their language acquisition was very low. We used to live in a secluded area, but now we live among Somali families. I think [that] now their Somali language is improving, gradually, and they are getting better because they have other people to speak with besides me. That's how they're picking up their language.

Faadumo (female, twenties, English, 2003)

When we moved here my parents tried to learn English. They used to talk to us in English, because we went to school and learned English [quickly]. Every time they tried to apply for jobs, the interviewers said, "Your English is bad; we can't talk to you." My parents tried to talk to us in English so they could improve their English. Sometimes now they speak Somali, but my brothers and sisters are so used to talking to each other in English that sometimes we talk to our parents in English and they respond in Somali, and then we respond in English.

Hassan (male, sixties, Somali, 1997)

I also want to stress the importance of the Somali language, because we cannot rely on our children learning [this] language on their own. For example, they [speak English at] school most of the day, and [when] they come back home maybe their parents don't speak English that well. There is a problem. There is miscommunication between the children and their parents, because the kids are growing up here and the parents grew up back home. Unless there is a collective effort among the community to address this issue, it will remain problematic.

Galad (male, sixties, Somali/English, 1995)

An African American was talking to me, and he said his biggest problem is that he knows he is from Africa, but he doesn't know which part of Africa. I told him that I can count all my ancestors' names, in Somali, up to thirty. I asked, "Do you know the name of your grand-grand-grand-grandfather?" I said if he told me that name, then maybe I would know which part of Africa he came from. He didn't know, because his name is a Christian name, a Western name. So I tell my sons every day they have to know their relatives ... and that they are from a great country with a great culture, even if we have civil war. I would like them to know Somali culture, Somali history ... and where they come from.

Ali (male, seventies, Somali, 1996)

There are a lot of things to miss about Somalia, such as going to the mosque, people reading the Qur'an, and just feeling the environment of the Islamic place. I also miss the food. I mean the meat we have here, we never know when it was slaughtered. It's just frozen meat. We don't know where it came from or how long it was there. In Somalia we used to get the fresh meat that had just been slaughtered right in front of you; or you see the blood, which indicates the meat was fresh. We used to have fresh milk, too, not just milk in gallons in the fridge. Over there milk came right from the cow every morning.

Idil (female, twenties, English, 2000)

Somali parents have power over their children, and I don't see that as a bad thing. Families' regulations vary. Like in my family, my dad is not strict at all, but my mother is more strict than my dad. Growing up, I was more afraid of my mother than I was of my father, but it's the other way around in some families.

Ebyan (female, thirties, Somali, 2005)

Raising children is really hard in this country ... you need to put in a lot of effort and work. ... It wasn't like that in Somalia. When they are at home, their [only] example is me, so I have to practice my culture and religion in order for them to imitate me and act like me. I have to start with myself first. When they go to schools and see something strange, they always come and ask me, "What is that?" Basically, I tell them what is right and what is wrong. If it is right, they do it. If it is wrong, they stay away from it.

When you come to the United States, your kids have more rights, and they demand a lot from you. When you are in Africa, the kids are basically living in the environment you want them to live in, the environment you think is good for them. You don't want them to mix with the native people that are here.

Group interview (three males)

They tell us, "If you want to have babies in the future, we can give you a house." But because I am young, I want to make a baby every single year. They say, "No," because that's not the culture here. In our culture, you have to make babies until you become sixty. But in America you have to have two children and one dog. There's a big difference in culture. They say, "We will give you this apartment, but you have to keep to eight people. No more children." But we have to proceed from our culture—we have to keep our culture—so we have to stay separate, me and my wife, otherwise we would make a baby as soon as we can.

Haweeya (female, teenager, English, 1992)

Our generation gets criticized a lot because we don't know as much as we should. My uncle called me the other day and [asked], "Do you know who I am?" I told him, "No," because I didn't. Nobody told me. If you don't tell me, I am not going to go look for it. He was my dad's first cousin. My mom was like, "Kids who grow up here have no clue of what's going on." I would have known if they had said, "There's this uncle, there's that uncle."

Somali kids grow up faster than kids here. When you bring a kid [here] from Somalia, the way he acts and talks is a lot smarter than a regular American because he has been expected to grow up faster.... From a young age [kids in Somalia] have responsibilities, so they carry themselves as adults. My cousin, who is with us here now, brought her five boys to Africa, and they stayed there for two years. My brother went to their house and he started speaking English. "Why is this grown man speaking English?" they asked. "He has no shame." He was sixteen at the time and they said, "You're an old man. What are you playing games for?" The kids carry themselves as adults.

Galad (male, sixties, Somali/English, 1995)

In Somalia the parents had the power, full power. Maybe there was a television, but only one channel. Here it is different, [with many] channels [available] twenty-four hours. I don't even know our children. They don't want to learn their culture; they are not interested. Maybe when they grow up. When I say to my son, "You are from Africa," he says, "No, I am not from Africa. I am from Georgia." He thinks in English, and he can't speak the Somali language.

Sahra (female, thirties, Somali/English, 1994)

When my kids watch the History Channel or the Discovery Channel about Africa or [when they see] what sometimes people portray in the media here, [it seems as if] Africa is a place where animals walk around—wild animals, lions and giraffes and all of those things. Sometime they are scared, and I tell them that's not how it is there. I tell them these are not realistic videos, they are just intended for safari purposes or for media promotions [and are] not necessarily real life, what we grew up with.

Haweeya (female, teenager, English, 1992)

Adults are afraid that when they die we won't be able to teach our children anything, that we'll forget. My mom was saying the other day that people who come here know the many generations that lived before them. And then their children just adapt to the American culture. They end up being Americans, and the generations are lost. But if you're in Africa, you carry your parents' memory. My mom knows information about her great-great-great grandparents. [She knows] who they are, and [her] family expects that. But she's afraid if we live here long enough we'll just forget about them.

Religious and Ethnic Identity

Halima (female, twenties, English, 2001)

I love being Somali, and I never regret it or ask myself, "Why was I born Somali?" or "Why am I Somali?" or anything like that. I like being Somali.

Rashid (male, forties, English, 1985)

Somali people live in Somalia and Djibouti, Ethiopia, and Kenya. At one time there was something called Somali nationalism and identity. I don't think this exists anymore, at least not for me. Basically, when I see a Somali person I see somebody who maybe has a language and a culture and a religion, but I don't identify myself anymore with Somali nationalism or country or anything like that. If I go to my father and he says, "Are you proud to be Somali?" I would say, "No." I'm proud, of course, to be Muslim. I'm proud to be a human being. But Somalis and what they did to one another—what they are still doing to one another—how they divide themselves into groups and clans and don't learn from their past mistakes: that is not something to be proud of.

Faadumo (female, twenties, English, 2003)

Being Muslim and being Somali are two different things. A lot of people associate them together. They think, "All good Somali people do this or don't do that." I was born in Somalia, I have seen how it is. I have seen the land. I have experienced it. I have experienced the war. I have seen everything. I mean, *I'm Somali,* you know?

Ali (male, seventies, Somali, 1996)

Culture is something that people . . . did over time, and they just got used to it. They do it [over and over] until it becomes normal in their life. . . . There is a saying in Somali that says, "Quitting the tradition makes Allah mad." But that's absolutely false, because what makes Allah mad is disobeying him by [practicing] other religions. Culture is just something people came up with, and it became the tradition to do it.

Caaliya (female, twenties, English, 2004)

A lot of Somalis tend to be cultural Muslims. Some of the things that Somalis tend to think are Islamic are actually just their own cultural manifestations or a distortion of the religion. For me the two identities are very separate. I'm proud to be a Muslim and I'm proud to be a Somali. But I have found that I don't want to be a cultural Muslim, because as I am becoming educated I would like . . . to be an educated consumer of whatever I believe. My Somali identity was something that was drilled into me, and I like the sense of comfort it gives me. I don't have to wonder where I'm from. My Islamic identity is something I had to learn—I had to relearn it, actually, because some of the things I thought were Islamic were [really] culture, and at times they're at odds. I try to have clear ideas of what is culture and what is religion.

Hassan (male, sixties, Somali, 1997)

I also believe in the freedom of religion. If people want to choose whatever religion or ideology they want to choose, that's their business. We should respect people's choices and also understand that people are different. We don't force people into our religion. I know that Christianity and other religions feel the same way . . . I don't really see a conflict coming from religion or different civilizations. But people misunderstand the texts or [are misled by] other things—and that's a problem. I have lived with people who are different [from me] for a long time. I remember I saw British [people] and Americans before I even came to the United States. I never saw people having problems with [those] who have different religions. But recently the world has changed, and all of a sudden you see people fighting, and allegedly people are fighting based on religion.

FIGURE 33. The Qur'an

Ladan (female, twenties, English, 2004)

We go to the mosque a lot. It's the only special place where we can be and meet other people.

Group interview (three females, two males)

One of the first things my parents were looking for [when visiting the University of Maine] was the mosque, so we went to the mosque even though it was closed. We stood in front looking in. They were happy.

Bashir (male, fifties, Somali, 2004)

When we moved to the United States things changed for the better. But as far as educating the kids, we always emphasized religious education. We thought everything else would come after, would take the back seat. We thought that if they had a good grasp of their religion, then that would be a good start for them to continue to learn other things.

Mariam (female, twenties, English, 1991)

If I had a choice, I wouldn't want to raise my kids in the United States, but that is something that I probably [can't] change. But my mom, you know, she made the best of it. She takes the kids to *dugsi*. She keeps them in line with religion.

Faiza (female, fifties, Somali/English, before 1986)

[For Ramadan] we cooked a lot of meat, a lot of lamb—a lot of different kinds of food. There were times of food and celebration and families coming together. Even men cooked sometimes, especially the meat. It's different here than [in] Somalia, because back home people would all break the fast together, because they finished work earlier. But here, sometimes some members of the family are working late or [have] gone to school or whatever, so you would have people breaking the fast on their own [and] not together.

Hassan (male, sixties, Somali, 1997)

Before you finish my interview I want to make sure that I raise a point that I feel is important. As you know, in the past there have been religious wars and civil wars. With increasing globalization, people are really interdependent upon each other ... we shouldn't relapse to a state of war. I tell my kids that it doesn't matter what peoples' religions or differences are—you can always reconcile with them, and you can always live with them peacefully side by side.

FIGURE 34. Islamic Center of Maine (Orono, Maine)

Sahra (female, thirties, Somali/English, 1994)

Being a Muslim is universal. Anybody could be a Muslim. But being Somali is just ethnicity, something that you are born into.

Gender Identity

Ladan (female, twenties, English, 2004)

The gender roles back in Africa are mostly women doing the cooking and cleaning and the men going out and working to bring in the money. It's just how it is. When you come here you know things are going to be equal. Everybody goes to work and then shares the work at home. My husband and I both work so, you know, you have to give me a day off, too. So he will cook and do the dishes and all the housework. We do share the work here. After the war some of the men would have to cook—maybe they were on their own, or they didn't have their family, or they didn't have their mom or sisters. It's a struggle for them if they don't know how to cook or how to iron their shirts. I think it's very important that everybody knows how to do these things.

Omar (male, thirties, English, 1999)

The naming ceremony is just a bit gender biased, too. If it's a male, they slaughter a goat. I don't know how many people remember this now. If a male is born to the family, the announcement is made by the attendant, who is usually female. She says, "A boy has been born." Then they go into celebration, "Lulululu!" But they don't do that if it's a girl—which is how social construction starts, very early.

Haweeya (female, teenager, English, 1992)

You can't get rid of whatever used to be there before the religion was there. Take circumcision, for example, which was in East Africa way before Islam got to East Africa or North Africa. For women, that is, not for men. They used to do it during the pharaoh's time, and that was way before the prophet Mohamed (Peace Be Upon Him). It's still done today by a lot of Eastern Africans, people in Kenya, etc. Circumcision was good for the men's health. That's why they started doing it. The religion directs Muslims to circumcise their sons. So when they started doing it, during the prophet's time, they said the girls got jealous. I guess the prophet said, "Okay. Don't do too much. Just show them their blood if they want this." The whole extreme mutilation had been happening way before the religion, and some people kept doing it. Somalis would say, "It's good for the women," you know what I mean. And some people would say, "It's in the religion," and yet, you can't find it anywhere in the Qur'an. Just once the prophet said, "Just show her the blood, but it's not mandatory." That's one of the traditions that just kind of crept into the religion.

Rashid (male, forties, English, 1985)

In Somali culture having a baby out of wedlock means basically you destroy your life.

Haweeya (female, teenager, English, 1992)

Dating, religiously, is not allowed. If [two people] were to date, they are supposed to be getting married soon, and their father would be there between them, monitoring. Somebody has to be there, whether it's your little brother or somebody [else]. And the girl has to be fully covered.

Haweeya (female, teenager, English, 1992)

I've also noticed people [in Somalia] don't practice their religion as well as they do after they leave Somalia. When my mom was younger she wouldn't wear a headscarf, but now she does. She [knows] the Qur'an, but generally boys studied the Qur'an more than girls when she was younger. But then, with our generation, even if we lived in Somalia now we would study the Qur'an. Back then it wasn't necessary for girls to learn.

Idil (female, twenties, English, 2000)

I was tabling in the Union at school every Wednesday. One day I was sitting there doing homework. This lady came up to me and said, "I think Islam oppresses women." I asked, "Why is that?" She said, "Well, I'm very ignorant, but I think Islam oppresses women." I said, "Why don't you go find out, and then come back to me next week." I gave her all the informational brochures [I had], and she's still coming back for more information.

Caaliya (female, twenties, English, 2004)

My family's pretty supportive, especially my grandfather, in terms of education for both females and males. Education just runs in our family, I guess.

And with men going away to different countries to work, women tend to take up positions of leadership and have to be the ones who are primary caregivers. Being a woman, I was always socialized to believe that education is important. Someone once told me that if you want to live life by your rules, you have to be independent. The only way you can be independent is through financial independence through education.

Halima (female, twenties, English, 2001)

Most families worry more about their boys. Somali girls are more mature, in a way. Most of the families that moved to Lewiston had teenage boys; all the girls were good students and respected their parents' opinions. This was true for Lewiston. In Minnesota I have seen Somali girls in gangs and doing drugs. What is sad is the fact that these girls hide what they do, and there is no one to help them. It is more shameful for girls to stand in the streets, so they do drugs and go to clubs and private parties at night.

Rashid (male, forties, English, 1985)

At the time of the civil war, guess who was doing better? It was the families who had daughters outside of the country, because girls take care of their families. When I went back there I saw people talking. When they see a beautiful house, they say, "They must have a daughter somewhere in Europe or in America." Even my own father said, "Nowadays it is better to have girls than boys." I kind of stepped away from my father when he said that, but I understood. My younger sister helped the family more than I did. The norms change. If you go to Somalia and you ask a family which one they prefer, a girl or a boy, I guarantee you most of them will tell you, a girl.

Racial Identity

Rashid (male, forties, English, 1985)

I think I was in New York then. And I remember people talking about black and white and it hit me. It hit me down here in my gut and I was like, "So now they are going to call me black."

Cawo (female, twenties, English, 1996)

When I arrived that was my first time to meet with a white man, a white person. But now, you know, now I know how to behave with a white man, how to talk to them and how to work with them, because I have been working for four years in the United States. Now I know how to behave.

Group interview (three young women)

Being a minority in Maine, you notice the little things as well as the big things—like being the only person of color in a classroom, or having your religion being obvious to everyone because women wear headscarves. You feel like you stand out more. I think little things like people talking down to you at stores and awkward moments with strangers is what I experienced the most. But no one has personally discriminated against me for my religion or race. In Georgia, there was a lot of hostility from the African Americans. I suppose it's because they did not understand our culture and religion, and that led to fights and miscommunication. In the beginning in Maine, even until this day, whites have stared and made comments, but that's understandable because they have never seen people like Somalis walking the streets. Personally, other than a few dirty looks and a few arguments, I haven't had any personal attacks on me due to my race.

Halima (female, twenties, English, 2001)

When the conflict happened [the incident resulting from the mayor's letter—see Nadeau, chapter 3, this volume], I went to the rally. In my high school, people from the Civil Rights Team went from class to class telling students to show up for the Many and One rally to let the people know what they want and what they think. There were a lot of high school kids on the Civil Rights Team. I even helped at the rally in the morning telling people where to go. A lot of people showed up to demonstrate to the other people that they were wrong and that not everybody from Maine hated Somalis. It did turn out positive, because a lot of people showed up to the Many and One rally and not many people supported the other side [anti-Somali].

Group interview (three young women)

I don't really know why my family came here, but we lived around African Americans and Hispanics. There were no Somalis, so maybe my mom wanted us to grow up around our people and learn our culture and language. I don't know. But when I came here it was the most racist place I've ever seen. Where I was before, it didn't matter who you were or what you were. Everyone ... hung out [together] and were friends. I mean you had white people using the "n" word ... because they grew up in that culture. It didn't matter to [us] because we knew they were not racist, it was just a word. I mean everyone used it: black, white, Chinese, it didn't matter. But coming to Maine and hearing it was a lot different, because these people were actually racist. I felt like I was fighting in the civil rights movement. Every day I was in a fight, and I was getting suspended a lot. I mean, this place was crazy for a while. There were many times when I just wanted to pack my stuff and go, but my mom wouldn't let me.

Rashid (male, forties, English, 1985)

We [Somalis] have a superiority complex; we think we are better than many people. One of the things that really used to amuse me when I [first] came here—I used to watch Phil Donahue. He would bring all of these [racist] people [on his show]. I'm like, "Okay. So he is saying he is better than me. He must be dreaming!" This white racist is talking about how they are better than me, and I'm [thinking], "What an idiot. Don't you know? I'm Somali."

Clan Identity

Caaliya (female, twenties, English, 2004)

The sense of pride [among Somalis] is not so much coming from my ethnic group, so to speak. It's more from socialization, I believe. My mother and my father would say, "You're a Somali, this is who you are, and these are your ancestors." It's about knowing two hundred years' worth of history as opposed to saying, "I'm proud, I'm in this tribe." It just gives me that kind of grounding.

With being Somali comes a set of morals, of values, of cultural ideas. [But while] Somalis look homogeneous, we really aren't. [The differences] can be huge at times, in terms of our culture and the way we do things. Some Somali cultures are more restrictive than others. What is okay for a certain tribe is not okay for another tribe. "You're a Somali" is what they use to inculcate those cultural ideals that should give me the cultural framework within which I can operate.

Ali (male, seventies, Somali, 1996)

As Somalis we have certain cultural traditions. In one tribe, people outside of that tribe don't marry into that tribe. It has nothing to do with religion, it's just cultural, and that's wrong. But people do it because they became used to it and it became normal for them to do.

Haweeya (female, teenager, English, 1992)

In Lewiston I hardly ever know who is [from what tribe]. I knew Muna before I knew what type of tribe she was from, and I'm not even familiar with like 90 percent of the tribe names. One time Muna asked, "Can you figure out what tribe I am?" I've known Muna for almost six years and I did not know. I just picked one and said it. Muna got mad and I'm like, "You never told me, so don't expect me to know." I am my tribe, and that's all that matters to me. I don't see [why] it's necessary for me to know other people's tribes.

Ladan (female, twenties, English, 2004)

Over there the clans are very important, but here, I don't know if [they're] positive or negative. But in a way, it's good to know where you are from. You don't have to focus too much on the clan thing, but it's very important to know where you are from, who your people are.

Haweeya (female, teenager, English, 1992)

Our name is very unique—our last name, Sharif. We are known among the Somalis because historically, we are descendants of the prophet's daughter. The Sharifs are considered [to be] the sheiks, just like priests, religious people. We are more religious. If you don't know [the] Qur'an, you are definitely not in the Sharif family. It is very rare to see a Sharif who is not religious. We are respected by the larger Somali community. [People say,] if you have troubles, go to the Sharifs, they might help you.

Editors' Note: *Many immigrants—especially those who were forced to leave their homelands—feel nostalgic longing for their home country, a feeling that can be accentuated when there is little chance of repatriation. Refugees who have been ripped from their moorings and scattered throughout the world often exist in "in-between" spaces where they feel as though they belong neither here nor there.*

How then, do refugees recreate meanings of home when living in exile? For Somalis, home means many different things depending on the person, their circumstances, and characteristics such as age of immigration, language proficiency, and level of education.

For some, home will always be Somalia, while for others, the meaning of home is evolving and multi-faceted with orientations in the past, present, and future. Research with Iranian immigrants speaks to this multiplicity of home: Iranians differentiate between their nostalgic home of the past (their original homeland), their practical home in the present (the place they currently live), and their imagined final home in the future (where they see themselves living eventually).[19] Speaking to the temporal and multidimensional conceptions of home, one Somali refugee in Maine differentiated between her "home" (where she was currently living while attending college), her "home home" (where her family lived a few hours away), and her "home home home" (Somalia).

The concept of home is often thought of as concrete and bounded rather than as fluid and symbolic. Yet, home can refer to a physical place where one lives—one's domicile—or an imagined place that exists in one's mind. Moreover, the boundaries between these two realms blend into one another, as Somalis recreate and negotiate aspects of their remembered home in their new locations. They do this in their households through food, language, and décor, and in their communities by creating ethnic enclaves whereby they live amongst other Somalis, surrounding themselves with the familiar. In Lewiston, there are currently over a dozen Somali-run stores that sell traditional Somali foods and wares, including halal *meat, camel's milk, colorful* hijabs, *Middle Eastern furniture, as well as Somali music, books, and videos—items that help keep them connected to their homeland and each other.*

One's relationship to place and the meanings of home shifts with the passage of time. As one becomes more acculturated and integrated in a new location, it may begin to feel more like home. The feeling of being-at-home is also affected by the degree to which one is accepted and welcomed in the new community. As Barbara Settles points out, "the right to be in a place and to be accepted and not harassed is fundamental to having a home."[20] Since their arrival, Somalis in Lewiston have faced a mixture of harassment, discrimination, and acceptance, but by some accounts—and largely the result of hard work by many Somalis and non-Somalis—this mixed welcome has begun to change. Assessing how things have changed in Lewiston, one Somali woman recently said that today when she walks down the street in Lewiston many people say hello and smile at her, whereas just five years ago, she was often confronted by hostile people on the streets who sometimes told her to "go back to Africa."[21] The excerpts that close this volume capture some of the emotions, nuances, and complexities of home for Somalis in Maine, thus illustrating how there is no singular, simple, or static definition of home.

Meanings of Home

Mariam (female, twenties, English, 1991)

Right now I feel I don't want to call America home. But that is the only place that I know. I don't remember Somalia. I wish I could, you know. But hopefully one day I will call that home.

Rashid (male, forties, English, 1985)

This, of course, is my home, but it's not 100 percent home. There is something missing. What's missing is [that] I cannot see my parents; I cannot see some of my relatives that I really admire and love. I cannot walk down the road and eat in a Somali restaurant and go to a mosque for every prayer.

Group interview (three females, two males)

My grandmother passed away in 2005, and she's buried in Boston. My mom and I went to see her grave. One time I remember my parents were consid-

FIGURE 35. Young Somali women (Northport, Maine)

ering moving to Texas and my mom worried, "My mother's grave is in Boston. How can I live so far away?" I never thought about people getting attached to graves and all that.

Caaliya (female, twenties, English, 2004)

Right now Lewiston-Auburn is my home. I had a hard time adjusting here and I still struggle, but I like my life here. I like what it has become, and I like the new experiences that I have [had]. I think that the biggest part of that would be this college. The Somali friends I've made—I met them here. My white friends—I met them here; my African American friends—I met them here. So this is like my nexus of everything coming together. The faculty and everybody here push you to be who you are, to think the way you would like to think. Original thought is the most important thing. They don't want you to regurgitate things that they have taught you. And if you disagree, you're completely entitled to disagree. It's that environment that I have found here that I'm going to miss when I move from here.

Group interview (three females, two males)

My whole family moved back to Atlanta this summer. I've lived in Maine the past six years, but I was born in Atlanta. My dad lived there the whole time. Now that my family's back in Atlanta, I [will] go to my aunt's house, because she lives in Lewiston. . . . I haven't lived in Atlanta for six years. But Lewiston is not my home, because my family is not there. I definitely don't consider the dorm my home. I guess I consider all three of those places home. As long as I'm around family, it's home. It's the environment basically . . . and food— it contributes to everything.

Group interview (three females, two males)

I was in Atlanta nine years, now [I've been] in Maine almost nine years. My parents say we have to move to Bangor, because they've been in Lewiston too long now. I asked, "Can't you stay put in one place?" Every time they are there for a really long time, the first thing they think of is moving. They say, "We're going to move this summer. No, we're going to move next summer. We just want to move." They don't care where they're moving to.

Caaliya (female, twenties, English, 2004)

My home is where the people I love are. At this point it's California, because most of my family lives in California. I learned quickly that a physical place doesn't matter if the people you love aren't there.

Ahmed (male, thirties, English, 2000)

Life in Maine is good. It might take another ten years [to bring peace to Somalia] even if there is a government in Somalia. People need somebody educated who can help them out. If I have a good degree, then I can help Somalia. Maybe I can go back home. That's one of my plans.

Afterword

Escape from Hell—What Now?

Ahmed I. Samatar

Ama Yurub, Ama Yaxas ("Europe or the Sharks")

—Folk saying[1]

"What do we know but that we face
One another in this place."[2]

"The citizen ... is the calculating egoist educated to public judgment; the citizen is the corrupt merchant induced to virtue; the citizen is the bigoted individual conditioned to tolerance; the citizen is the impulsive actor trained to deliberateness; the citizen is the adversary taught to seek common ground with her [or his] opponent."[3]

I. Introduction

The last twenty years have witnessed many profound human tragedies. Some of these were primarily as a result of devastating natural events; others were attributable, to a significant degree, to human choices and actions. The first type brings to mind the calamitous tsunami that took the lives of hundreds of thousands in South Asia and the Indian Ocean region, as well as the killer earthquakes in Iran, Haiti, and Chile. The latter type is evidenced by such examples as the chronic violence in Colombia, Mexico, and Sri Lanka; bloodletting in Rwanda, the Democratic Republic of the Congo, and Liberia; savage wars in Sierra Leone; and the mayhem in Darfur. Though the quantitative loss of lives in Somalia has not been as large as in some of these situations, the Somali condition has become one of the most bewildering, durable, and deepest in its impact. Its paramount consequences include the hollowing out of civic spirit and a decampment of around 10 percent of the population to neighboring countries and as far afield as the remotest corners of the world—including Alaska and the most southern parts of New Zealand. This epilogue to *Somalis in Maine* is divided into brief segments: an articulation of what drove many Somalis to despair and flight and an explanation of some of the challenges facing those who have started all over again in the United States.

II. Ruination

In an earlier writing, I had proffered that the Somali situation could best be described as a *catastrophe*—defined as a historical moment that captures the confluence of multiple crises.[4] The roots could be traced to at least six main factors: a difficult—but not hopeless—environment; colonial dismemberment of contiguous territories; high levels of ignorance; a divided political elite; a tug-of-war between superpowers; and civil war.

Situated between the equator and the 15th parallel north, the Somali-inhabited ecology has always been a hard context in which to sustain life—a condition that has kept most Somalis both on the edge and on the move. Though one could discern four seasons, primarily determined by the northwestern and southwestern monsoon winds, the brief (March–June) *Gu* and even shorter *Der* are the only months in which a modicum of rainfall is expected—though uneven among the regions, the average never exceeds a dozen inches at the best of times. Even during these two seasons, however, the likelihood of consecutive years of meager rains, if not outright droughts, are not uncommon. Thus, a reliable availability of water has been the source of constant and high anxiety for the Somalis of the Horn. An exception to this perpetual harsh weather and climate has been the land between and around the only two rivers in the country—the more reliable Juba and the shallower Shabelle. In addition to the most northwestern area, this is also the only part of the Somali territory that has sustained productive farming activities. For the rest of this vast terrain, sustenance of life has traditionally been sought through pastoralism, with a few fishing communities along the three-thousand-kilometer coastline—the longest in the continent. In brief, the Somali people have a continuing history of contending with an environment legendary for its niggardliness. This does not rule out the potential for improvement in either maximizing what is already available or discovering hidden treasures. But a realization of either one of the them, or both, will depend on a rightful mixture of intelligent and stable political leadership, competent socioeconomic institutions, and a harnessing of appropriate technical (i.e., scientific) skills—a far cry from the prevailing circumstances.

Colonial conquest of the Somali-inhabited region of the Horn of Africa was a supremely disastrous dismemberment. The colonial powers (France, Britain, and Italy) and the collaborating Abyssinian feudal monarchy agreed to arbitrarily divide among themselves the four hundred thousand square miles of contiguous territory of the Somali-speaking peoples. The upshot was this: France would take what would be named Côte Français des Somalis (present-day Republic of Djibouti); Britain acquired what would become British Somaliland and the Northern Frontier District of Kenya; Italy claimed Italian Somaliland on the Indian Ocean; and Emperor Menelik of Ethiopia was awarded the "Ogaden" region. Farah Nur, one of the notable poets of the era, expressed the onslaught this way:

> The British, the Ethiopians, and the Italians are squabbling,
> The country is snatched and divided by whomever is stronger,
> The country is sold piece by piece without our knowledge,
> And for me, this is the Teeth of the Last Days.[5]

By the time this agreement was concluded, the Somali people ended up as subjects to five different colonial administrations. Among the consequences has been a lasting damage to collective belonging, particularly induced through a malicious intention by the colonials to transmute kinship identities into tribalist definitions. Kinship identity, an indigenous invention, is known for its complex and interdigitating mixture of mutualities and reparative virtues to manage tensions and discord. Tribalism was designed by the imperialists to anchor the infamous paradigm of "divide and rule" and focused on at once vanquishing any local resistance to the pursuit of creating submissive clients and compounding, if not inventing, flammable splinters among kin groups. Put another way, the colonial impact was a sorrowful combination of geographical mutilation, with dire burdens for pastoralists; a fragmentation of consciousness; and a breeding of exclusionary devices among the Somalis in the competition for whatever political and economic crumbs had fallen from the table of the colonial actors. These will have enormous implications for the movements toward decolonization and Somali independence, the establishment of the state, and the contemporary era of dissolution and the resultant pulling up of stakes to move to distant lands.

The rise of the second phase of the resistance to colonialism in the 1940s (after Sayid Mohamed Abdille Hassan's Darwish campaign) culminated in the birth of the trans-zonal political party (the Somali Youth League, or SYL) that, together with three other smaller Northern organizations, succeeded in establishing the new Somali Republic on July 1, 1960. For a brief moment, marked by the final and quickly moving years of decolonization and the morrow of sovereignty, there was a palatable atmosphere of widespread jubilation—a feeling that the world could be made anew. Akin to Wordsworth's famed expression on the early effect and promise of the French Revolution, "bliss was it in that dawn to be alive," Somali's most eminent poet of the era, Abdillahi Sultan "Timaade," delivered one of his most memorable poems, "Kaa na Siib Kan na Saar" ("Take that one [colonial flag] down and mount this one [the new national flag]") at midnight on June 26, 1960, at the Freedom Garden in Hargeisa.

Despite the excitement, there were already at least five accompanying or waiting liabilities that would bode ill for the post-colonial era. First, there was a substantial political minority in Italian Somaliland that was in support of Italian rule and, therefore, was in hostile opposition to the nationalism of the SYL. Italophiles argued for many more decades of Italian suzerainty.

Second, among all the independence-seeking political organizations, there were many (if not the majority) who construed the new dispensation as an inauguration of a struggle for personal and sectarian enrichment. The commons was now to become a source of private or clan privilege—the politicization of kin.

Third, some voices in the North (ex-British) immediately interpreted the distribution of the senior state portfolios as a lopsided and unfair grab by the South. This suspicion, partially supported by some facts, was strengthened by the concentration of decision making in remote Mogadishu, the center of the South. For Northern Somalis, these points added up to the onset of a local version of "combined and uneven development." Here, then, lie the original seeds of the current alienation of the North from the South. The state's bombing of Hargeisa and Burao, two important towns of the North, by the regime of Siyaad Barre in 1988 has left behind bitter memories. As if that were not enough, events of the last two decades, including a monopolization by Southerners of the highest leadership portfolios of the numerous attempts to resurrect the national state, have only reaffirmed the discord. Yet, notwithstanding the forgoing, it is important to note this: though most

Northern Somalis are fully disillusioned with the old union, they are still cognizant of the deeper entwinement of histories and the continuing embroilment in each other's lives and fate.

Fourth, within the South, there were significant groups of Somali agriculturalists (some now identifying themselves as "Somali Bantu") whose rightful place was submerged by not-so-hidden discriminatory practices. They labored hard, with minimum compensation, first for the rapacious Italians and later for the new Somali ruling state and commercial class.[6] This, too, will become another fissure leading to the coming decomposition.

Finally, literacy and broader educational attainment have not been a historical endowment of the Somali people. With a negligible cluster of individuals who traveled to other Islamic lands in the late nineteenth and early twentieth centuries, formal schooling began after the conclusion of the Second World War. None of the colonials invested much in human development. The Italians, whose cruel fascism manifested itself in the expropriation of land and racial humiliation,[7] only moved toward creating educational opportunities for Somali subjects during the trusteeship period of the 1950s. The British, who were distant and miserly, were equally neglectful to an extent that Northerners would describe the colonial authorities as "the deaf government," whose intentions were "to have no ideas and spend no money."[8] The French and Ethiopians were even less attentive to the educational needs of the "natives" under their rule. All in all, on the eve of the independence of the Somali Republic, literacy rates were among the lowest in the continent, such that it became very difficult to staff the upper echelons of the incipient state.

Somalis have been entangled with the "modern world-system" ever since Middle Eastern Muslims came to trade and spread the faith. But perhaps it was Vasco de Gama's siege and setting ablaze of some coastal settlements, such as Brava and Mogadishu, and the rise of Indian Ocean mercantile trade that marks the Somali induction into the System. But, in addition to colonialism, the paramount Somali encounter with the powers of the outside was in the context of the now-defunct competition between the United States and the USSR during the decades of the 1960s, 70s, and 80s. In the pursuit of strategic outposts, each superpower saw the Somali peninsula as a valuable asset. For the Somali elite bent on the unification of the three Somalilands with the new Republic, the sponsorship of a superpower was the *single* most paramount foreign policy objective. The confluence of these two interests would become the basis of endless intrigue until the assassination of President Sharmarke (fueled by conspicuous corruption among the highest officers of the state—especially the prime minister and minister of the interior) and the subsequent coup headed by General Siyaad Barre in 1969. With this change to a leftist military dictatorship trained by the Soviets, the patronage was consummated. Already imbued with the desire to win back the missing Somali territories, particularly the Somali-inhabited region, Somali military forces, in conjunction with the local liberation movement, started a fierce military offensive in 1977, resulting in quick victories that came close to taking over the major city of Dire Dawa. However, that advance was brought to a halt in 1978 and later followed by a decimating defeat and retreat of the Somali forces. Victory was due to the regrouping of the Ethiopian army as well as the decisive switching of Soviet allegiance (accompanied by Cubans and Yemenis) to the Ethiopian side. With the destruction of the Somali military came a swift decline in the economy, the evaporation of the legitimacy of Siyaad Barre's regime, the rise of armed opposition, and the complete exhaustion of national institutions. By the beginning of the 1990s, the country descended into horrendous and sectarian chaos (with the exception of the North and the Northeast) from which it has yet to recover.[9]

This recapitulation affords one to meditate on its meaning for the Somali people and their sympathizers in the global society. From my perspective, the catastrophe has three fundamental dimensions: (a) the dissipation of civic belonging or *Somalinimo*, (b) the pulverization of national institutions—at the center of which is the state—and (c) the total absence of visionary, legitimate, and competent leadership. A look at some human development indicators (HDI), compared with neighboring countries (which themselves include some of the poorest in the world), gives a glimpse of the grinding wretchedness of Somali society. In income, life expectancy, and literacy, the country scores among the very lowest. Moreover, in the deficit measures—such as birth rate, total fertility rate, and population growth rate—the country scores among the highest.

III. Flight: Battling Out of the Catastrophe

With the sky having fallen on them and, thus, out of desperation, Somalis from all regions, ages, genders, and, to a limited extent, classes have resorted to all types of thinking and actions. These range from a retreat into retaliatory and violent bigotry, escape to areas within the country associated with one's kin, and seeking refuge beyond the borders of Somalia. In the case of the latter, Somali refugee camps are to be found in all the neighboring countries and some across the seas. In Kenya's north, Dadaab, the largest refugee camp in the world (with more than two hundred thousand inhabitants) and totally populated by as deep as three generations of Somalis, is a fixture in the work of international aid organizations.

The tens of thousands who have arrived in these United States have settled in many states. Minnesota, Ohio, Washington, Virginia, and California contain the largest concentrations. There are, however, smaller but notable clusters in Maine, Texas, Massachusetts, Utah, Arizona, and Oregon. Somalis appeared in the United States around the Second World War. The earliest were young men who took to the sea as part of merchant marine fleets and then, for one reason or another, went on shore and settled in ports such as New York. These extremely small numbers were later (after independence) joined by university students on various types of scholarships. Still, until the age of *Qaxootin* (exodus) in the late 1980s and early 1990s, when a combination of factors made it possible for Somalis to enroll in U.S. schools, Somalis were statistically miniscule in their presence in the United States. By the end of 2010, the picture had dramatically changed. A steep growth in numbers (perhaps as high as eighty thousand) and public awareness of the Somalis has brought both positive and negative attention—from touching hospitality to racist and religious hostility. Thus, the debate on how successfully Somalis have merged with the larger American society is being taken up in numerous contexts and will continue to be a topic of utmost interest for all involved.[10]

At first blush, and using the time of arrival as an index, the Somali American population could be disaggregated into three broad categories or generations: (a) those who had direct experiences of the glow of independence, the decay, and the subsequent violent sectarianism that engulfed the society; (b) those whose lives were primarily shaped by, and who came of age during, the civil war; and (c) those who either were brought here as very young children or were born in the United States. Before I elaborate on the differences and implications thereof, a comment on the concept of *generation* is in order. In one ordinary sense, it is a measure of time or age; in another, it connotes some common consciousness. It is this conjunction of a numerical accounting and the construction of a shared *mentalité* by way of ruptured event(s) that amount to a defining lived time that is sustained in thought and feeling, i.e., memory. As Wilhelm Dilthey writes:

> [A] generation is constituted of a restricted circle of individuals who are bound together into a homogenous whole by their dependence on the same great events and transformations that appeared in their age of [maximum] receptivity, despite the variety of other subsequent factors.[11]

The most consequential events of the post-colonial era among the Somalis are, as I mentioned earlier, the convergence of the erosion of civic identity, the death of the national state, and the abject failure of leadership. But it was not always like this. The generation of the late 1950s into the 1970s grew up in the *élan* of coming independence, its emotional afterglow, relatively available material rewards, and the visibility of individuals in high political leadership worthy of emulation—President Aden A. Osman, Prime Minister Abdirazak H. Hussein, and the lesser-known Michael Mariano. The memory of this ebullient formative period, as it flits in and out of their awareness, helps somewhat cushion their sensibilities from the full effects of the descent into the diabolical vulgarity that had ensued. In other words, they remember other times that favorably compare with the years of the catastrophe. A characteristic attitude of this cohort is a mixture of nostalgia and aghastness. This does not absolve them of their own failure to save the country from sliding into disaster during their watch. Nonetheless, this group's encounter with the American civilization is less problematic: they had matured while Somalia was a relatively functioning society in which codes of public conduct were observed, and they are now fading into the background as elderly retirees.

The second category is composed of those typically brought up in, if not born into, the collective defeat underscored by internecine barbarism and vanished civic belonging, and who had lived in the debris of crumbled institutions. This is the generation of the 1980s and 1990s (and still coming). They arrived in the United States and other regions of the world deeply marked by a complex interdigitation of a haunting Hobbesian background, years spent in degrading refugee camps, and vulnerably squandering a significant amount of time looking for succor. Such circumstances do not equip the average person to immediately and effectively swim in the swift and strong currents of American society. This cohort, still in the prime of life, continues to face major difficulties in finding its bearings and settling.

The third category is the American-born. Still very young and numerically less at the moment, they will become the majority in time. These are the least affected by the dissolution, although they are not immune to seeing and hearing about vivid reminders of the catastrophe—including the worsening condition of the kin back in Somalia. Yet, for them, opportunities (and wrong seductions) are comparatively more accessible and adaptation less onerous. The long-term future of Somali Americans depends on how successfully cosmopolitan they become.

Despite these differences, all three groups face the challenges of *critical adaptation*[12] to their American/global milieu. While gains in their endeavor require a genuine initial welcome, durable sympathy, and deep investment by the American people and institutions, the bulk of the responsibility for adjustment lies with the new arrivals. To be sure, many obstacles have and will readily present themselves. For the purpose of this essay, I identify and tersely comment on these challenges: language competency and educational advancement, cultural flexibility and the cultivation of civic-mindedness, and diasporic solidarity.

Language Competence and Educational Advancement

On arrival, most Somali refugees (particularly the second generation) speak, read, and write rudimentary English or none at all. This is a categorical liability in a national context, which is at once notoriously monolingual and highly competitive. In addition, the deficit in English language proficiency could make it easier for the intolerant to insert Somali Americans into existing racist stereotypes that are part and parcel of American reality. A quick command of the English language and educational ambition, then, lead to the acquisition of high skills, a vocation, and pride—an achievement that enables one to shed the burden of hopelessness associated with the old country and, conversely, facilitates exhibitions of rare Somali gifts and rehabilitates personal dignity and self-confidence. Moreover, with mastery of English, the Somali language could rise to work contrapuntally and, thus, offer new knowledge and wisdom—a position of distinct advantage over monolingualism.

Cultural Mutability

Despite the dark side of American history, this is still one of the few countries in the Global North (the other notable one is Canada) that publicly acknowledges that its national identity is made of the different many. On the Great Seal, since the inception of the Republic, has been etched the motto *E Pluribus Unum*. Even when such a credo is wantonly jettisoned (e.g., advocacy of English language only or forms of chauvinistic Eurocentrism), there is still a greater deal of undeniable truth in the claim that the United States is a cultural milieu where the recognition of difference and the possibilities for inclusion are distinctly promoted. In order to be an effective enabler of and contributor to multiculturalism at its best, then, Somalis will have to intelligently manage their transition into becoming also Americans. This implies an optimum degree of world openness and cultural mutability, if not reinvention—a task that begins with an avoidance of manufacturing a singular identity (e.g., religious or ethnic),[13] and a respectful attitude for the best traditions of the hosts. Otherwise, the end will be poisonous self-isolation resulting in mutual resentment and "othering." In such an environment, civic belonging will be badly damaged—a situation already detectable in the United States and other countries. Will Kymlicka notes:

> On the one hand, many ... groups are insisting that society officially affirm their difference, and provide various kinds of institutional support and recognition for their difference.... On the other hand, if society accepts and encourages more and more diversity, in order to promote cultural inclusion, it seems that citizens will have less and less in common. If affirming difference is required to integrate marginalized groups into the common culture, there may cease to be a common culture.[14]

The desired alternative demands creating space for encounters, reciprocal explorations, and opportunities for, in Etienne Balibar's muscular phrase, "dialectical resolution of antagonism." For Somalis to become stakeholding Americans, then, a redesigning of self begins with creative thinking and transformative actions that make it possible to distill the older heritage and filter the new. Such a success adds value to both parts and becomes a firm basis for individual capacitation and civic efficacy. This is the full meaning of robust citizenship. But the project is difficult, and there will be many occasions when a return to some form of militant nativistic authenticity, total surrender, or even deracination might seem easier to embark upon. In all three cases, however, the end result will be costly. Isaiah Berlin writes:

The new must be grafted on the old; that is the only alternative to pet-rifaction, or the miserable aping of some ill-understood foreign orig-inal. A [people] cannot be treated as an exotic plant for long if [they are] to grow; [they] can grow only in the open air, in the public world that is common to all; one cannot be forced to feed exclusively on what is gone and dead, in a carefully preserved artificial light, or achieve anything but a stunted growth.[15]

The moral of the statements by Will Kymlicka and Isaiah Berlin is this: lifetime exercises in synthesis pave the road to a successful critical adaptation or, in Gadamer's celebrated phrase, the "fusion of horizons"—the basis for civic virtue.

Diaporic Solidarity

Somali Americans of all generations have hardly let up posing and discussing the most supreme question of their lives: what went so wrong in the old country? Most of their responses include a narration of their personal or family experiences of the catastrophe and a somewhat predictable, if not banal, regurgitation of clanism as the determining factor. To be sure, there is a modicum of shallow truth to the latter point. However, what is important here is their preoccupation with the conditions back in Somalia. This obses-sion has two contradictory ramifications for the task of critical adaptation: (a) a re-living of the destructive pathologies in the new time, or (b) a use of the American arena to perhaps not forget but certainly to forgive and, sub-sequently, forge pan-Somali American mutualities. The first track is a loser of major proportions; the latter lends itself to collective and progressive rede-finition and empowerment—a trajectory that could at once help improve respective American communities (including the continuous struggle for social justice and the expansion and preservation of individual liberty) as well as build clout to become part of the solution in the now-hapless old country. Notwithstanding the formidable impediments, the choice is still this: grounded cosmopolitanism[16] or involutionary ghettoization.

Appendix A

Mayor Raymond's Letter to
the Somali Community

For some number of months, I have observed the continued movement of a substantial number of Somalis into the downtown area of our community. I have applauded the efforts of our city staff in making available the existing services and the local citizenry for accepting and dealing with the influx.

I assumed that it would become obvious to the new arrivals the effect the large numbers of new residents has had upon the existing staff and city finances and that this would bring about a voluntary reduction of the number of new arrivals—it being evident that the burden has been, for the most part, cheerfully accepted, and every effort has been made to accommodate it.

Our Department of Human Services has recently reported that the number of Somali families arriving into the city during the month of September is below the approximate monthly average that we have seen over the last year or so. It may be premature to assume that this may serve as a signal for future relocation activity, but the decline is welcome relief given increasing demands on city and school services.

I feel that recent relocation activity over the summer has necessitated that I communicate directly with the Somali elders and leaders regarding our newest residents. If recent declining arrival numbers are the result of your outreach efforts to discourage relocation into the city, I applaud those efforts. If they are the product of other unrelated random events, I would ask that the Somali leadership make every effort to communicate my concerns on city and school service impacts with other friends and extended family who are considering a move to this community.

To date, we have found the funds to accommodate the situation. A continued increased demand will tax the city's finances.

This large number of new arrivals cannot continue without negative results for all. The Somali community must exercise some discipline and reduce the stress on our limited finances and our generosity.

I am well aware of the legal right of a U.S. resident to move anywhere he/she pleases, but it is time for the Somali community to exercise this discipline in view of the effort that has been made on its behalf.

We will continue to accommodate the present residents as best as we can, but we need self-discipline and cooperation from everyone.

Only with your help will we be successful in the future—please pass the word: We have been overwhelmed and have responded valiantly. Now we need breathing room. Our city is maxed-out financially, physically and emotionally.

I look forward to your cooperation.

Laurier T. Raymond Jr.
Mayor, City of Lewiston
Source: *Lewiston Sun Journal,* 4 October 2002, A11.

Appendix B

Letter from Somali Elders

October 6, 2002
Mr. Laurier Raymond
Mayor, City of Lewiston
Re: Your letter dated October 1, 2002
Somalis in Lewiston

This letter is in response to your above referenced letter in regard to the move of Somali refugees/immigrants to the city of Lewiston. First of all, with due respect, we would like to indicate that your letter is not only untimely but is also inflammatory and disturbing, to say the least. Your letter is untimely because it is written and released at a time when the movement of Somalis to Lewiston has naturally dropped and as per records no Somali moved to Lewiston since the end of August 2002. The letter is also inflammatory and disturbing as we are dismayed to see such a letter from an elected official and leader who is supposed to show good leadership, co-existence and harmony among the residents of this humble city.

We react to your letter in mixed feelings ranging from dismay, astonishment and anger. This is because of the fact that you have never given us a chance to meet with you and discuss our future plans with you during your term in office. Your predecessor Mayor Kalleigh Tara perfectly understood us and was working with us as new additions to a city where she was the mayor. We also had and were given opportunities to meet with and discuss our future with elected and non-elected local and state officials. Most recently, such meetings included those we had with Governor Angus King on September 17 and with the gubernatorial candidate, Congressman John Baldacci on September 27th, among others.

During all such meetings, the officials indicated their satisfaction with our coming to live here in the state, they say, is sparsely populated and needs to attract more residents as both manpower and future electorates. Those officials, after listening to us, applauded our efforts to try and "Fit in" as much as we can. While we have had contacts with other leaders as stated above, you have never given us a chance to meet and explain ourselves to you. The first contact, which you ever had with us, is through your recent letter, which prompted this response; something which we never thought would happen and feel unwarranted at this time.

For your information therefore, our coming to Lewiston and living here have revitalized this city in certain ways. Our presence has turned Lewiston into a multi-ethnic, multi-racial city, which has embraced diversity and change. A city of thirty-six thousand people, in the middle of the "whitest" state in the country has suddenly become an international city. Lewiston's name appeared in papers and news clips around the country. We portrayed the facts about this place and its humble people who we consider, by and large, as generous Americans who understand our plight and are ready to help in our initial days of settling down. Our presence here have [sic] also attracted hundreds of thousands of dollars in state and federal funds to boost existing social services for all residents of Lewiston. This particular point was not stated in your letter.

Apartment units located in the Lewiston downtown area which were abandoned many years ago, were suddenly refurbished and made livable as the arrival of Somalis generated funds and put money in the pockets of landlords. This also raised the market value of real estate. Somalis were hired to work in businesses and plants making them to be able to contribute to the local economy as taxpayers. Back in April 2002, there were 249 able-bodied Somali men and women who could work, forty people worked at the time. Today out of the 416 able bodied men and women 215 persons are currently employed. This is over 50 percent of adults who could work. Also, there are three Somali businesses in Lewiston which opened in less than a year.

While we thank the city of Lewiston, and the general public for their understanding and accepting us in their midst, we would nevertheless like to bring to your attention and to the attention of others in your line of thinking, that we are citizens and/or legal residents of this country. Although we originally hail from the Eastern African state of Somalia, we renounced our Somali citizenship and [have] taken U.S. citizenship. Over 80 percent of our children are Americans by birth. Therefore, we believe we have every right to live anywhere in this country. So do other Somalis or any other legal residents who choose to come and live in Lewiston or in Alaska for that matter.

In view of the above, and with due respect we consider your letter Mr.

Mayor, as the writing of ill-informed leader who is bent towards bigotry. Therefore, by a copy of this letter we ask both the state government and law enforcement to guarantee our safety here. If any harm [or] form of an attack happens to any Somali-American man, woman or child in the wake of your letter, we hold you squarely responsible for any such acts. We think your letter is an attempt to agitate and incite the local people and a license to violence against our people physically, verbally and emotionally.

Hope this is clear and let God show all of us what is right.

Sincerely,
Elders of the Somali Community

CC: Office of Governor Angus King
William Welch, Lewiston Police Chief
Lewiston/Auburn Community Task Force
Pierrot Rugaba, State Refugee Coordinator
Jim Bennet, Administrator: City of Lewiston
Source: *Lewiston Sun Journal*, 8 October 2002, A8.

Appendix C

The Many and One Coalition

Many People, Many Colors, One Community: Lewiston/Auburn, Maine

Welcome!

The Many and One Coalition invites concerned citizens to denounce hatred and work together to shape a community of peace, love and acceptance.

What We Stand For:

We affirm, support, and welcome those of our communities who are native born and from away.

We desire to create a community of peace, love, and trust among neighbors.

We desire to dispel all forms of hatred from among us as well as within us and provide a secure environment where people will not have to live in fear and terror.

We invite fellow citizens to work with us toward building community.

The Many and One Coalition is a group of citizens and community leaders who formed in response to news that a national organization had plans to rally in the city of Lewiston, Maine.

National attention was brought to the area because of a letter from a city leader requesting that the influx of Somali immigrants be slowed down to give the city room to breathe. The letter upset many local people who have grown to love and respect their new neighbors; neighbors who had been displaced from their national homeland *because* of war and terror.

The national attention that this letter brought, also made white supremacist groups take notice. They made their plans to hold a rally on January 11, 2003 where they hoped to recruit new members for their organization.

The race toward January 11 was on and large numbers of concerned citizens began to come together to denounce, diffuse, and dispel the work of the groups who were planning on convening in Lewiston.

Area communities began to demonstrate their support for the Coalition's efforts and people from all over Maine showed their willingness to become involved in rejecting a message of hate and embracing the empowering message of love & peace.

Source: http://www.promorevolution.com/frontpage.cfm? ProgramID=2797

Notes

Part I

1. As an introduction to immigrant stories, students read excerpts from a collection by teenagers who came from Somalia, Iraq, Sudan, and Iran: a publication that emerged from a nonprofit writing center in Portland, Maine. The Telling Room Story House Project, *I Remember Warm Rain.*

Chapter 1

1. The World Factbook, https://www.cia.gov/library/publications/the-world -factbook/geos/so.html (accessed July 12, 2010); Samatar and Samatar, "Transition and Leadership," 2.
2. Ahmed Samatar, "Beginning Again: From Refugee to Citizen," 10–11.
3. Schlee, "Redrawing the Map of the Horn: The Politics of Difference," 356.
4. Lewis, *A Modern History;* Ahmed Samatar, "A Paradoxical Gift" (accessed July 12, 2010).
5. Besteman, *Unraveling Somalia,* 17.
6. Ahmed Samatar, "The Porcupine Dilemma," 56.
7. Kaplan, "The Society and Its Environment," 81.
8. Mohamoud, *State Collapse and Post-Conflict Development in Africa,* 18.
9. Samatar, "The Curse of Allah," 111.
10. Gardner with Warsame, "Women, Clan Identity and Peace-building," 154.
11. Kaplan, "The Society and Its Environment," 86.
12. Mohamoud, *State Collapse and Post-Conflict Development in Africa,* 54.
13. Kaplan, "The Society and Its Environment," 93. This complex system is described in Kaplan, ibid., 81–105.
14. As one contemporary poet commented, "Poetry is the heart of our culture. We are nothing if not a nation of poets," and as hip-hop artist K'Naan stated, "We recite, not write." "Interview with Professor Said Sheikh Samatar," 7; http://austincitylimits.org/3510-knaan-mos-def (accessed March 1, 2010). See also Lewis, *A Modern History,* 25.
15. Rinehart, "Historical Setting," 52.
16. Cassanelli, "The Partition of Knowledge in Somali Studies," 7, 8.
17. Touval, *Somali Nationalism,* 27. Ahmed I. Samatar notes that "given the harsh economic ecology of the Somali areas, a few, mostly men, have

always left for journeys into distant lands. This was usually the case when long-lasting droughts engulfed the Somali territories." The Somali word is *tacabbir*: "temporary adventures to improve one's material life and the ultimate return to either the place of origin or one of the more enterprising towns with a degree of worldliness uncommon among contemporaries." "Beginning Again," 10.

18. Lewis, *A Modern History*, 40.
19. Touval, *Somali Nationalism*, 1. The British claimed northern Somalia as a protectorate, which required little expenditure.
20. Lyons, "Crises on Multiple Levels: Somalia and the Horn of Africa," 192.
21. The Anglo-Ethiopian Treaty took from Somalia "half of the fertile northern highlands and vital season grazing area of the Haud." Touval, *Somali Nationalism*, 16, 46.
22. Turton, "Somali Resistance to Colonial Rule," 126, 124.
23. Lewis, *A Modern History*, 83.
24. Touval, *Somali Nationalism*, 54; Quoted from the poem, "The Will" in "Interview with Professor Said Sheikh Samatar," 10.
25. "Ismail Mire, the dervish general . . . stated in an interview that the Sayyid's men would ride up to a herdsman and say, 'Join me and my brother and bring all your sheep and goats and camels,' and if he agreed, they let him come and, if he did not, they killed him and took the stock.'" Quoted in Jama Mohamed, "The Political Economy of Colonial Somaliland," 539. Hassan appears in every text on the history of Somalia. See for example Lewis, *A Modern History*, 63–91.
26. Jama Mohamed, "The Political Economy of Colonial Somaliland," 540, 541.
27. Lewis, *A Modern History*, 11.
28. Touval, *Somali Nationalism*, 71.
29. Said Samatar, "A Country Study: Somalia."
30. Rinehart, "Historical Setting," 38.
31. French Somaliland voted against independence. It would not become the independent state of Djibouti until 1977.
32. Rinehart, "Historical Setting," 38.
33. The World Factbook, https://www.cia.gov/library/publications/the-world-factbook/geos/so.html (accessed July 7, 2010).
34. Samatar and Samatar, "International Crisis Group Report on Somaliland," 114; Ahmed Samatar, "The Curse of Allah," 113.

35. Lee Cassanelli makes a convincing argument that the partition of the region created an intellectual partition and that the consequences of this were profound. "Partition of Knowledge in Somali Studies," 5.

36. Besteman, *Unraveling Somalia*, 12.

37. Female Genital Mutilation (FGM), or Female Genital Cutting (FGC), was not a focus of our study. The global attention and humanitarian response to it, however, has been huge. The terms refer to the partial or total removal of the female genitalia. There are three forms. The least invasive (clitoridectomy or *sunna*) removes the clitoral hood with or without a part of the clitoris. The most severe (infibulation) involves the total removal of the external genitalia and stitching the sides of the vaginal opening together to leave a small opening "about the size of a match stick to allow for the flow of urine and menstrual blood" (http://fgmnetwork.org/intro/world.php). Estimates of the prevalence of the practice in Somalia—which is performed on girls between the ages of four and eleven—range from 90 percent (UNICEF) to 98 percent (Amnesty International). Eighty percent of these are of the most extreme form (infibulation).

FGM or FGC is practiced in approximately twenty-seven other countries in Africa and the Middle East. Although many of these countries are Islamic, not all Islamic countries practice it and not all who practice it are Islamic. UNICEF notes that "while UNICEF is firmly committed to respecting the cultural identity and tradition of the countries in which it works, it is clear about the unacceptability of traditional practices that violate human rights, and specifically the rights of children. Action eliminating harmful traditional practices is specifically mandated by the Convention of the Rights of the Child and FGM is clearly such a practice" ("Eradication of Female Genital Mutilation in Somalia," UNICEF, www.unicef.org/somalia/SOM_FGM_Advocacy_Paper.pdf).

Although Siyad Barre initiated a campaign to eliminate the practice in 1988 and a year later the government supported an international conference in Mogadishu on "Female Circumcision: Strategies to Bring About Change," the collapse of the state halted any organized effort to end the practice. In March 2004, three Somali women's networks announced a nationwide campaign to eradicate the practice and to address the role of religion in the fight against it. Isabel Candela, Programme Manager of Oxfam, Netherlands who had worked with grassroots women organizations in Somalia since 1995, noted, "although Islam does not advocate FGM, there is rising misconception among Somali religious leaders that FGM is a religious rite" (News from Africa, March 2004, www.newsfromafrica.org/newsfromafrica/articles/art_3744.html). In November 2009, Somalia's Transitional Federal Government announced that it intended to become a party of the Convention of the Rights of the Child (CRC), thus acknowledging that FGM or FGC violates a child's rights. Somalia had been one of two countries not to ratify the CRC. The United States prohibited the practice in 1995.

For different Somali women's views on the practice see Barnes and Boddy, *Aman: The Story of a Somali Girl;* Dirie, *Desert Flower;* Korn with Eichhorst, *Born in the Big Rains.*

38. Lewis, *A Modern History,* 217.
39. Roble and Rutledge, *The Somali Diaspora* 21; Besteman, *Unraveling Somalia,* 14. In 1962 the Soviet Union agreed to loans to equip and train Somalia's armed forces. By the late 1960s, eight hundred Somalis had received military training in the Soviet Union while a large number of Soviet personnel had served in Somalia as military advisors. Rinehart, "Historical Setting," 40.
40. Besteman, *Unraveling Somalia,* 14.
41. Farah, *Yesterday, Tomorrow,* 52.
42. Lewis, *A Modern History,* 262.
43. For a detailed account of the disintegration of Somalia see Lewis, *A Modern History,* chapter XI.
44. Lewis, *A Modern History,* 267.
45. Farah, *Yesterday, Tomorrow,* 44.
46. Farah, *Yesterday, Tomorrow,* 16.
47. Ibid., 20.
48. Ibid., 2,16.
49. Ahmed Samatar, "Beginning Again," 5.
50. Awa Abdi, "In Limbo," 18.
51. Kapteijns and Arman, "Educating Immigrant Youth," 20.
52. This replaced the Transitional National Government, which was formed four years earlier. For a detailed account of the recent politics of Somalia see Mohamoud, *State Collapse and Post-Conflict Development in Africa,* chapters 8 and 9.

53. Samatar and Samatar, "Transition and Leadership," 2; The World Factbook, https://www.cia.gov/library/publications/the-world -factbook/geos/so.html (accessed July 7, 2010).
54. Besteman, *Unraveling Somalia*, 19.
55. Little, "Reflections on Somalia," 96.
56. Ibid., 65.
57. Said, *Orientalism*, 325.

Chapter 2

1. In 2008 it was estimated that 3,300 of the estimated refugee population of 3,500 Somalis were secondary migrants. The small remainder were direct refugee resettlements (see Nadeau, "The Flawed U.S. Refugee Workforce Development Strategy"). The hub of Somali activity is in Lewiston, although many Somalis also reside in neighboring Auburn. Current estimates suggest that there are more than 4,000 Somalis in Lewiston today.
2. The legal term "secondary migrant" refers to individuals who are initially resettled in one geographic location in the United States but decide to relocate to another location within the first eight months of settlement. When refugees relocate to a new location within the first eight months of settlement, they are still eligible for refugee resettlement benefits. After eight months they are no longer eligible for refugee benefits but can apply for public assistance. See Timberlake, "Municipal Collaboration." In this chapter, the term "secondary migration" is applied to refugees who move to a new location regardless of the amount of time that has passed.
3. Nadeau, "The Flawed U.S. Refugee Workforce Development Strategy."
4. Alaska, Arkansas, Delaware, Hawaii, Montana, West Virginia, and Wyoming. See U.S. Department of Health & Human Services, "Fiscal Year 2001 Refugee Arrivals."
5. Kapteijns and Arman, "Educating Immigrant Youth in the United States," 18; Fuglerud and Engebrigtsen, "Culture, Networks and Social Capital," 1126.
6. Goza, "The Somali Presence in the United States," 262.
7. Ibid., 255–275; Schaid and Grossman, "The Somali Diaspora in Small Midwestern Communities," 296–319.
8. Shandy and Fennelly, "A Comparison of the Integration Experiences," 23–45; Schaid and Zoltan, "The Somali Diaspora in Small Midwestern Communities," 295–319; Semple, "A Somali Influx."

9. Horst, "The Somali Diaspora in Minneapolis," 275–94; Mattessich and Hope, *Speaking for Themselves*.
10. Kapteijns and Arman, "Educating Immigrant Youth in the United States," 18–43.
11. Goza, "The Somali Presence in the United States," 263.
12. U.S. Census Bureau, "Summary File 1 and Summary File 3."
13. Timberlake, "Municipal Collaboration."
14. Nadeau, "The Flawed U.S. Refugee Workforce Development Strategy"; Rabrenovic, "When Hate Comes to Town," 349–60.
15. Nadeau, "The Flawed U.S. Refugee Workforce Development Strategy."
16. Focus groups took place in community centers and office conference rooms, whereas the majority of the interviews took place in the homes of participants in Lewiston and Auburn, Maine. Two of the interviews took place over the phone with Somalis who had moved out of Maine. The interviews and focus groups lasted between one and two hours. Participants were offered the option of speaking in Somali, English, or a combination, and trained bilingual interviewers were present. During the interviews and focus groups, people often showed up after an interview or focus group was underway, sometimes flowing in and out of the room and the conversation. This occurred more often in people's homes, which were fluid environments characterized by children, extended family members, or neighbors coming and going. Only those who participated in the dialogue were included as research subjects. Six additional interviews were conducted after data for this article was analyzed.
17. The English interviews and focus groups were transcribed in full by trained research assistants. Those interviews and focus groups conducted in Somali or both Somali and English were first translated verbatim by trained bilingual student research assistants and then transcribed in English. Quotations used in this chapter were minimally edited for clarity and readability. Excessive redundancies such as "you know" and "um" were eliminated; passages and phrases—marked by ellipses—were abridged in the interest of condensing and clarifying; and grammatical changes were made to improve the flow and clarity of the subjects' stories. In addition, pseudonyms were used to protect the anonymity of the interviewees.
18. The findings of this study are not generalizable; they are specific to the local context in which the data were gathered. Moreover, those findings are limited by our particular contacts in the Somali community. The diverse Somali community is cleaved along a number of social, political,

and cultural lines, and given our limited contacts, we were unable to access entire segments of the community. For example, this chapter does not necessarily represent the secondary migration experiences of Somali Bantu, a minority group that has migrated to Lewiston in recent years.

19. Fuglerud and Engebrigtsen, "Culture, Networks and Social Capital," 1126.
20. See Timberlake, "Municipal Collaboration."
21. See Nadeau, "The Somalis of Lewiston," 105–46.
22. Rabrenovic, "When Hate Comes to Town," 349–60.
23. See Buckley, "The Political Economy of Immigration Policies," who points to a relationship between secondary migration and welfare availability particularly among refugees. See also Zimmerman and Fix, "Immigrant Policy in the States," who reported that welfare generosity influences refugees' migration decisions, although to a lesser extent than jobs and family ties.
24. Shandy, *Nuer-American Passages*.
25. Macarthy, "Significance of Race."
26. Ibid.
27. See Shandy, *Nuer-American Passages*, 170, Table A.6. Resettlement States by Level of Welfare Benefits, for more details. See Macarthy, "Significance of Race," for an analysis of time limits and racial composition of states. See also Ihuto Ali, "Staying off the Bottom of the Melting Pot," and Peterson, "African Immigrants Set Pace to Get Off Welfare," who both provide evidence that counters the perception that large numbers of Somalis are on welfare.
28. Macarthy, "Significance of Race"; Shandy, *Nuer-American Passages*.
29. See Kapteijns and Arman, "Educating Immigrant Youth in the United States," 28.
30. Section 8 housing vouchers are a form of financial assistance that is provided by the U.S. Department of Housing and Urban Development (HUD) to very low-income families, the elderly, and the disabled so they can rent homes or apartments in the private market. Voucher-holders are permitted to move and use their vouchers anywhere in the United States.
31. The Many and One rally was organized by a community-based coalition in response to a poorly attended rally organized by the neo-Nazi group National Alliance, who came to Lewiston after the mayor published an inflammatory letter in the local newspaper asking Somalis to stop moving there. See Rabrenovic, "When Hate Comes to Town."

32. Somali immigrants are sometimes perceived as a threat to native-born racial minorities, which is not unfounded. In her research with immigrants and employers in New York City, Nancy Foner found that employers were more inclined to hire minority immigrants over native-born blacks and Hispanics, largely because of racist attitudes toward blacks and Hispanics and the perception that immigrant workers would be more docile and harder working. Foner, *From Ellis Island to JFK*.

33. See Al-Sharmani, "Diasporic Somalis in Cairo."

34. See Portes, "Social Capital: Its Origins and Applications in Modern Sociology."

35. Shandy, *Nuer-American Passages,*134.

36. Ibid., 5.

37. Ibid., 134.

38. Somali clan structure is extremely complex. There are six main clan-families with numerous subclans. The majority of Somalis trace their lineage to the four main pastoral nomadic clans (the Dir, Darod, Isaq, and Hawiye), whereas the minority trace their lineage to the two major agricultural clans (the Digil and Rahanweyn). See Lewis, *A Modern History,* for more detail.

39. Putman, *Bowling Alone*.

40. "1.5 generation" refers to immigrants who grew up in two cultures—born outside of the United States and immigrating to the United States at a young age. "Second generation" refers to children who were born in the United States to immigrant parents.

41. See Langellier (chapter 7, this volume) for an analysis of identity.

42. Putman, *Bowling Alone*.

Chapter 3

1. Miller, "Census: Maine Oldest, Whitest State in Nation."

2. "What is the American Dream?" *The Library of Congress*, December 19, 2002, www.loc.gov/teachers/classroommaterials/lessons/american -dream/students/thedream.html.

3. Hodgkin, *Lewiston Memories*.

4. Lewiston Historical Commission, *Historic Lewiston: Its Architectural Heritage*; Leamon, *Historic Lewiston: A Textile City in Transition*, 10–34.

5. Rand, *The Peoples Lewiston-Auburn Maine 1875–1975*.

6. Leamon, *Historic Lewiston: A Textile City in Transition*, 10–34.

7. Lewiston Historical Commission, *Bales to Bedspreads;* Judd, Churchill, and Eastman, *Maine: the Pine Tree State.*

8. 2009–2010 unemployment has since increased to levels not seen since 1983, as the average rate of unemployment has consistently hovered between 8.8 percent and 9.5 percent (Maine Department of Labor, *Historical Unemployment Rates for Lewiston Maine and the United States,* Augusta: Division of Labor Market Information Services, Local Area Unemployment Statistics Program, June 16, 2003; Dennison, "Civilian Labor Force Estimates."

9. U.S. Bureau of the Census, Census 2000 Summary File 3: Sample Data of 111 Communities—Poverty Rates, generated by Philip Nadeau using American Factfinder; 2002 figures showing Lewiston with the highest poverty rate in the state are from Census Tract 201, which depicts the downtown area of the city roughly bordered east to west by Birch Street and Lowell Court and north to south by Blake Street down to the Androscoggin River.

10. Lincoln Jeffers (Assistant to the City Administrator), *Lewiston Economic Development Highlights,* August 2010. Available upon request from Phil Nadeau.

11. "2003 Statistical Issue." Authorized refugee numbers will almost always differ from those actually relocated. Under the Refugee Act of 1980, the president, in consultation with Congress and the U. S. Department of State, authorizes a set number of eligible refugees, as determined by the Department of Homeland Security's Bureau of Citizenship and Immigration Services (formerly the Immigration and Naturalization Service) to relocate into the United States. Additionally, security clearances, funding, and other variables may impact a refugee's ability to relocate into the United States.

12. Phil Nadeau, *Report to Governor Angus King.*

13. "Secondary migrants" is a phrase utilized by many federal, state, and local agencies to identify those immigrants who have arrived as refugees— technically in country thirty-six months or less—who move from their initial community of resettlement to another community somewhere in the U.S. This chapter will define *all* resettled refugees who move from one U.S. community of resettlement to another as such.

14. "Annual Report to Congress—2000," *U.S. Department of Health and Human Services.*

15. Nadeau, *Report to Governor Angus King.*
16. Tilove, "Somali Migration Transforms Lewiston"; Bixler, "From Clarkstown to Lewiston." See also Huisman, chapter 2, this volume.
17. "Housing: Sustaining Portland's Future."
18. Sue Charron (Director, General Assistance Office), interviews with author, Lewiston, Maine, January–April 2001.
19. Ibid.
20. "Maine Looks Like Home to Somali Immigrants."
21. Charron interviews, January–April 2001.
22. Grossman, "Somali Immigrant Settlement."
23. Ibid.
24. "Economics and Demographics – Employment Patterns of Somali Immigrants to Lewiston."
25. Charron interviews, January–April 2001.
26. Reardon, "A Yankee Mill Town Globalizes"; Ron Claiborne, "ABC News," September 15, 2002; Matthew Bell, "The World," *Public Radio International,* July 22, 2002; Douglas Kennedy, "Fox Report with Shepard Smith," *Fox News,* August 6–7, 2002.
27. *The Letter* is also the title of a film documentary produced by Hamzeh Mystique Films focusing on the weeks and months following the issuance of Mayor Raymond's letter. Information about the documentary can be found at www.hamzehmystiquefilms.com/theletter.
28. Dot Perham-Whittier (Coordinator, Lewiston Community Relations), interview with author, Lewiston, Maine, February 4, 2003.
29. Abley, "Somalis Caught in Storm." Citizens also expressed this view in assorted emails, available by request from author.
30. Dot Perham-Whittier, 2006 & 2007 All-America City Award Applications. Available upon request from author.
31. Community Public Health Steering Committee, *Meeting Summary,* April 13, 2007. Available upon request from author.
32. Nadeau, "The New Mainers."
33. The genesis of "New Mainers" and its use to describe new immigrants and refugees taking up residence in Maine can be traced as far back as 2002 to the Portland area based CITE (Community Improvement Through Employment) initiative's "New Mainers" subcommittee and their work around immigrant employment barriers. Since that time, the term "new Mainers" has been used by many as an alternate descriptor to positively

emphasize a relocated refugee's status as a new Maine resident: as opposed to someone who is simply in-state as a dislocated person from another country.

34. Dennison, "Historical Unemployment Rates."
35. Rector, *An Analysis of the Employment Patterns of Somali Immigrants.*
36. Allen, "Employment and Earnings Outcomes."
37. Ibid.
38. Rector, *An Analysis of the Employment Patterns of Somali Immigrants.*
39. Allen, "Employment and Earnings Outcomes."
40. Burt, Peyton, and Adams, "Reading and Adult English Language Learners."
41. McKay and Weinstein-Shr, "English Literacy in the U.S."
42. Allender, "Australia's Migrants and Refugees."
43. Sue Martin (Director, Lewiston Public School ELL Director), interview conducted by telephone on October 11, 2007.
44. Calabria, "Somalia's Woes."
45. Ann Kemper (ESL Programming Director, Lewiston Adult Education), telephone interviews with author, October 7, 2008 and October 23, 2008.
46. "Promoting Cultural Sensitivity."
47. Nadeau, "Summary of City Meetings." See also Toner and Hough, chapter 8, this volume.
48. Kemper interviews, October 7 & 23, 2008.
49. Lewiston Adult Education, *ESOL Report 2002-2003-3/12/08,* March 27, 2008. Report available upon request from author.
50. The Lewiston Adult Education program utilizes the CASAS program to evaluate the placement of individuals into their ESL program. "CASAS—Comprehensive Adult Student Assessment Systems—is the most widely used system for assessing adult basic reading, math, listening, writing, and speaking skills within a functional context. CASAS is the only adult assessment system of its kind to be approved and validated by the U.S. Department of Education and the U.S. Department of Labor to assess both native and non-native speakers of English" (CASAS, no date). Lewiston Adult Education's scales levels of English proficiency employing the CASAS Student Performance Level (SPL) designations.
51. Kemper interviews, October 7 & 23, 2008.
52. Sue Martin, memo to Phil Nadeau, *Thoughts About Federal Support,* October 10, 2007.

53. Mamgain and Collins, "Off the Boat, Now Off to Work."
54. Muir, "English and Literacy Teaching and Learning Strategies."
55. Duffy, Harmon, Ranard, Thao, and Yang, "The Hmong: An Introduction to Their History and Culture."
56. "How Refugees Come to America."
57. Nadeau, "The Somalis of Lewiston."
58. Kemper interviews, October 7 & 23, 2008.
59. Ibid.
60. Ibid.
61. Mchugh, Gelatt, and Fix, "Adult English Language in the United States."
62. "Office of Refugee Resettlement, Refugee Assistance Division, ORR Budget."
63. McHugh, Gelatt, and Fix, "Adult English Language in the U.S."
64. "Office of Refugee Resettlement, Refugee Assistance Division, Targeted Assistance Discretionary Program."
65. Ibid.
66. Lordeman, "The Workforce Investment Act (WIA)."
67. "Summary of the Adult Education and Family Literacy Act."
68. Kemper interviews, October 7 & 23, 2008.
69. "Immigrants and Employment: Workforce Development."
70. "WIA Title 1 Strategic Plan Modification."
71. Allender, "Australia's Migrants and Refugees."
72. "Australian TESOL Training Centre."
73. Allender, "Australia's Migrants and Refugees."
74. Muir, "English and Literacy Teaching."
75. "Beginning a Life in Australia-Welcome to Queensland."
76. "Workplace English Language and Literacy (WELL) Program."
77. See New Mainers Workforce Partnership-L/A. (no date). *Synopsis.* Handout provided by James Baumer, Director of Business Services, Central Western Maine Workforce Development Board.
78. Ibid.
79. Ibid. See also "Implementation Guidelines."
80. "Implementation Guidelines."
81. James Baumer (Central Western Maine Workforce Investment Board, Director of Business Services), telephone interview with author on October 24, 2008.
82. Nancy Dolan, email correspondence with author, February 29, 2008.

Chapter 4

1. This chapter is based on Ismail Ahmed, "Somali Leadership in Lewiston: How It Impacts the Community's Acculturation Process" (Master's thesis, University of Southern Maine, 2005).

2. Although the concept of social capital is contested and defined in a variety of ways across disciplines, in this study it pertains to the resources and benefits that are accrued and exchanged through participation in culturally marked social networks. For more information on social capital, see, for example, Putnam, *Bowling Alone*, Bourdieu, "The Forms of Capital," and Taylor, *Unleashing the Potential: Bringing the Residents to the Center of Regeneration*.

3. See Huisman, chapter 2, this volume and Nadeau, chapter 3, this volume.

4. Harris, *The Rise of Anthropological Theory*.

5. Lewis, *A Modern History*, and Kapteijns with Ali, *Women's Voices in a Man's World*.

6. See Lewis, *A Modern History*.

7. This author was reprimanded and threatened with dire consequences if he further pursued why the mayor wrote the letter.

8. Harris, *The Rise of Anthropological Theory*.

9. Mutual assistance associations, or MAAs, are grassroots, community-based organizations managed primarily by and for members of particular resettled refugee groups.

10. The communal living of the Somalis in Lewiston made it necessary to have prior and special arrangements for times when and places where the informants were available for the interviews. I mostly interviewed the informants in their apartments, in a comfortable and familiar setting, while having a cup of Somali tea.

11. These Somali women were perceived as leaders and were already involved in advocacy of the community. They offered case management, were mentoring other women, and were recognized as de facto Somali leaders in Lewiston. In the public sphere they influenced decision making.

12. Ages and length of stay in Maine varied widely for all twenty participants. Their mean age was thirty-three years, and the average length of stay in Maine was 3.4 years. Some of them reported to have had an average education by Somali standards (at least elementary schooling); fifteen reported that they were first generation with a high-school education, and that their fathers and mothers had no formal education beyond the

Qur'anic schools. Eighteen of the informants affirmed that they had attended Lewiston Adult Education classes some time during their stay in Lewiston. Fifteen of them were married and had children. Seven of them were naturalized United States citizens. And two of the participants were also entrepreneurs who owned small businesses in downtown Lewiston.

13. The following topics formed the basis of questions for the interviews: personal philosophy of leadership, perception of community leadership, and influence on his/her leadership beliefs. Defining leadership concretely was a difficult and abstract process for the respondents. I asked numerous probing questions in order to allow the participants to articulate their personal definitions of leadership, such as: "Name a leader you are familiar with," "What does leadership mean to you?" "What are its religious implications?" and "Do you consider yourself as a leader and what does that mean?"

14. Hammersley, *Reading Ethnographic Research.*

15. For example, most of the informants worked in an American environment. They report that while they try to get along with their American colleagues, they cannot express themselves easily. One commented, "When I communicate with my American colleagues, I cannot relax; I have to be on guard all the time. I am always afraid of saying or doing the wrong thing that would offend them or embarrass myself. It makes me really tired. When [I am] with Somalis, I feel like [a] fish in the water. [I] feel at ease." However, the majority of the Somali leaders were also working in environments where their clientele are mostly Somali.

16. Nzelibe, "The Evolution of African Management Thought."

17. Putman, *Bowling Alone.*

18. Ibid.

19. Nzelibe, "The Evolution of African Management Thought."

20. Dia, "Indigenous Management Practices."

21. See, for example, Taylor, *Unleashing the Potential;* Thake, *Staying the Course;* and Thake and Staubach, *Investing in People.*

22. Examples in Lewiston are the partnership between the Somali United Women of Maine and Community Concepts (initially) and Catholic Charities Maine (later); and Daryeelka and Sisters of Charity, to name just a few.

23. Mayo, "Partnerships for Regeneration and Community Development."

24. Hannerz, *Exploring the City.*
25. Dees, *The Meaning of Social Entrepreneurship.*
26. The history of the world, according to some leadership scholars, is the history of "great men" who created what the masses of people could accomplish. See Jennings, *An Anatomy of Leadership,* and Nahavandi, *The Art and Science of Leadership.*
27. At the core of what must be done is what public educators Harry C. Boyte and Nancy Kari describe as popular civic education in *Building America.* See also Chrislip and Larson, *Collaborative Leadership.*

Chapter 5

1. Roble and Rutledge, *The Somali Diaspora,* 24; Awa Abdi, "In Limbo."
2. Roble and Rutledge, *The Somali Diaspora,* 26.

Chapter 6

1. I would like to acknowledge all the people who have helped me with resources, guidance, and feedback in the writing of this piece. I am indebted to the University of Maine faculty members of the Somali Narrative Project, particularly Dr. Kimberly Huisman and Dr. Carol Toner, who continuously and tirelessly supported me with their invaluable feedback. I would also like to thank my family and recognize their contribution to my success and ability to undertake this project, especially my father, Jirde Warsame, my mother, Fatuma Nur, and my sister, Nasra Warsame. Furthermore, my uncle, Mohammed Warsame, generously offered his extensive knowledge of the sociopolitical evolution of the Somali people. I would like to thank Professor Seth Singleton, who has always encouraged me to reach my full potential in academia and inspired me to connect my undergraduate education in International Affairs with my graduate studies in Education. I would to like to thank Dr. John Maddaus and Dr. Owen J. Logue from the College of Education and Human Development as well as the faculty of the Higher Education Program at the University of Maine for their support and passion in empowering me throughout my college career. Finally, thanks to Connie Smith and others in the Financial Aid Office whose expertise helped me negotiate financial matters.
2. Since the 1954 *Brown v. Board of Education of Topeka, Kansas* ruling, many improvements have taken place to address inequality and segregation in education. However, some daunting challenges still remain. See Blake,

"The Full Circle."

3. The Upward Bound Program was launched in 1965 as part of President Johnson's War on Poverty, and was one of the TRIO programs. See Maddaus and Liu, "Rising Against All Odds."

4. Citing Richard Rothstein, Sonia Nieto claims that "during the immigration period from 1880–1915, few Americans succeeded in school, least of all immigrants; immigrants of all backgrounds did poorly." Nieto, *Language, Culture, and Teaching*, 42.

5. Mohamed, "Wasted Talent."

6. Kapteijns and Arman, "Educating Immigrant Youth in the United States."

7. See Abada and Tenkorang, "Gender Differences in Educational Attainment"; Feliciano and Rumbaut, "Gendered Paths"; Lopez, *Hopeful Girls, Troubled Boys;* Zhou and Bankston, "Family Pressure."

8. See Sotomayor, "The Role of Ethnic Networks"; Bennett and Lutz, "How African American Is the Net Black Advantage?"; Kroneberg, "Ethnic Communities and School Performance"; Thomas, "The Effect of Family Immigration History."

9. Kapteijns and Arman, "Educating Immigrant Youth in the United States," 31.

10. Chickering and Reisser, *Education and Identity.*

11. Kapteijns and Arman, "Educating Immigrant Youth," 23.

12. Ibid.

13. Nieto, *Language, Culture, and Teaching*, 33–34.

14. For example, at the University of Maine, a friend of mine introduced me to the Somali Narrative Project, which was composed of four University of Maine faculty members. They all come from different educational backgrounds and have only their interest in the Somalis and Somali students in common. The fact that there were advocates for Somali students on campus, and that they were interested in both the culture and history of my native country, was very reassuring to me and to the other Somali students who were involved in the project.

Chapter 7

1. Caaliya is a pseudonym. This essay is adapted from Kristin M. Langellier, "Performing Somali Identity in the Diaspora: 'Wherever I Go I Know Who I Am,'" *Cultural Studies* 24 (2010): 66–94. (www.informaworld.com)

2. Caaliya's interview was conducted in the summer of 2006 in Lewiston, Maine. It is part of the larger, ongoing Somali Narrative Project, a

collaborative of faculty and Somali students at the University of Maine that began in 2004. I acknowledge the ongoing contributions of all project members and other students with whom we have worked over the years. We thank the Somali community for their generosity with their stories, with special gratitude to Caaliya (pseudonym) for her generative story on Somali identity in the diaspora.

3. Pollock, "A Response to Dwight Conquergood's Essay," 38.

4. Conquergood, "Beyond the Text," 25–36.

5. Lewis, *Understanding Somalia and Somaliland*, 25. Somali verbal skills emerge within their long, abundant, and rich oral traditions of poetry, narrative, and history.

6. This question about being "like us" is asked in Kapteijns and Arman, "Educating Immigrant Youth in the United States," 19. The quotation on the "sense of self" is from McGown, *Muslims in the Diaspora*, 97.

7. Barbara Myerhoff calls these cultural performances "definitional ceremonies." Myerhoff, *Remembered Lives*.

8. Murray Forman argues that the command that the refugee perform the "plight and flight" narrative to audiences is "reminiscent of the colonial · condition in which the voice of the subjugated subject is contained within the authoritative structures of the dominant class" and that "living to tell the tale may thus produce a prison of another, discursive form." Forman, "'Straight Outta Mogadishu,'" 44–45.

9. Although I have considered that such a large and mixed audience so complicated, even contaminated, the interview as to render it anomalous, I argue instead that the situation offers certain advantages. It reflects the collectivistic nature of Somali culture and their preference for group interactions. And it mirrors normative conditions of Somali experience in the diaspora, that is, narrating and negotiating identity in intercultural and intracultural spaces that cannot escape the changing constraints of bodies, situation, and discourse. Indeed, the group interview setting seems to create more than contain possibilities for identity construction.

10. Riessman, *Narrative Methods for the Human Sciences*,105. I excerpted and transcribed key narrative moments and examined them more closely for how they create and negotiate Caaliya's identity in a performance that is co-produced and discursively driven. Transcriptions highlight performance features that mark embodiment and retain the joint production of the narrative by listeners. The ordering of key identity moments retains

fidelity to the sequence in which they emerged in the interview event. The analysis follows Caaliya's trail in the trajectories and turns of its telling, foregrounding her agency and linking stories of dramatized identities.

11. In the transcripts, I preserve false starts, repetitions, and self-interruptions while segmenting the story into lines that reflect the narrator's rhythms and meaning units. Lines in the transcript suggest where the storyteller took brief pauses in a thought unit. Indented lines are used to group phrases on a single topic that were spoken together. A dash [—] at the end of a word indicates an abrupt cut-off of sound, often a self-interruption or shift in direction of thought. Short pauses are noted in brackets as [pause]; longer pauses are also noted in brackets. Italics denote emphasis. Other notes in brackets [laughter] provide information by describing vocal or gestural qualities or other clarification. I further describe performance features in the discussion of the storytelling.

12. Kapteijns, "Women and the Crisis of Communal Identity."

13. The ethnic limits of the Somali nation are signified in the five-pointed star adopted at the time of independence in 1960. They include French Djibouti, British Somaliland, Italian Somalia, British north Kenya, and the Ethiopian portion of the Somali Ogaden. For a brief overview of precolonial Somalia, colonial partition and re-partition, and postcolonial Somalia, see Lewis, *Understanding Somalia and Somaliland*.

14. Kapteijns and Arman, "Educating Immigrant Youth in the United States," 28.

15. McGown, *Muslims in the Diaspora*, 28–30; Lewis, *Understanding Somalia and Somaliland*.

16. Kapteijns and Arman, "Educating Immigrant Youth in the United States," 33–34.

17. See Jordan, "An African Presence in Europe."

18. Quote is by Ibrahim, "One is Not Born Black," 78. Catherine Besteman makes the argument that Somalia has a history of social stratification on the basis of race, status, region, and language in which she focuses on the 'Bantu' heritage and enslavement in Somalia. Some tensions between Bantu and ethnic Somalis have migrated to Lewiston, according to some informants. Besteman, *Unraveling Somalia*.

19. For classic statements of Somali clanism, see Lewis, *Blood and Bone: The Call of Kinship in Somali Society* and *Understanding Somalia and Somaliland*. For alternative readings of clanism, see Ahmed Samatar, "The

Curse of Allah" and Kapteijns, "Women and the Crisis of Communal Identity."

20. Among the reasons for the injunction not to talk about clans is the intense and continuing trauma of the civil war. Efforts to reduce clan ties in favor of a pan-Somali national identity after independence, followed by the campaign under dictator Siyad Barre's "scientific socialism" to eradicate clan loyalties, have not extinguished the meaning of tribe and kin in personal identities. Additional pressures in the diaspora include appeals to modernity and global Islam as anchors of Somali identity.

21. One Somali interviewee suggested that as cultural outsiders, Somalis of different clans might be more forthcoming with us than with a native interviewer. For a fuller discussion, see Langellier, chapter 9, this volume.

22. Kapteijns with Ali, *Women's Voices in a Man's World*; Cawo Abdi, "Convergence of Civil War and the Religious Right"; Korn with Eichhorst, *Born in the Big Rains*.

23. In her bestselling memoir *Infidel*, Somali refugee Ayaan Hirsi Ali describes wearing pants and riding a bicycle in the Netherlands: "one Somali said, 'you are putting us all to shame with your bicycle. When you ride toward us with your legs spread we can see your genitals.'" Ali, *Infidel*, 202.

24. Leila Ahmed, *Women and Gender in Islam*, 247.

25. Forman, "'Straight Outta Mogadishu,'" 33–60.

26. *The Letter: An American Town and the "Somali Invasion,"* a film directed by Ziad H. Hamzeh (2003), documents this incident. See also Finnegan, "New in Town: The Somalis of Lewiston" and Jones, "The New Yankees." Caaliya arrived in Lewiston after the episode but was familiar with its occurrence and aftermath.

27. Kapteijns and Arman, "Educating Immigrant Youth in the United States," 28.

28. Ibrahim, "One is Not Born Black."

29. Forman, "'Straight Outta Mogadishu.'"

30. Jordan, "An African Presence in Europe," 343.

31. Lewis, *Understanding Somalia and Somaliland*, 25.

32. This practice—as well as what to name it—has a complex politics. In the discussion here I use the term "female genital cutting" in order to discuss the different linguistic choices that Caaliya makes as she talks about the practice in her storytelling. See Hough, chapter 1, note 37, this volume, for further discussion of this practice.

33. Kapteijns and Arman, "Educating Immigrant Youth in the United States," 35.
34. See, for example, McGown, *Muslims in the Diaspora,* 150. Female genital cutting is a difficult and unresolved issue within Somali culture. For memoirs, see Dirie, *Desert Flower* and Korn with Eichorst, *Born in the Big Rains.*
35. See the full-length version of this essay for explication of possible readings of Caaliya's covering that draws on a range of scholarship on wearing the veil.
36. Duits and van Zoonen, "Headscarves and Porno-Chic," 115.
37. Madison, "Performance, Personal Narratives, and the Politics of Possibility." Shahnaz Kahn describes the Muslim feminist as unavoidably situated in this hybridized space that moves "away from overdetermined subjectivity to a creative critical space" for identity construction in the diaspora in *Muslim Women: Crafting a North American Identity,* 125.
38. Interview 12 with an anonymous male, August 23, 2006.
39. Bateson, "Joint Performance Across Cultures."

Chapter 8
1. While migration theories have become more complex in recent decades, the search for better economic opportunities remains central to understanding migration. See Suarez-Orozco, "Right Moves? Immigration, Globalization, Utopia, and Dystopia." For the migration and acculturation of French Canadians in Lewiston, see Richard, *Loyal But French.*
2. Quoted in Farah, *Yesterday, Tomorrow,* 118; Adam and Ford, *Mending Rips in the Sky: Options for Somali Communities in the 21st Century,* 449–50.
3. Interview 8, 2006, 8–10. The University of Maine Somali Narrative Project conducted the interviews quoted in this paper. See Langellier, chapter 9, this volume, for details on this project and the interviews.
4. Interview 33, June 2009, 6.
5. Rector, "An Analysis of the Employment Patterns of Somali Immigrants." This unemployment rate may be inflated, given that it includes all parents with small children. Many of these parents are not technically unemployed but are, in fact, choosing to stay at home to care for their children. Further, it is unclear whether or not this figure includes seasonal occupations. For a thoughtful response to this DOL report, see Bates College Department of Anthropology, "Perceived Barriers to Somali Immigrant Employment in Lewiston."

6. "Five Years After Somalis Migrated to Lewiston, Maine USA."
7. See, for example, Mamgain and Collins, "Off the Boat, Now Off to Work"; Allen, "Employment and Earnings Outcomes"; Nadeau, chapter 3, this volume; and Rector, "An Analysis of the Employment Patterns of Somali Immigrants to Lewiston."
8. Interview 35, June 2009, 11. Interview 38, May 27, 2010. Workplace discrimination based on dress is common elsewhere as well. See Guerin and Guerin, "Relocating Refugees in Developed Countries."
9. Interview 39, March 18, 2010, 2.
10. Doug Rutledge points to the Somalis' desire to participate in the social and economic life of the United States without assimilating. Roble and Rutledge, *The Somali Diaspora*, 14.
11. L.L. Bean Inc. Company Profile, www.globalsources.com/PEC /PROFILES/LLBEAN.HTM (accessed on June 2, 2010).
12. Interview 40, August 19, 2009, 11–13.
13. Ibid., 11.
14. Ibid., 13.
15. Ibid., 9–10.
16. Interview 41, September 3, 2009, 3. While we were on the L.L. Bean campus taking pictures, we witnessed many pleasant cross-cultural exchanges in both English and Somali.
17. Ibid., 5, 7.
18. Interview 40, August 19, 2009, 4.
19. Ibid., 3.
20. L.L. Bean Careers, http://llbeancareers.com/inclusion.htm (accessed on June 7, 2010). For more on the Diversity Hiring Coalition of Maine, go to http://maine.gov/mdot/disadvantaged-business-enterprises/pdf /Diversity%20Hiring%20Coalition%20of%20Maine.htm. Interview 40, August 19, 2009, 16.
21. Interview 35, June, 2009, 9.
22. Interview 41, September 3, 2009, 24.
23. Allen, "Employment and Earnings Outcomes," 95.
24. Interview 5, July 11, 2006, 5–12.
25. The Somali Bantu who were approved for resettlement in the United States are a particular subset of Bantu whose ancestors were brought as slaves from Kenya, Malawi, Mozambique, and Tanzania. When slavery ended in the early twentieth century, many created lives for themselves in

farming villages along the Juba River. See UNHCR, "The Somali Bantu"; Stephen and The Cultural Orientation Africa Project, "Somali Bantu Report"; Lehman and Eno, *Somali Bantu: Their History and Culture* (accessed July 7, 2010); Besteman, *Unraveling Somalia;* and the National Somali Bantu Project, www.somalibantu.org.

26. Lehman and Eno, "Somali Bantu."
27. Little, "Reflections on Somalia," 69.
28. "U.S. a Place of Miracles for Somali Refugees," as quoted in Ahmed Samatar, "Beginning Again," 15; USCRI, *Refugee Reports* 23, 1.
29. Stephen and The Cultural Orientation Africa Project, "Somali Bantu Report," 21.
30. Ibid., 6.
31. Each year, from ten to twelve thousand migrant workers enter Maine to help harvest blueberries, cranberries, apples, and broccoli in addition to performing other agricultural work. Adam, "Maine Migrant Farm Workers' Exhibit to Travel Through Region."
32. Interview 29, October 24, 2008, 20.
33. "Besteman, as quoted in "Single Somali-Bantu Mothers Farm in Maine."
34. "Phone conversation with Daniel Ungier on July 9, 2010."
35. Kurtz, "Differentiating Multiple Meanings of Garden and Community," 658. For a history of community gardens see Lawson, *City Bountiful.*
36. Phone interview with Andrew Marshall, MOFGA, July 9, 2010.
37. The rough terrain, short growing season, and indifferent soil forced farmers to supplement and diversify their sources of income. Farmers cut ice, processed hides, and produced handmade items in order to survive. "Most farmers were not completely self sufficient, rather they were part of a 'complex economy,' that included bartering and trading for locally and regionally produced goods and services." Smith-Mayo, "Maine: The State of Local Food," 3.
38. Russell Libby, quoted in "Maine: The State of Local Food," 6.
39. Interview with Bob Sullivan, 2007, as quoted in "Maine: The State of Local Food," 8.
40. Interview 42, May 27, 2010. Lots to Gardens describes itself as "a youth and community driven organization that uses sustainable urban agriculture to create access to fresh food, and to nurture healthy youth and a healthy community. We teach people how to grow their own food, provide affordable access to fresh food, and involve youth as leaders. We help fami-

lies and youth develop skills and build power for lifelong and community-wide change." www.stmarysmaine.com/Nutrition-Center-of-Maine /lots-to-gardens.html (accessed 7 July 2010).

41. "New American Sustainable Agriculture Project" (accessed July 7, 2010).
42. www.cei.maine.org.While the Maine NASAP was started by Coastal Enterprises Incorporated, it is now funded by the Department of Labor. CEI was incorporated in 1977 with a commitment to sustainability, which it describes as "meeting the needs of the current generation without compromising the ability or opportunity for future generations to meet their needs." www.cei.maine.org. See also Packard-Littlefield Farm at http://www.cultivating community.org/agriculture/packard-littlefield -farm.html.
43. Coastal Enterprises Inc., www.ceimaine.org.
44. Stitely, "Cultivating New Americans," accessed July 7, 2010.
45. Giraud, "Shared Backyard Gardening," 168, 170.
46. Gilbert, "Mayor's Corner: A Response to No Comparison between Somalis and Francos." The mayor listed other jobs Somalis hold as well: "As for Somalis working, here are some of the places where they work in L-A and this doesn't count those who travel to Portland, Freeport and other places. The list of some is as follows and it is by no means all inclusive: Wal-Mart Super Store, Wal-Mart Distribution Center, Dingley Press, staff/management at Tambrands, L.L. Bean (20 year round & 300 seasonal), 13 hotels and motels, Catholic Charities, City of Lewiston staff, hospitals and health care facilities, pharmacies, Hudson Bus Lines, Department of Health & Human Services, School department, Dunkin Donuts distribution, Bates College, Central Maine Community College as a professor of Mathematics. There are twelve store owners, eight truck drivers, three Somali restaurants and cafeteria, Somali home/health care (two of which sub-contract a total of seventy-five employees), twelve who provide Somali interpreter services, one who owns a cell phone company. There are between five and ten Somali property owners and five Somali owners of rental units."
47. Roble and Rutledge, *The Somali Diaspora*, 1.
48. Roble and Rutledge, *The Somali Diaspora*, 101.
49. Interview 41, September 3, 2009, 22.
50. Damooei, "Analyzing Somalia's Past and Present Economic Constraints," 275.

51. Ismail Ahmed, "Remittances and Their Economic Impact in Post-War Somaliland," quoted in Jacobsen, *The Economic Life of Refugees*, 60. To put that figure into a larger context, worldwide remittances in 2007, money sent from all migrants to their home countries, was an estimated $318 billion. See Fagen, "Migration, Development and Social Services" (accessed June 9, 2010). Western governments scrutinize these payments due to the potential support for radical organizations. See Horst, "The Transnational Political Engagements of Refugees."

52. Hammond, "Obliged to Give." (accessed June 7, 2010): n.p.

53. Ibid.

54. Interview 39, March 18, 2010, 2.

55. Roble and Rutledge, *The Somali Diaspora*, 4.

56. For women working in Somalia as traders, see Warsame, "Crisis or Opportunity?"; Farah, *Yesterday, Tomorrow*, 71–72; Interview 4, 7.

57. Citing U.S. Census figures, the *Bangor Daily News* reported that Maine has the oldest median age (forty-two years old) in the United States and with 95.3 percent of the population reported as "white," the state is also the least diverse. Miller, "Census: Maine Oldest, Whitest State in Nation." See also *The Growing Latin American Influence*, and Allen, "Employment and Earnings Outcomes."

Chapter 9

1. This chapter is a revision of Kristin M. Langellier, "Negotiating Somali Identity in Maine," in *Applied Communication in Organizational and International Contexts*, ed. Elizabeth C. Fine and Berndt Schwandt (St. Ingbert: Röhrig Universitätsverlag, 2008), 97–106.

2. See Hamzeh, *The Letter: An American Town and the "Somali Invasion."* See also Finnegan, "New in Town" and Jones, "The New Yankees."

3. Local supporters of diversity might be more likely to attend a public rally than might critics of the Somali migration. Negative local comments about Somalis often occur in online formats, for example, newspaper readers' comments to articles in the *Lewiston Sun*.

4. Lewiston was identified as a model for The New Migration Project to work in cities in strife after immigrants have moved in, including Boise, ID; Fort Wayne, IN; Frederick, MD; and Manchester, NH. The project is based on the Center for Preventing Hate, a public education program focused on reducing anti-immigrant bias in neighborhoods across the United States with programs designed to foster relationships between

long-term residents and new resettled immigrants in an effort to create safe, inclusive communities. See www.preventinghate.org.

5. See Ihuto Ali, "Staying off the Bottom of the Melting Pot."

Chapter 10

1. Bickman, *Minding American Education*, 2.
2. Freire, *Pedagogy of the Oppressed*.
3. We received many small grants from various sources that allowed us to buy books for our reading group, to pay for student travel to conferences, to buy food for some of our events, and to a limited extent to pay students for some of their work with us. We have thanked our funding sources in the acknowledgments to this book.
4. In this reading group, we read: Lewis, *A Modern History of the Somali, Nation and State in the Horn of Africa* 4th ed.; novels by Farah including *From a Crooked Rib, Gifts, Secrets, Links*, and *Yesterday, Tomorrow: Voices from the Somali Diaspora*; Gardner and Bushra, eds., *Somalia, The Untold Story—The War Through the Eyes of Somali Women*; Dirie and Miller, *Desert Flower: The Extraordinary Journey of a Desert Nomad*.
5. Boal, *Theatre of the Oppressed*. We drew from the following sources for the Readers Theater script: Ahrens and Hashi-Aldus, eds., *The Night You Were Born, Cherished One*; Barnes and Boddy, *Aman: The Story of a Somali Girl*; Dirie and Miller, *Desert Flower*; Farah, *Yesterday, Tomorrow*; Gardner and Bushra, eds., *Somalia—The Untold Story*; Inness, ed., *Running for Their Lives*; Laurence, *The Prophet's Camel Bell*.
6. For a discussion on the terminology used for this practice see Hough, chapter 1, note 37, this volume.

Chapter 11

1. Originally published as Kimberly Huisman, "Readers' Theater as Public Pedagogy," *Theory in Action* 2, no. 3 (July 2009): 6-30, www.transformativestudies.org. All Rights Reserved.
2. Mills, *The Sociological Imagination*, 3.
3. Mills, *The Sociological Imagination*.
4. In subsequent semesters, we have offered a class for the students so they could earn some academic credit for their participation.
5. See Kemmis and McTaggart, "Participatory Action Research," 563.
6. For a discussion on the terminology used for this practice see Hough, chapter 1, note 37, this volume.
7. Boal, *Theatre of the Oppressed*.

8. This also raises concerns and limitations of the research findings because the gender and age differences between the interviewer and the interviewee may affect what the interviewee is willing to disclose.

9. McIntyre, Chatzopoulos, Politi, and Roz, "Participatory Action Research: Collective Reflections."

10. Freire, "Education and Conscientizacao," 45.

11. Ibid. See also Freire, *Pedagogy of the Oppressed*, 69.

12. Conquergood, "Performing as a Moral Act," 10.

13. Alexander, "Performance Ethnography," 414.

14. McIntyre, Chatzopoulos, Politi, and Roz, "Participatory Action Research: Collective Reflections," 753–54.

15. Mills, *The Sociological Imagination*.

16. Alexander, "Performance Ethnography: The Reenacting and Inciting of Culture," 416.

17. Denzin, *Performance Ethnography*; Glass, "On Paulo Freire's Philosophy of Praxis."

18. Denzin, *Performance Ethnography*, 7.

19. Habermas, *Between Facts and Norm*.

20. Denzin, *Interpretive Ethnography*, xxi.

21. Ibid., 225.

22. Denzin, *Performance Ethnography*. See Conquergood, "Performing as a Moral Act"; McCall, "Performance Ethnography; Denzin, *Performance Ethnography*.

Part V

1. See Ihuto Ali, "Staying off the Bottom of the Melting Pot."

2. Lewis, *Understanding Somalia*, 25.

3. Over this time period, we conducted thirty-three interviews and logged numerous observation hours in Somali homes and in various locations in the Somali community. We also conducted eight focus-group interviews (ranging from four to eight participants) in order to focus on a more specific topic—for example, work and employment or reasons for moving to and leaving Maine. Most of the individual interviews took place in people's homes, and most focus groups took place in an office conference room. We secured funding to hire and train three Somali students to conduct interviews, and with their help, about half of the interviews were conducted in

either the Somali language or a combination of Somali and English. The interviews and focus groups lasted between one and two hours.

4. All but two of the interviewees were refugees from the civil war beginning in the early 1990s. Ladan and Rashid were immigrants who came to the United States in the early 1980s.

5. The excerpts are based on transcriptions of audiotapes and digital files of the interviews. When interviews were in Somali, an SNP student provided an oral translation in English, which was then transcribed. To enhance readability, we removed the repetitions, false starts, self-interruptions, and digressions that characterize all speaking. In some places we add references or information in brackets [ ] as a way to clarify meaning.

6. Pollock, "Memory, Remembering, and Histories of Change," 89.

7. United Nations High Commissioner for Refugees. 2007 "Global Trends: Refugees, Asylum-Seekers," 2007.

8. Both refugees and asylees are recognized by the government as having a "well-founded fear of persecution." The difference between the two is based on their physical location. Refugees obtain permission to enter a country before relocating whereas asylees seek refuge in a country after they arrive.

9. Singer and Wilson, "From 'There' to 'Here.'"

10. U.S. Department of Health & Human Services. Fiscal Years 2001-2007 Refugee Arrivals.

11. For a theoretical analysis of identity formation see Jenkins, *Rethinking Ethnicity.*

12. Grealy, "The Country of Childhood," 80.

13. The intersectional and multiplicative views of identity were developed by Crenshaw, "Demarginalizing the Intersection of Race and Sex," and Wing, "Brief Reflections toward a Multiplicative Theory of Praxis and Being." For an explication of identity as a cake made from inseparable ingredients, see DeFrancisco and Palczewski, *Communicating Gender Diversity,* 9.

14. McGown, *Muslims in the Diaspora,* 97. See also Kapteijns and Arman, "Educating Immigrant Youth in the United States," 17.

15. For classic statements of Somali clanism, see Lewis, *Blood and Bone* and *Understanding Somalia.* For alternative readings of clanism, see Ahmed Samatar, "The Curse of Allah" and Kapteijns, "Women and the Crisis of Communal Identity."

16. Other terms for this practice are "female genital cutting" and "female circumcision." See Hough, chapter 1, this volume, note 37.
17. See Kapteijns, *Women's Voices in a Man's World*; Cawo Abdi, "Convergence of Civil War and Religious Right"; and the bestselling memoir by Ayaan Ali, *Infidel*.
18. For race in the diaspora, see, for example, Forman, "'Straight Outta Mogadishu'"; Ibrahim, "One Is Not Born Black"; and IhutoAli, "Staying off the Bottom of the Melting Pot."
19. Graham and Khosravi, "Home is Where You Make It."
20. Settles, "Being at Home in a Global Society."
21. See "Lewiston's Somali Community Turns 10."

Afterword
1. Lindley, *The Early Morning Phone Call*, 32.
2. Yeats, *The Collected Works of W. B. Yeats*, 354.
3. Barber, *A Passion for Democracy*, 12.
4. Samatar, ed., *The Somali Challenge*, 8.
5. Andrzejewski and Lewis, *Somali Poetry*.
6. Besteman, "Land Tenure, Social Power and the Legacy of Slavery in Southern Somalia." See also Besteman and Cassanelli, eds., *The Struggle for Land in Southern Somalia* and Menkhaus, "Rural Transformation and the Roots of Underdevelopment in Somalia's Lower Juba Valley."
7. Hess, *Italian Colonialism in Somalia*.
8. Geshekter, "Entrepreneurs, Livestock, and Politics: British Somaliland, 1920–1950," 10.
9. Samatar, "The Curse of Allah: Civic Disembowelment and the Collapse of the State in Somalia." 95–146.
10. For instance, see Lidwien Kapteijns and Abukar Arman, "Educating Immigrant Youth in the United States: An Exploration of the Somali Case," 18–43.
11. Cited in Schorske, *Thinking with History*, 155. For further articulation of this point, see Wilhelm Dilthey in *The Formation of the Historical World in the Human Sciences*, Vol. III, edited by Rudolf A. Makkreel and Frithjof Rodi, particularly "The Structural Nexus of Knowledge," 45–90.
12. Ahmed I. Samatar, "Beginning Again: From Refugee to Citizen," 1–17.
13. Amartya Sen warns against the deadly dangers of this narrowing of the self. Its immediate cost, he writes, is "the miniaturization of human beings"—a slippery slope to violence. (Sen, *Identity and Violence*.)

14. Will Kymlicka and Wayne Norman, "Return of the Citizen: A Survey of Recent Work on Citizenship Theory," in *Theorizing Citizenship*, 6.
15. Berlin, et. al., *The Sense of Reality*, 260.
16. Delanty, *The Cosmopolitan Imagination*.

Bibliography

"2003 Statistical Issue." *Refugee Reports* 24, no. 9 (December 31, 2003). http://72.3.131.88/data/refugee_reports/archives/2003/RRDec.pdf.

Abada, Teresa, and Eric Yeboah Tenkorang. "Gender Differences in Educational Attainment among the Children of Canadian Immigrants." *International Sociology* 24, no. 4 (July 2009): 580–608.

Abdi, Awa M. "In Limbo: Dependency, Insecurity, and Identity Amongst Somali Refugees in Dadaab Camps." *Bildhaan: An International Journal of Somali Studies* 5 (2005): 17–34.

Abdi, Cawo Mohamed. "Convergence of Civil War and Religious Right: Reimagining Somali Women." *Signs* 33 (2007): 183–207.

Abley, Mark. "Somalis Caught in Storm." *Montreal Gazette,* January 11, 2003.

Adam, Glenn. "Maine Migrant Farm Workers' Exhibit to Travel through Region." *Associated Press,* February 23, 2008.

Adam, Hussein M., and Richard Ford. *Mending Rips in the Sky: Options for Somali Communities in the 21st Century.* Lawrenceville, NJ, and Asmara, Eritrea: The Red Sea Press, 1997.

Ahmed, Ismail. "Somali Leadership in Lewiston: How It Impacts the Community's Acculturation Process." Master's thesis, University of Southern Maine, 2005.

Ahmed, Ismail. "Remittances and Their Economic Impact in Post-War Somaliland." *Disasters* 24 (2000): 380–83.

Ahmed, Leila. *Women and Gender in Islam.* New Haven, CT: Yale University Press, 1992.

Ahrens, Joy, and Awralla Hashi-Aldus, eds. *The Night You Were Born, Cherished One: Habeynkaad Dhalatay Dhooko.* Portland, ME: Portland Adult Education, 2001.

Alexander, Brian Keith. "Performance Ethnography: The Reenacting and Inciting of Culture." In *The Sage Handbook of Qualitative Research,* edited by Norman. K. Denzin and Yvonne. S. Lincoln, 411–41. Thousand Oaks, CA: Sage, 2005.

Ali, Ayaan Hirsi. *Infidel.* New York: Free Press, 2007.

Ali, Ihuto. "Staying Off the Bottom of the Melting Pot: Somali Refugees Respond to a Changing U.S. Immigration Climate." *Bildhaan: The International Journal of Somali Studies* 9 (2009): 82–114.

Allen, Ryan. "Employment and Earnings Outcomes for Recently Arrived Refugees in Portland, Maine." Maine Department of Labor, 2006. www.maine.gov/labor/lmis /publications/pdf/RefugeeReport.pdf.

Allender, Susan Chou. "Australia's Migrants and Refugees: Opening the Door to Lifelong Learning." U.S. Department of Education. www2.ed.gov/pubs / HowAdultsLearn/Allender.pdf.

Al-Sharmani, Mulki. "Diasporic Somalis in Cairo: The Poetics and Practices of Soomaalinimo." In *From Mogadishu to Dixon: The Somali Diaspora in a Global Context,* edited by Abdi M. Kusow and Stephanie R. Bjork, 71–94. Trenton, NJ: The Red Sea Press, 2007.

Andrzejewski, B. W. and I. M. Lewis. *Somali Poetry: An Introduction.* Oxford: Oxford University Press, 1964.

"Annual Report to Congress—2000." *U.S. Department of Health and Human Services, Office of Refugee Resettlement.* September 26, 2002. www.acf.dhhs.gov/programs/orr/policy/00arc8.htm.

"Australian TESOL Training Centre—Adult Migrant Teacher Preparation Course." *Australian TESOL Training Centre & ACL Adult Migrant English Program.* 2007. http://mail.acl.edu.au/documents/AdultMigrantTeacher -PreparationCoursebrochure2007.pdf.

Barnes, Virginia Lee, and Janice Boddy. *Aman: The Story of a Somali Girl.* New York: Pantheon Books, 1994.

Bates College Department of Anthropology. "Perceived Barriers to Somali Immigrant Employment in Lewiston, A Supplement to Maine's Department of Labor Report." Maine Department of Labor. www.maine.gov/labor/lmis/laus.html.

Bateson, Mary Catherine. "Joint Performance across Cultures: Improvisation in a Persian Garden." *Text and Performance Quarterly* 13 (1993): 113–21.

"Beginning a Life in Australia-Welcome to Queensland." *Australian Government—Department of Immigration and Citizenship.* November 2007. www.immi.gov.au/media/publications/settle/beginning-life -texts/qld/eng.pdf.

Bennett, Pamela R., and Amy Lutz. "How African American is the Net Black Advantage? Differences in College Attendance Among Immigrant Blacks, Native Blacks, and Whites." *Sociology of Education* 82, no. 1 (January 2009): 70–100.

Berlin, Isaiah, Henry Hardy, and Patrick Gardiner. *The Sense of Reality: Studies in Ideas and Their History.* New York: Farrar, Straus and Giroux, 1996.

Besteman, Catherine. "Land Tenure, Social Power and the Legacy of Slavery in Southern Somalia." PhD diss., University of Arizona, 1991.

———. *Unraveling Somalia: Race, Violence, and the Legacy of Slavery.* Philadelphia: University of Pennsylvania, 1999.

Besteman, Catherine and Lee V. Cassanelli, eds. *The Struggle for Land in Southern Somalia: The War Behind the War.* Boulder, Col.: Westview Press, 1996.

Bickman, Martin. *Minding American Education, Reclaiming the Tradition of Active Learning.* New York: Teachers College Press, Columbia University, 2003.

Bixler, Mark. "From Clarkstown to Lewiston: Concerns About Crime, Kids' Future Led to Move." *Atlantic Journal-Constitution,* August 18, 2002.

Blake, J. Herman. "The Full Circle: TRIO Programs, Higher Education, and the American Future—Toward a New Vision of Democracy." *The Journal of Negro Education* 67, no. 4 (Autumn 1998): 329–32.

Boal, Augusto. *Theatre of the Oppressed.* Translated by Charles. A. McBride and Maria-Odilia L. McBride. New York: Theatre Communication Group, 1985.

Bourdieu, Pierre. "The Forms of Capital." In *Handbook of Theory and Research for the Sociology of Education,* edited by John G. Richardson, 241–58. New York: Greenwood, 1986.

Boyte, Harry C., and Nancy Kari. *Building America: The Democratic Promise of Public Work.* Philadelphia: Temple University Press, 1996.

Buckley, Francis H. "The Political Economy of Immigration Policies." *International Review of Law and Economics* 16 (1996): 81–99.

Burt, Miriam, Joy Kreeft Peyton, and Rebecca Adams. "Reading and Adult English Language Learners: A Review of the Research." *Center for Applied Linguistics.* 2003. http://www.cal.org/caela/research/RAELL.pdf.

Calabria, Karen. "Somalia's Woes Grow in Kenyan Refugee Camps." *Mail and Guardian.* October 10, 2006. www.mg.co.za/article/2006-10-10-somalias-woes-grow-in-kenyan-refugee-camps.

Cassanelli, Lee. "The Partition of Knowledge in Somali Studies: Reflections on Somalia's Fragmented Intellectual Heritage." *Bildhaan: An International Journal of Somali Studies* 9 (2009): 4–17.

Chanoff, Sasha, Linmei Li, and Andrew Hopkins. "The Somali Bantu." *Refugees* 3, no. 128 (2002): 4–31.

Chickering, Arthur W., and Linda Reisser. *Education and Identity.* San Francisco: Jossey-Bass, 1993.

Chrislip, David D., and Carl E. Larson. *Collaborative Leadership: How Citizens and Civic Leaders Can Make a Difference.* San Francisco: Jossey-Bass, 1994.

Conquergood, Dwight. "Beyond the Text: Toward a Performative Cultural Politics." In *The Future of Performance Studies: Visions and Revisions,* edited by Sheron J. Dailey, 25–36. Annandale, VA: National Communication Association, 1998.

———. "Performing as a Moral Act: Ethical Dimensions of the Ethnography of Performance." *Literature in Performance* 5, no. 2 (1985): 1–13.

Crenshaw, Kimberlé. "Demarginalizing the Intersection of Race and Sex: A Black Feminist Critique of Antidiscrimination Doctrine, Feminist Theory, and Antiracist Politics." *University of Chicago Legal Forum* (1989): 139–67.

Damooei, Jamshid. "Analyzing Somalia's Past and Present Economic Constraints and Opportunities for Creating a Conducive Economic Environment." In *Mending Rips in the Sky,* edited by Hussein M. Adam and Richard Ford, 271–97. Lawrenceville, TN: The Red Sea Press, 1997.

Dees, J. Gregory. *The Meaning of Social Entrepreneurship: Working Paper.* Palo Alto, CA: Stanford University Press, 1998.

DeFrancisco, Victoria Pruin, and Catherine Helen Palczewski. *Communicating Gender Diversity: A Critical Approach.* Thousand Oaks, CA: Sage Publications, 2007.

Delanty, Gerard. *The Cosmopolitan Imagination: The Renewal of Critical Theory.* Cambridge: Cambridge University Press, 2009.

Dennison, Gerard, "Civilian Labor Force Estimates with Unemployment Rate Comparisons, Lewiston, Maine, and the United States by Month." n.d. Maine Department of Labor.

———. "Historical Unemployment Rates, Lewiston-Auburn MSA." April 1, 2010. Maine Department of Labor.

Denzin, Norman K. *Interpretive Ethnography: Ethnographic Practices for the 21st Century.* Thousand Oaks, CA: Sage, 1997.

———. *Performance Ethnography: Critical Pedagogy and the Politics of Culture.* Thousand Oaks, CA: Sage, 2003.

Dia, Momadou. "Indigenous Management Practices: Lessons from Africa's Management in the 90s." In *Culture and Development in Africa,* edited by

Ismail Serageldin and June Taboroff, 169–91. Washington, DC: World
Bank, 1994.

Dirie, Waris, and Cathleen Miller. *Desert Flower: The Extraordinary Journey of a
Desert Nomad.* New York: William Morrow, 1998.

Duffy, John, Roger Harmon, Donald R. Ranard, Bo Thao, and Kou Yang.
"The Hmong: An Introduction to Their History and Culture." *Center for
Applied Linguistics.* 2004. www.cal.org/co/hmong/hmong_fin.pdf.

Duits, Linda, and Liesbet van Zoonen. "Headscarves and Porno-Chic: Disciplining Girls' Bodies in the European Multicultural Society." *European
Journal of Women's Studies* 13 (2006): 103–17.

"Economics and Demographics – Employment Patterns of Somali Immigrants
to Lewiston." *Maine State Planning Office.* April 1, 2008.
http://www.maine.gov/spo/economics/release.php?id=97815.

Fagen, Patricia Weiss. "Migration, Development and Social Services." ISIM,
Institute for the Study of International Migration (February 2009).

Farah, Nuruddin. *From a Crooked Rib.* London: Heinemann, 1970.

———. *Gifts.* New York: Penguin, 2000.

———. *Links.* New York: Riverhead Books, 2000.

———. *Secrets.* New York: Penguin, 1999.

———. *Yesterday, Tomorrow: Voices from the Somali Diaspora.* London:
Cassell, 2000.

Feliciano, Cynthia, and Ruben G. Rumbaut. "Gendered Paths: Educational and
Occupational Expectations and Outcomes among Adult Children of
Immigrants." *Ethnic and Racial Studies* 28, no. 6 (November 2009):
1087–1118.

Finnegan, William. "New in Town: The Somalis of Lewiston." *New Yorker,*
December 11, 2006, 46–58.

"Five Years after Somalis Migrated to Lewiston, Maine USA." *Washington Post,*
March 2, 2006.

Foner, Nancy. *From Ellis Island to JFK: New York's Two Great Waves of Immigration.* New York: Russell Sage Foundation, 2000.

Forman, Murray. "'Straight Outta Mogadishu:' Prescribed Identities and
Performative Practices among Somali Youth in North American Schools."
TOPIA: Canadian Journal of Cultural Studies 5 (2001): 33–60.

Freire, Paulo. "Education and Conscientizacao." In *Education for Critical
Consciousness,* edited by Paulo Friere, 41–58. New York: Crossroad Publishing Company, 1973.

———. *Pedagogy of the Oppressed*. New York: Seabury Press, 1970.

Fuglerud, Oivind, and Ada Engebrigtsen. "Culture, Networks and Social Capital: Tamil and Somali Immigrants in Norway." *Ethnic and Racial Studies* 29, no. 6 (2006): 1118–1134.

Gardner, Judith, and Judy el Bushra, eds. *Somalia, the Untold Story: The War through the Eyes of Somali Women*. London: Pluto Press, 2004.

Gardner, Judith, with Amina Mohamoud Warsame. "Women, Clan Identity and Peace-Building." In *Somalia, the Untold Story: The War through the Eyes of Somali Women*, edited by Judith Gardner and Judy El-Bushra, 153–65. London: Pluto Press, 2004.

Geshekter, Charles. "Entrepreneurs, Livestock, and Politics: British Somaliland, 1920–1950." In *The Robert L. Hess Collection on Ethiopia and the Horn of Africa*, 10. Berkeley: Stanford African Studies, 1982.

Gilbert, Larry. "Mayor's Corner: A Response to No Comparison between Somalis and Francos." *Twin City Times*, April 1, 2010.

Giraud, Deborah D. "Shared Backyard Gardening." In *The Meaning of Gardens: Idea, Place, and Action*, edited by Mark Francis and Randolph T. Hester, Jr., 166–71. Cambridge, MA: MIT Press, 1991.

Glass, Ronald. "On Paulo Freire's Philosophy of Praxis and the Foundations of Liberal Education." *Educational Researcher* 30 (2001): 15–25.

Goza, Franklin. "The Somali Presence in the United States: A Socio-Economic and Demographic Profile." In *From Mogadishu to Dixon: The Somali Diaspora in a Global Context*, edited by Abdi M. Kusow and Stephanie R. Bjork, 255–74. Trenton, NJ: The Red Sea Press, 2007.

Graham, Mark, and Shahram Khosravi. "Home Is Where You Make It: Repatriation and Diaspora Culture among Iranians in Sweden." *Journal of Refugee Studies* 10, no. 2 (September 2006): 115–33.

Grealy, Lucy. "The Country of Childhood." In *Becoming American: Personal Essays by First Generation Immigrant Women*, edited by Meri Nana-Ama Danquah, 76–84. New York: Hyperion, 2000.

Grossman, Zoltán. "Somali Immigrant Settlement in Small Minnesota and Wisconsin Communities." *University of Wisconsin, Eau Claire*. 2003. http://academic.evergreen.edu/g/grossmaz/somali.html.

The Growing Latin American Influence, Opportunities for Maine's Economy. Augusta, ME: Maine Center for Economic Policy, 2009.

Guerin, Pauline B., and Bernard Guerin. "Relocating Refugees in Developed Countries: The Poverty Experiences of Somali Resettling in New Zealand."

In *5th International APMRN Conference, Fiji, 2002: Selected Papers,* edited by K. Lyon and C. Voight-Graf, 64–70. Wollongong: University of Wollongong, 2002.

Habermas, Jurgen. *Between Facts and Norm.* Translated by William Rehg. Cambridge, MA: MIT Press, 1996.

Hammersley, Martyn. *Reading Ethnographic Research: A Critical Guide.* London: Longman, 1990.

Hamzeh, Ziad H. *The Letter: An American Town and the "Somali Invasion."* Hamzeh Mystique Films, 2003.

Hannerz, Ulf. *Exploring the City: Inquiries Towards an Urban Anthropology.* New York: Columbia University Press, 1980.

Harris, Marvin. *The Rise of Anthropological Theory.* New York: Crowell, 1968.

Hess, Robert L. *Italian Colonialism in Somalia.* Chicago: University of Chicago Press, 1966.

Hodgkin, Douglas I. *Lewiston Memories: A Bicentennial Pictorial.* State College, PA: Jostens Printing & Publishing, 1994.

Horst, Cindy. "The Somali Diaspora in Minneapolis: Expectations and Realities." In *From Mogadishu to Dixon: The Somali Diaspora in Global Context,* edited by Abdi M. Kusow and Stephanie R. Bjork, 275–94. Trenton, NJ: The Red Sea Press, 2007.

———. "The Transnational Political Engagements of Refugees: Remittance Sending Practices Amongst Somalis in Norway." *Conflict, Security & Development* 8, no. 3 (2008): 317–39.

"Housing: Sustaining Portland's Future." *City of Portland.* 2002. http://www.ci.portland.me.us/planning/housingplan.pdf.

"How Refugees Come to America." *U.S. Committee for Refugees and Immigrants (USCR).* 2010. www.refugees.org/about-us/faqs.html

Huisman, Kimberly. "Readers' Theater as Public Pedagogy: Putting Culture into Motion to Foster Dialogue, Democracy and Understanding About Somali Immigrants in Maine." *Theory in Action* 2, no. 3 (2009): 6–30.

Ibrahim, Awad. "One Is Not Born Black: Becoming and the Phenomenon(ology) of Race." *Philosophical Studies in Education* 35 (2004): 77–87.

"Immigrants and Employment: Workforce Development." *National Immigration Law Center.* 2003. http://www.nilc.org/immsemplymnt/wrkfrc_dev /wrkfrc_dev003.htm.

"Implementation Guidelines: Measures and Methods for the National Reporting System for Adult Education." *National Reporting System.* 2010.
www.nrsweb.org.

Inness, Sherrie A., ed. *Running for Their Lives: Girls, Cultural Identity, and Stories of Survival.* Lanham, MD: Rowman & Littlefield, 2000.

"Interview with Professor Said Sheikh Samatar at the 2005 Annual Meeting of
the African Studies Association, Washington, D.C." *Bildhaan: An International Journal of Somali Studies* 6 (2006): 1–24.

Jacobsen, Karen. *The Economic Life of Refugees.* Bloomfield, CT: Kumarian
Press, 2005.

Jenkins, Richard. *Rethinking Ethnicity: Arguments and Explorations.* Thousand
Oaks, CA: Sage Publications, 1997.

Jennings, E. E. *An Anatomy of Leadership: Princes, Heroes, and Supermen.* New
York: Harper, 1960.

Jones, Maggie. "The New Yankees." *Mother Jones,* March/April 2004, 65–69.

Jordan, Glenn. "An African Presence in Europe: Portraits of Somali Elders."
Cultural Studies 22 (2008): 328–53.

Judd, Richard W., Edwin A. Churchill, and Joel W. Eastman. *Maine: The Pine
Tree State from Prehistory to the Present.* Orono, ME: University of Maine
Press, 1995.

Kahn, Shahnaz. *Muslim Women: Crafting a North American Identity.*
Gainesville, FL: University of Florida Press, 2000.

Kaplan, Irving. "The Society and Its Environment." In *Somalia: A Country
Study,* edited by Harold D. Nelson, 133–78. Area Handbook Series. Washington, DC: American University, 1982.

Kapteijns, Lidwien. "Women and the Crisis of Communal Identity: The Cultural Construction of Gender in Somali History." In *The Somali Challenge:
From Catastrophe to Renewal?,* edited by Ahmed I. Samatar, 211–32. Boulder, CO: Lynne Rienner Publisher, 1994.

Kapteijns, Lidwien, with Maryan Omar Ali. *Women's Voices in a Man's World:
Women and the Pastoral Tradition in Northern Somali Orature, c. 1899–
1980.* Portsmouth, NH: Heinemann, 1999.

Kapteijns, Lidwien, and Abukar Arman. "Educating Immigrant Youth in the
United States: An Exploration of the Somali Case." *Bildhaan: An International Journal of Somali Studies* 4 (2004): 18–43.

Kemmis, Stephen, and Robin McTaggart. "Participatory Action Research:
Communicative Action and the Public Sphere." In *The Sage Handbook of*

Qualitative Research, edited by Norman K. Denzin and Yvonne S. Lincoln, 559–603. Thousand Oaks, CA: Sage, 2005.

Korn, Fadumo, with Sabine Eichhorst. *Born in the Big Rains: A Memoir of Somalia and Survival.* New York: The Feminist Press, 2006.

Kroneberg, Clemens. "Ethnic Communities and School Performance Among the New Second Generation in the United States: Testing the Theory of Segmented Assimilation." *The Annals of the American Academy of Political and Social Science* 620 (November 2008): 138–60.

Kymlicka, Will and Wayne Norman. "Return of the Citizen: A Survey of Recent Work on Citizenship Theory," in *Theorizing Citizenship*, edited by Ronald Beiner, 6. Albany, N.Y.: State University of New York Press, 1995.

Kurtz, Hilda. "Differentiating Multiple Meanings of Garden and Community." *Urban Geography* 22 (2001): 656–70.

The Lanes Island Blog. "Single Somali-Bantu Mothers Farm in Maine." www .lanesisland.com/news/2010/02/the_somali_bantu_farmers_of_fr.html.

Langellier, Kristin M. "Performing Somali Identity in the Diaspora: 'Wherever I Go, I Know Who I Am.'" *Cultural Studies* 24 (2010): 66–94.

———. "Negotiating Somali Identity in Maine." In *Applied Communication in Organizational and International Contexts*, edited by Elizabeth C. Fine and Bernd Schwandt, 97–106. St. Ingbert: Röhrig Universitätsverlag, 2008.

Laurence, Margaret. *The Prophet's Camel Bell.* Toronto: McClelland and Stewart, 1963.

Lawson, Laura J. *City Bountiful: A Century of Community Gardening in America.* Berkeley: University of California Press, 2005.

Leamon, James S. *Historic Lewiston: A Textile City in Transition.* Auburn, ME: Maine Vocational Institute, Lewiston Historical Commission, 1976.

Lehman, Daniel Van, and Omar Eno. "Somali Bantu: Their History and Culture." Center for Applied Linguistics, Cultural Orientation Resource Center. http://www.cal.org/co/bantu/sbtoc/html.

Lewis, Ioan M. *Blood and Bone: The Call of Kinship in Somali Society.* Lawrenceville, NJ: The Red Sea Press, 1994.

———. *A Modern History of the Somali: Nation and State in the Horn of Africa* 4th ed. Athens, OH: Ohio University Press, 2002.

———. *Understanding Somalia and Somaliland: Culture, History, Society.* New York: Columbia University Press, 2008.

Lewiston Historical Commission. *Bales to Bedspreads.* Auburn: Central Maine Technical College, 2000.

Lewiston Historical Commission. *Historic Lewiston: Its Architectural Heritage.* Lewiston, ME: Lewiston Historical Commission, n.d.

"Lewiston's Somali Community Turns 10." *Maine Watch,* MPBN, February 12, 2010.

Library of Congress, "Somalia," Country Studies Series. http://lcweb2.loc.gov/frd/cs/sotoc.html.

Lindley, Anna. *The Early Morning Phone Call: Somali Refugees' Remittances.* Oxford: Berghahn Books, 2010

Little, Peter D. "Reflections on Somalia, or How to Conclude an Inconclusive Story." *Bildhaan: An International Journal of Somali Studies* 3 (2003): 61–74.

Lopez, Nancy. *Hopeful Girls, Troubled Boys: Race and Gender Disparity in Urban Education.* New York: Routledge, 2003.

Lordeman, Ann. "The Workforce Investment Act (WIA): Program-by-Program Overview and FY2007 Funding of Title I Training Programs." *UNT Digital Library.* March 2, 2006. http://digital.library.unt.edu/ark:/67531/metacrs9992/.

Lyons, Terrence. "Crises on Multiple Levels: Somalia and the Horn of Africa." In *The Somali Challenge: From Catastrophe to Renewal?,* edited by Ahmed I. Samatar, 189–207. Boulder, CO: Rienner, 1994.

Macarthy, Nailah. "Significance of Race: Comparative Analysis of State Time Limit Policies Under the Personal Responsibility and Work Opportunity Reconciliation Act of 1996." PhD diss., Howard University, 2006.

Maddaus, John, and X. Liu, "Rising Against All Odds: Impact of an Upward Bound Site on Disadvantaged Rural Youth." Paper presented at the annual meeting of the American Educational Research Association, San Diego, August 12, 2009.

Madison, D. Soyini. "Performance, Personal Narratives, and the Politics of Possibility." In *The Future of Performance Studies: Visions and Revisions,* edited by Sheron J. Dailey, 276–86. Annandale, VA: National Communication Association, 1998.

"Maine Looks Like Home to Somali Immigrants." *Somalia Watch News.* www.somaliawatch.org/archivejun02/020802102.htm.

Makkreel, Rudolf A. and Frithjof Rodi, eds. *The Formation of the Historical World in the Human Sciences,* Vol. III. Princeton: Princeton University Press, 2002.

Mamgain, Vaishali, and Karen Collins. "Off the Boat, Now Off to Work:

Refugees in the Labour Market in Portland, Maine." *Journal of Refugee Studies* 16, no. 2 (2003): 113–46.

Mattessich, Paul W., and Ginger Hope. *Speaking for Themselves: A Survey of Hispanic, Hmong, Russian and Somali Immigrants in Minneapolis-Saint Paul.* Amherst H. Wilder Foundation. 2000. www.wilder.org/download.0.html?report=1151.

Mayo, Marjorie. "Partnerships for Regeneration and Community Development: Some Opportunities, Challenges, and Constraints." *Critical Social Policy* 17 (1997): 3–26.

McCall, Michael M. "Performance Ethnography: A Brief History and Some Advice." In *Handbook of Qualitative Research,* edited by Norman K. Denzin and Yvonna S. Lincoln, 421–34. Thousand Oaks, CA: Sage, 2000.

McGown, Rima Berns. *Muslims in the Diaspora: The Somali Communities of London and Toronto.* Toronto: University of Toronto Press, 1999.

McHugh, Margie, Julia Gelatt, and Michael Fix. "Adult English Language in the U.S.: Determining Need and Investing Wisely." *Migration Policy Institute, National Center on Immigration Integration Policy.* July 2007. http://www.migrationpolicy.org/pubs/NCIIP_English_Instruction073107.pdf.

McIntyre, Alice, Nikolos Chatzopoulos, Anastasia Politi, and Julieta Roz. "Participatory Action Research: Collective Reflections on Gender, Culture, and Language." *Teaching and Teacher Education: An International Journal of Research and Studies* 23, no. 5 (2007): 748–56.

McKay, Sandra Lee, and Gail Weinstein-Shr. "English Literacy in the U.S.: National Policies, Personal Consequences." *University of Southern California.* 1995. www.usc.edu/dept/education/CMMR/PolicyPDF /English_Literacy_in_the_US.pdf.

Menkhaus, Kenneth. "Rural Transformation and the Roots of Underdevelopment in Somalia's Lower Juba Valley." PhD diss., University of South Carolina, 1989.

Miller, Kevin. "Census: Maine Oldest, Whitest State in Nation." *Bangor Daily News,* May 14, 2009.

Mills, C. Wright. *The Sociological Imagination.* New York: Oxford University Press, 1959.

Mohamed, Abdirizak. "Wasted Talent: The Absence of Somali Students from Post-Graduate Education." www.hiiraan.com/op2/2008/aug/wasted _talent_the_absence_of_somali_students_ from_post_graduate _education.aspx

Mohamed, Jama. "The Political Economy of Colonial Somaliland." *Africa* 74, no. 44 (2004): 534–66.

Mohamoud, Abdullah A., *State Collapse and Post-Conflict Development in Africa: The Case of Somalia (1960–2001).* East Lafayette, IA: Purdue University Press, 2006.

Muir, Dawn. "English and Literacy Teaching and Learning Strategies for Newly Arrived Humanitarian Refugee Students from Sudan." *Sudanese Online Research Organization (SORA).* http://sora.akm.net.au/publish.php.

Myerhoff, Barbara. *Remembered Lives: The Work of Ritual, Storytelling, and Growing Older.* Ann Arbor, MI: University of Michigan Press, 1992.

Nadeau, Phil. "The Flawed U.S. Refugee Workforce Development Strategy for Somali Economic Self-Sufficiency in Lewiston." Paper presented at the Race, Ethnicity and Place Conference IV, Miami, Florida, November 6, 2008.

———. "The New Mainers: State and Local Agencies Form Partnerships to Help Somali Immigrants." *National Civic Review* 96, no. 2 (Summer 2007): 55–57.

———. *Report to Governor Angus King: New Somali Arrivals and Other Issues Relative to Refugee/Secondary Migrants/Immigrants and Cultural Diversity in the City of Lewiston.* Lewiston: City of Lewiston, May 9, 2002.

———. "The Somalis of Lewiston: Effects of Rapid Migration to a Homogeneous Maine City." *Southern Maine Review* (1995): 105–46.

———. "Summary of City Meetings with Federal Refugee Agencies and Congressional Delegation." *City of Lewiston.* November 13, 2007. www.ci.lewiston.me.us/news/2007/2007files/11-15-07WashingtonDCSummaryof11-13-07.pdf.

Nahavandi, Afsaneh. *The Art and Science of Leadership.* Upper Saddle River, NJ: Prentice Hall, 2003.

National Somali Bantu Project. www.somalibantu.org.

"New American Sustainable Agriculture Project." www.cultivatingcommunity.org/programs/nasap.html.

Nieto, Sonia. *Language, Culture, and Teaching: Critical Perspectives.* New York: Routledge, 2010.

Nzelibe, C. O. "The Evolution of African Management Thought." *International Studies in Management and Organization* 16 (1986): 6–16.

"Office of Refugee Resettlement, Refugee Assistance Division, ORR Budget." *U.S. Department of Health and Human Services-Administration for*

Children and Families. May 13, 2009.
www.acf.hhs.gov/programs/orr/about/divisions.htm.

"Office of Refugee Resettlement, Refugee Assistance Division, Targeted Assistance Discretionary Program," *U.S. Department of Health and Human Services-Administration for Children and Families.* May 13, 2009. www.acf.hhs.gov/programs/orr/about/divisions.htm#1.

Peterson, David. "African Immigrants Set Pace to Get Off Welfare." *StarTribune.com,* Dec. 27, 2006.

Pollock, Della. "Memory, Remembering, and Histories of Change." In *The Sage Handbook of Performance Studies,* edited by D. Soyini Madison and Judith Hamera, 87–105. Thousand Oaks, CA: Sage Publications, 2006.

———. "A Response to Dwight Conquergood's Essay 'Beyond the Text: Towards a Performative Cultural Politics.'" In *The Future of Performance Studies: Visions and Revisions,* edited by Sheron J. Dailey, 37–46. Annandale, VA: National Communication Association, 1998.

Portes, Alejandro. "Social Capital: Its Origins and Applications in Modern Sociology." *Annual Review of Sociology* 24 (1998): 1–24.

"Promoting Cultural Sensitivity: A Practical Guide for Tuberculosis Programs That Provide Services to Persons from Somalia." *Centers for Disease Control and Prevention.* 2008. www.cdc.gov/tb/publications/guidestoolkits/EthnographicGuides/Somalia/default.htm.

Putman, Robert. *Bowling Alone: The Collapse and Revival of American Community.* New York: Simon & Schuster, 2000.

Rabrenovic, Gordana. "When Hate Comes to Town: Community Response to Violence Against Immigrants." *American Behavioral Scientist* 5, no. 2 (2007): 349–60.

Rand, John. *The Peoples Lewiston-Auburn Maine 1875-1975.* Freeport, MA: The Bond Wheelwright Company, 1975.

Reardon, Patrick T. "A Yankee Mill Town Globalizes." *Chicago Tribune,* June 13, 2002.

Rector, Amanda K. "An Analysis of the Employment Patterns of Somali Immigrants to Lewiston from 2001 through 2006." Center for Workforce Research and Information, Maine Department of Labor, www.maine.gov/labor/lmis/publications/pdf/LewistonMigrantReport.pdf.

Richard, Mark Paul. *Loyal but French: The Negotiation of Identity by French-Canadian Descendants in the United States.* East Lansing, MI: Michigan State University Press, 2008.

Riessman, Catherine K. *Narrative Methods for the Human Sciences.* Thousand Oaks, CA: Sage Publications, 2008.

Rinehart, "Historical Setting." In *Somalia: A Country Study,* edited by Harold D. Nelson, 1–60. Area Handbook Series. Washington, DC: American University, 1982.

Roble, Abdi, and Doug Rutledge. *The Somali Diaspora: A Journey Away.* Minneapolis, MN: University of Minnesota Press, 2008.

Said, Edward. *Orientalism.* New York: Vintage Books, 1978.

Samatar, Abdi I. "Empty Bowl: Agrarian Political Economy in Transition and the Crises of Accumulation." In *The Somali Challenge: From Catastrophe to Renewal?,* edited by Ahmed I. Samatar, 65–92. Boulder, CO: Rienner, 1994.

Samatar, Abdi Ismail, and Ahmed I. Samatar. "International Crisis Group Report on Somaliland: An Alternative Response." *Bildhaan: An International Journal of Somali Studies* 5 (2005): 107–124.

———. "Transition and Leadership: An Editorial." *Bildhaan: An International Journal of Somali Studies* 5 (2005): 1–17.

Samatar, Ahmed I. "Beginning Again: From Refugee to Citizen." *Bildhaan: An International Journal of Somali Studies* 4 (2004): 1–17.

———, ed. *The Somali Challenge: From Catastrophe to Renewal?* Boulder, CO: Lynne Reinner Publishers, 1994.

———."Introduction and Overview." In *The Somali Challenge: From Catastrophe to Renewal?,* edited by Ahmed I. Samatar, 3–19. Boulder, CO: Rienner, 1994.

———. "The Curse of Allah: Civic Disembowelment and the Collapse of the State of Somalia." In *The Somali Challenge: From Catastrophe to Renewal?,* edited by Ahmed I. Samatar, 95–146. Boulder, CO: Rienner, 1994.

———. "A Paradoxical Gift." H-Net Reviews in the Humanities & Social Sciences (December 2003).

———. "The Porcupine Dilemma: Governance and Transition in Somalia." *Bildhaan: An International Journal of Somali Studies* 7 (2007): 39–90.

Samatar, Said. "A Country Study: Somalia." Washington, DC: Federal Research Division, Library of Congress. http://lcweb2.loc.gov/frd/cs/sotoc.html.

Schaid, Jessica, and Zoltan Grossman. "The Somali Diaspora in Small Midwestern Communities: The Case of Barron, Wisconsin." In *From Mogadishu to Dixon: The Somali Diaspora in a Global Context,* edited by Abdi M. Kusow and Stephanie R. Bjork, 295–319. Trenton, NJ: The Red Sea Press, 2007.

Schlee, Gunther. "Redrawing the Map of the Horn: The Politics of Difference." *Africa* 73, no. 3 (2003): 343–368.

Schorske, Carl E. *Thinking with History: Explorations in the Passage to Modernism.* Princeton, N.J.: Princeton University Press, 1998.

Semple, Kirk. "A Somali Influx Unsettles Latino Meatpackers." *New York Times,* October 15, 2008.

Sen, Amartya. *Identity and Violence: The Illusion of Destiny.* New York: W.W. Norton, 2006.

Settles, Barbara H. "Being at Home in a Global Society: A Model for Families' Mobility and Immigration Decisions." *Journal of Comparative Family Studies* 32, no. 4 (2001): 627–45.

Shandy, Dianna J. *Nuer-American Passages: Globalizing Sudanese Migration.* Gainesville, FL: University Press of Florida, 2007.

Shandy, Dianna J., and Katherine Fennelly. "A Comparison of the Integration Experiences of Two African Immigrant Populations in a Rural Community." *Journal of Religion & Spirituality in Social Work* 25, no. 1 (2006): 23–45.

Singer, Audrey, and Jill H. Wilson. "From 'There' to 'Here': Refugee Resettlement in Metropolitan America." Metropolitan Policy Program, The Brookings Institution: Living Cities Census Series (September, 2006), www.brookings.edu /metro/pubs/ 20060925_singer.pdf.

Smith-Mayo, Jennifer. "Maine: The State of Local Food." Unpublished paper, University of Maine, December 16, 2009.

Sotomayor, Alberto Alvarez de. "The Role of Ethnic Networks in the Educational Attainment of Children of Immigrant: Resources or Obstacles?" *Migraciones* 23 (June 2008): 45–77.

Stephen, Pindie, and The Cultural Orientation Africa Project. "Somali Bantu Report." Nairobi, Kenya: International Organization for Migration, 2002.

Stitely, Amy. "Cultivating New Americans: Refugee Garden and Farm Projects." http://architecture.mit.edu/class/nature/student_projects/2007/astitely /urban-nature/index.html.

Suarez-Orozco, Marcelo M. "Right Moves? Immigration, Globalization, Utopia, and Dystopia." In *The New Immigration,* edited by Carola Suarez-Orozco and Desiree Baolian Qin, 3–21. New York: Brunner-Routledge, 2005.

"Summary of the Adult Education and Family Literacy Act." *Iowa Literacy Resource Center.* 1999. http://readiowa.org/AD_ED_FAM_LIT_ACT.htm.

Taylor, Martin. *Unleashing the Potential: Bringing the Residents to the Center of Regeneration.* York: York Publishing Services, 1995.

The Telling Room Story House Project. *I Remember Warm Rain: 15 Teenagers, 15 Coming to America Stories.* Portland, ME: The Telling Room, 2007.

Thake, S. *Staying the Course: The Role and Structure of Community Regeneration Organizations.* York: York Publishing, 1995.

Thake, S., and R. Staubach. *Investing in People: Rescuing Communities from the Margin.* York: Joseph Roundtree Foundation, 1993.

Thomas, Audrey Alforque. "The Effect of Family Immigration History on Blacks in Higher Education." *Sociology Compass* 3, no. 5 (September 2009): 836–46.

Tilove, Jonathan. "Somali Migration Transforms Lewiston." *Kennebec Journal Morning Sentinel,* September 8, 2002.

Timberlake, Sharon E. "Municipal Collaboration in Response to Secondary Migration: A Case Study of Portland and Lewiston, Maine." PhD diss., University of Southern Maine, 2007.

Touval, Saadia. *Somali Nationalism: International Politics and the Drive for Unity in the Horn of Africa.* Cambridge, MA: Harvard University Press, 1963.

Turton, E. R. "Somali Resistance to Colonial Rule and the Development of Somali Political Activity in Kenya 1893–1960." *Journal of African History* 13, no. 1 (1972): 119–43.

United Nations High Commissioner for Refugees. "Global Trends: Refugees, Asylum-Seekers, Returnees, Internally Displaced and Stateless Person." June 17, 2008. http://www.unhcr.org/4852366f2.html.

———. "The Somali Bantu" *Refugees* 2, no.128 (2002): 4–11.

"U.S. A Place of Miracles for Somali Refugees." *New York Times,* July 20, 2003.

U.S. Census Bureau. "Summary File 1 and Summary File 3." 2000. http://factfinder.census.gov/servlet/DatasetMainPageServlet.

———. Committee for Refugees and Immigrants (USCRI). *Refugee Reports* 23, no.8 (November 2002).

———. Department of Health & Human Services. Fiscal Years 2001–2007 Refugee Arrivals. Edited by The Office of Refugee Resettlement: U.S Department of Health & Human Services' Administration of Children & Families. www.hhs-stat.net/scripts/topic.cfm?id=237.

Warsame, Amina Mohamoud. "Crisis or Opportunity? Somali Women Traders and the War." In *Somalia, the Untold Story: The War Through the Eyes of*

Somali Women, edited by Judith Gardner and Judy el Bushra, 116–38. London: Pluto Press, 2004.

"WIA Title 1 Strategic Plan Modification." *Maine Focus.org - Central Western Maine Workforce Board.* 2008. http://mainefocus.org/documents/master.pdf.Wing, Adrien Katharine. "Brief Reflections toward a Multiplicative Theory of Praxis and Being." In *Critical Race Feminism: A Reader,* edited by Adrien Katharine Wing, 27–34. New York: New York University Press, 1997.

"Workplace English Language and Literacy (WELL) Program." www.deewr.gov.au/Skills/Programs/LitandNum /WorkplaceEnglishLanguageandLiteracy/Pages/default.aspx.

Yeats, William Butler. "Man and the Echo." In *The Collected Works of W. B. Yeats,* edited by W. B. Yeats, Richard J. Finnerman, and George Mills Harper. London: Macmillan, 1977.

Zhou, Min, and Carl L. Bankston. "Family Pressure and the Educational Experience of the Daughters of Vietnamese Refugees." *International Migration* 39, no. 4 (2001): 133–51.

Zimmerman, Wendy, and Michael Fix. "Immigrant Policy in the States: A Wavering Welcome." In *Immigration and Ethnicity: The Integration of America's Newest Arrivals,* edited by Barry Edmonston and Jeffrey S. Passel, 287–316. Washington, DC: Urban Institute Press, 1994.

List of Contributors

Ismail Ahmed resides in Columbus, Ohio. Prior to relocating, he lived in Lewiston, Maine, where he ran STTAR Consultancy Services and worked for Catholic Charities Maine Refugee and Immigration Services. He has also worked in Baltimore, Maryland, for Lutheran Immigration & Refugee Services' RefugeeWorks. Ismail earned a master's degree in leadership and organizational studies from the University of Southern Maine's Lewiston-Auburn College, and currently works as an educational consultant and social commentator.

Mazie Hough, Associate Director of Women in the Curriculum and Women's Studies Program at the University of Maine, is a historian who specializes in nineteenth century social and women's history, oral history, and the history of sexuality. She teaches a variety of courses including women and globalization, women's studies methodologies, and women's history.

Kimberly A. Huisman is an Associate Professor in the Sociology Department at the University of Maine. She has been working with immigrants since 1991. Her research focuses on immigration, race, and gender. She teaches courses on immigration, microsociology, social deviance, and social inequality. Along with the other three editors of this volume, she founded the Somali Narrative Project in 2004 to address the rapid change and cultural tensions that emerged in response to the migration that brought Somalis to Maine.

Kristin M. Langellier, Professor of Communication and Journalism at the University of Maine, has a research program on personal narrative, family storytelling, culture, and identity. She teaches undergraduate and graduate courses in narrative, women and communication, and intercultural communication. She also teaches courses in communication theory and is a faculty in Women's Studies and Franco-American Studies.

Nasra Mohamed, a founding student member of the Somali Narrative Project, was born in Mogadishu, Somalia. She moved to the United States in February of 2001. Ms. Mohamed graduated from the University of Maine in 2007 with a BA in International Affairs and Political Science. She is currently pursuing a master's of social work at the University of Minnesota. She is also a Fellow in LEND (Leadership Education and Neurodevelopment Disabilities), an interdisciplinary leadership training program at the University of Minnesota. Ms. Mohamed is very passionate about working with families and children and hopes to work in the field of Human Services serving families, especially immigrant and refugee families.

Phil Nadeau has been serving as Lewiston, Maine's Deputy City Administrator for eleven years and has been in the profession for sixteen years. He holds a Masters in Public Policy and Management from the University of Southern Maine. His refugee policy research and his role as the city's refugee liaison has been recognized in the book *Sharing the Dream,* authored by Dominic Pulera and cited by journalists and academics. He has worked at the state and federal level in the refugee policy area and has spoken nationally regarding Lewiston's refugee story.

Dr. Ahmed I. Samatar is the James Wallace Professor of Political Science and Dean of the Institute for Global Citizenship at Macalester College, St. Paul, Minnesota. Professor Samatar is the founding editor in chief of *Bildhaan: An International Journal of Somali Studies.* His expertise is in the areas of global political economy, political and social thought, and African development, and is the author/editor of five books and over thirty articles, including *The African State: Reconsiderations* (Heinemann, 2002) and *Somalia: State Collapse, Multilateral Intervention, and Strategies for Political Reconstruction* (Brookings Institution, 1995).

Storytellers *Gulaid, Kay Ahmed, Liban Abu, Bashir Mohamed, Khalid Mohamed, Elham Sala, Aisha Mohamed, Sadia, Fartuna Hussein, Kalteezy Kali, Ubah Bashir, Nawal Wali, Fathiya Sharif Mohamed, Faiza Ahmed, and Britney Harris* are student authors of the personal experience stories. Most are current or former students from the University or other colleges in Maine who participated in storytelling retreats with the Somali Narrative Project.

Carol Nordstrom Toner is the Maine Studies Program Director and Research Associate in History at the University of Maine. She teaches courses in history, Maine studies, women's studies, and interdisciplinarity. Her research includes labor and women's history with a focus on Maine.

Ismail Warsame is one of the founding student members of the Somali Narrative Project. After completing his BA in International Affairs and Political Science, he recently earned his masters in Higher Education at the University of Maine. He is currently working at Oregon State University as an international student advisor.

Permissions

The following sources were reprinted with permission of the publisher:

Chapter 2, "Why Maine," is adapted from Kimberly A. Huisman,"Why Maine? Secondary Migration Decisions of Somali Refugees," *Ìrìnkèrindò: a Journal of African Migration* (forthcoming, June 2011).

Chapter 3, "A Work in Progress: Lewiston Responds to the Rapid Migration of Somali Refugees," includes material that was first published by University of Southern Maine's *Southern Maine Review* (2005): "The Somalis of Lewiston: Effects of Rapid Migration to a Homogeneous Maine City," *Southern Maine Review* (1995): 105–46.

Chapter 7, "Caaliya's Storytelling," is adapted from Kristin M. Langellier, "Performing Somali Identity in the Diaspora: 'Wherever I Go, I Know Who I Am,'" *Cultural Studies* 24 (2010): 66–94.

Chapter 9, "Collaborating with the Community," is adapted from Kristin M. Langellier, "Negotiating Somali Identity in Maine," in *Applied Communication in Organizational and International Contexts,* ed. Elizabeth C. Fine and Bernd Schwandt, 97–106 (St. Ingbert: Röhrig Universitätsverlag, 2008).

Chapter 11, "Readers Theater as Public Pedagogy," is adapted from Kimberly A. Huisman, "Readers' Theater as Public Pedagogy: Putting Culture into Motion to Foster Dialogue, Democracy and Understanding About Somali Immigrants in Maine," *Theory in Action* 2: 3 (2009): 6–30. (© 2009). Transformative Studies Institute, all rights reserved. www.transformativestudies.org

The map used in figure 1 was reproduced with permission by International and Ethnic Boundaries of Somalia. From Ioan M. Lewis, *Understanding Somalia and Somaliland: Culture, History, Society* (New York: Columbia University Press, 2008).

The map used in figure 2, Islam in Africa, is CIA Map #801208.

The cover photograph was reproduced with permission from Samantha Appleton.

The following photographs in this book were taken by Jason Crain and were reproduced with permission: figures 3, 7, 19, 20, 21, 22, 33, 34.

The following photograph in this book was taken by Rhea Côté Robbins and was reproduced with permission: figure 26.

The following photographs in this book were taken by Kevin Johnson and were reproduced by permission: 16, 17, 18, 25, 27, 29, 30.

The following photographs in this book were taken by Nasra Mohamed and were reproduced by permission: 10, 11, 12, 31.

Index

9/11: anti-Muslim sentiments following, 131, 133, 199; and Somali refugees, xxvi, 18, 227

Abdullahi, Muna, 205 fig. 24
Abu, Liban, 136–39
Adams, James Truslow, 53
Adult Education and Family Literacy Act, 67, 69
Adult Education Center, 64, 65, 66, 69
Adult Migrant English Program (AMEP), 70, 71
Africa: colonization of, xxiii; consequences of colonialism in, 11–13, 14; defining social identity in, 151; map of Islam in, xiv fig. 2; migration to U.S. from, 23, 256; prejudice against other Africans in, 150
African Americans, 30, 36, 150–51, 155, 156
Ahmad, 130
Ahmed, 36
Ahmed, Faiza, 73–76
Ahmed, Hassan Osman, 17
Ahmed, Ismail, 202–203
Ahmed, Kay, 20–22
Ahmed, Leila, 154
Akiwumi, Fenda, 61
Alexander, Brian Keith, 237
Allen, Ryan, 63
Allender, Susan Chou, 63–64, 70
Aman, 31, 33–34, 36, 37, 45
AMEP. see Adult Migrant English Program

American Folk Festival, readers theater performance, 230 fig. 27, 234 fig. 20 and 30
Amina, 211
Anglo-Ethiopian Treaty, 12
Arab League, xxiii, xxvi
Arizona, 29, 33, 293
Arman, Abukar, 25, 129, 150
ARS. see Re-Liberation of Somalia assimilation, 256
Atlanta, GA, 27, 30, 36, 56, 170
Auburn, ME, 24, 55
Australia, xxvi, 53, 70–71, 72

Baldacci, John, 301
Balibar, Etienne, 296
Bantus: agricultural skills among, 178, 181; and agricultural work in Maine, 183–85, 188; discrimination and marginalization experienced by, 179, 186; and identity, 181; and Islam, 180; in Lewiston, xxvi, 25, 53, 64–65; lineage of, 9–10; self-identified by place of residence, 179; special challenges faced by, 179–81; term, 178; viewed by Samaal, 10
Barre, Mohamed Siyad, 18, 160, 179, 183, 290; control of Somalia exerted by, 15, 16; military coup by, xxiii, 14, 292; overthrow of, xxiv, 7, 16; reforms implemented by, 14–15; and written Somali language, 201
Barron, WI, 25
Bashir, Ubah, 143–44

Bates College, 59, 60, 61, 183, 217
Berlin, Isaiah, 296–97
Besteman, Catherine, 8, 16, 18–19, 61, 180–81
Bickman, Martin, 211
biil, 186–87, 189
Bildhaan, 215
Boal, Augusto, 213
Boise, ID, 185, 186
Boston, MA, 26
Boston Globe, 59
Britain, 11, 13–14, 289
British Somaliland, xxiii, 12, 13, 14, 289
Brown University, 60–61
Bush, George H. W., xxv

Caaliya, 40, 45; autobiographical details, 147; dress worn by, 145; home viewed by, 39; interview with, 147–48; on living in Lewiston, 32, 35–36; narrative of identity, 41, 148–65, 266; performance of identity, 145–46; on Somali social networks, 38, 43–44
Calvary United Methodist Church, 59
Canada, xxvi, 295
CARE, 107
Carrington, Amy, 185
CASAS. *see* Comprehensive Adult Student Assessment Systems
Cassanelli, Lee, 10
Catholic Charities Maine (CCM), 61, 64, 67, 177; Office of Refugee and Immigration Services, 55, 201
Cawo, 27, 30, 39, 42
CCM. *see* Catholic Charities Maine

cell phones, 42, 43
Central/Western Maine Workforce Investment Board, 71
clans: and Barre, 16–17; blamed for current catastrophe in Somalia, 8, 266, 297; communication taboo about, 152–53; in contemporary Somalia, 18–19; depicted by Western media, 266; and external agencies, 19; and family, 39–40; gathering around wells, 10; and genealogy, 9, 10, 150, 266; and Islam, 157; and protection and military support, 16–17; relations among, 152; and social capital, 41; subclans within, 9; viewed by Somalis, 178–79
Clinton, Bill, xxv
Coastal Enterprises, 185
Cold War, 8, 15, 291
colonialism, 154; consequences of, 11–13, 14, 289–891, 294; and female genital mutilation, 159, 161; and Somalia's contemporary catastrophe, 289, 290–91; and Somali literacy, 291
Columbus, OH, 25, 26, 56, 99
community agriculture, 170–71
community gardens, 181, 182
Comprehensive Adult Student Assessment Systems (CASAS), 65
Cultivating Community, 185
culture: defined, 84; identity as, 164; internal and external forces in, 237; oral (*see* oral tradition); and SNP readers theater, 232–35; as a verb, 234–35, 237, 239

Dadaab refugee camp, Kenya, xxiv, 7, 107, 293; photographs of, 112 fig. 10, 118 fig. 12, 253 fig. 31
Dagahley refugee camp, Kenya, 107
Damooei, Jamshid, 187
Democratic Republic of Somalia, xxiii
Denzin, Norman, 237, 238, 239
desocialization, 83
Dia, Momadou, 95
dialogue, 233
Dilthey, Wilhelm, 293
discrimination, 133; and the Bantus, 179, 180, 186; faced by immigrants, 218, 256, 282; and the *hijab*, 171–72
Diversity Hiring Coalition of Maine, 177
Djibouti, 11, 17, 26
dress, 25; and employment, 171–72, 180; male, and Western youth, 156, 267; women wearing Western, 237
Duits, Linda, 163

education (*see also* pedagogy); and active learning, 211; and female Somalis, 160; higher (*see* education, higher); and immigrants, 129, 131; and racism, 131; viewed by Somalis, 130
education, higher: and communication within the Somali community, 135; and female Somali students, 131; internal barriers to, 129–31; Ismail Warsame's experience, 125–29; recommendations for educators, 134–35; societal and institutional barriers to, 129, 131–33; and the Somali Narrative Project, 219; Somali students absent from, 129
Eid ul-Fitr, 87, 172, 215
employment, 170; and the Bantus, 179–80; challenges, 62–65, 72, 170–73; and highly trained professionals, 178; and leaving Maine, 189; in Lewiston, 53–54; and refugee needs, 53–54, 70; strategies used to overcome barriers to, 170, 173; and women, 188–89
Engebrigtsen, Ada, 25, 26
English as a second language. *see* ESL
English Language Learners, 64
Epic of America, The (Adams), 53–54
ESL (English as a second language), 62, 63; alternative approaches to funding, 70–72; and funding, 65–72, 171; funding for, in Lewiston, 62; Ismail Warsame's experience, 126–27; and native language illiteracy, 63, 65–66, 171; offered by L.L. Bean, 176
Estaville, Lawrence, 61
Ethiopia, 11; and the Ogaden and Haud territories, xxiii, xxiv, 12, 289; and Somalia, 13–14, 15, 16, 18; and Somali refugees, 17, 26; and the Soviet Union, 15, 16, 292; supported by the US, 15
ethnicity, 149, 156, 164
ethnography, 238, 239

Faadumo, 32
family, 39–40, 266–64; genealogy, 40–41; nuclear, 89; and polygamy, 40; size, 32; and social capital, 41; and U. S. refugee policy, 180–81

famine, xxiv, 18
Farah, Nuruddin, 17, 212, 213, 237
Farham, 33, 35
farmers' markets, 182, 185
female circumcision. *see* female genital
    mutilation
female genital mutilation, 15, 161, 266;
    as cultural rather than religious,
    158–59, 160, 214; discussed by
    Caaliya, 158–60; and SNP readers
    theater, 214, 230, 233
feminism, 154, 161, 266
Forman, Murray, 156
France, xxiv, 11, 289
Franco-American Heritage Center,
    readers theater performance, 200
    fig. 23, 217
Franco Americans, 169, 218
Freeport, ME, 33, 173
Freire, Paulo, 212, 233
French Somaliland, xxiii, xxiv, 14, 289
    (*see also* Republic of Djibouti)
Fuglerud, Oivind, 25, 26

Galad, 39, 40
GAO. *see* General Assistance Office
gender: joke on Somali culture regard-
    ing, 153–54; new roles in U. S., 189;
    and parental fears, 156–57, 267; and
    secondary migration, 44–45; and
Somali culture and Islam, 157–61, 162,
    164–65, 266
genealogy, 9, 10, 40–41, 150
General Assistance Office (GAO), 56,
    58
generation, 293–94
Georgia, 26, 27, 29, 56

Gilbert, Larry, 186
Giraud, Deborah, 186
Glass, Ronald, 237
Good Life, The (Nearing), 182
Gulaid, 3–6
Guleed, 26–27, 32, 33

Hagardhere refugee camp, Kenya, 107
Halima, 30, 31, 33, 35, 45
Hammond, Laura, 187–88
Harris, Britney, 195–96, 195 fig. 21, 196
    fig. 22, 197

Hassan, Mohamed Abdille, 290 (*see
    also* Hassan, Muhammed Abdille)

Hassan, Muhammed Abdille, xxiii, 12–
    13 (*see also* Hassan, Mohamed
    Abdille)
Haud region, xxiii, 12, 14
Hibo, 36
higher education. *see* education, higher
hijab, 25; as barrier to employment,
    171–72, 215; and Caaliya, 145–46,
    159, 161–62, 163; and choice, 163;
    and identity, 156; and safety on the
    job, 174; viewed in the West, 145,
    162
Hillview, 201
Hmong, 63
home, 281–82
Houston, TX, 179
Hussein, Abdirazak H., 293
Hussein, Fartuna, 103–5

Ibrahim, Awad, 156
identity: and Caaliya, 41, 148–65; com-

munal, 149; contradictory narratives, 152; and culture, 148–57, 160, 164; ethnic, 164; and expanding social networks, 42; hyphenated, 256, 257; of immigrants, 256, 257; interlocking facets of, 265–66; kinship, 289; national or religious, 40, 41; and race, 156; and refugee as victim, 146–47; and religion, 40, 41, 148, 157–65, 266; and SNP readers theater, 232–33; and Somali American adaptation, 146, 296–97; and Somalis in higher education, 132–33; and stories, 146; transforming in US context, 41–42

Ifo refugee camp, Kenya, 107

IGAD. *see* Intergovernmental Authority on Development

illiteracy, 63–66, 99, 171, 291, 292

immigrants: French Canadian, 169, 217, 218, 230; and identity, 256, 257; Iranian, 282; Irish, 54, 169; migration patterns of, 169; and nostalgia for home, 281; Somali (*see* refugees, Somali)

Immigration and Naturalization Act, 23

individualism, 34, 88, 158

infibulation, 15, 160 (*see also* female genital mutilation)

Intergovernmental Authority on Development (IGAD), 18

International Conference on Immigration, 214

International Organization for Migration, 179–80

International Women's Day, xxiii

iPods, 175, 176, 179

Islam: apologists, 161–62; arrival in Somalia, xxiii, 10; and the Bantus, 180; and clan divisions, 157; and collective decision-making, 9; and culture, 266; and female genital mutilation, 158–61; and gender, 157–61; and identity, 40, 41, 148, 157–65, 266; and leadership, 86, 89–90; map of, in Africa, xiv fig. 2; practices of, and employment, 171–73, 173–74, 180; and resistance against colonizers, 12–13; and Somalia's relationship to the wider community, 10; and Somali creation myth, 150; viewed by Caaliya, 161; viewed in the West, 162, 266

Islamic Center of Maine, 190 fig. 19, 275 fig. 34; men praying at, 192 fig. 20; young women at, 196 fig. 22

Islamic Courts Union, 18

Italian Somalia: and the Bantus, 179; creation of, xxiii, 12, 289; independence of, 14; and the post-colonial era, 290; and World War II, 13

Italy, xxiii, 11, 13, 26, 289

Juba River, 8, 11, 183, 288

Kali, Aisha, 242–43, 244
Kali, Hakeem, 243
Kali, Kalteezy, 240–44
Kali, Maariyah, 240–41, 242, 243
Kapteijns, Lidwien, 25, 129, 150
Kemmis, Stephen, 229
Kemper, Ann, 65, 67
Kenya: Bantu refugees in, 179; refugees

in, xxiv, 17, 18, 23, 26, 107, 236, 293; and Somalia, 14 (*see also* Northern Frontier of Kenya)

Khalid, 27, 32

King, Angus, 56, 57, 58, 301

Know-Nothing, 54

Kurtz, Hilda, 181

Kymlicka, Will, 296, 297

L.L. Bean, 175 fig. 18; awards received by, 177; cross-cultural understanding promoted by, 176–77; mentioned, 182, 188, 189; and Somali Bantu, 179; Somali employees, 173 fig. 16, 175 fig. 17; Somali response to, 177–78; strategies to overcome barriers to Somali employment, 173–77, 186

Ladan, 35, 40

language: and employment, 62–65, 171, 175; English as second (*see* ESL); and leadership, 57, 98–99; Maay Maay (Bantu), 183; oral (*see* oral tradition); Somali, xxiii, 15, 42, 89, 171, 176, 201, 295; training in, using iPod technology, 175, 176

leadership: and communication, 89; and community-based citizenship, 100–102; and community partnership, 86, 95–100; and continuity, 84; defined by Somali refugees, 83, 88–90; emerging, 92–93, 94–95, 95–96; and further studies, 99; and Islam, 86, 89–90; and language, 57, 98–99; in Lewiston, 83, 85–86, 90–92, 94, 95; new paradigm, 100, 101–2; and pastoralism, 84; qualities for effective, 101; and social capital, 93–94;

and the Somali language, 98–99; traditional, 84–85, 90–91, 93, 94–95, 97, 100–101; and transition into American society, 89, 90–91

Letter, The, 199

Lewis, I. M., 8, 12, 247

Lewiston, ME: and Bantu employment, 178; benefits to, of Somali migration, 189, 302; community response to Somali refugees, 53, 57–61, 72; economic and cultural profile, 24–25, 54, 55, 87, 227; economic opportunity in, 33–34, 46, 62, 169; housing in, 25, 32–33; immigrant history, 54–55, 60 fig. 6, 217, 218; Lisbon Street, 28 figs. 4 and 5, 29, 42, 87 fig. 9, 260 fig. 32; media coverage of, 58–59, 156, 199; and public assistance, 27; racism and lack of diversity in, 34–36, 46, 59; and refugee employment, 53; refugee population, 24, 25, 56, 58; refugee resettlement funding in, 67; refugee workforce funding in, 68–70; relationship with Somali leaders, 57–58; and safety and social control, 30–31, 46; sharing of information in, 42–43; Somali businesses in, 25, 28 figs. 4 and 5, 282; Somali departure from, 33–37, 47; Somali migration to, xxvi, 53, 227, 301; as stepping stone, 47; study on secondary migration to, 25–26; town hall meeting, 58; unemployment in, 55, 62, 170

Lewiston-Auburn College, 59, 60

Lewiston-Auburn Public Health Committee, 61

Leyla, 4, 5

Libaan, 34, 43
Libby, Russell, 182
Lisbon Street, Lewiston, ME, 29, 42, 87
  fig. 9; photographs, 28 figs. 4 and 5,
  260 fig. 32
literacy, 291, 295
Little, Peter D., 19
local foods movement, 182
Lots to Gardens, 61, 183, 184–85

Mahamoud, Omar, 173, 176, 178
Maine: benefits from Somali migration
  to, 189, 302; character of, 189; economy in, 170; farming in, 182–83,
  185; lack of diversity in, 53; lack of
  economic opportunities in, 33–34;
  migration of natives from, 34; and
  quality of life, 30; racism and lack of
  diversity in, 34–36; refugee work
  force training funding, 69; response
  to Somali migration to, 199; and
  safety and social control, 30–31;
  Somali migration to, 23, 27, 256;
  State Planning Office, 62; viewed by
  Somali refugees, 170; welfare benefits in, 27, 29; winters in, 25
Maine Department of Labor, 62, 63,
  170
Maine Organic Farmers and Gardeners
  Association (MOFGA), 182
Many and One Coalition, 35, 59, 61,
  199, App. C 305–6
Mariano, Michael, 293
Marshall, Andrew, 182
Martin, Sue, 64, 66
mayor's letter. see Raymond, Laurier T.
  Mcintyre, Alice, 233
McKay, Sandra Lee, 63

McTaggart, Robin, 229
media: and clan divisions, 247, 266;
  and Lewiston's Somali refugees, 58–59,
  156, 199, 201
Memphis, TN, 56
Menelik II, 11, 289
Miller, Kevin, 63
Mills, C. W., 227, 236, 239
Minneapolis, MN, 26, 56, 57, 99, 129,
  256
Minnesota, 29, 293
MOFGA. see Maine Organic Farmers
  and Gardeners Association
Mogadishu, xxv, 3–6, 16, 17
Mohamed, Abdirizak, 129
Mohamed, Aisha, 79–82
Mohamed, Bashir, 48–51
Mohamed, Fathiya Sharif, 190–92
Mohamed, Khalid, 221–25
Mohamed, Nasra, 107, 112 fig. 11
Mohammed, 26
Mohammed, Prophet, 9, 90
Mohamoud, Abdullah A., 9
multiculturalism, 296
Mumina, 183
Muna, 30
myth, creation, 150

Nadeau, Phil, 27
narrative, 201
NASAP. see New American Sustainable
  Agricultural Project
Nashville, TN, 56, 179
National Assembly, 14
National Civic League, 61
National Civic Review, 61
National Immigration Law Center, 69
nationalism, 11, 12

National Training Reform Agenda, 70
National Women's Studies Association, 215
Nearing, Scott and Helen, 182
New American Sustainable Agricultural Project (NASAP), 181, 183–85, 186, 188
"New Mainers Partnership," 61
New Mainers Workforce Alliance project, 72
New Mainers Workforce Project, 61
New Mainers Work Ready project, 71–72
New Orleans, LA, 56
Nieto, Sonia, 129, 134
nomadicism, 38–39, 169
Northern Frontier of Kenya, 12, 14, 289
Nuer refugees, Somali, 39
Nur, Farah, 289

Obama, Barack, 72
Office of Refugee Resettlement (ORR), 53, 70; and funding, 64, 68–69, 72; and secondary migration, 56, 61
Ogaden region, xxiii, xxiv, 12, 13, 15
Omar, 29, 30, 37, 42; on secondary migration, 34–35, 40, 43, 44
Operation Restore Hop, xxv
oral tradition, 10, 150, 153, 160 (*see* also storytelling); and social networks, 42–43, 44
ORR. *see* Office of Refugee Resettlement
Osman, Aden A., 293

Parrit, Sharon, 173, 174, 176, 177
pastoralism, 10, 288; and leadership,

84, 89; and the Samaal, 9; undermined by European boundaries, 11–12, 289
pedagogy, 212, 229, 231, 232, 238
performance ethnography, 238
piracy, xxvi, 7
political correctness, 153, 155–56
polygamy, 40, 180–81, 266
Portland, ME, 55, 178; housing in, 25, 56; secondary migration to, 23, 55, 56, 61
postcolonial theory, 154
pre-Somali inhabitants, 9, 10
Puntland region, xxv, 18
Putnam, Robert, 41, 94

Qur'an, 90, 160, 274 fig. 33
Quraysh, 9

race, 151, 155, 156, 164–65, 267
racism: and African Americans, 36; in the educational system, 131; and English illiteracy, 295; in Lewiston, 34–36, 35–36; and political correctness, 156; Somali resistance to, 130, 133, 156
Ramadan, 172, 174
Rashid, 36, 39
Raymond, Laurier T.: open letter to Somali community, 58–59, 86–86, 156, 199, App. A 299–300; Somali elder response to, 85, 97, App. B 301–3
readers theater: audiences, 228, 230, 232, 237–38; context created in, 238–39; and democratization, 229, 231, 232–33, 239; development of

Shabeelle River, 8, 11 (*see also* Shabelle River)

Shabelle River, 288 (*see also* Shabeelle River)

Shandy, Dianna, 38–39

Sharmarke, Omar Abdinashiid Ali, 292 (*see also* Shermaarke, Omar Abdinashiid Ali)

Shermaarke, Omar Abdinashiid Ali, xxiii, 14 (*see also* Sharmarke, Omar Abdinashiid Ali)

slave trade, 9, 10

small businesses, Somali-owned, 25, 28 figs. 4 and 5, 171, 186, 260 fig. 32

SNP. *see* Somali Narrative Project

social capital, 95; bonding and bridging, 41–42, 93–94, 100; defined, 41, 83; and gender, 45; and identity, 41–42, 100; and leadership, 83–84, 93, 97–99, 101, 102

Social Service, 68

sociological imagination, 227, 228, 235, 236

Somalia: civil war in, xxiv, 152, 157, 160, 169, 179; during the cold war, 291; colonization of, 11–13, 289; constitution, 14, 15; current catastrophe in, 287–88; economy of, and biil, 187; ethnic groups in, 8–9; as a failed state, 7, 8; foreign aid to, 15–16; human development indicators (HDI), 292; independence of, xxiii, 14, 15, 160; and the international trade route, 8, 10; map of ethnic, xxiii fig. 1; militarization of, 15–16; mistrust of government in, 16, 130; national flag, 14; partitioning of,

xxiii, 11–12, 13–14, 289 (*see also* Italian Somalia; British Somaliland; French Somaliland; Haud region; Ogaden region); political involvement in, 10–11; prior to European colonization, 8–11, 13; refugees from (*see* refugees, Somali; Somali Americans); relationship to wider Muslim community, 10; roots of catastrophe in, 288–92; and travel, 10–11; and the United States, 291; unprecedented exodus from, 7; and the USSR, 291–92; and Western narratives of modernity, 157

Somali Americans, 55, 293, 293–97 (*see also* refugees, Somali)

Somali Democratic Republic, xxiii

Somali Independence Day, 87, 201, 216

Somaliland Republic, xxiv

Somali Narrative Project (SNP), 61; and active learning, 211, 220; contributions of UM Somali students to, 211, 212–13, 214, 215, 216, 218, 219–20; first project, 212; first years of, 200–204; and gender norms, 202; goals of, 199, 200, 227; and higher education, 215; impact on student participants, 211, 215, 216–17, 219, 220, 235–37; interviews and focus groups conducted by, 216–17, 227, 247–48; members of, 199, 205 fig. 24, 211; readers theater (*see* readers theater); reading group established by, 212–13, 227, 228; Somali participants advice for, 204

Somali Republic, 179, 290

Somalis: behavior toward strangers,

146, 247; character of, 129–30, 158, 247; conversion to Islam, xxiii; cross-cultural misunderstandings by, 130–31; diversity among, 247; ethnic pride retained by, 146, 150, 266; family size, 32; generations of, in U.S., 293–95; group valued over individual, 34; historical mobility of, 26; identification with race resisted by, 156; morals and values, 152, 153, 154; photograph of young men, 5 fig. 3; photographs of young women, 76 fig. 7, 78 fig. 8, 283 fig. 35; reactions to current catastrophe, 292–93; refugees (*see* refugees, Somali); speech and argument organized by, 164; traditions among, 170–71, 186–88, 217, 229; unique in the African context, 150

Somali Youth League (SYL), 290

Southern Somalia, xxv

Soviet Union, 8, 291–92

stereotypes, 232, 295

Stitely, Amy, 185

storytelling, 2, 201, 229, 248 (*see also* oral tradition)

Suez Canal, xxiii, 11

Sufia, 27

Sufis, 10

sustainable agriculture movement, 182

SYL. *see* Somali Youth League

symbolic interaction theory, 232

Tara, Kalleigh, 301

Targeted Assistance, 68, 69, 70

TFG. *see* Transitional Federal Government

Theatre of the Oppressed, 215

"Timaade," Abdillahi Sultan, 290

Toner, Carol, 233

Transitional Federal Government (TFG), xxv, xxvi; current, 18

tribalism, 14–15, 16, 289

tribes. *see* clans

UIC. *see* Union of Islamic Courts

UN. *see* United Nations

unemployment, 170, 178, 188

Ungier, Daniel, 181, 184, 185, 188

UNHCR. *see* United Nations High Commissioner for Refugees

Union of Islamic Courts (UIC), xxv

United Nations (UN), 13, 16, 18, 19; and Somali refugees, xxiv, xxv, xxvi

United Nations High Commissioner for Refugees (UNHCR), 17, 107, 255

United Somali Congress, 16

United Somali Women of Maine, 201

United States: African immigration to, 23; and Bantus, 179; black-white relations in, 151, 155; Department of Labor, 72; Ethiopia supported by, 15, 18; multiculturalism acknowledged in, 295–96; refugees in, 255–56; and Somalia, xxiv, xxv, 8, 14, 15–16, 291; Somali immigration to, xxvi, 23–24, 55, 107, 146, 293, 295

United States Committee for Refugees and Immigrants, 66–67

University of Maine, 61, 127–28, 134, 218; and the Somali Narrative Project, 201, 211, 219, 220

University of Southern Maine, 61, 176

Upward Bound Program, 127, 128, 131, 134

urban gardens, 181, 182

van Zoonen, Liesbet, 163

Walter, Kirsten, 183

Warsame, Ismail, 125–29, 195 fig. 21, 196, 197

Weinstein-Shr, Gail, 63

WIA. *see* Workforce Investment Act

women (*see also* gender); and employment, 188–89; and leadership, 87, 90, 94, 97, 100; and literacy, 160; and marriage, 9; paying *biil*, 188; and peacekeeping, 9; photograph of young, 76 fig. 7, 78 fig. 8, 165 fig. 14, 168 fig. 15, 196 fig. 22; and SNP readers theater, 213, 214; viewed in Somalia, 157; and Western dress, 237

Workforce Investment Act (WIA), 67, 69

Workplace English Language and Literacy Program, 71

"WorkReady" program, 71

World Church of the Creator, 199

World War I, 181

World War II, xxiii, 13, 181, 293

Yearwood, Emily, 205 fig. 24